Wirtschaftsenglisch

Wirtschaftssprachen by

Wirtschaftsenglisch
(Englisch und Amerikanisch)

von

Alfred FONTENILLES
Claude CHAPUIS
Peter DUNN

Deutsche Bearbeitung von
Susanne GAGNEUR
in Zusammenarbeit mit
Bärbel RENNER

Illustrationen von J.L. GOUSSÉ

ASSiMiL
Postfach 47
52388 Nörvenich
DEUTSCHLAND

© Assimil 1996   ISBN: 3-89625-004-3

**Der Assimil-Verlag
bietet folgende Sprachlernmethoden an:**

Grundkurse: Reihe "ohne Mühe"
Arabisch
Chinesisch (2 Bände)
Chinesische Schrift
Deutsch (als Fremdsprache)
Englisch
Französisch
Italienisch
Japanisch (2 Bände)
Kanji-Schrift
Neugriechisch
Niederländisch
Polnisch
Portugiesisch
Russisch
Schwedisch (2 Bände)
Spanisch
Türkisch
Ungarisch

Vertiefungskurse: Reihe "in der Praxis"
Englisch
Französisch
Italienisch
Spanisch

Weitere Titel in Vorbereitung

Die Ton-Aufnahmen sämtlicher Lektionen und Übungen aus diesem Buch (insgesamt 250 Minuten Spieldauer) können Sie bei Ihrem Buchhändler bestellen:
"English for the Business World"
auf **4 Audio-CDs** - ISBN 2-7005-1211-1
oder
auf **4 Ton-Cassetten** - ISBN 2-7005-1162-x

ASSiMiL
B.P. 25 - F-94331 Chennevières-sur-Marne Cedex

VORWORT

Der vorliegende Kurs richtet sich an Personen, die bereits über einen umfangreichen englischen Wortschatz verfügen und die wichtigsten Redewendungen und sprachlichen Mechanismen des Englischen kennen, und die sich auf mühelose Weise die Wirtschafts- und Handelssprache des britischen bzw. amerikanischen Englisch aneignen möchten.

Wir haben uns dafür entschieden, Sie an die für die Bereiche Wirtschaft und Handel spezifischen Begriffe und Ausdrücke heranzuführen, indem wir Kapitel für Kapitel den beruflichen Werdegang einer jungen englischen Universitätsabgängerin verfolgen. Die schrittweise Einführung von Susan Edwards in die Geschäfts- und Arbeitswelt schien uns das beste Mittel zu sein, die im englischen bzw. amerikanischen Sprachgebrauch verwendete Wirtschafts- und Handelsterminologie authentisch und zusammenhängend darzustellen.

Die Kapitel, aus denen sich dieser Kurs zusammensetzt, sind allesamt Dialoge, die sich vor einem realistischen und lebensnahen Hintergrund abspielen und daher für den Lernenden in hohem Maße praxisorientiert sind.

IST DIES EIN KURS IN SPRACHWISSENSCHAFT ODER IN WIRTSCHAFT?

Dieser Kurs kann und will keinen Anspruch auf Vollständigkeit stellen. Wir haben aber versucht, Ihnen die wichtigsten Inhalte des Bereichs Wirtschaft zugänglich zu machen, wenn diese auch an bestimmten Stellen extrem vereinfacht dargestellt werden, um das allgemeine Verständnis nicht zu erschweren.

Wir halten es für wichtig, daß beim Lernenden bereits in der Muttersprache ein gutes Verständnis der Wirtschaftsterminologie vorhanden ist. Es versteht sich von selbst, daß man sich die Übersetzung eines Wortes wie z.B. "Bilanz" oder "Inkassobeauftragter" leichter einprägen kann, wenn man die Bedeutung dieses Wortes bereits in seiner Muttersprache kennt.

HABEN WIR DEM BRITISCHEN ODER DEM AMERIKANISCHEN ENGLISCH DEN VORZUG GEGEBEN?

Da Susan Edwards eine internationale Karriere macht, ist es unerläßlich, auf gewisse **Unterschiede** zwischen **angelsächsischem** und **amerikanischem** Sprachgebrauch einzugehen, wobei sogar gelegentlich die "australische Variante" erwähnt wird. Beachten Sie in diesem Zusammenhang, daß wir im Interesse der Vereinheitlichung durchgehend in den Episoden, die sich in Großbritannien oder in Australien abspielen (und auch im Index), der Orthografie des britischen Englisch den Vorzug gegeben haben. In den anderen Episoden finden Sie die amerikanische Schreibweise vor. Im britischen Englisch lautet also die Endsilbe von Wörtern wie z.B. labour -*our*, im amerikanischen Englisch -*or*. Ebenso lautet das englische Suffix bei entsprechenden Verben -*ise*, das amerikanische Suffix -*ize*.

Die Aufnahmen der Dialoge und der Verständnisübungen machen die Unterschiede zwischen den beiden Aussprachevarianten klar. Durch aufmerksames und regelmäßiges Anhören der Aufnahmen kann der Lernende sein Gehör für die wichtigsten vokalischen und konsonantischen Unterschiede schulen und verfeinern. (Für die Übungen sollten Sie Ihr Wiedergabegerät zwischen den einzelnen Sätzen auf "Pause" stellen, damit Sie genügend Zeit haben, sich die entsprechenden Antworten zu überlegen und sie zu formulieren.)

WIE IST DIESER KURS AUFGEBAUT?

Alle **40 Kapitel** dieses Kurses sind gleich aufgebaut. Sie umfassen

• einen **Dialog auf Englisch** mit der entsprechenden Übersetzung auf der gegenüberliegenden Seite. (Für die idiomatischen Ausdrücke haben wir statt einer Wort-zu-Wort-Übersetzung meistens eine Äquivalentübersetzung angeboten, die zwar vom Sinn her etwas freier ist, jedoch unter sprachwissenschaftlichen Gesichtspunkten dem englischen Wortlaut näher kommt.)

• **ANMERKUNGEN** in deutscher Sprache, die einzelne, im Dialog verwendete Begriffe oder geschilderte Sachverhalte erklären. Ergänzend hierzu enthalten viele **ANMERKUNGEN** synonyme oder verwandte Terminologie zum jeweiligen Begriff.

• ein **Beispieldokument** in englischer Sprache, das das im jeweiligen Kapitel behandelte Thema illustriert und verdeutlicht.

• **themenbezogene Zusatzinformationen** auf Deutsch, die mit dem Symbol [i] gekennzeichnet sind. Hier finden Sie ergänzende Informationen zu landesüblichen Eigenheiten, die in bezug auf das im jeweiligen Kapitel behandelte Thema von Interesse sind.

• Außerdem bieten wir Ihnen verschiedene Arten von **Übungen** an:

* Verständnisübungen: Ausgehend von bestimmten Fragen sollen Sie – schriftlich oder mündlich – Antworten in ganzen Sätzen formulieren, deren Inhalt Sie dem Dialog entnehmen können.

* Übersetzungsübungen: In diesen Übungen, in denen Sie aus dem Deutschen ins Englische übersetzen sollen, trainieren Sie die Anwendung des Vokabulars und der im Kapitel enthaltenen Ausdrücke und Redewendungen.

* Wortschatztests: Hierbei handelt es sich entweder um Lückentexte, bei denen Sie fehlende Wörter ergänzen müssen, oder um Zuordnungstests, bei denen Sie z.B. einer Frage eine passende Antwort zuweisen müssen, wobei Sie immer mehrere Auswahlmöglichkeiten haben.

* Falsch oder wahr? Hier müssen Sie über den Wahrheitsgehalt bestimmter Aussagen entscheiden. Halten Sie Aussagen für falsch, so sollten Sie dies durch eine kurze Begründung auf Englisch belegen.

* Praktische Übungen: Dies sind z.T. sehr anspruchsvolle Übungen, bei denen es um das Verfassen von Lebensläufen, Briefen, Memos oder Berichten bis hin zu differenzierteren Übungen im Zusammenhang mit der Interpretation und Verwendung der in den Kapiteln enthaltenen Dokumente geht.

Für jede Übung finden Sie die entsprechende Lösung auf der gegenüberliegenden Seite:

* die Übersetzung, in der der Wortschatz des betreffenden Kapitels verwendet wird,

* eine mögliche Antwort auf die gestellte Frage (die jedoch nicht die einzig richtige Antwort sein muß!),
* ein Lösungsvorschlag für praktischen Übungen.

Zögern Sie nicht, alle Übungen mehrmals durchzuarbeiten, um zu überprüfen, ob und mit welcher Geschwindigkeit Sie gewisse Lernziele erreichen. Lassen Sie sich nicht durch die praktischen Übungen entmutigen, bei denen Sie z.B. einen Text verfassen müssen: eine unbefriedigende Leistung zieht keinerlei Konsequenzen nach sich. Machen Sie sich jedoch klar, daß diese Übungen Ihnen helfen, sich in realen Situationen zu bewähren, z.B. bei der Suche nach einer Arbeitsstelle, und daß sie Ihnen einen schnellen Einstieg in die berufliche Praxis erleichtern.

Und um Ihnen nach all diesen Übungen ein bißchen Gelegenheit zum Luftholen zu geben, sagt Ihnen am Schluß jedes Kapitels eine kleine Rubrik ("Do" und "Don´t"), wie man sich in Großbritannien, den USA usw. in bestimmten Situationen angemessen verhält.

Am Ende des Kurses finden Sie einen **deutsch-englischen Index**, in dem noch einmal alle wichtigen Begriffe des Kurses aufgelistet sind. Er gibt Ihnen die Möglichkeit,

● die Bedeutung bestimmter Wörter oder Ausdrücke zu ermitteln, die in den Dokumenten oder in bestimmten Übungen auftauchen und zu denen es keine gesonderte Anmerkung gab,

● die englischen Entsprechungen bestimmter deutscher Wörter zu finden, ohne ein zusätzliches Buch oder eine andere Form der Sekundärliteratur hinzuziehen zu müssen.

So, machen Sie nun die Bekanntschaft von Susan und ihren vielen Freunden, Kollegen und Gesprächspartnern auf der ganzen Welt.

*****

Die Autoren von Assimil danken der Barclays Bank sowie Marks & Spencer für die Erlaubnis, ihren Namen sowie bestimmte Dokumente verwenden zu dürfen, zu denen sie die Autoren inspiriert haben.

INHALT

Seite

I	VORWORT	III-VI
II	ÜBERSICHT ÜBER DIE KAPITEL:	
1	Der Universitätsabschluß	1
2	Das Vorstellungsgespräch	11
3	Eingestellt	21
4	Der erste Arbeitstag	31
5	Die Firma kennenlernen (I)	41
6	Die Firma kennenlernen (II)	51
7	Praktische Berufserfahrung	61
8	Einführung in das Finanzwesen	71
9	Die Wahl des Arbeitsplatzes	81
10	Die Personalverwaltung	91
11	Der Streik	101
12	Karriereausbau	111
13	Die Arbeit einer Sekretärin	121
14	Das High-Tech-Büro	131
15	Unterstützung der örtlichen Gemeinde	143
16	Geschafft	153
17	Studium in den Vereinigten Staaten	163
18	Marktstudien	175
19	Von der Theorie zur Praxis	185
20	Kulturelle Unterschiede	197
21	Produktänderungen	207
22	Der richtige Marketing-Mix	219
23	Kontaktaufnahme mit einer Werbeagentur	229
24	Qualitätskontrolle	239
25	Produktwerbung	249

26	Das Leben eines Verkäufers	261
27	Verantwortlich für den Export	271
28	Exportfinanzierung	281
29	Eine Geschäftsverhandlung	291
30	Risikobegrenzung	303
31	Politische Probleme	313
32	Den Markt beachten	323
33	Ein Boykott droht	333
34	Leben auf vollen Touren	343
35	Zurück in Großbritannien	353
36	Analyse der Firmenbuchhaltung	363
37	Fehler der Vergangenheit	373
38	Leveraged Management Buy-Out (LMBO)	383
39	Diversifikation	393
40	Die verdiente Belohnung	403

III ÜBERSICHT ÜBER DIE DOKUMENTE

- Job offer — 5
- Higher education in management (UK) — 15
- Letter of appointment — 25
- Types of business structrure (UK) — 35
- Organisation chart of United Chocolate Inc — 45
- Organisation chart of United Chocolate Ltd — 55
- Site plan of United Chocolate Ltd's plant at Filton — 65
- British banking and Barclays — 75
- Confidential letter from Milton Keynes to Filton (about absenteeism) — 85
- Reply to confidential letter — 95
- Trade unions in Great Britain — 105
- Internal memorandum (from Manager, Human Resources, about career development project) — 115

- Stationery order form — 125
- The information super highway — 137
- Anniversary celebrations programme — 147
- The MBA (Master of Business Administration) — 157
- Map of Texas — 169
- Market research questionnaire — 179
- Computers in our lives — 191
- A student's first impression of the USA (letter) — 201
- Product development — 213
- Marketing mix and pricing — 223
- Advertising and society — 233
- Quality, quality control and accreditation — 243
- Public relations — 255
- A salesperson's report — 265
- Organization chart : North America, domestic and Canada — 275
- Draft memo (from Export Manager to Sales Manager, Pacific Rim) — 285
- Understanding Australia — 307
- International trade (Balance of trade/Balance of payments) — 317
- Protecting the consumer and the environment — 327
- Congratulatory letter — 337
- Working abroad (letter) — 347
- How to run a meeting (Internal memo) — 357
- Birtwhistle's Profit and Loss Account — 367
  Birtwhistle's Balance Sheet — 368
- Summary of Birtwhistle's capital ownership before and after takeover — 377
- Financing of LMBO and capital structure of Birtwhistle Finance Holding (BFH) — 387
- Minutes of a board meeting — 397
- A clipping from the "Yorkshire Telegraph" : Woman in charge at Birtwhistle's — 407

IV ÜBERSICHT ÜBER DIE THEMENBEZOGENEN ZUSATZINFORMATIONEN 🛈

*	Gruß- und Schlußformeln in Briefen	6
*	"Frauen"	16
*	Die Telefonnummern	26
*	Das "Duzen" bei Engländern und Amerikanern	36
*	Die Zeitzonen	46
*	Wer trinkt was?	56
*	Vertrautheit erzeugt nicht immer Verachtung	66
*	Die Schotten und das liebe Geld	76
*	Die Geschäftswelt: Ein Schlachtfeld	86
*	Arbeitskräfte oder Personal	96
*	Der Autofahrer auf der anderen Seite des Kanals	106
*	Die Berufsausbildung	116
*	Der Tag der Sekretärinnen	126
*	Die Sekretärin: ein aussterbender Berufszweig?	138
*	Die Wohltätigkeitseinrichtungen	148
*	Fortbildung	158
*	Die Texaner	170
*	Die Euphemismen	180
*	Die Tortendiagramme	192
*	Die Entspanntheit der Amerikaner	202
*	Brainstorming	214
*	Die Rolle des Marketing in unserem Leben	224
*	Die Werbeslogans	234
*	Weinverkostung	244
*	Wettbewerbe, Spiele und Lotterien	256
*	Der Sport und die Firma	266
*	Das Geschäftsessen	276
*	Frank und frei	286
*	Australien	298
*	Risiko-Management	308
*	Die Multis, Unternehmen ohne Grenzen	318
*	Die Marktbeherrschung	328

*	Wirtschaft und Unternehmen (Einige historische Zitate)	338
*	Statussymbole	348
*	Golf	358
*	Der Kontenplan	371
*	Die "Golden Boys"	378
*	Die Beteiligung der Angestellten am Unternehmensgewinn	388
*	Eine gelungene Diversifikation: Eiscremeriegel	398
*	Eine Frage der Etikette	408

V ÜBERSICHT ÜBER DIE PRAKTISCHEN ÜBUNGEN

¤	**Bewerbungsschreiben**	9
¤	**Lebenslauf**	19
¤	**Verfassen eines tabellarischen Lebenslaufs**	59
¤	**Verfassen einer Dienstanweisung**	199
¤	**Verfassen und Lesen von Telex-Nachrichten**	141
¤	**Verfassen einer Bilanz**	381

VI DEUTSCH-ENGLISCHER INDEX   414

CHAPTER 1

Graduating from university

Susan Edwards will soon be graduating from university with a BA Honours degree in modern languages. She is with two fellow students who are also in their final year: Paula is reading chemistry, Catherine English literature and history. They are having dinner at Paula's flat. **(1) (2) (3) (4)**

1. **Susan:** So how are things going, you two?

2. **Catherine:** Well it depends what things you're talking about, doesn't it?

3. **Susan:** Work, of course. We all know that things are going very well between you and David!

4. **Paula:** Yes, I wish I could say the same about me and Jeremy!

5. **Catherine:** Well if you cooked him 'chili con carne' as hot as this last weekend, I'm not surprised you scared him off.

6. **Paula:** Thanks very much!

7. **Catherine:** I'm sorry Paula; I was only joking. I think your 'chili con carne' is fantastic. No seriously, work is going OK, but when I think that we'll soon have to start revising for finals, the mind boggles! I suppose I'll have to make a start during the Easter vacation. **(5) (6)**

8. **Susan:** I haven't started yet, either. I've been so busy applying for jobs and attending interviews. What about you, Paula?

9. **Paula:** Well actually I've already started revising. There's so much to remember in chemistry that it's impossible to leave everything till the last minute. I'll really have to get a first, if I'm going to work as a research chemist. **(7)**

10. **Catherine:** For a company or at the university?

KAPITEL 1

Der Universitätsabschluß

Susan Edwards wird bald ihren Universitätsabschluß mit einem Prädikatsexamen als Bakkalaureus der Geisteswissenschaften in modernen Sprachen machen. Sie trifft sich mit zwei Kommilitoninnen, die ebenfalls gerade ihr letztes Jahr an der Universität absolvieren: Paula studiert Chemie, Catherine englische Literatur und Geschichte. Sie essen in Paulas Wohnung zu Abend.

1. **Susan:** Wie sieht's denn aus bei euch beiden?
2. **Catherin:** Naja, das hängt davon ab, wovon du sprichst, nicht wahr?
3. **Susan:** Vom Arbeiten natürlich. Wir alle wissen, daß es zwischen David und dir sehr gut läuft!
4. **Paula:** Ja, ich wünschte, ich könnte das Gleiche von mir und Jeremy behaupten!
5. **Catherine:** Naja, wenn du ihm ein so scharfes 'Chili con carne' gekocht hast wie letztes Wochenende, wundert es mich nicht, daß du ihn vergrault hast.
6. **Paula:** Vielen Dank!
7. **Catherine:** Tut mir leid, Paula, ich hab doch nur einen Witz gemacht. Ich finde, dein 'Chili con Carne' ist ausgezeichnet. Nein, mal im Ernst: mit dem Studium ist alles OK, aber bei dem Gedanken, daß ich bald mit dem Lernen für die Abschlußprüfungen beginnen muß, wird mir schwindlig! Ich glaube, ich werde in den Osterferien damit beginnen müssen.
8. **Susan:** Ich hab auch noch nicht angefangen. Ich hatte so viel mit Bewerbungen und Vorstellungsgesprächen zu tun. Und was ist mit dir, Paula?
9. **Paula:** Nun ja, ich habe schon mit dem Lernen begonnen. Man muß sich so viel merken in der Chemie, daß es unmöglich ist, alles bis zur letzten Minute aufzuschieben. Wenn ich als Chemikerin in der Forschung arbeiten will, muß ich unbedingt eine Eins machen.
10. **Catherine:** Für eine Firma oder an der Universität?

ANMERKUNGEN

(1) **BA** (GB) ist die Kurzform für *Bachelor of Arts*, ein Universitätsabschluß, der etwa unserem Diplom entspricht. Mit *Arts* sind hier die Geisteswissenschaften gemeint.
(2) **Honours degree** (GB) ist ein Examen mit Auszeichnung (vgl. auch *first*, Anmerkung 7). Ein *pass degree* ist dagegen ein Examen ohne Prädikat.
(3) **to read** ist ein anderer Ausdruck für "studieren".
(4) **flat:** Umgangssprachlich für *apartment* "Wohnung".
(5) **finals** ist die Kurzform für *final examinations* "Abschlußprüfungen (an der Universität)".
(6) **the mind boggles:** "bei dem Gedanken wird mir schwindlig"; *to boggle at/over sth.* "das übersteigt die Vorstellungskraft", "das ist Wahnsinn" usw.
(7) **first** ist die beste Note bei einem *BA Honours degree* in Großbritannien. Danach folgt *second (-class honours)* und *third (-class honours)*.

CHAPTER 1

11. **Paula:** For a company, definitely. It's much more challenging, and better paid, too!

12. **Catherine:** Money's not everything, you know. I still intend to do postgraduate research and get my PhD. Then I'll be able to get a university teaching job. I know there's not much money in it, but when David's a chartered accountant, he'll be raking it in. **(8) (9) (10) (11)**

13. **Susan:** Have you been to any interviews yet, or applied for any jobs, Paula?

14. **Paula:** Not as such. I'm in the process of writing to the big chemical firms, enclosing my CV, in the hope that they'll be interested in me. I've heard nothing definite yet. What about you? **(12)**

15. **Susan:** I've applied for several jobs I've seen advertised and had five interviews already through the Careers Office. They are all big companies either in the food industry or in retail distribution. I'm still waiting like you, though; they take so long to give you an answer. **(13)**

16. **Catherine:** And you still want to work in marketing? A proper businesswoman, eh!

17. **Susan:** Why not? Or maybe personnel management. I'm looking forward to next Monday. I've got another interview, with United Chocolate this time, and that's the company I've really set my sights on.

18. **Catherine:** I'm not surprised; you get through so many of their products!

19. **Paula:** Talking of chocolate, clear away the dishes and I'll bring in the dessert. I've made a chocolate mousse!

20. **Susan:** Mmm, lovely!

KAPITEL 1

11. **Paula:** Sicherlich für eine Firma. Das ist eine größere Herausforderung und wird auch besser bezahlt!
12. **Catherine:** Geld ist nicht alles, weißt du. Ich habe immer noch vor, in die Postgraduiertenforschung zu gehen und meinen Doktor zu machen. Ich kann dann eine Dozentenstelle an der Universität bekommen. Ich weiß, daß dabei nicht viel herausspringt, aber wenn David beeidigter Wirtschaftsprüfer ist, wird er ordentlich Geld scheffeln.
13. **Susan:** Hast du schon irgendwelche Vorstellungsgespräche gehabt oder dich für irgendwelche Stellen beworben, Paula?
14. **Paula:** Nicht so richtig. Ich bin gerade dabei, die großen Chemieunternehmen anzuschreiben, und ihnen meinen Lebenslauf zu schicken, in der Hoffnung, daß sie an mir interessiert sind. Bis jetzt habe ich noch nichts Definitives gehört. Was ist mit dir?
15. **Susan:** Ich habe mich für mehrere Jobs beworben, die ich in Anzeigen gesehen habe, und hatte bereits fünf Vorstellungsgespräche, die über das Berufszentrum liefen. Es handelt sich bei allen um große Unternehmen entweder in der Lebensmittelindustrie oder dem Einzelhandel. Ich warte aber noch, genau wie du; die brauchen so lange, bis sie mal antworten.
16. **Catherine:** Und du willst immer noch im Marketing arbeiten? Eine richtige Geschäftsfrau, he!
17. **Susan:** Warum nicht? Oder vielleicht Personalverwaltung. Ich bin gespannt auf nächsten Montag. Ich habe ein weiteres Vorstellungsgespräch, diesmal bei United Chocolate, und das ist das Unternehmen, das ich wirklich angepeilt habe.
18. **Catherine:** Das wundert mich nicht; du ißt so viele von ihren Produkten!
19. **Paula:** Wo wir gerade über Schokolade reden: räumt die Teller weg und ich bringe den Nachtisch. Ich habe Mousse au Chocolat gemacht!
20. **Susan:** Mmmh, lecker!

ANMERKUNGEN (Fortsetzung)

(8) Der **postgraduate** in Großbritannien entspricht dem *graduate* in den USA; gemeint ist der Akademiker bzw. Absolvent einer Hochschule. Ein Student, der noch nicht das Niveau des *bachelor* erreicht hat, wird *undergraduate* genannt.

(9) **PhD:** *Doctor of Philosophy*, der Doktortitel in den anglophonen Ländern, der auf der Forschung und der Verteidigung einer Doktorarbeit basiert, wobei das Fachgebiet entweder Wissenschaft oder Philologie sein kann, allerdings nicht Medizin (siehe Kapitel 16, Anmerkung 2).

(10) Der **chartered accountant (CA)** in Großbritannien entspricht dem *certified public accountant (CPA)* in den USA: "Wirtschafts-, Buchprüfer". *Accountancy* ist das "Rechnungswesen" im weitesten Sinne, *accounting* die "Buchführung, Buchhaltung".

(11) **to rake in** ist ein umgangssprachlicher Ausdruck, der "Geld scheffeln" bedeutet und von *rake*, der "Geldharke" der Croupiers in Spielcasinos, kommt.

(12) **CV** ist in Großbritannien die Kurzform für *curriculum vitae*; in den USA sagt man eher *résumé*.

(13) Das **Careers Office** ist eine Art Berufsberatungszentrum mit Services für Studienabgänger, das man an vielen britischen und amerikanischen Universitäten findet.

CHAPTER 1　　　　　　　　　　　　　　　　　　　　DOCUMENT

Job Offer

John CHARTRES Plc
UK leader in marmalade and quality preserves

JUNIOR MARKETING MANAGER

You will be graduating from a good British university this year with a BA Honours degree. Your are looking for a challenging career in FMCG* marketing, with considerable prospects for the future. Your have a good command of French and one other major European language, and are prepared for frequent travel.

We are a medium-sized, but rapidly-expanding company, whose registered trademark is a household name within the UK. We are looking for a Junior Marketing Manager to help us launch our range of marmalades
and quality preserves in France, initially, and subsequently in other EU countries.

After a trial period of 6 months, the successful candidate will report directly to the Marketing Director. The position carries an excellent remuneration and benefits package (private health insurance, company car, etc.).

Please write, enclosing a comprehensive CV to:

Ms Ruth Newland, Personnel Dept, John CHARTRES Plc, Seville Road, HAVANT, Hants PO9 2TN

---

* **fast-moving consumer goods.**

KAPITEL 1

 Gruß- und Schlußformeln in Briefen

Gruß- und Schlußformeln in Briefen sind Höflichkeitsfloskeln, die besonders in offiziellen Schreiben sehr wichtig sind und die man unbedingt kennen sollte, wenn man an eine Privatperson oder eine Behörde oder Firma im Ausland schreibt. Im englischen Sprachgebrauch heißt die goldene Regel, daß man sagen soll, was man zu sagen hat, und das möglichst klar und einfach.

Schreibt man in Großbritannien einen Brief und kennt man den Namen des Adressaten (auch dann, wenn man ihn noch nicht persönlich kennengelernt hat), beginnt man das Schreiben mit *Dear Mr Robertson* oder *Dear Ms Edwards*. Man beendet den Brief mit der lakonischen Formel *Yours sincerely*. Kennt man dagegen den Namen des Empfängers nicht, schreibt man in der Anrede *Dear Sir* (oder *Sirs*, wenn sich das Schreiben allgemein an eine Firma richtet). Die Schlußformel lautet in diesem Fall *Yours faithfully*.

In den Vereinigten Staaten liegen die Dinge noch einfacher. Das Komma hinter *Dear (...)*, kann durch einen Doppelpunkt (:) ersetzt werden, z.B. *Dear Mr Robertson:*. Anstelle von *Dear Sirs* tritt im Amerikanischen *Gentlemen*. Als Schlußformeln kann *Yours sincerely, Sincerely yours* oder einfach *Sincerely*, unter Freunden oder guten Bekannten *Yours*, verwendet werden.

CHAPTER 1

EXERCISES

Comprehension

Lesen Sie den Dialog aufmerksam durch. Beantworten Sie dann die nachfolgenden Fragen, und zwar immer in ganzen Sätzen:

1. Where does this dialogue take place? **2.** Will Paula and Catherine soon be graduating from university? **3.** Are things going well between Catherine and David? **4.** Does Catherine really like Paula's *chili con carne*? **5.** Has Susan started revising for her finals yet? **6.** Why does Paula prefer to work for a company? **7.** Why do you think that Catherine is not worried about being well paid? **8.** How has Paula set about looking for a job? **9.** Why is Susan particularly looking forward to the interview with United Chocolate? **10.** Do you think that Susan is fond of chocolate? Why?

Translation

1. Paula und Catherine studieren nicht moderne Sprachen an der Universität. **2.** Es läuft nicht sehr gut zwischen Jeremy und mir. **3.** Mein *Chili con Carne* war zu scharf, und das hat ihn vergrault. **4.** Catherine meinte es nicht ernst; sie hat nur einen Witz gemacht. **5.** Ich werde während der Osterferien mit dem Lernen beginnen müssen. **6.** Ich war so beschäftigt mit Lernen, daß ich noch keine Stelle gesucht habe. **7.** Ich würde gerne Forschung an der Universität betreiben, aber mit Chemie ist das etwas anderes. **8.** Ich schreibe große Lebensmittelfirmen an und sende ihnen meinen Lebenslauf. **9.** Susan ißt viel Schokolade. **10.** Räumt die Teller weg, ihr beiden, und ich bringe den Kaffee.

KAPITEL 1

LÖSUNGSVORSCHLÄGE

Verständnisübung

1. This dialogue takes place in Paula's flat. 2. Yes, Paula and Catherine are both in their final year. 3. Yes, they seem to be going well. 4. Yes, Catherine was only joking; she thinks Paula's *chili con carne* is fantastic. 5. No, she hasn't. She's been too busy applying for jobs and attending interviews. 6. Paula prefers to work for a company because it's more challenging and better paid. 7. Because her boyfriend, David, will earn a lot of money when he's a chartered accountant. 8. Paula has been writing to big chemical firms, enclosing her CV. 9. Because United Chocolate is the company she would really like to work for. 10. Susan is probably fond of chocolate, because Catherine says she eats a lot of UC's products. She also thinks that a chocolate mousse is lovely.

Übersetzungsübung

1. Paula and Catherine are not reading modern languages at university. 2. Things are not going very well between Jeremy and me. 3. My *chili con carne* was too hot and that scared him off. 4. Catherine was not serious; she was only joking. 5. I'll have to start revising during the Easter vacation. 6. I've been so busy revising that I haven't looked for a job yet. 7. I'd rather do research at the university, but for chemistry it's different. 8. I'm writing and sending my CV to big food companies. 9. Susan gets through a lot of chocolate. 10. Clear away the dishes, you two, and I'll bring in the coffee.

CHAPTER 1

Application letter

Lesen Sie dieses Schreiben gründlich durch und setzen Sie dann jeweils eines der folgenden Wörter in die numerierten Lücken ein: ***keen, sincerely, advertised, apply for, interview, graduating, suited, knowledge, currently, experience.***

Ms Susan Edwards,
1 Welburn Ave,
LEEDS LS16 5HJ

Ms Ruth Newland,
Personnel Dept,
John Chartres Plc,
Seville Road,
HAVANT,
Hants PO9 2TN

2nd April 199.

Dear Ms Newland,
    I would like to (**1.** ...) the post of Junior Marketing Manager which was (**2.** ...) in this month's edition of ***University Graduate***.

    I am (**3.** ...) in my final year of a BA Honours degree in modern languages (Spanish and French) at the University of Leeds and will be (**4.** ...) in June. I am very (**5.** ...) to make my career in marketing, in a company such as yours, whose products are so well known. I feel that my (**6.** ...) of French and Spanish and my work (**7.** ...) make me particularly well (**8.** ...) for this position.

    I enclose a comprehensive CV which I hope will interest you. I look forward to being able to meet you and answer your questions during an (**9.** ...).

    Yours (**10.** ...),

    Susan Edwards

Encl: Curriculum Vitae

KAPITEL 1

Diese Wörter hätten Sie einsetzen sollen:

1. apply for
2. advertised
3. currently
4. graduating
5. keen
6. knowledge
7. experience
8. suited
9. interview
10. sincerely

DO!

Pronounce *Mister*, but write *Mr*.

DON'T!

Don't say:
- 'Lord David', but 'Lord (David) Werrett'.
- 'Sir Stafford', but 'Sir Peter (Stafford)'.

CHAPTER 2 📼

Being interviewed

Susan Edwards is being interviewed by United Chocolate (UK), which regularly tours the top UK universities to recruit graduates to work as trainee managers. **(1)**

1. **Mr Robertson:** Well, I think we've covered nearly everything. So let me now ask you a rather difficult question. What would you say are the weak points in your CV?

2. **Susan:** *(After a moment's hesitation)* Well, I suppose my lack of experience of the corporate world – apart from one or two summer vacation jobs! But I didn't study business at university. There's also the fact that I'm a girl! **(2)**

3. **Mr Robertson:** Our company has always made a point of taking part in what is commonly called the 'milk round'. Not because we make a lot of milk chocolate, I hasten to add! *(Amusement)* We have always believed that if we can find young talent, we can do the management training ourselves. Or pay for our brightest hopes to return to university later on... **(3)**

4. **Susan:** To obtain some sort of specialist qualification?

KAPITEL 2

Das Vorstellungsgespräch

Susan Edwards hat ein Vorstellungsgespräch bei der Firma United Chocolate (UK), die regelmäßig die besten englischen Universitäten besucht, um Studienabgänger als Trainee Manager einzustellen.

1. **Herr Robertson:** Gut, ich denke, wir haben fast alles besprochen. Jetzt will ich Ihnen eine etwas schwierige Frage stellen. Was, würden Sie sagen, sind die Schwachpunkte in Ihrem Lebenlauf?

2. **Susan:** *(Nach kurzem Zögern)* Ich denke, mein Mangel an Erfahrung in der Unternehmenswelt – mit Ausnahme von ein oder zwei Jobs in den Sommerferien! Aber ich habe nicht Wirtschaft studiert. Und dann ist da noch die Tatsache, daß ich eine Frau bin!

3. **Herr Robertson:** Unser Unternehmen hat immer Wert darauf gelegt, sich an dem zu beteiligen, was gemeinhin als die "Eliteauswahl" ("Runde des Milchmanns") bezeichnet wird. Natürlich nicht, weil wir so viel Milchschokolade herstellen! *(Lacht)* Wir waren immer der Meinung, daß wir, falls wir junge, talentierte Menschen finden können, die Management-Ausbildung selber übernehmen könnten. Oder unseren größten Hoffnungsträgern später ein Aufbaustudium bezahlen...

4. **Susan:** Um eine Art Spezialqualifikation zu erlangen?

ANMERKUNGEN

(1) **trainee**: Vorsicht! Dieser Begriff kann im Englischen zwei unterschiedliche Bedeutungen haben: "Praktikant" (bzw. "Volontär"), also ein Student, der im Rahmen seines Studiums ein Praktikum absolviert, oder "Auszubildender, Nachwuchskraft", ein bereits fest angestellter, jedoch noch in der Ausbildung befindlicher Arbeitnehmer. Daher auch *training period*: "Praktikum" oder "Ausbildung(szeit)". Für "Praktikum" sagt man in Großbritannien auch oft *placement* und in den Vereinigten Staaten *internship* (*intern* "Praktikant").

(2) **corporate**: Im Englischen ein Adjektiv, wird jedoch im Deutschen meistens mit "Unternehmens-", "Betriebs-", "Firmen-" wiedergegeben. Es bezieht sich auf Kapitalgesellschaften (im US-Amerikanischen *corporation*), aber auch auf andere Unternehmen im allgemeinen. Man spricht von *corporate world* "Unternehmenswelt", *corporate headquarters* "Firmensitz", *corporate lawyer* "Firmenanwalt" und *corporate jet* "Firmenflugzeug".

(3) **milk round** ist ein umgangssprachlicher Ausdruck für die jährliche Runde der großen Unternehmen durch die höheren Bildungseinrichtungen Großbritanniens, bei der – und hier wird klar, warum von *milk*, also "Milch" die Rede ist – sozusagen die "Creme" der jungen Hochschulabsolventen für eine Stelle in diesen Unternehmen angeworben wird.

CHAPTER 2

5. **Mr Robertson:** Exactly. Like an MBA, for example. Oh, I know a lot of companies now prefer graduates with business or joint degrees. The former Polytechnics probably started that trend... **(4) (5) (6)**

6. **Susan:** And I noticed in France, for example, that most managers are recruited from business schools.

7. **Mr Robertson:** That's quite true. But we have always been successful with our policy. As for your being a girl, that's certainly not a disadvantage. United Chocolate has always tried to give an equal place to women. After all, a considerable number of our customers, throughout the world, are women. Are there any questions you would like to ask me?

8. **Susan:** Could you say a little about what being a trainee manager with United Chocolate would entail?

9. **Mr Robertson:** Certainly. Should you come and work with us, you will have a trial period of six months. During that time, you will get to know the company, its products, its activities... You will also see what the various functions of management involve. Then, after six months, if we are still satisfied with you, we will let you choose the area you want to work in. For example, maybe personnel or marketing in your case. **(7)**

10. **Susan:** You mentioned, just now, sending people back to university...

11. **Mr Robertson:** Yes I did. But I said only our 'brightest hopes'! United Chocolate will pay for their tuition fees too, provided that they stay with the company for a certain number of years after that.

12. **Susan:** That's only normal.

13. **Mr Robertson:** Quite so. Well, I think we've said enough. I must see another candidate. *(They both stand)* So, it's been very nice speaking to you, Susan. *(Shaking hands and seeing her out)* And I hope to be able to give you an answer within a month,
at the latest.

14. **Susan:** Thank you very much. Goodbye.

15. **Mr Robertson:** Goodbye.

KAPITEL 2

5. **Herr Robertson:** Genau. Wie zum Beispiel ein MBA. Oh, eine Menge Unternehmen bevorzugen jetzt Hochschulabsolventen mit kaufmännischen oder Doppelabschlüssen. Diesen Trend haben wahrscheinlich die ehemaligen technischen Hochschulen in Gang gesetzt ...
6. **Susan:** Und ich habe in Frankreich zum Beispiel bemerkt, daß die meisten Manager auf Wirtschaftshochschulen angeworben werden.
7. **Herr Robertson:** Das ist völlig richtig. Wir hatten aber immer Erfolg mit unserer Strategie. Was die Tatsache betrifft, daß Sie eine Frau sind, so ist dies sicher kein Nachteil. United Chocolate hat immer versucht, Frauen einen gleichberechtigten Platz einzuräumen. Und eine beträchtliche Anzahl unserer Kunden auf der ganzen Welt sind ja Frauen. Gibt es irgendwelche Fragen, die Sie mir gerne stellen würden?
8. **Susan:** Könnten Sie etwas dazu sagen, wie es konkret aussehen würde, als Trainee Manager bei United Chocolate zu arbeiten?
9. **Herr Robertson:** Sicher. Sollten Sie bei uns anfangen, so haben Sie eine Probezeit von sechs Monaten. Während dieser Zeit lernen Sie das Unternehmen, seine Produkte, seine Aktivitäten kennen. Sie werden auch sehen, was zu den verschiedenen Management-Funktionen gehört. Wenn wir nach sechs Monaten immer noch zufrieden mit Ihnen sind, können Sie den Bereich wählen, in dem Sie gerne arbeiten würden. In Ihrem Fall zum Beispiel Marketing oder Personalwesen.
10. **Susan:** Sie haben eben erwähnt, daß Sie Leute an die Universität zurückschicken...
11. **Herr Robertson:** Ja, das habe ich. Aber ich sagte 'nur unsere größten Hoffnungsträger'! United Chocolate wird auch ihre Studiengebühren tragen, vorausgesetzt, sie bleiben danach eine Reihe von Jahren im Unternehmen.
12. **Susan:** Das ist ganz normal.
13. **Herr Robertson:** Genau. Nun, ich denke, wir haben genug geredet. Ich muß nun einen weiteren Bewerber empfangen. (*Sie stehen beide auf.*) Es war sehr nett, mit Ihnen zu sprechen, Susan. (*Er schüttelt ihre Hand, während er sie hinausbegleitet.*) Ich hoffe, daß ich Ihnen spätestens in einem Monat eine Antwort geben kann.
14. **Susan:** Vielen Dank. Auf Wiedersehen.
15. **Herr Robertson:** Auf Wiedersehen.

ANMERKUNGEN (Fortsetzung)

(4) **MBA** *Master of Business Administration:* "Graduierter Betriebswirt". Ein an den US- und mittlerweile auch an den britischen Hochschulen zu erwerbendes Diplom. Inhabern dieses Abschlusses, die eine ihrer Qualifikation entsprechende Stelle suchen, stehen in den meisten Unternehmen sämtliche Türen offen. (Siehe auch Kapitel 16, Dokument.) Im Deutschen hat sich mittlerweile der Begriff MBA eingebürgert.

(5) **Joint (Honours) Degree**: Bei dieser Art von Studiengang belegt der Student zwei gleichwertig zu beurteilende Hauptfächer, z.B. Spanisch und Wirtschaft.

(6) **Polytechnic**: Siehe Dokument.

(7) **trial period**: Wie bei uns gibt es auch in Großbritannien eine Probezeit. Dieser Begriff sollte nicht mit *training period* (Anmerkung 1) verwechselt werden.

CHAPTER 2 DOCUMENT

Higher Education in Management (UK)

Traditionally, British universities were never active in the field of management education. They believed, rightly or wrongly, that such subjects as marketing or finance had no place in academia: at most, they would teach economics and perhaps some accounting. At the same time, there seemed to be the feeling in British companies – probably born of military experience and public-school[1] education – that you could not learn to be a manager: you either had the necessary qualities or you did not. They believed that if they could find talented youngsters, they could do the management education themselves, even if this meant sending the high-flyers[2] back to school later to obtain some management qualification.

British companies would therefore be content to recruit graduates from universities, not on the basis of the subjects they had studied but of their proven intellectual ability and potential social skills. This annual search for talent, during which the big companies hold recruiting sessions in the best institutions, became known as the 'milk round', because their aim was to cream off the brightest graduates. There was also, of course, the old-boy[3] network, in which former public-school pupils, or graduates of Oxbridge[4], would give priority to people from their former institutions.

Then in 1966, Polytechnics were created and did a very good job in offering courses and degrees in business and management. For a long time, however, students with the best 'A' level results preferred universities, and British companies continued to spurn[5] these business studies graduates. It was not really until the eighties that the universities gradually became interested in management education. First, the newer universities and then the older ones started creating new courses, which were often joint Honours degrees (eg[6] French and business studies). Finally, in 1991, with the passage of the Further and Higher Education Act, Polytechnics were allowed to adopt university titles, and so the distinction between the two types of institution should now disappear.

---

[1] *public-school*: "Privatschule" (in Großbritannien bezeichnet dieser Ausdruck entgegen dem englischen Wortlaut die teuren Privat- oder Eliteschulen wie z.B. Eton, Harrow usw.).
[2] *high-flyer*: "Hochbegabter, Überflieger, Ehrgeizling".
[3] *old boy*: "Ehemaliger" (einer Schule, Universität,...)
[4] *Oxbridge*: Zusammengezogener Ausdruck aus Oxford und Cambridge.
[5] *to spurn*: "zurückweisen, abweisen".
[6] *eg* (exempli gratia): "zum Beispiel".

KAPITEL 2

"Frauen"

Die Männer reden gerne über Frauen, aber manchmal muß "man" seine Worte mit sehr viel Bedacht wählen.
Im Dialog sagt Susan, die Engländerin ist, zu Herrn Robertson: *'(...) I'm a girl!'*. In den USA, wo die Sprache in beruflichen Beziehungen mehr und mehr *politically correct* sein muß, könnte das Wort *girl*, vor allem, wenn es von einem Mann ausgesprochen wird, als abwertend aufgefaßt werden.
In Großbritannien lernen die Kinder schon früh, daß man nicht *woman*, sondern *lady* sagt, wenn von einer Frau (Dame?) die Rede ist, aber keine *lady* würde Anstoß an dem Wort *female* "Weibchen" nehmen, während diese Bezeichnung im Deutschen vollkommen unmöglich wäre, da hier eindeutig Bezug auf die Tierwelt genommen wird.
Der folgende kleine Dialog soll zeigen, wie schwierig es ist, auf diesem Gebiet das richtige Wort zu treffen:
Two men meet. The first says to the second: 'Who was that lady I saw you with last night?' The second replies: 'That was no lady, that was my wife!'

CHAPTER 2

EXERCISES

Comprehension

Lesen Sie den Dialog aufmerksam durch. Beantworten Sie dann die nachfolgenden Fragen, und zwar immer in ganzen Sätzen:

1. Where do you think this interview is taking place? **2.** Has this interview only just begun? **3.** What does Susan think her weak points might be? **4.** What is the meaning of the 'milk round'? **5.** Why has United Chocolate always been in favour of the 'milk round'? **6.** What trend did the former Polytechnics start? **7.** What is United Chocolate's policy concerning women? **8.** What are the terms of a trainee manager's contract? **9.** What does United Chocolate usually do with its 'brightest hopes'? **10.** What is Mr Robertson going to do after this interview?

Translation

1. Susan hat ein Vorstellungsgespräch bei der Firma United Chocolate, die regelmäßig Absolventen an den besten Universitäten Großbritanniens anwirbt. **2.** Was, würden Sie sagen, sind die Schwachpunkte in Ihrem Lebenslauf? **3.** Mir fehlt Erfahrung in der Unternehmenswelt, weil ich nie ein Praktikum gemacht habe. **4.** Wenn wir begabte junge Leute finden können, können wir sie selbst ausbilden. **5.** In Frankreich werden die meisten Führungskräfte von Wirtschaftshochschulen angeworben. **6.** Viele unserer Kunden weltweit sind Frauen. **7.** Wenn Sie für uns arbeiten würden, hätten Sie eine sechsmonatige Probezeit. **8.** Was gehört zu den verschiedenen Management-Funktionen in einem Unternehmen? **9.** Wir sind bereit, ihre Studiengebühren zu bezahlen, vorausgesetzt, sie bleiben einige Jahre bei uns. **10.** Ich werde Sie hinausbegleiten! Ich hoffe, daß ich Ihnen innerhalb eines Monats eine Antwort geben kann.

DO!

Start a letter to a woman by 'Dear Ms So-and-so' or 'Dear Madam'.

KAPITEL 2

LÖSUNGSVORSCHLÄGE

Verständnisübung

1. This interview is no doubt taking place somewhere at Leeds University. **2.** No. They've already covered nearly everything. **3.** She thinks her weak points might be her lack of experience of the corporate world and the fact that she's a girl. **4.** It refers to the tour of top British universities that big companies make in order to recruit graduates. **5.** Because it can find young talent to train as managers. **6.** The former Polytechnics started the trend of putting onto the job market graduates with business or joint degrees. **7.** Its policy is to give an equal place to women. **8.** A trainee manager has a trial period of six months, before choosing the area he (*or* she) wants to work in. **9.** It sends them back to university to obtain some sort of specialist qualification. **10.** Mr Robertson is going to interview another candidate.

Übersetzungsübung

1. Susan is being interviewed by United Chocolate, which regularly recruits graduates from the top UK universities. **2.** What would you say are the weak points of your CV? **3.** I lack experience of the corporate world, as I've never carried out a placement. **4.** If we can find talented young people, we can train them ourselves. **5.** In France, most executives are recruited from business schools. **6.** Many of our customers, throughout the world, are women. **7.** If you were to work for us, you would have a six-month trial period. **8.** What do the various functions of management in a company involve? **9.** We are prepared to pay their tuition fees, provided they stay with us for a certain number of years. **10.** I'll see you out! I hope to be able to give you an answer within a month.

 DON'T!

Don't address a woman as 'Miss' or 'Mrs' (pronounced: Missiz) but 'Ms' (pronounced: Miz).

CHAPTER 2

Application

Sehen Sie sich Susans Lebenslauf aufmerksam an. Setzen Sie jeweils eines der folgenden Wörter in die Lücken ein.

skills, born, experience, department, nationality, fluent, road, Spanish, mother, address, education, wine, references, employee, merchants, awarded, sports, BA, jazz, languages

Curriculum Vitae

Susan Anne EDWARDS
(1. ...): 2nd February 1971, Bristol (UK)
Current (2. ...): 1 Welburn Ave, LEEDS LS16 5HJ
Telephone: 0113 275 2706
(3. ...): British

(4. ...)

1982-89 – Thornbury Grammar School, Avon County
GCE 'A' Levels:
    Spanish (Grade A)
    French (Grade B)
    Modern history (Grade A)

1989-93 – University of Leeds
(5. ...) (Hons) in Modern Languages ([6. ...] and French)
    to be [7. ...] June 1993)

WORK (8. ...)

August 1989: Waitress – The Severn View Inn, Tockington

July-August 1990:
    Shop Assistant – Bennett & Wilson Ltd, Wine (9. ...), Bristol

July-August 1991:
    Temporary (10. ...), packing department
      Soboca, Plombières-lès-Dijon, France

September 1991-June 1992:
    Language assistant, Collegio San José,
      Plaza Santa Cruz 29, Valladolid 47002, Spain

KAPITEL 2

July-August 1992:
   Shop assistant – Bennett & Wilson Ltd, Wine merchants, Bristol

(11. ...)

English: (**12.** ...) tongue
Spanish : Very (**13.** ...)
French: Fluent
Japanese: Beginner

Travel: Spain (10 months), France (2 months), Germany (2 weeks), USA (3 weeks)

SPECIAL (14. ...)

Current driving licence
Conversant with word-processing software (Works, Word)

INTERESTS

Music: saxophonist in amateur (**15.** ...) band, modern dancing, rock 'n' roll
(**16.** ...): aerobics, horseriding, windsurfing

(17. ...)

Professor Peter Mann
(**18.** ...) of Modern Languages
University of Leeds
LEEDS LS2 9JT

Mr James Bennett
Bennett & Wilson Ltd
(**19.** ...) Merchants
21 Old Bath (**20.** ...)
BRISTOL BS1 5NG

Diese Wörter hätten Sie einsetzen sollen:

1. born **2.** address **3.** nationality **4.** education **5.** BA **6.** Spanish **7.** awarded
8. experience **9.** merchants **10.** employee **11.** languages **12.** mother **13.** fluent
14. skills **15.** jazz **16.** sports **17.** references **18.** department **19.** wine **20.** road

CHAPTER 3

Getting the job

Following her interview with United Chocolate (UK), Susan has at last received a positive answer. She is naturally delighted, and phones her parents to tell them the good news.

1. **Mrs Edwards:** Bristol 754622.
2. **Susan:** Hello Mum, it's Susan.
3. **Mrs Edwards:** Hello, dear. What a nice surprise!
4. **Susan:** I got the job, Mum!
5. **Mrs Edwards:** Which one, Susan? You've been applying for so many!
6. **Susan:** United Chocolate, of course! As a trainee manager.
7. **Mrs Edwards:** *(Without enthusiasm)* Well, congratulations, Susan. Have you accepted yet?
8. **Susan:** No, but I intend to write the letter this weekend.
9. **Mrs Edwards:** You must be very pleased.
10. **Susan:** Of course I am, Mum. But you don't sound very pleased.
11. **Mrs Edwards:** Oh, of course I am. I just hope you're doing the right thing, that's all!
12. **Susan:** I suppose you'd rather I went into the Civil Service like Dad. Or found a husband and started a family. **(1)**
13. **Mrs Edwards:** Now don't be unfair! Your father has had a very good career in the Civil Service. And what's wrong with getting married and having children?
14. **Susan:** Look Mum, we've been through all this before. I don't want to work in the Civil Service and I don't want to settle down. Not for the time being at least. I want a challenging career. I want to travel and meet people. Job satisfaction, Mum, plus a good salary and prospects for the future.

KAPITEL 3

Eingestellt

Nach ihrem Vorstellungsgespräch bei United Chocolate (UK) hat Susan schließlich eine positive Antwort erhalten. Sie freut sich natürlich und ruft ihre Eltern an, um ihnen die gute Nachricht mitzuteilen.

1. **Frau Edwards:** Bristol 754622.

2. **Susan:** Hallo Mami, ich bin's, Susan.

3. **Frau Edwards:** Hallo Liebes. Was für eine nette Überraschung!

4. **Susan:** Ich hab den Job gekriegt, Mami!

5. **Frau Edwards:** Welchen, Susan? Du hast dich für so viele Jobs beworben!

6. **Susan:** Bei United Chocolate, natürlich! Als Trainee Manager.

7. **Frau Edwards:** *(Ohne Begeisterung)* Na, gratuliere, Susan. Hast du ihn schon angenommen?

8. **Susan:** Nein, aber ich habe vor, dieses Wochenende den Brief zu schreiben.

9. **Frau Edwards:** Du must sehr zufrieden sein.

10. **Susan:** Natürlich bin ich das, Mami. Aber du klingst nicht so zufrieden.

11. **Frau Edwards:** Oh, sicher bin ich zufrieden. Ich hoffe nur, daß du richtig handelst, das ist alles!

12. **Susan:** Ich nehme an, du hättest es lieber gehabt, wenn ich die Beamtenlaufbahn eingeschlagen hätte, wie Papi. Oder geheiratet und eine Familie gegründet hätte.

13. **Frau Edwards:** Jetzt sei mal nicht ungerecht! Dein Vater hat im Staatsdienst eine sehr gute Karriere gemacht. Und was ist falsch daran, zu heiraten und Kinder zu bekommen?

14. **Susan:** Guck mal, Mami. Wir haben das alles schon mal durchgesprochen. Ich möchte nicht im Staatsdienst arbeiten, und ich möchte nicht häuslich werden. Zumindest nicht im Moment. Ich möchte eine herausfordernde Karriere. Ich möchte reisen und Leute treffen. Zufriedenheit im Job, Mami, plus ein gutes Gehalt und Aussichten für die Zukunft.

ANMERKUNGEN

(1) **Civil Service** (GB): "Staatsdienst, öffentlicher Dienst". In den USA spricht man eher von *government workers*.

CHAPTER 3

15. **Mrs Edwards:** What sort of terms of employment are they offering you?
16. **Susan:** Well, I told you the salary,...
17. **Mrs Edwards:** Yes. Almost as much as your father earns now!
18. **Susan:** ... and then, of course, I'll have a six-month trial period,...
19. **Mrs Edwards:** That's what worries me. What if they decide they don't want you after six months? You know what these big companies are like.
20. **Susan:** But they will want me Mum; I'm going to succeed. They even pay for their best young managers to go back to university.
21. **Mrs Edwards:** Mmm...
22. **Susan:** Is Dad there? I'd like to break the news to him.
23. **Mrs Edwards:** I'll go and get him; he's watching a football match on TV.

    A short pause.

24. **Mr Edwards:** *(With enthusiasm)* Hello, Susan. Congratulations! Your mother told me the news. We're really proud of you!
25. **Susan:** Mum didn't sound too pleased, though. She'd rather I went into the Civil Service.
26. **Mr Edwards:** Well, your mother only wants what's best for you. She doesn't know what working in the Civil Service is really like. You go ahead and be a businesswoman. I can just imagine all the perks. **(2)**
27. **Susan:** Look Dad, I won't get many fringe benefits at the beginning, but... **(3)**
28. **Mr Edwards:** Listen Susan. I must ring off now. Someone has just scored a goal. It's been lovely speaking to you. Congratulations, and we'll see you on graduation day. **(4)**

KAPITEL 3

15. **Frau Edwards:** Welche Beschäftigungsbedingungen bieten sie dir?
16. **Susan:** Naja, ich sagte dir ja: das Gehalt...
17. **Frau Edwards:** Ja, fast so viel wie dein Vater jetzt verdient!
18. **Susan:** ... und dann habe ich natürlich eine sechsmonatige Probezeit...
19. **Frau Edwards:** Das ist es, was mich beunruhigt. Was ist, wenn sie sich nach sechs Monaten entschließen, daß sie dich nicht mehr wollen? Du weißt doch, wie diese großen Firmen sind.
20. **Susan:** Aber sie werden mich wollen, Mami; ich werde Erfolg haben. Sie bezahlen den besten jungen Führungskräften sogar noch ein Studium...
21. **Frau Edwards:** Mmmh....
22. **Susan:** Ist Papi da? Ich würde ihm die Neuigkeit gerne mitteilen.
23. **Frau Edwards:** Ich gehe ihn holen; er guckt sich ein Fußballspiel im Fernsehen an.

Kurze Pause.

24. **Herr Edwards:** *(Begeistert)* Hallo Susan. Herzlichen Glückwunsch! Deine Mutter hat mir die Neuigkeit erzählt. Wir sind wirklich stolz auf dich!
25. **Susan:** Mami hat aber nicht allzu zufrieden geklungen. Sie hätte es lieber, wenn ich Beamtin würde.
26. **Herr Edwards:** Naja, deine Mutter will immer nur das Beste für dich. Sie weiß nicht, wie es wirklich ist, im Staatsdienst zu arbeiten. Mach du nur so weiter und werde Geschäftsfrau. Ich kann mir gut all die Sondervergünstigungen vorstellen.
27. **Susan:** Naja, Papi, ich werde am Anfang nicht viele Gehaltsnebenleistungen bekommen, aber ...
28. **Herr Edwards:** Hör mal zu, Susan. Ich muß jetzt aufhören. Gerade hat einer ein Tor geschossen. Es war nett, mir dir zu sprechen. Herzlichen Glückwunsch, wir sehen uns bei der Diplomverleihung.

ANMERKUNGEN (Fortsetzung)

(2) **perks**: Kurzform für *perquisites* "Sondervergünstigungen". Man sagt auch:
(3) **(fringe) benefits**: Führungskräfte kommen häufig in den Genuß von Sonderleistungen wie z.B. einem Firmenwagen *(company car)* oder einer privaten oder Zusatzkrankenversicherung *(private health insurance)*, die es ihm in Großbritannien erlaubt, Krankenversicherungsleistungen in Anspruch zu nehmen, die über die des *National Health Service* hinausgehen. Manchmal erhält der Angestellte auch die Möglichkeit, Firmenanteile *(stock options)* zu kaufen. In diesem Zusammenhang muß auch das *non-contributory pension scheme* erwähnt werden, eine beitragsfreie Betriebspension, die vollständig vom Arbeitgeber finanziert wird. (Im *contributory pension scheme* zahlt der Arbeitnehmer in eine beitragspflichtige Pensionskasse.)
(4) **graduation day**: Ein wichtiger Tag im Leben britischer und amerikanischer Hochschulabgänger, an dem die Diplomierten, bekleidet mit einem Talar *(gown)* und einem Barett *(mortar-board)* auf dem Kopf, in einer feierlichen Zeremonie ihr Diplom entgegennehmen.

CHAPTER 3

DOCUMENT

Letter of Appointment

UNITED CHOCOLATE (UK) Ltd
Thornbury House
Arlington Row
MILTON KEYNES
Bucks, MK2 5BQ
Tel: 01908 956384
Fax: 01908 956122

Ms Susan Edwards,
1 Welburn Ave,
LEEDS LS16 5HJ

20th May 199.

Dear Ms Edwards,
    Further to the interview which you had with my assistant, Mr Keith Robertson at the University of Leeds last month, I am pleased to inform you that we should like to offer you a position in our company as trainee manager.

    You will find enclosed two copies of the contract which specifies the conditions of employment. Please read this document carefully, and if you are in agreement with its terms, sign both copies and return them to me. We will then send you your copy in due course.

    We should like you to take up your position between 1st and 15th July if this is convenient for you. Please let us know your starting date as soon as possible.

    Let me take this opportunity of congratulating you. I look forward to meeting you and welcoming you to United Chocolate.

    Yours sincerely,

Alexander Romer-Lee
Director of Human Resources

Encl.: Employment contract

KAPITEL 3

Die Telefonnummern

Während man sich in Deutschland mit dem Familiennamen am Telefon meldet, nennt man in Großbritannien seine Telefonnummer. Dies ist vor allem bei Privatpersonen sehr gängig, auch wenn man über den Nutzen dieses Brauchs streiten kann. Denn oft wird die Nummer so schnell aufgesagt, daß man Mühe hat, sie zu verstehen, vor allem, wenn man kein Engländer ist.
Susans Mutter teilt, wie dies in Großbritannien üblich ist, die Nummer in 3er- oder 4er-Einheiten ein (754-622) und nicht, wie man es bei uns machen würde, in 2er-Einheiten (75 46 22). In diesem speziellen Fall können die drei letzten Ziffern entweder *six-two-two* oder *six-double-two* gelesen werden.
Beachten Sie, daß anstelle der Ortsvorwahl (*local dialling code* in Großbritannien, *area code* in den USA) sehr häufig die entsprechende Stadt genannt wird. Man sagt also *Bristol 754-622* anstelle von *0272-754-622*.
Wenn Ihnen Ihr Gesprächspartner in Großbritannien seine komplette Telefonnummer mit Ortsvorwahl gibt, so verhält es sich hier wie in Deutschland: Sie brauchen die erste Null nicht zu wählen, wenn Sie vom Ausland aus anrufen. Für "Null" sagt man entweder *zero* (immer häufiger) oder *O* (wie der Buchstabe O).

CHAPTER 3

EXERCISES

Comprehension

Lesen Sie den Dialog aufmerksam durch. Beantworten Sie dann die nachfolgenden Fragen, und zwar immer in ganzen Sätzen:

1. Why has Susan phoned her parents? 2. Was Mrs Edwards expecting Susan to call? 3. When is Susan going to accept the post she has been offered? 4. Do you think Susan's mother is happy to hear the news? 5. Does Susan intend to get married and start a family? 6. How does Susan see her immediate future? 7. Do United Chocolate pay their trainee managers well? 8. Do you think Susan's father is pleased to hear the news? 9. Do you think he enjoys being a civil servant? 10. When will Susan next see her parents?

Translation

1. Auf den Brief, den sie an Petrochem Plc schrieb, erhielt Susan eine abschlägige Antwort. 2. Ich weiß, daß sie schließlich einen Job bekommen hat, aber welchen? Sie hat sich für so viele beworben. 3. Ich habe vor, dieses Wochenende meine Eltern anzurufen. 4. Herr Edwards klang nicht zufrieden. Er hörte sich ein Fußballspiel im Radio an. 5. Nach der Probezeit wird Susan mehr als ihr Vater verdienen. 6. Geld ist nicht alles, weißt du. Zufriedenheit im Job und Aussichten für die Zukunft sind auch wichtig. 7. Im Staatsdienst hast du nicht oft so viele Sondervergünstigungen. 8. Ich muß auflegen; wir sehen dich in den Osterferien. 9. Wenn Catherine wüßte, wie Forschungsarbeit an der Universität wirklich ist, bin ich sicher, sie würde es vorziehen, Führungskraft in einer Firma zu sein. 10. Oft wollen die Firmen nach einigen Monaten die jungen Leute, die sie eingestellt haben, nicht mehr.

KAPITEL 3

LÖSUNGSVORSCHLÄGE

Verständnisübung

1. Susan has phoned her parents to tell them she'd got the job with UC. 2. No, she wasn't. She says it's a nice surprise. 3. She is going to accept the post this weekend. 4. She probably is, but she doesn't want Susan to do the wrong thing. 5. No, she doesn't want to get married and start a family, for the time being at least. 6. She sees her immediate future in a challenging career. 7. Yes, from what Mrs Edwards says, we can assume that UC pay their trainee managers well. 8. Yes, he seems very pleased to hear the news. 9. Probably not. He seems to contradict his wife. 10. She will see them next on graduation day.

Übersetzungsübung

1. Following the letter she wrote to Petrochem Plc, Susan received a negative answer. 2. I know she has at last got a job, but which one? She's been applying for so many. 3. I intend to phone my parents this weekend. 4. Mr Edwards didn't sound pleased. He was listening to a football match on the radio. 5. After the trial period, Susan will earn more than her father. 6. Money's not everything, you know. Job satisfaction and prospects for the future are important, too. 7. You don't often have as many fringe benefits in the Civil Service. 8. I must ring off; we'll see you during the Easter vacation. 9. If Catherine knew what doing research at the university was really like, I'm sure she'd prefer to be a company executive. 10. Often, after a few months, companies no longer want the young people they've recruited.

CHAPTER 3

Application

Hier ist ein neuer Typ von Übung, der Ihre Kreativität ein bißchen fordern soll. Seien Sie aber ehrlich mit sich selbst und versuchen Sie, nicht auf das vorbereitete Modell zu sehen, es sei denn, Sie wissen gar nicht mehr weiter. Sehen Sie sich noch einmal den Brief an, den Susan an John Chartres Plc (Kapitel 1, Übung 3) geschrieben hat. Verfassen Sie einen Brief auf der Basis der Vorlage und antworten Sie abschlägig auf Susans Anfrage. In Ihrer Antwort sollten Sie unter anderem:

* Susan für ihr Schreiben danken;
* ihre Bewerbung ablehnen und diese Ablehnung begründen (z.B. wegen nicht ausreichender Französischkenntnisse);
* den Brief mit einer höflichen Formel schließen.

DO!

**On meeting someone for the first time, the response to 'How do you do?' must be 'How do you do?'
On meeting again: 'How are you?'
'Fine, thank you. And you?'**

KAPITEL 3

Praktische Übung

John CHARTRES Plc
Seville Road
HAVANT
Hants PO9 2TN

Ms Susan Edwards,
1 Welburn Ave,
LEEDS LS16 5HJ

                                   23rd April 199.

Dear Ms Edwards,
      Thank you so much for applying for the post of Junior Marketing Manager within this company. I am sorry to have been so long giving you an answer, but as you can imagine, we received a large number of applications.

      We gave much attention to your CV, but I regret to inform you that we have decided not to offer you the post. We found your profile very interesting, but feel that your level in French is not sufficient to meet our requirements.

      We wish you luck in the search for your first post, and feel convinced that you will find what you are looking for with another company.

      Yours sincerely,

      Ruth Newland
      Personnel Assistant

DON'T!

In letter-writing, don't forget to practise the three C's:
be clear, concise and courteous.

CHAPTER 4 🖭

Starting work

Susan has now graduated from the University of Leeds and has started her job with United Chocolate (UK) Ltd. This is her first day at the company's registered office in Milton Keynes, north of London. She is being officially welcomed by Mr Romer-Lee, Director of Human Resources. **(1)**

1. **Mr Romer-Lee:** So, welcome to United Chocolate, Susan. I'm very pleased you decided to come and work for us. Gosh! You didn't get that sun tan in England, I know!

2. **Susan:** No! I've just got back from a holiday in Corfu.

3. **Mr Romer-Lee:** Lucky you! Well, I'm afraid the holiday is over now, for some time too! We're going to keep you pretty busy here!

4. **Susan:** I know you're very busy, anyway. It is very good of you to go out of your way to welcome me this morning.

5. **Mr Romer-Lee:** Well, I always make a point of welcoming trainee managers. I feel it's important. Now I see Mr Robertson has already given you an information pack to read about United Chocolate.

6. **Susan:** Yes. *(Rapidly going through it)* Annual report, company accounts, pressbook, brochures about the products, examples of advertising campaigns...

7. **Mr Romer-Lee:** Do you have any questions?

8. **Susan:** Well, I'm sure I'll have lots of things to ask when I've read it all. There is one thing I don't really understand, though.

9. **Mr Romer-Lee:** What's that?

10. **Susan:** It's just that Mr Robertson referred to the company as United Chocolate *Ltd.* I always thought that big companies had the initials *Plc,* like Marks and Spencer *Plc,* for example. **(2)**

KAPITEL 4

Der erste Arbeitstag

Susan hat nun ihr Diplom an der Universität von Leeds erworben und ihre Stelle bei United Chocolate (UK) Ltd. angetreten. Dies ist ihr erster Tag an der Hauptniederlassung des Unternehmens in Milton Keynes nördlich von London. Sie wird offiziell von Herrn Romer-Lee, dem Personalchef, begrüßt.

1. **Herr Romer-Lee:** Na dann, willkommen bei United Chocolate, Susan. Ich freue mich sehr, daß Sie sich entschieden haben, bei uns zu arbeiten. Mein Gott! Diese Bräune haben Sie sich bestimmt nicht in England geholt!?

2. **Susan:** Nein! Ich komme gerade vom Urlaub aus Korfu zurück.

3. **Herr Romer-Lee:** Sie Glückliche! Nun ja, ich fürchte, die Ferien sind nun vorüber, und das für eine ganze Weile! Wir werden Sie hier schön beschäftigen!

4. **Susan:** Ich weiß ja, daß Sie sehr viel zu tun haben. Es ist sehr nett von Ihnen, daß Sie sich Zeit genommen haben, mich heute morgen zu begrüßen.

5. **Herr Romer-Lee:** Nun ja, ich lege immer großen Wert darauf, Trainee Manager zu begrüßen. Ich finde, das ist wichtig. Ich sehe gerade, daß Herr Robertson Ihnen schon eine Informationsmappe über United Chocolate zum Lesen gegeben hat.

6. **Susan:** Ja. *(Sie blättert sie schnell durch.)* Jahresbericht, Firmenbuchhaltung, Pressemappe, Produktbroschüren, Beispiele für Werbekampagnen...

7. **Herr Romer-Lee:** Haben Sie irgendwelche Fragen?

8. **Susan:** Naja, ich bin sicher, daß ich eine Menge fragen werde, wenn ich alles durchgelesen habe. Aber es gibt etwas, das ich wirklich nicht verstehe.

9. **Herr Romer-Lee:** Und das wäre?

10. **Susan:** Es geht nur darum, daß Herr Robertson vom Unternehmen als 'United Chocolate *Ltd.*' gesprochen hat. Ich habe immer gedacht, daß große Unternehmen den Firmenzusatz *Plc* haben, wie 'Marks and Spencer *Plc*', zum Beispiel.

ANMERKUNGEN

(1) Ltd. ist die Abkürzung von *Limited* und kennzeichnet in Großbritannien eine *Private Limited Company*, die in etwa unserer deutschen GmbH (Gesellschaft mit beschränkter Haftung) entspricht (siehe Dokument).

(2) Plc steht für *Public Limited Company* und ist in etwa vergleichbar mit unserer AG (Aktiengesellschaft; siehe Dokument). Andere Gesellschaftsformen sind *sole trader* "Einzelkaufmann, Einzelfirma" und *partnership* "offene Handelsgesellschaft, Personengesellschaft".

CHAPTER 4

11. **Mr Romer-Lee:** Unfortunately, it's a little more complicated than that, Susan. Basically, there are two main types of company in the UK. Private limited companies and public limited companies. You mustn't confuse that with the notion of the *private* or *public* sector, by the way. All it really means is that a company's shares can or cannot be traded publicly. **(3) (4) (5)**

12. **Susan:** And United Chocolate's can't?

13. **Mr Romer-Lee:** No, not in the UK. You see, United Chocolate (UK) is a wholly-owned subsidiary of the US parent company. The Americans control all the stock – capital stock as the accountants call it. *(After a pause)* Incidentally, talking of Marks and Spencer, they're a very big customer of ours. **(6) (7)**

14. **Susan:** But I thought they only sold their own products.

15. **Mr Romer-Lee:** Of course, they do. But who makes those products for them? Own-brand products for big retail chains are an important part of our turnover.

16. **Susan:** I can see I'm going to have an awful lot to learn!

17. **Mr Romer-Lee:** Yes, but during your six-month trial period you'll spend some time working in each of the company's departments: Financial and Legal, Marketing and so on.

18. **Susan:** And Personnel, too, I hope.

19. **Mr Romer-Lee:** Human Resources, too, naturally. OK, Susan. Let's go for lunch, if you're ready.

KAPITEL 4

11. **Herr Romer-Lee:** Leider ist es ein bißchen komplizierter, Susan. Im Grunde gibt es zwei Haupttypen von Gesellschaften in Großbritannien, die *Private Limited Company* und die *Public Limited Company*. Sie dürfen das übrigens nicht mit dem Begriff des *privaten* oder *öffentlichen* Sektors verwechseln. Es bedeutet lediglich, daß die Aktien eines Unternehmens öffentlich gehandelt werden können oder nicht.

12. **Susan:** Und das kann United Chocolate nicht?

13. **Herr Romer-Lee:** Nein, nicht in Großbritannien. Sehen Sie, United Chocolate (UK) ist eine hundertprozentige Tochtergesellschaft der US-Muttergesellschaft. Die Amerikaner kontrollieren das gesamte Kapital – das Grundkapital, wie die Buchhalter sagen. *(Nach einer Pause)* Nebenbei bemerkt, wo wir gerade von Marks and Spencer sprechen: das ist ein sehr großer Kunde von uns.

14. **Susan:** Aber ich habe gedacht, sie verkaufen nur ihre eigenen Produkte.

15. **Herr Romer-Lee:** Natürlich tun sie das. Aber wer stellt diese Produkte für sie her? Hausmarkenprodukte für große Einzelhandelsketten stellen einen wichtigen Teil unseres Geschäftsumsatzes dar.

16. **Susan:** Ich sehe schon: Ich habe noch schrecklich viel zu lernen!

17. **Herr Romer-Lee:** Ja, aber Sie werden während Ihrer sechsmonatigen Probezeit jede Abteilung des Unternehmens durchlaufen: Finanz- und Rechtsabteilung, Marketing usw.

18. **Susan:** Und die Personalabteilung auch, hoffe ich.

19. **Herr Romer-Lee:** Die Personalabteilung natürlich auch. Gut, Susan. Gehen wir zum Mittagessen, wenn Sie fertig sind.

ANMERKUNGEN (Fortsetzung)

(3) **private sector**: Die Summe aller wirtschaftlichen Aktivitäten, die von juristischen oder natürlichen Personen unternommen werden, und deren Ziel der private Gewinn ist. Gegenteil von:

(4) **public sector**: Alle wirtschaftlichen Aktivitäten, die vom Staat, d.h. von Staatsbetrieben, unternommen werden.

(5) **shares** ist der angelsächsische Sammelbegriff für "Aktien", während die Amerikaner *stock* sagen. Entsprechend heißt der "Aktionär" in Großbritannien *shareholder* und in den USA *stockholder*.

(6) **parent company**: "Muttergesellschaft". Ein Unternehmen, das die direkte oder indirekte Mehrheit oder sogar das gesamte Kapital besitzt und aufgrund dessen ein oder mehrere andere Unternehmen, die sog. "Tochtergesellschaften" *(subsidiaries)*, kontrolliert.

(7) **capital stock**: "Grundkapital" eines Unternehmens, also alle Besitztitel einer Gesellschaft (Aktien und Anteile) zum Nennwert *(nominal value (GB), par value (US))*. Nicht zu verwechseln mit *shareholders's funds (GB)* bzw. *stockholders' equity (US)* "Eigenkapital", bei einer AG das Grundkapital samt offener Rücklagen. (Siehe Kapitel 36, Dokument).

CHAPTER 4

DOCUMENT

Types of Business Structure (UK)

In the UK, there are three basic types of business structure: the *sole trader*, the *partnership* and the *limited company*. Let's try and understand the very big differences which exist between them.

* The *sole trader* – This is the simplest form of business organisation and it can be set up without any legal formalities. The trader must obviously comply with national laws *(Acts of Parliament)* and local laws *(by[e]-laws)*. This simple structure is suitable for shopkeepers or craftsmen. They are entitled to all the profits, but will pay income tax on these. They also have unlimited liability for any debts the business incurs.

* The *partnership* – This form of business organisation, governed by the Partnership Acts 1890 and 1907, is most commonly used by professional people, eg accountants, solicitors, doctors, etc. With a few exceptions, twenty is the maximum number of partners.
Normally, all partners have unlimited liability, both jointly and severally *(general partnership)*, but provided there is at least one unlimited partner, it is possible to have limited partners *(limited partnership)*.
Profits are shared equally or in any other way which is specified in the *Deed of Partnership*.

* The *limited company* – The Companies Acts 1985, amended in 1989, consolidated current company law. There are about a million limited companies, which may be either *public* or *private:*

Public Limited Company (Plc): The word *public* here means that the shares and debentures of a Plc can be bought and sold by members of the general public. Even if numerically Plcs represent a tiny minority of UK companies, they are obviously, because of their size, the country's most important companies. Moreover, only about one third of them are quoted on the London Stock Exchange, some of the rest being traded on other smaller markets.

Profits are distributed in the form of dividends, and liability is limited to the shareholding a person has in the company. A minimum of two members are required, but there is no upward limit.

Private Limited Company (Ltd): This type of company is governed by the same rules and regulations as the Plc. Its shares and debentures, however, cannot be bought and sold by the general public and it will not be quoted, therefore, on the Stock Exchange. Since 1992, when the Twelfth EC Company Law Directive came into effect, it has even been possible for an individual person to form what is known as a Single Member Private Company.

KAPITEL 4

Das "Duzen" bei Engländern und Amerikanern

Das englische *you* ("Du", "Sie") erlaubt keine Unterscheidung zwischen "duzen" und "siezen". Es ist neutral und gibt keinen Hinweis darauf, wieviel Nähe oder Distanz man zu seinem Gesprächspartner hat.
Wie machen also die Engländer bzw. die Amerikaner diesen subtilen Unterschied zwischen Personen, die sie siezen, und solchen, die sie duzen? Natürlich indem sie den Vornamen der jeweiligen Person verwenden oder eben den Nachnamen, dem dann *Mr., Miss, Ms* oder *Mrs.* vorangestellt wird. In der Arbeitswelt geht es in Großbritannien und in den USA etwas weniger steif zu als in Deutschland; dort sprechen sich Kollegen in den meisten Fällen mit dem Vornamen an.
Man braucht also nicht erstaunt zu sein, wenn Herr Romer-Lee *Susan* sofort bei ihrem Vornamen nennt, anstatt *Miss Edwards* zu sagen. Susan dagegen muß warten, bis ihr Vorgesetzter ihr das "Du" anbietet, indem er sagt: *"Call me Alex"*. Aber es wird bestimmt nicht lange dauern, bis das geschieht.

CHAPTER 4

EXERCISES

Comprehension

Lesen Sie den Dialog aufmerksam durch. Beantworten Sie dann die nachfolgenden Fragen, und zwar immer in ganzen Sätzen:

1. Did Susan go to work for United Chocolate immediately after graduation? **2.** Who is the first person that Susan meets at United Chocolate? **3.** Has Susan read the literature she has been given about United Chocolate yet? **4.** Does she have many questions to ask Mr Romer-Lee? **5.** What doesn't Susan really understand about United Chocolate? **6.** Why is United Chocolate (UK) not referred to as a Plc? **7.** Who owns United Chocolate (UK)? **8.** Give a synonym for stockholders' equity. **9.** Do Marks and Spencer only sell their own products? **10.** How will Susan get to know about business in general at United Chocolate in particular?

Translation

1. Die Hauptniederlassung befindet sich in Slough, westlich von London. **2.** Herr Romer-Lee, der Personalchef, heißt alle künftigen Führungskräfte persönlich (selbst) willkommen. **3.** In der Informationsmappe, das sein (ihr) Kollege ihm (ihr) gegeben hat, fehlt die Firmenbuchhaltung, die vertraulich ist. **4.** Aber ich dachte, daß sich *public company* auf einen staatseigenen Betrieb bezieht. **5.** Unsere Aktien können nicht öffentlich gehandelt werden. **6.** UC besitzt drei hundertprozentige Tochtergesellschaften in verschiedenen europäischen Ländern. **7.** Hausmarkenprodukte für große Einzelhandelsketten stellen keinen wichtigen Teil unseres Geschäftsumsatzes dar. **8.** Unter unseren bedeutendsten Kunden sind jedoch einige große Einzelhandelsketten. **9.** Ich würde lieber in der Marketingabteilung als in der Finanzabteilung arbeiten. **10.** Das Grundkapital des Unternehmens wird von der Muttergesellschaft in Großbritannien gehalten.

KAPITEL 4

LÖSUNGSVORSCHLÄGE

Verständnisübung

1. No, she went on holiday in Corfu first. 2. The first person that Susan meets at UC is Mr Romer-Lee, the Director of Human Resources. 3. No, she hasn't read it all yet. 4. No, but she'll have lots of things to ask when she's read all the literature. 5. She doesn't understand why UC (UK) is referred to as *Ltd* and not *Plc*. 6. Because it is a private company, whose shares cannot be traded publicly. 7. UC (UK) is fully owned by the US parent company. 8. A synonym for stockholders' equity is shareholders' funds. 9. Yes, M&S only sell their own products. 10. During her six-month trial period, she'll spend some time working in each of the company's departments.

Übersetzungsübung

1. The company's registered office is in Slough, west of London. 2. Mr Romer-Lee, the Director of Human Resources, welcomes all the future executives himself. 3. In the information pack which his (*or* her) colleague gave him (*or* her), the company accounts, which are confidential, are missing. 4. But I thought that *public company* referred to a state-owned company. 5. Our shares cannot be traded publicly (*or* bought or sold by the general public). 6. UC has three fully-owned subsidiaries in various European countries. 7. Own-brand products for retail chains do not represent a large part of our turnover. 8. Several large retail chains, however, are among our biggest customers. 9. I'd rather work in the marketing department than in the finance department. 10. The company's (capital) stock is held by the parent company in the UK.

CHAPTER 4

Application

Lesen Sie sich die folgenden Aussagen aufmerksam durch und entscheiden Sie, welche wahr und welche falsch sind. Korrigieren Sie die falschen Aussagen auf Englisch.

1. The status of *sole trader* is usually preferred by small shopkeepers.
2. The principal advantage of being a sole trader is that you do not have to pay income tax.
3. To form a general partnership, you need a minimum of twenty partners.
4. In a general partnership, all partners have unlimited liability.
5. Limited companies are governed by the Companies Acts 1980 amended in 1907.
6. There are about a billion limited companies in the UK.
7. Only a public limited company can be quoted on the Stock Exchange.
8. A private limited company has between two and fifty shareholders.
9. The notion of public and private limited companies should not be equated with that of the public and private sectors.
10. It is impossible to form a private company with only one person.

DO!

*When you go abroad, show self-discipline.
Consider that you are an ambassador of your country.*

KAPITEL 4

Praktische Übung

1. *Wahr.*
2. *Falsch:* The principal disadvantage of being a sole trader is that you pay income tax on your profits.
3. *Falsch:* This is normally the maximum number of partners for any partnership.
4. *Wahr.*
5. *Falsch:* Limited companies are governed by the Companies Acts 1985, amended in 1989.
6. *Falsch:* There are about 4,000 public limited companies (Plc) in the UK.
7. *Wahr.*
8. *Wahr.*
9. *Wahr.*
10. *Falsch:* Since 1992, it has been possible to form a single member private company.

DON'T!

Don't shake hands every time you meet an American (or a Briton, for that matter). In America and Britain, people shake hands when they first meet.

CHAPTER 5

Getting to know the company (I)

After having lunch in the Managers' dining-room with Mr Romer-Lee, Director of Human Resources, Susan is being briefed by the Assistant Director, Mr Robertson, on the structure and organisation of the company. **(1)**

1. **Mr Robertson:** You are already aware that our parent company, United Chocolate Inc, is a multinational corporation headquartered in Philadelphia, Pennsylvania. **(2) (3) (4)**

2. **Susan:** *(Smiling)* Also known as the Quaker State. **(5)**

3. **Mr Robertson:** Indeed. William Penn, a famous Quaker, fled to America at the end of the XVIIth century to escape religious persecutions in England. He founded a colony which was named after him.

4. **Susan:** I seem to remember, from my university history and literary readings, that the Quakers were most active in the development of the chocolate trade in Britain during the XVIIIth century, in order to counter the consumption of tea, which they considered an intoxicating beverage!

5. **Mr Robertson:** *(Impressed)* A relevant remark, showing extensive general culture.

6. **Susan:** Thank you! *(Humorously)* The study of the humanities may not be a waste of time after all!

7. **Mr Robertson:** We certainly owe a lot to the Quakers, who pioneered in what we now describe as the food industry and, generally speaking, the agri-business. The ways of the Lord are impenetrable!

8. **Susan:** *(After a short pause)* To return to your original point, am I right to assume that all the decisions made in the home office, here, have to be approved in Philadelphia?

KAPITEL 5

Die Firma kennenlernen (I)

Nachdem Sie mit Herrn Romer-Lee, dem Personalchef, in der Kantine für Führungskräfte ihr Mittagessen eingenommen hat, wird Susan vom stellvertretenden Direktor, Herrn Robertson, über die Struktur und Organisation des Unternehmens unterrichtet.

1. **Herr Robertson:** Sie wissen bereits, daß unsere Muttergesellschaft, United Chocolate Inc., ein multinationales Unternehmen mit Sitz in Philadelphia, Pennsylvania, ist.
2. **Susan:** *(Lächelt)* Auch als Quäker-Staat bekannt.
3. **Herr Robertson:** Genau. William Penn, ein berühmter Quäker, flüchtete Ende des 17. Jahrhunderts nach Amerika, um der religiösen Verfolgung in England zu entgehen. Er gründete eine Kolonie, die nach ihm benannt wurde.
4. **Susan:** Ich glaube, ich erinnere mich aus den Geschichts- und Literaturvorlesungen an der Universität, daß die Quäker während des 18. Jahrhunderts in der Entwicklung des Schokoladenhandels in Großbritannien sehr aktiv waren, um gegen den Konsum von Tee anzugehen, den sie für ein giftiges Getränk hielten!
5. **Herr Robertson:** *(Beeindruckt)* Eine wichtige Bemerkung, die von sehr gutem Allgemeinwissen zeugt.
6. **Susan:** Danke! *(Belustigt)* Das Studium der Geisteswissenschaften ist wahrscheinlich doch keine Zeitverschwendung!
7. **Herr Robertson:** Wir haben den Quäkern sicherlich viel zu verdanken, da sie Pionierarbeit in dem Bereich geleistet haben, den wir heute als Lebensmittelindustrie oder allgemein Agrarindustrie bezeichnen. Die Wege des Herrn sind unergründlich!
8. **Susan:** *(Nach einer kurzen Pause)* Um zum Ausgangspunkt zurückzukommen: Liege ich richtig, wenn ich annehme, daß alle Entscheidungen, die am hiesigen Sitz getroffen werden, in Philadelphia genehmigt werden müssen?

ANMERKUNGEN

(1) **to brief:** "unterweisen, unterrichten, informieren". *Briefing* "Unterrichtung, Instruktionen, Anweisungen" (siehe Kapitel 23, Anmerkung 2).
(2) **Inc.** ist die Abkürzung von *incorporated* "als Aktiengesellschaft eingetragen".
(3) **corporation (US):** "Kapital-, Aktiengesellschaft". Dieser Ausdruck deckt die beiden angelsächsischen Gesellschaftsformen *Ltd* und *Plc* bzw. die beiden deutschen Gesellschaftsformen GmbH und AG ab.
(4) **to be headquartered** bedeutet "seinen Firmensitz ... haben". Das US-Synonym zu "Firmensitz" lautet *registered office* oder *corporate headquarters*, das angelsächsische Synonym *company headquarters*.
(5) **Quaker:** Die "Quäker", deren Name vom Verb *to quake* "zittern" kommt, waren Mitglieder einer protestantischen Sekte im England des 17. Jahrhunderts. Die Quäker glauben an die unmittelbare Erleuchtung der Gläubigen durch Gott. Sie verwerfen Sakramente, Priestertum, Eid, Krieg und Lustbarkeiten und wirkten in und nach den Weltkriegen durch ihre großzügige Wohltätigkeit.

CHAPTER 5

9. **Mr Robertson:** Things are not that simple. Our company, originally founded in the USA in the second half of the XIXth century, currently operates almost all over the world, which implies the defining and implementing of a global strategy at a certain level. That strategy must integrate the organisation's objectives into a cohesive whole...
(A discreet knock on the door)

10. **Mr Robertson:** Come in!

11. **Gladys:** *(Mr Robertson's secretary)* Sorry sir. A long-distance call from Mr Van Gulik of corporate headquarters. Should I say you are temporarily engaged?

12. **Mr Robertson:** No, it's 2 pm. I was expecting that call. With Susan's permission, I will take it right now. Put him through to me in the conference room and ask him to hold the line.
(To Susan) Will you please excuse me? I won't be long. In the meantime, do examine the organisation chart and prepare your questions.
(About ten minutes later) I must apologise for the interruption. That was my corresponding number in Philadelphia. *(Looking at his watch)* I'm afraid I'm going to have to leave you soon and shoot down to Heathrow, too. By the way, Susan, did Mr Romer-Lee tell you that before you start your trial period, as such, we're going to send you to work a month in one of our factories down near Bristol? Starting next Monday, if that's convenient for you.

13. **Susan:** Sounds interesting!

14. **Mr Robertson:** We'll put you up in a hotel of course.

15. **Susan:** Well actually, my parents live in Thornbury...

16. **Mr Robertson:** Of course, I'd forgotten...

KAPITEL 5

9. **Herr Robertson:** So einfach sind die Dinge nicht. Unser Unternehmen, das ursprünglich in der zweiten Hälfte des 19. Jahrhunderts in den USA gegründet wurde, arbeitet gegenwärtig weltweit, was das Definieren und die Umsetzung einer globalen Strategie auf einer bestimmten Ebene beinhaltet. Diese Strategie muß die Ziele der Organisation in ein zusammenhängendes Ganzes einbetten...
(Jemand klopft diskret an die Tür)

10. **Herr Robertson:** Herein!

11. **Gladys:** *(Herrn Robertsons Sekretärin)* Entschuldigen Sie. Ein Ferngespräch von Herrn Van Gulik von der Unternehmenszentrale. Soll ich sagen, daß Sie vorübergehend beschäftigt sind?

12. **Herr Robertson:** Nein, es ist 14 Uhr. Ich habe diesen Anruf erwartet. Mit Susans Erlaubnis nehme ich den Anruf gleich entgegen. Stellen Sie ihn zu mir in den Konferenzraum durch und bitten Sie ihn, dranzubleiben.
(Zu Susan) Würden Sie mich bitte entschuldigen? Es wird nicht lange dauern. Sehen Sie sich in der Zwischenzeit doch das Organisationsschema an und bereiten Sie Ihre Fragen vor.
(Etwa 10 Minuten später) Ich muß mich für die Unterbrechung entschuldigen. Das war mein Ansprechpartner in Philadelphia. *(Sieht auf seine Uhr)* Ich fürchte auch, ich muß Sie bald verlassen und schnell nach Heathrow fahren. Übrigens, Susan, hat Herr Romer-Lee Ihnen gesagt, daß wir Sie, bevor Ihre eigentliche Probezeit anfängt, für einen Monat zum Arbeiten in eine unserer Fabriken in der Nähe von Bristol schicken werden? Ab nächsten Montag, wenn's Ihnen recht ist.

13. **Susan:** Klingt interessant!

14. **Herr Robertson:** Selbstverständlich bringen wir Sie in einem Hotel unter.

15. **Susan:** Naja, also meine Eltern wohnen in Thornbury...

16. **Herr Robertson:** Natürlich, das hatte ich vergessen...

CHAPTER 5 DOCUMENT

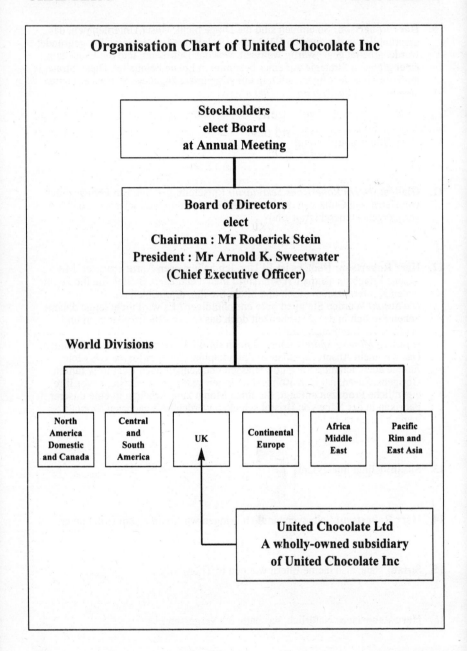

KAPITEL 5

Die Zeitzonen

In der Wirtschaftswelt geht die Sonne niemals unter. Die 24 Zeitzonen *(time zones)* sind also eine Realität, über die man sich in der Geschäftswelt ständig bewußt sein muß.
Wenn es in London 12 Uhr mittags GMT *(Greenwich Mean Time – Greenwich-Zeit)* ist, ist es in Philadelphia 7 Uhr morgens und in Los Angeles 4 Uhr morgens. In Paris ist es dann 13 Uhr, in Hongkong 20 Uhr und in Tokio 21 Uhr. Ebenfalls berücksichtigen muß man die saisonalen Zeitvarianten, also Sommerzeit und Winterzeit *(summer time, winter time)*, die je nach Land an unterschiedlichen Daten beginnen und enden.

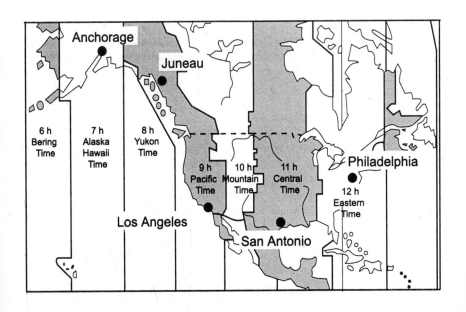

CHAPTER 5

EXERCISES

Comprehension

Lesen Sie den Dialog aufmerksam durch. Beantworten Sie dann die nachfolgenden Fragen, und zwar immer in ganzen Sätzen:

1. Where and with whom did Susan have lunch? 2. Where is UC Inc headquartered? 3. Why is Pennsylvania also known as the Quaker State? 4. For what reason were the Quakers so active in the development of the chocolate trade in the XVIIIth century? 5. Why is Mr Robertson so impressed by Susan? 6. Does Susan really think that the study of the humanities may be a waste of time? 7. In what sector can the Quakers be considered as pioneers? 8. Why does United Chocolate Inc need to define and implement a global strategy at a certain level? 9. Why does Gladys interrupt Mr Robertson's conversation with Susan? 10. Does Mr Robertson refuse to take Mr Van Gulik's call?

Translation

1. Es ist Herr Robertson, der Susan Anweisungen gibt. 2. Die Tochtergesellschaft hat ihren Firmensitz nicht in Philadelphia. 3. Ich glaube, ich erinnere mich, daß die Kolonie nach ihm benannt wurde. 4. Durch die Entwicklung des Schokoladenhandels wollten die Quäker gegen den Konsum von Tee angehen. 5. Das ist eine Bemerkung, die ich für recht wichtig halte. 6. Das Studium von Fremdsprachen ist bestimmt keine Zeitverschwendung. 7. Was wir jetzt als Lebensmittelindustrie oder Agrarindustrie bezeichnen, ist ein wichtiger Wirtschaftssektor. 8. Muß man davon ausgehen, daß alle Entscheidungen, die in Großbritannien getroffen werden, in den USA genehmigt werden müssen? 9. Unser Unternehmen, das ursprünglich [ein] amerikanisch[es] Unternehmen] war, arbeitet gegenwärtig fast weltweit. 10. Bitten Sie ihn, dranzubleiben, und stellen Sie ihn zu mir ins Büro durch.

KAPITEL 5

LÖSUNGSVORSCHLÄGE

Verständnisübung

1. She had lunch in the Managers' dining-room with Mr Romer-Lee. **2.** It is headquartered in Philadelphia, Pennsylvania. **3.** It is known as the Quaker State because it was founded, as a colony, by a famous Quaker. **4.** The Quakers were trying to counter the consumption of tea which they considered an intoxicating drink. **5.** He is impressed by Susan's extensive general culture. **6.** No, her remark is meant humorously. **7.** They were pioneers in what we now describe as the food industry and, generally speaking, the agri-business. **8.** Because it currently operates almost all over the world. **9.** Because there is the long-distance call for Mr Robertson from Mr Van Gulik. **10.** No, he tells Gladys to put him through to him in the conference room.

Übersetzungsübung

1. It is Mr Robertson who is going to brief Susan. **2.** The subsidiary is not headquartered in Philadelphia. **3.** I seem to remember that the colony was named after him. **4.** By developing the chocolate trade, the Quakers wanted to counter the consumption of tea. **5.** It's a remark I consider quite relevant. **6.** The study of foreign languages is certainly not a waste of time. **7.** What we now describe as the food industry or agri-business is an essential economic sector. **8.** Must one assume that all the decisions made in Britain have to be approved in the US? **9.** Our company, originally American, currently operates almost all over the world. **10.** Ask him to hold the line, and put him through to me in my office.

CHAPTER 5

Application

Lesen Sie sich die folgenden Aussagen aufmerksam durch und entscheiden Sie, welche wahr und welche falsch sind. Korrigieren Sie die falschen Aussagen auf Englisch.

1. Pennsylvania was named after its founder, a famous Quaker.
2. The Quakers were not hostile to the consumption of tea.
3. A subsidiary is controlled by its parent company.
4. United Chocolate Ltd is an independent company.
5. The stockholders of a corporation meet every two years.
6. The stockholders elect the board of directors.
7. The stockholders also elect the chairman.
8. Stockholder is the US equivalent of shareholder.
9. A US corporation is the equivalent of a private limited company (Ltd) in Britain.
10. In the organisation of United Chocolate Inc, America forms a single division.

DO!

Make a point of meeting deadlines.

KAPITEL 5

Wahr oder falsch?

1. *Wahr.*
2. *Falsch:* They considered it an intoxicating beverage and wanted to counter its consumption.
3. *Wahr.*
4. *Falsch:* It is a wholly-owned subsidiary of United Chocolate Inc.
5. *Falsch:* They meet every year.
6. *Wahr.*
7. *Falsch:* The chairman is elected by the Board.
8. *Wahr.*
9. *Falsch:* A US corporation may be a public or private limited company.
10. *Falsch:* North America (Domestic and Canada) is distinct from Central and South America.

DON'T!

Don't make empty promises. Commit yourself.

CHAPTER 6

Getting to know the company (II)

Mr Robertson had to go to Heathrow Airport to meet a senior executive from the US home office. He has turned Susan over to Phil Irwin, his young assistant. **(1)**

1. **Phil Irwin:** So, Mr Robertson said you'd have lots of questions for me on the subject of global company strategy and objectives.

2. **Susan:** It seems to me, Phil, that considering the nature of our organisational structure, under US control, and the extreme geographical diversification of our activities, both in terms of production and of sales, the objectives of the parent company and of some of its subsidiaries might, in some circumstances, become contradictory.

3. **Phil Irwin:** That's a good point. I can't deny that, on occasions, disagreements, even conflicts, may arise. There are times, for instance, when it is difficult to reconcile the quest for profit and shareholder satisfaction with social, environmental or even national priorities. But whatever our individual position in the organisation chart, we all seek, ultimately, to achieve a common goal or set of goals, once agreed upon by our top management.

4. **Susan:** How do things work, then?

5. **Phil Irwin:** Our US corporate structure is topped by a Board of Directors, currently chaired by Mr Roderick Stein. The Chairman, or Chairperson, is elected by the Board members. **(2)**

6. **Susan:** Could you explain the role of the Board in that highly sensitive context?

7. **Phil Irwin:** Basically, it makes long-term policy decisions on all matters affecting the life of the company at large. It is then the task of the President or Chief Executive Officer, also known as the CEO, to see that those decisions are turned into positive actions. **(3)**

KAPITEL 6

Die Firma kennenlernen (II)

Herr Robertson mußte nach Heathrow fahren, um einen leitenden Angestellten der US-Zentrale zu treffen. Er hat Susan Phil Irwin, seinem jungen Assistenten, anvertraut.

1. **Phil Irwin:** So, Herr Robertson sagte, daß Sie eine Menge Fragen zum Thema globale Unternehmensstrategie und -ziele an mich haben.
2. **Susan:** Es scheint mir, Phil, daß die Zielsetzungen der Muttergesellschaft und die einiger Tochterunternehmen sich in bestimmten Situationen widersprechen könnten, wenn man die Art unserer Organisationsstruktur unter US-Kontrolle und die extreme geographische Vielfalt unserer Aktivitäten sowohl in Sachen Produktion als auch in Sachen Verkauf betrachtet.
3. **Phil Irwin:** Das ist eine gute Bemerkung. Ich kann nicht leugnen, daß gelegentlich Meinungsverschiedenheiten, ja sogar Konflikte, auftreten können. Es gibt z.B. Zeiten, in denen es schwierig ist, das Streben nach Gewinn und die Zufriedenheit der Aktionäre mit sozialen, umweltpolitischen oder sogar nationalen Prioritäten in Einklang zu bringen. Aber egal, wo der Einzelne im Organisationsschema steht, wir alle versuchen letztendlich, ein gemeinsames Ziel oder eine Gruppe von Zielen zu erreichen, sobald die Unternehmensleitung dem zugestimmt hat.
4. **Susan:** Wie funktioniert das dann?
5. **Phil Irwin:** An der Spitze unserer US-Unternehmensstruktur steht der Firmenvorstand, dessen Vorsitz momentan Herr Roderick Stein hat. Der Vorsitzende, oder Präsident, wird von den Vorstandsmitgliedern gewählt.
6. **Susan:** Könnten Sie die Rolle des Vorstands in diesem hochsensiblen Zusammenhang erklären?
7. **Phil Irwin:** Er trifft hauptsächlich langfristige Strategieentscheidungen in allen Fragen, die die Existenz des Unternehmens insgesamt betreffen. Es ist dann die Aufgabe des Präsidenten oder des Generaldirektors, der auch CEO genannt wird, dafür zu sorgen, daß diese Entscheidungen in positive Maßnahmen umgesetzt werden.

ANMERKUNGEN

(1) **senior executive:** "leitender Angestellter".
(2) **chairperson:** "Vorstandsvorsitzende(r)". In den Vereinigten Staaten ersetzt dieser Ausdruck immer häufiger den Ausdruck *chairman*, da die Nachsilbe *-man* als zu patriarchalisch empfunden wird.
(3) **chief executive officer (CEO):** "Generaldirektor". Eine Person, die im Vorstand die Verantwortung für die Ausführung *(implementing)* der gefällten Entscheidungen übernimmt. Werden Entscheidungsfindung und Umsetzung der Entscheidungen von ein und derselben Person wahrgenommen, sagt man in den USA *chairman* oder *CEO*, in Großbritannien *chairman* oder *managing director*. Sind beide Funktionen getrennt, sagt man zum Generaldirektor in den USA *president* und in Großbritannien *managing director*.

CHAPTER 6

8. **Susan:** Where do we, the British company, stand in that structure?

9. **Phil Irwin:** We are separate and almost equal! **(4)**

10. **Susan:** That rings a bell!

11. **Phil Irwin:** No, it's not what you think. Our boss, Lord Werrett, is Chairman of the Board and Managing Director of United Chocolate Ltd. He is also an active and influential member of the US Board. His position at the head of our company calls for extensive travel, to America, of course, but also to various other areas of the world, where it is important that he represent the interests and explain the role of the British component of our multinational entity. **(5) (6)**

12. **Susan:** Are all foreign subsidiaries represented on that board?

13. **Phil Irwin:** No, only the most important ones, that have their say about their respective role in the management and development of the firm.

14. **Susan:** It must be no easy task to harness energies so widely scattered.

15. **Phil Irwin:** For sure. Undoubtedly, the firm's basic performance measure is, of course, profit. But it can only be achieved by effective coordination, appraisal, planning and, above all, by knitting together the total resources – material, financial and human – of the enterprise. And now, never mind the Quakers. Let's have a nice cup of tea! **(7) (8)**

KAPITEL 6

8. **Susan:** Wo stehen wir, das britische Unternehmen, in dieser Struktur?

9. **Phil Irwin:** Wir sind eigenständig und fast gleichberechtigt!

10. **Susan:** Das erinnert mich an etwas!

11. **Phil Irwin:** Nein, es ist nicht so wie Sie denken. Unser Chef, Lord Werrett, ist Vorsitzender des Vorstands und Generaldirektor von United Chocolate Ltd. Er ist auch ein aktives und einflußreiches Mitglied des US-Vorstands. Seine Position an der Spitze unseres Unternehmens erfordert ausgedehnte Reisen, natürlich in die USA, aber auch in viele andere Gebiete der Welt, wo es wichtig ist, daß er die Interessen vertritt und die Rolle des britischen Unternehmensteils unseres multinationalen Unternehmens erläutert.

12. **Susan:** Sind alle ausländischen Tochtergesellschaften in diesem Vorstand vertreten?

13. **Phil Irwin:** Nein, nur die bedeutendsten, die ein Mitspracherecht bei ihrer jeweiligen Rolle im Management und in der Entwicklung der Firma haben.

14. **Susan:** Es muß keine leichte Aufgabe sein, derart weit verstreute Energien zu bündeln.

15. **Phil Irwin:** Sicher. Ohne Zweifel ist der Gewinn die Basis für alle Leistungsmaßnahmen der Firma. Aber dies kann nur erreicht werden durch effektive Koordination, Bewertung, Planung und vor allem die enge Verknüpfung aller Unternehmensressourcen – materieller, finanzieller und personeller. Und jetzt wollen wir die Quäker vergessen und eine schöne Tasse Tee trinken gehen!

ANMERKUNGEN (Fortsetzung)

(4) **separate and almost equal** ist eine ironische Anspielung auf die rassendiskriminierenden Gesetze, die in den USA etwa um 1880 aufkamen und die für die Schwarzen die Doktrin "getrennt, aber gleichberechtigt" propagierten. Sie wurden durch die Bürgerrechtsgesetze *(Civil Rights Acts)* abgeschafft, die nacheinander in den Jahren 1957-68 eingeführt wurden.

(5) **chairman (of the board):** "Präsident, Vorstandsvorsitzender". Der *board of directors* ist die von den Aktionären gewählte höchste Aufsichts- und Verwaltungsinstanz der angloamerikanischen Aktiengesellschaften und ist Vorstand und Aufsichtsrat in einem, während es bei deutschen Aktiengesellschaften einen Vorstand (geschäftsführendes Organ) und einen Aufsichtsrat (Kontrollorgan) gibt. *Board member* "Vorstandsmitglied".

(6) **represent** ist hier ein Konjunktiv *(it is important that...)*, der sich durch das Fehlen des "s" bei der 3. Person Singular auszeichnet.

(7) **profit:** "Gewinn, Ertrag, Erlös"; *profitability* "Wirtschaftlichkeit, Rentabilität"; *benefit(s)* "Vergünstigung, Vorteil", auch: "(Versicherungs-)leistung, Rente". (Vgl. auch Kapitel 3, Anmerkung 3.)

(8) **appraisal:** "Bewertung, Wertbestimmung, Beurteilung". *To appraise* "abschätzen, bewerten, taxieren".

CHAPTER 6   DOCUMENT

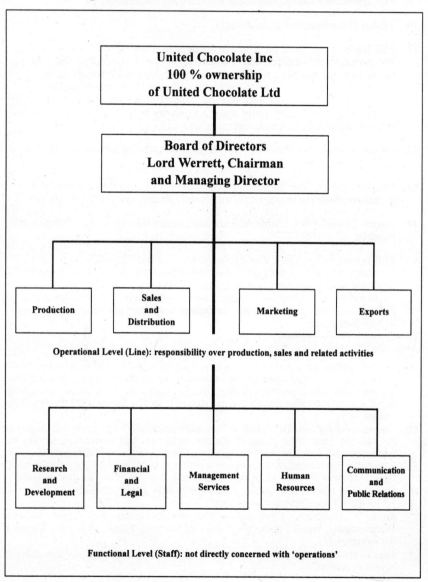

Organisation Chart of United Chocolate Ltd

KAPITEL 6

Wer trinkt was?

Zwar ist den Engländern ihr Tässchen Tee *(tea time)*, das zu den unterschiedlichsten Tageszeiten getrunken wird, nach wie vor heilig (Experten haben errechnet, daß die Engländer drei Jahre ihres Lebens vor einer Teetasse bzw. Teekanne verbringen!), jedoch macht die Kaffeepause *(coffee break)* der Teepause *(tea break)* während des Arbeitstages immer häufiger Konkurrenz. Während die Teepause hauptsächlich im Arbeitermilieu verbreitet ist, findet man die Kaffeepause eher bei den Führungskräften. Dennoch wird der Tee noch lange ein Symbol für England und der Kaffeelöffel noch lange ein *tea spoon* bleiben. In den Vereinigten Staaten ist die Kaffeepause während des Arbeitstages weit mehr verbreitet als in England.

High tea ist eine Art Abendbrot in Arbeiterkreisen, das am späten Nachmittag oder am frühen Abend eingenommen wird. Das Abendessen *(dinner)*, das später am Abend gegessen und zu dem häufig Wein getrunken wird, ist für die englische Mittelklasse eine Art Statussymbol *(status symbol)*.

Sie kennen vielleicht den Ausdruck *"That's not my cup of tea"*. Er ist übersetzbar mit "Das ist nicht mein Bier", "Das geht mich nichts an". Da sieht man, wo die Vorlieben bei den einzelnen Nationen liegen...

CHAPTER 6

EXERCISES

Comprehension

Lesen Sie den Dialog aufmerksam durch. Beantworten Sie dann die nachfolgenden Fragen, und zwar immer in ganzen Sätzen:

1. Why did Mr Robertson turn Susan over to his young assistant? **2.** What sort of questions does Susan want to ask Mr Irwin? **3.** In Susan's opinion, are the objectives of the parent company and of those of some of its subsidiaries necessarily compatible? **4.** On what occasion may disagreements or conflicts arise between parent company and subsidiaries? **5.** Who ultimately decides what the common goal, or set of goals, of the company will be? **6.** What is the exact role of the board of directors? **7.** Why is the word chairperson commonly used in the US instead of chairman, at least when applied to a woman? **8.** Describe the exact task of the CEO, president or managing director. **9.** Does Lord Werrett play an important role in the multinational corporate structure? **10.** Are all foreign subsidiaries represented on the US board?

Translation

1. Susan hat eine Menge Fragen zur Unternehmensstruktur. **2.** Die Einführung einer neuen Strategie wird keine leichte Aufgabe sein. **3.** Sie sollten lieber einen Firmenanwalt konsultieren, falls eine schwerwiegende Meinungsverschiedenheit auftreten sollte. **4.** Das Organisationsschema des Unternehmens zeigt klar den Unterschied zwischen der Verwaltungs- und der Fertigungsebene. **5.** Wir können nicht leugnen, daß es gelegentlich schwierig ist, das Streben nach Gewinn und den Umweltschutz miteinander in Einklang zu bringen. **6.** Wie auch immer die Umstände sein mögen, sie müssen jetzt versuchen, die Ziele zu erreichen, auf die man sich auf der letzten Konferenz geeinigt hat. **7.** Unser Vorsitzender und Generaldirektor ist ebenfalls ein einflußreiches Mitglied des Vorstands unserer Muttergesellschaft. **8.** Ihre neue Tätigkeit wird ausgedehnte Reisen in verschiedene Gebiete der Welt erfordern. **9.** Der CEO muß dafür Sorge tragen, daß die Entscheidungen des Vorstandes umgesetzt werden. **10.** Durch das Verknüpfen aller Ressourcen des Unternehmens wird man die Rentabilität verbessern.

KAPITEL 6

LÖSUNGSVORSCHLÄGE

Verständnisübung

1. He had to go to the airport to meet a senior executive from the US home office. 2. She wants to ask questions on the subject of global company strategy. 3. No, it seems to her that they might, in some circumstances, become contradictory. 4. Disagreements or conflicts may arise over the difficulty of reconciling the quest for profit and shareholder satisfaction with social, environmental or national priorities. 5. It is the company's top management. 6. It makes long-term policy decisions on all matters affecting the life of the company at large. 7. Chairperson is used because chairman is considered a sexist word. 8. He or she sees to it that the decisions made by the board are turned into positive actions (*or* implemented). 9. Yes, he is not only the Chairman and Managing Director of United Chocolate Ltd, but also an active and influential member of the US board. 10. No, only the most important ones like United Chocolate Ltd are represented.

Übersetzungsübung

1. Susan has lots of questions on the company's structure. 2. The implementing of a new strategy will be no easy task. 3. You had better consult a corporate lawyer, if a serious disagreement were to arise. 4. The company's organisation chart clearly shows the difference between staff and line (*or* functional and operational) levels. 5. We can't deny that it is, on occasions, difficult to reconcile the quest for profit and environmental protection. 6. Whatever the circumstances, they must now seek to achieve the goals agreed upon at the last meeting. 7. Our chairman and managing director is also an influential member of the parent company's board. 8. Your new job will call for extensive travel to various areas of the world. 9. The CEO (*or* president, *or* managing director) must see to it that the decisions of the board are implemented. 10. It is by knitting together the total resources of the firm that one will improve profitability.

CHAPTER 6

Application

Hier wieder eine Übung, bei der Scharfblick gefordert ist. Es wird für Sie sehr nützlich sein, wenn Sie lernen, wie man einen tabellarischen Lebenslauf auf Englisch verfaßt. Verwenden Sie als Vorlage das nachfolgende "Porträt" von Phil Irwin und erarbeiten Sie auf seiner Grundlage einen tabellarischen Lebenslauf, wie er auf der gegenüberliegenden Seite gezeigt wird:

Phil Irwin is twelve years Susan's senior. He was born in Manchester on St Patrick's Day, which made his grandparents very happy, as they had left Ireland to settle in this part of England.

Phil very quickly proved to be a bright child and won a scholarship to attend Manchester Grammar School. After obtaining his 'A' levels, he went to study economics and accounting at University College, London, and obtained a first-class Honours degree. He was immediately 'snapped up'* by the Halifax Building Society who recognised him as a potential high-flyer.

For five years, he worked in accounting and finance, before returning to the University of Warwick to study for an MBA. Upon completion of this degree, he was delighted to be offered a job with United Chocolate to work in their Financial and Legal Department. Yet after only a few months, UC, impressed by his managerial skills and human qualities, offered him his current position, Manager, Human Resources, ie assistant to Mr Robertson. Phil readily accepted the challenge.

He has always prided himself on his French, and regularly spends his summer holidays with his wife and two daughters in the house they own in the Lubéron. He practises rock-climbing, skiing and also several water-sports, especially sailing. He loves to go to the opera in London, when his job allows him to do so.

* 'snapped up' ist hier ein sehr salopper Ausdruck, der etwa unserem "sich unter den Nagel reißen", "sich jdn. oder etw. schnappen", "bei etw. zugreifen" entspricht.

DO!

Learn from your mistakes instead of learning only not to make mistakes by not trying anything.

KAPITEL 6

Phil IRWIN

Born 17th March 1959, Manchester (UK)
British Passport
Married with 2 children

EDUCATION

1985-86 – University of Warwick
  MBA (Option: Finance)

1977-80 – University College, London
  BSc, Economics and Accounting (first-class Honours)

1970-77 – Manchester Grammar School (Timothy O'Brien scholarship)

PROFESSIONAL EXPERIENCE

1986- ***United Chocolate (UK) Ltd***
  Junior Financial Manager
  Manager, Human Resources

1980-85 – ***Halifax Building Society***
  Junior Manager, Accounting Department

SPECIAL SKILLS

Computers: IBM PC and Macintosh; conversant with most standard word-processing, spreadsheet and database software

Foreign languages: fluent in written and spoken French

INTERESTS

Sports: rock-climbing, skiing, sailing
Leisure: going to the opera

DON'T!

***Don't be afraid of questioning yourself.
Trips abroad and encounters with foreigners
will necessarily challenge your beliefs.***

CHAPTER 7

Getting some hands-on experience

As Mr Robertson promised, Susan has been sent to a United Chocolate factory in Filton, near Bristol, to be given a taste of work on the production line. She's chatting during the afternoon tea break with Daphne, a fellow production worker.

1. **Daphne:** You're new here, aren't you, love? **(1)**

2. **Susan:** Yes, this is my first day.

3. **Daphne:** Working during the summer holidays, are you?

4. **Susan:** Actually, no. I'm a trainee manager. Mr Robertson sent me here to get some 'hands-on' experience.

5. **Daphne:** *(Jokingly)* Start at the bottom and see how the other half lives, eh! Or sent to spy on us, maybe! Who's Mr Robertson, anyway? **(2)**

6. **Susan:** He's the Assistant Director of Human Resources of United Chocolate (UK). Have you ever met him?

7. **Daphne:** I've heard the name. Seen it on notices and things. But you know, love, in my thirty-one years in this factory, I've seen a few managers come and go!

8. **Susan:** Thirty-one years! That's a lot of seniority! You must have seen a lot of changes in your work, too. **(3)**

9. **Daphne:** Not as many as you'd think. We still make the same products, bars of chocolate. Except that now we use grams and kilos, whereas before it was ounces and pounds. The chocolate's not as good either.

10. **Susan:** Can you really remember what it used to taste like?

11. **Daphne:** I most certainly can! In my opinion, it's because of all these EC regulations: all the things they make us or won't let us put in it. **(4)**

KAPITEL 7

Praktische Berufserfahrung

Wie Herr Robertson versprochen hat, wurde Susan in ein United Chocolate-Werk in Filton in der Nähe von Bristol geschickt, um einen Vorgeschmack davon zu erhalten, wie die Arbeit in der Fertigung vor sich geht. In der nachmittäglichen Teepause unterhält sie sich mit Daphne, einer in der Produktion tätigen Kollegin.

1. **Daphne:** Du bist neu hier, nicht wahr?
2. **Susan:** Ja, das ist mein erster Tag.
3. **Daphne:** Ist das ein Job für die Sommerferien?
4. **Susan:** Nein, ich bin Trainee Manager. Herr Robertson hat mich hierhergeschickt, damit ich einige "praktische" Erfahrung sammeln kann.
5. **Daphne:** *(In scherzhaftem Ton)* Fängst ganz unten an und guckst, wie die anderen leben, eh?! Oder vielleicht sollst du uns auspionieren! Wer ist eigentlich Herr Robertson?
6. **Susan:** Er ist stellvertretender Personalchef von United Chocolate (UK). Haben Sie ihn schon mal getroffen?
7. **Daphne:** Ich habe den Namen schon gehört. Hab ihn auf Aushängen und so gelesen. Aber weißt du, während der 31 Jahre, die ich in dieser Fabrik bin, habe ich schon so manchen Manager kommen und gehen sehen!
8. **Susan:** 31 Jahre! Das ist ein ganz hübsches Dienstalter! Sie müssen auch eine ganze Menge Veränderungen in Ihrer Arbeit erlebt haben.
9. **Daphne:** Nicht so viele wie du vielleicht denkst. Wir stellen nach wie vor die gleichen Produkte her, Schokoladenriegel. Mit der Ausnahme, daß wir jetzt in Gramm und Kilo rechnen, während wir zuvor in Unzen und Pfund gerechnet haben. Die Schokolade ist auch nicht mehr so gut.
10. **Susan:** Können Sie sich wirklich erinnern, wie sie geschmeckt hat?
11. **Daphne:** Sicher kann ich das! Meiner Meinung nach liegt es an all diesen EG-Richtlinien: all diese Sachen, die wir hineintun sollen oder nicht hineintun dürfen!

ANMERKUNGEN

(1) **love** ist in Großbritannien eine saloppe und nettgemeinte Anrede, mit der vor allem Frauen angesprochen werden. Für diesen Ausdruck gibt es im Deutschen keine direkte Übersetzung. Man hört auch häufig *dear*.

(2) In **the other half** "die anderen" schwingt ein leicht sozialkritischer Unterton mit. Dieser Ausdruck kann je nach Kontext den besserverdienenden Teil der Bevölkerung oder den Teil der Bevölkerung bezeichnen, der weniger Geld, Macht usw. besitzt.

(3) **seniority:** "höheres Dienstalter, höherer Rang" beschreibt die Zeit, die eine Person in einem Unternehmen oder auf einer bestimmten Stelle beschäftigt ist und mit der im Laufe der Zeit bestimmte Vergünstigungen, Sonderleistungen usw., insbesondere hinsichtlich des Gehalts, verbunden sind.

(4) **EC (European Community):** Der Ausdruck *EEC, European Economic Community*, deutsch EWG, Europäische Wirtschaftsgemeinschaft, wird offiziell seit dem 1. November 1993 nicht mehr verwendet. Auch wenn der Vertrag von Maastricht die *EU (European Union* – Europäische Union) gegründet hat, wird dennoch weiterhin in der Wirtschafts- und Rechtssprache der Ausdruck *EC* verwendet.

CHAPTER 7

12. **Susan:** Yes, the Factory Manager mentioned that too, this morning, when he was showing me round. Explaining the lay-out of the factory, the various machines and so on. **(5)**

13. **Daphne:** Mr Evans. He's not a bad bloke, really. Been here almost as long as I have! He's a bit obsessed about safety and hygiene, if you ask me, but I suppose you have to be now. All this special clothing you have to wear. **(6)**

14. **Susan:** Well, you can't afford to take any risks with hygiene when you're making food products, I suppose.

15. **Daphne:** You're beginning to sound like Mr Evans already! Always on about BS 5750, quality circles, – TQM, now, – computerised production management and the like. Sometimes I don't even know what he's talking about! Mind you, it's easier now to make the chocolate, with all these new machines.
    When I first came, the machines were British, from a firm in Birmingham, I remember. Now they're all German or Japanese. Computer-controlled. I kid my grandchildren that I operate a computer! **(7) (8) (9) (10) (11)**

16. **Susan:** They do send you on training courses, I hope.

17. **Daphne:** Oh, yes, they do. And I love going on them, too. I may think the chocolate is not as good as it used to be, but don't think I'm against progress. How else do you think I could stay for thirty-one years in the same firm?!

KAPITEL 7

12. **Susan:** Ja, der Werksleiter hat das auch heute morgen erwähnt, als er mich herumgeführt hat. Er hat mir die Aufteilung des Betriebs, die verschiedenen Maschinen usw. gezeigt.
13. **Daphne:** Herr Evans. Er ist eigentlich ein netter Typ. Ist fast schon so lange hier wie ich. Er ist ziemlich pingelig, was Sicherheit und Hygiene angeht, wenn du mich fragst, aber ich nehme an, das muß man jetzt sein. Diese ganze Spezialkleidung, die man jetzt tragen muß.
14. **Susan:** Naja, ich denke, wenn man Lebensmittel herstellt, kann man sich nicht leisten, irgendwelche Risiken bei der Hygiene einzugehen.
15. **Daphne:** Du fängst schon an, wie Herr Evans zu reden! Er spricht ständig von BS 5750, Qualitätskreisen – mittlerweile "Totale Qualitätskontrolle" – rechnergestützter Produktionsverwaltung und all diesen Dingen. Manchmal weiß ich nicht einmal, wovon er überhaupt spricht! Aber ich sag dir, es ist jetzt leichter, Schokolade herzustellen, mit all diesen neuen Maschinen. Als ich hier anfing, waren es englische Maschinen von einer Firma in Birmingham, das weiß ich noch. Jetzt haben wir nur deutsche und japanische Maschinen. Computergesteuert. Ich sage immer spaßeshalber zu meinen Enkeln, daß ich an einem Computer arbeite!
16. **Susan:** Ich hoffe, man schickt Sie auf Schulungen.
17. **Daphne:** Oh ja, das tun sie. Und ich gehe auch sehr gerne da hin. Ich mag vielleicht denken, daß die Schokolade nicht mehr so gut ist wie sie mal war, aber glaube nicht, daß ich gegen Fortschritt bin. Wie sonst, denkst du, konnte ich 31 Jahre lang in der gleichen Firma arbeiten?!

ANMERKUNG (Fortsetzung)

(5) **to show someone round**: "jdn. herumführen". Merken Sie sich auch *to show someone in* "jdn. hinein-/hereinführen" und *to show someone out* "jdn. hinaus-/ herausgeleiten oder -begleiten".

(6) **bloke** ist in Großbritannien eine saloppe und nettgemeinte Bezeichnung für eine andere Person, in etwa vergleichbar mit unserem "Typ, Kerl". Die Amerikaner sagen eher *guy*.

(7) **BS 5750**: Ein Qualitätsstandard, der vom *British Standards Institute (BSI)* festgelegt wird. Mittlerweile erfolgt in der internationalen Wirtschaft die Harmonisierung der Qualitätsnormen fast nur noch durch die ISO-Norm *(International Standards Organization).*

(8) **quality circles:** "Qualitätskreise" sind Teams, die aus fünf bis zehn Angestellten eines Unternehmens bestehen, und die sich regelmäßig zusammenfinden, um kritisch ihre Arbeitsmethoden zu erörtern, mit dem Ziel, die Qualität der Produkte zu verbessern und die Produktivität zu steigern.

(9) **TQM (Total Quality Management):** Alle Aktivitäten, die dazu dienen, zum Zweck einer höheren Kundenzufriedenheit qualitativ hochwertige Güter herzustellen und diese gemeinsam mit Qualitätsdienstleistungen auf den Markt zu bringen.

(10) **computerized production management**: Bei der rechner- (oder computer)gestützten Produktionsverwaltung werden sämtliche Fertigungsabläufe mit Hilfe der elektronischen Datenverarbeitung optimiert und überwacht. Dies ermöglicht, die Kosten so gering wie möglich zu halten und trotzdem die Produktivität und Qualität der Produkte zu steigern.

(11) **computer-controlled (machines)**, die mittlerweile in fast allen modernen Industriebetrieben die Norm sind, werden von einem Computer gesteuert.

CHAPTER 7 — DOCUMENT

Site plan of United Chocolate Ltd's plant at Filton

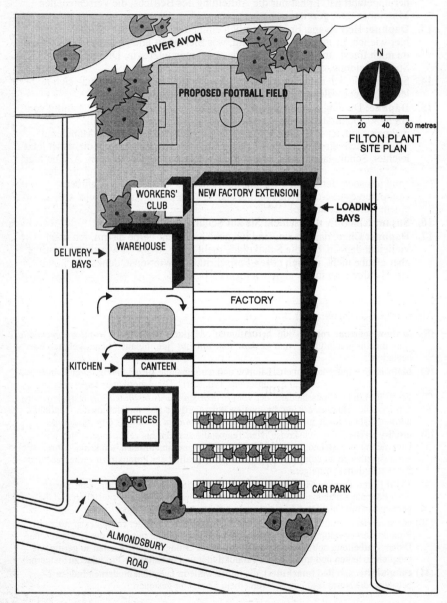

KAPITEL 7

Vertrautheit erzeugt nicht immer Verachtung

Welcher Deutsche wäre nicht überrascht, von einer unbekannten Person mit *love* angeredet zu werden, z.B. auf der Straße oder von einer Verkäuferin im Geschäft? Die Engländer, egal ob Männer oder Frauen, lieben diese nette Art der Anrede, die, obwohl sie sehr familiär und salopp ist, durchaus nicht den Beigeschmack von Geringschätzung oder Verachtung hat. (Dennoch gibt es ein bekanntes englisches Sprichwort: *Familiarity breeds contempt.*)
Die Aussprache des Wortes *love* ist nicht überall in England gleich. Je mehr man sich von Südengland entfernt, desto weniger klingt *love* wie die letzte Silbe von *above*, sondern nähert sich eher an die Aussprache von *look* an. Man schreibt auch oft *luv*, um den Unterschied deutlich hervorzuheben.
In der gleichen Kategorie von Anreden hört man auch oft *dear, duck(ie)* oder *sweetheart*; auch *mate* ist sehr geläufig, jedoch eher unter Männern.
Schließlich sollten Sie sich noch merken, daß das Wort *cheers*, das in erster Linie die Bedeutung von "Prost!" oder "Auf Dein Wohl!" hat, in der Umgangssprache immer häufiger im Sinne von "danke!" benutzt wird (Beispiel: *"Cheers, mate!"*). Und wenn Ihnen jemand etwas gibt oder schenkt ("Hier, bitte schön!"), hört man neuerdings immer häufiger *there you go* anstelle von *here you are*.

CHAPTER 7

EXERCISES

Comprehension

Lesen Sie den Dialog aufmerksam durch. Beantworten Sie dann die nachfolgenden Fragen, und zwar immer in ganzen Sätzen:

1. What, in your opinion, is 'hands-on' experience? 2. What do you think Daphne means by the 'other half'? 3. Has Daphne ever met Mr Robertson? 4. Explain what is meant by the word 'seniority'. 5. Have many things changed since Daphne started working for United Chocolate? 6. What changes does Daphne mention concerning the bars of chocolate made in the factory? 7. To what does Daphne attribute her judgement that the chocolate does not taste as good as before? 8. Do you think that Daphne has a good opinion of Mr Evans, the factory manager? 9. How have the machines changed since Daphne first started working in the factory? 10. What, according to Daphne, shows that she is not against progress?

Translation

1. Herr Robertson hatte Susan versprochen, sie zum Arbeiten in eine Produktionseinheit westlich von London zu schicken. 2. Während der Pause unterhielt sie sich mit Daphne, die ein hohes Dienstalter hatte. 3. Sie arbeitet seit mindestens 30 Jahren in derselben Fabrik. 4. In 31 Jahren hat es wenig Veränderungen gegeben. Das Produkt ist immer noch das gleiche, aber es schmeckt nicht mehr so gut. 5. Früher wogen die Schokoladenriegel vier Unzen; nun wiegen sie 125 Gramm. 6. Der Manager führte Daphne in der Fabrik herum und erläuterte ihr die Anordnung der verschiedenen Maschinen. 7. Der Werksleiter ist ein bißchen pingelig mit der Hygiene, aber das ist in der Lebensmittelindustrie ganz normal. 8. Die Arbeiter müssen Spezialkleidung tragen, da man keine Risiken eingehen darf. 9. Dank rechnergestützter Produktionsverwaltung und Qualitätskreisen haben wir viele Fehler ausgeschaltet. 10. Daphne ist zu Schulungskursen gegangen, um zu lernen, wie man computergesteuerte Maschinen bedient (verwendet).

KAPITEL 7

LÖSUNGSVORSCHLÄGE

Verständnisübung

1. 'Hands-on' experience is practical experience, acquired by actually doing something. **2.** Daphne is no doubt referring to the workers, as opposed to the managers. **3.** No, but she says she's heard and seen his name. **4.** 'Seniority' means the length of time, the number of years someone has worked for a firm or organisation. **5.** Daphne suggests that fewer things have changed than Susan might expect. **6.** The fact that their weight is now metric, and that the chocolate doesn't taste as good as it used to. **7.** She attributes this judgement to EC regulations concerning what can or cannot be used in the manufacturing process. **8.** On the whole, her opinion seems to be fairly good. **9.** They used to be British. Now they are either German or Japanese, and are computer-controlled. **10.** The fact that she attends all the training courses to learn new techniques.

Übersetzungsübung

1. Mr Robertson (had) promised to send Susan to work in a production unit west of London. **2.** During the break, she chatted with Daphne, who had a great deal of seniority. **3.** She's been working in the same factory for at least thirty years. **4.** There have been few changes in thirty-one years. The product is still the same, but it doesn't taste as good. **5.** Before, the bars of chocolate used to weigh four ounces; now they weigh 125 grams. **6.** The manager showed Daphne round the factory and explained to her the lay-out of the various machines. **7.** The Factory Manager is a bit obsessed with hygiene, but that's quite only normal in the food industry. **8.** The workers have to wear special clothing, as you can't take any risks. **9.** Thanks to computerised production management and quality circles, we have eliminated many defects. **10.** Daphne has gone on training courses to learn how to use computer-controlled machines.

CHAPTER 7

Application

Sehen Sie sich den Plan des Betriebsgeländes an. Lesen Sie sich dann die folgenden Aussagen aufmerksam durch und entscheiden Sie, welche wahr und welche falsch sind. Korrigieren Sie die falschen Aussagen.

1. Deliveries of raw materials are made on the west side of the plant site.
2. Motorists have to turn right when they come in through the main gates.
3. The office building forms a rectangle.
4. It is sometimes possible to park your car in the shade.
5. As you would expect, the kitchen is adjacent to the staff canteen.
6. Lorries load at the oldest part of the factory.
7. The in-house football team always plays its home games on the plant site.
8. The factory itself is the building which occupies the largest surface area on the site.
9. Originally the factory building was larger than it is today.
10. The workers' club is in front of the warehouse.

DO!

*In your business relations with people,
be prepared to adapt.*

KAPITEL 7

Wahr oder falsch?

1. *Wahr.*
2. *Wahr.*
3. *Falsch:* It forms a square.
4. *Wahr.*
5. *Wahr.*
6. *Falsch:* The loading bays are in the new factory extension.
7. *Falsch:* The football field does not exist at the present time ('proposed').
8. *Wahr.*
9. *Falsch:* On the contrary, it has been extended.
10. *Falsch:* It is behind the warehouse.

DON'T!

***Don't hesitate to look facts in the face:
be realistic and pragmatic.***

CHAPTER 8

Introduction to finance

Susan's second assignment during her trial period is meant to familiarise her with the company's overall financial procedures. Harold Mc Duff, a senior executive in the Financial and Legal Department, is in charge of the preliminary briefing.

1. **Mr McDuff:** Nowadays, just like individuals, companies – whether small or big – cannot do without the services, and, occasionally, the help of a bank.

2. **Susan:** Of that I am well aware!

3. **Mr McDuff:** You must also understand that when we refer to the financial operations of a large company like UC, we don't simply mean writing cheques, cashing them or transferring money from one place to another. **(1) (2)**

4. **Susan:** Untrained as I am in all financial skills, I can imagine that one relies on one's bank for a multitude of other services.

5. **Mr McDuff:** Quick thinking! As the case may be, the company will have to finance itself, short term through commercial paper, notes or certificates of deposit, also called CDs, or long term by issuing bonds. Yet it must also be in a position to maximise profit on its available or expected cash by resorting to various financial instruments. That's the task of cash management. **(3) (4) (5)**

6. **Susan:** I'm anxious to learn more about that.

7. **Mr McDuff:** You'll have an opportunity to spend some time with our back-office staff. But you can already see that the bank is our privileged partner and adviser. That's why most of our banking operations are now performed through Barclays or their associates. **(6)**

KAPITEL 8

Einführung in das Finanzwesen

Auf Susans zweitem Posten im Laufe ihrer Probezeit soll sie sich mit den allgemeinen Abläufen der Finanzbuchhaltung des Unternehmens vertraut machen. Harold McDuff, ein leitender Angestellter der Finanz- und Rechtsabteilung, ist für die Ersteinführung verantwortlich.

1. **Herr McDuff:** Ebenso wie Einzelpersonen können Unternehmen – egal ob große oder kleine – heutzutage nicht ohne die Dienste und manchmal auch die Hilfe einer Bank auskommen.
2. **Susan:** Darüber bin ich mir völlig im klaren!
3. **Herr McDuff:** Sie müssen auch verstehen, daß, wenn wir von den finanziellen Abläufen eines großen Unternehmens wie UC sprechen, wir nicht nur das Ausstellen und Einlösen von Schecks oder das Überweisen von Geld von einem an einen anderen Ort meinen.
4. **Susan:** Unerfahren wie ich in allen finanziellen Dingen bin, kann ich mir vorstellen, daß man sich noch bei einer Vielzahl von anderen Dienstleistungen auf seine Bank verläßt.
5. **Herr McDuff:** Das haben Sie schnell erfaßt! Je nachdem, wie der Fall liegt, muß das Unternehmen sich selbst kurzfristig durch Warenwechsel, Schuldscheine oder Hinterlegungsscheine oder langfristig durch die Ausgabe von [festverzinslichen] Wertpapieren finanzieren. Dennoch muß es auch in der Position sein, aus seinen verfügbaren oder zu erwartenden Barmitteln einen maximalen Gewinn zu ziehen, indem es auf verschiedene Kreditinstrumente zurückgreift. Dies ist die Aufgabe des Finanzmanagements.
6. **Susan:** Ich möchte unheimlich gerne mehr darüber lernen.
7. **Herr McDuff:** Sie werden die Gelegenheit haben, einige Zeit mit unseren Verwaltungsmitarbeitern zu verbringen. Aber Sie können schon erkennen, daß die Bank unser bevorzugter Partner und Ratgeber ist. Das ist der Grund, warum die meisten unserer Bankgeschäfte jetzt durch Barclays oder ihre Partner abgewickelt werden.

ANMERKUNGEN

(1) **cheque** ist die in Großbritannien gebräuchliche Schreibweise, während man in den USA *check* schreibt. *Cheque book* "Scheckbuch"; *bearer cheque* "Inhaberscheck"; *crossed cheque* "gekreuzter Scheck, Verrechnungsscheck".
(2) **to cash** "einlösen, einziehen" (Scheck); *cash* "Bargeld, Barmittel".
(3) **commercial paper:** "Handels-/Warenwechsel"; *note of hand* oder *promissory note* "Schuldschein".
(4) **certificate of deposit (CD):** "Hinterlegungsschein, Depositenquittung". Im Gegensatz zu dem unter (3) genannten *commercial paper* muß der Hinterlegungsschein immer von einem Finanzinstitut ausgegeben werden.
(5) **bond:** "(festverzinsliches) Wertpapier, Obligation, Pfandbrief". In Großbritannien sagt man hierzu *debenture*.
(6) Das **back-office** bezeichnet das Verwaltungspersonal, das sich, wie der Name sagt, im "hinteren Teil" des Büros befindet, und daher keinen direkten Kundenkontakt hat. Der Gegensatz hiervon ist das *front-office*, wo das Personal unmittelbarer Ansprechpartner für den Kunden ist.

CHAPTER 8

8. **Susan:** Does the 'now' imply that this hasn't always been the case?

9. **Mr McDuff:** Indeed! Until recently we dealt with different banking institutions in the different countries or regional areas where we trade or manufacture.

10. **Susan:** It must have made the management of it very complex.

11. **Mr McDuff:** Yes, very much so! However, the reasons for our choice of a single institution are to be found elsewhere.

12. **Susan:** Please explain.

13. **Mr McDuff:** Well, until a few years ago, capital markets tended to be mostly national rather than international. Today, borders have become irrelevant to the world of finance. Instant satellite communications and computerised quotes have made global markets possible. **(7) (8)**

14. **Susan:** I know from experience that Hong-Kong has become as easily accessible as London, provided you take into account time differences.

15. **Mr McDuff:** Consider also the growing internationalisation of our company, and you will understand that we found it more practical, and less costly, to turn our business over to a single banking institution with an extensive worldwide network.

16. **Susan:** That's the case with Barclays. It has branches, subsidiaries or partner banks all over the world. *(Smiling)* It happens to be my 'own' bank too...! **(9)**

17. **Mr McDuff:** It is clear that by doing business with a single bank, we have considerably reduced, or at least simplified, our paperwork and, thereby, improved our productivity.

18. **Susan:** Am I right to assume that the savings must be substantial?

19. **Mr McDuff:** Sure enough! And remember, I am a Scotsman!

KAPITEL 8

8. **Susan:** Heißt "jetzt", daß dies nicht immer der Fall war?
9. **Herr McDuff:** Genau! Bis vor kurzem haben wir mit verschiedenen Kreditinstituten in den verschiedenen Ländern oder Regionen gearbeitet, in denen wir unsere Waren vertreiben oder fertigen.
10. **Susan:** Das muß die diesbezügliche Verwaltung sehr kompliziert gemacht haben.
11. **Herr McDuff:** Ja, genau so war's! Die Gründe dafür, warum wir uns ein einzelnes Institut ausgesucht haben, müssen jedoch woanders gesucht werden.
12. **Susan:** Erklären Sie das bitte.
13. **Herr McDuff:** Nun ja, bis vor einigen Jahren waren die Kapitalmärkte eher national als international. Heute sind die Landesgrenzen für die Finanzwelt nicht mehr wichtig. Unmittelbare Übertragungen per Satellit und die Übertragung von Kursnotierungen per Computer haben Weltmärkte möglich gemacht.
14. **Susan:** Ich weiß aus Erfahrung, daß man zu Hongkong genauso leicht Zugang erhält wie zu London, vorausgesetzt, man berücksichtigt den Zeitunterschied.
15. **Herr McDuff:** Bedenken Sie auch die wachsende Internationalisierung unseres Unternehmens, und Sie werden verstehen, daß wir es praktischer und kostengünstiger fanden, unsere Geschäfte an ein einziges Bankinstitut mit einem umfassenden weltweiten Netzwerk zu übergeben.
16. **Susan:** Das trifft auf Barclays zu. Sie haben Filialen, Tochtergesellschaften oder Partnerinstitute in der ganzen Welt. *(Lächelt)* Es ist zufällig auch "meine" Bank...
17. **Herr McDuff:** Es versteht sich, daß wir dadurch, daß wir nur mit einer Bank Geschäfte abwickeln, unseren Verwaltungsaufwand erheblich reduziert oder zumindest vereinfacht und somit unsere Produktivität gesteigert haben.
18. **Susan:** Liege ich richtig, wenn ich annehme, daß die Einsparungen beträchtlich sind?
19. **Herr McDuff:** Sicher! Und vergessen Sie nicht: ich bin Schotte!

ANMERKUNGEN (Fortsetzung)

(7) **capital market:** "Kapitalmarkt, Finanz-, Geldmarkt". Man sagt auch *financial market*.
(8) **quote** (oder **quotation**): "Kurs, Kursnotierung, Börsennotierung"; *to quote* "Preis ansetzen; Kurse börsenmäßig notieren, Kurse feststellen".
(9) **branch:** "Filiale, Zweigstelle, Nebenstelle". Handelt es sich um eine sehr kleine Verkaufsstelle, sagt man *outlet*.

CHAPTER 8

DOCUMENT

British Banking and Barclays

In the last few years, **British banking** has undergone great changes dictated by:
– the steady growth of international trade
– the fast development of computer technology providing a variety of new financial services to individual or corporate customers.
Worldwide deregulation and harmonisation of banking rules and practices – at least within the European Union – have led to aggressive foreign competition.
The Bank of England – also known as the old lady of Threadneedle Street – remains the country's Central Bank. But the traditional distinction between commercial (deposit) banks, merchant (investment) banks and savings banks tends to become less clear as each one tries to broaden the scope and range of services offered.

The origins of the **Barclays** Group go back to the City of London in the 18th century.
Today, the group holding company is quoted in London, New York and Tokyo, and is the first banking group in the United Kingdom. It also occupies a leading position amongst European and international banks.
Barclays is present in 77 countries including the other members of the European Union where it maintains 325 branches and outlets.
In each case the bank attempts to take account of the specific characteristics of the national market.
Barclays has constantly developed its activities to provide a universal banking service for both private and corporate customers.

KAPITEL 8

Die Schotten und das liebe Geld

Der Ruf, der den Schotten vorauseilt, sei er nun berechtigt oder nicht, hat längst die Grenzen Großbritanniens überschritten und ist auf der ganzen Welt Gegenstand zahlloser Witze geworden. Ihre Sparsamkeit *(frugality)* und ihr übertrieben wirtschaftliches Denken *(frugal* "wirtschaftlich, ökonomisch") sind sprichwörtlich. Sie "drehen jede Mark zweimal um" *(they look twice at every penny)*, denn für sie gibt es keine kleinen Einsparungen, sondern nur große Ausgaben, wie aus dem Sprichwort *"Take care of the pennies and the pounds will take care of themselves"* (etwa vergleichbar mit unserem "Kleinvieh macht auch Mist") hervorgeht.

Aus diesem Grund wird die Haltung der Schotten zum Geld sehr schnell mit Geiz gleichgesetzt *(stinginess* "Knauserigkeit"; *stingy* "knauserig").

Dafür – oder gerade deshalb – eignen sich die Schotten sehr gut für alle finanzbuchhalterischen Positionen; man findet z.B. viele Schotten unter den Wirtschaftsprüfern.

CHAPTER 8

EXERCISES

Comprehension

Lesen Sie den Dialog aufmerksam durch. Beantworten Sie dann die nachfolgenden Fragen, und zwar immer in ganzen Sätzen:

1. What is the purpose of Susan's second assignment? **2.** Who, this time, is in charge of briefing her? **3.** How can the company finance itself short term? **4.** When does a company normally issue bonds? **5.** Whose responsibility is it to maximise profit on available or expected cash? **6.** Has Barclays always been the privileged partner and adviser of United Chocolate? **7.** What was to be noted about capital markets until a few years ago? **8.** Why have borders become irrelevant to the world of finance? **9.** If you want to telephone to Hong-Kong, what must you take into account? **10.** What's the advantage for United Chocolate of doing business with a single bank?

Translation

1. Die Probezeit ist dazu gedacht, den Praktikanten mit allen Abläufen des Unternehmens vertraut zu machen. **2.** Die Ursprünge unserer Bank gehen zurück bis ins 18. Jahrhundert. **3.** Schreiben Sie den Scheck aus; ich werde selbst gehen und ihn bei der Bank einlösen. **4.** So klein das Unternehmen auch sein mag, es hat eine wichtige Position in seinem Bereich. **5.** Ich könnte nicht mehr ohne meinen Computer auskommen. **6.** Um Ihr Projekt zu finanzieren, werden Sie die Dienste einer Bank benötigen. **7.** Wir werden Ihnen die Gelegenheit geben, bei unserem Verwaltungspersonal zu arbeiten. **8.** Dank Kommunikation per Satellit und Übertragungen von Kursnotierungen per Computer sind die Finanzmärkte leicht zugänglich geworden. **9.** Unsere Privatkunden sind so wichtig für uns wie unsere Firmenkunden. **10.** Durch Vereinfachung unserer Verfahren haben wir es geschafft, unsere Produktivität zu steigern.

KAPITEL 8

LÖSUNGSVORSCHLÄGE

Verständnisübung

1. It is meant to familiarise her with the company's current financial procedures. **2.** It is Mr Harold McDuff, a senior executive in the Financial and Legal Department. **3.** It can finance itself short term through commercial paper and certificates of deposit. **4.** It issues bonds when it needs to finance itself long term (*or* when it needs long-term financing). **5.** It is the responsibility of the company's cash management. **6.** No, until recently United Chocolate dealt with different banks in the different countries where it trades or manufactures. **7.** They tended to be mostly national rather than international. **8.** They have become irrelevant because of instant satellite communications and computerised quotes. **9.** You must take into account time differences. **10.** It reduces paperwork and improves productivity.

Übersetzungsübung

1. The trial period is meant to familiarise the trainee with all the company('s) procedures. **2.** The origins of our bank go back to the XVIIIth century. **3.** Write the cheque; I will go and cash it myself at the bank. **4.** Small as the company may be, it occupies an important position in its field. **5.** I could no longer do without my computer. **6.** (In order) to finance your project, you will need the services of a bank. **7.** We will give you the opportunity to work in our back-office. **8.** Thanks to satellite communications and to computerised quotes, the financial markets have become easily accessible. **9.** Our private customers are as important to us as our corporate customers. **10.** By simplifying our procedures we have managed to improve our productivity.

CHAPTER 8

Application

*Lesen Sie den Dialog, die **ANMERKUNGEN** und das Dokument aufmerksam durch und fassen Sie die Gründe zusammen, die United Chocolate dazu bewogen haben, sämtliche Transaktionen nur über eine einzige Bank abzuwickeln, und nennen Sie die Vorteile, die das Unternehmen daraus gezogen hat (ca. 80-100 Wörter).*

DO!

***Develop your sense of psychology:
observe, notice, listen, remember.***

KAPITEL 8

Lösungsvorschlag

United Chocolate, both as a corporation (US) and a private limited company (UK), has grown more and more international: it currently manufactures and trades all over the world.

On the other hand, capital markets have experienced the same internationalisation. Satellites and computers have made financial transactions possible in real time around the clock.

It became obvious then to have all United Chocolate operations performed by Barclays, a leading banking institution with an extensive worldwide network.

The advantages are numerous:
* simplification of management
* improved productivity
* and, as a result, considerable savings to United Chocolate.

DON'T!

Don't forget that the British are more interested in facts and in the means to reach their goals than in ideas. So are the Americans.

CHAPTER 9

Choosing where to work

Susan has successfully completed her six-month trial period. Mr Robertson has asked to see her to talk about where she is now going to work. They are discussing the inner workings of United Chocolate Ltd. **(1)**

1. **Mr Robertson:** *(Pointing to the United Chocolate [UK] organisation chart on the wall behind his desk)* As I told you in one of our first discussions – and as you've been able to see for yourself over the past six months, of course! – our company structure is relatively simple: operational or line departments on the one hand, functional or staff departments on the other. **(2)**

2. **Susan:** Isn't that too rigid or too military an approach to management?

3. **Mr Robertson:** *(Smiling)* You're beginning to talk like an experienced manager already! On paper, perhaps; but in practice, by providing exceptional work flexibility and cooperation among departments, we have developed an innovative atmosphere which stimulates employees' motivation, from the bottom to the top of the hierarchy, blue-collar workers as well as white-collar workers. This, by the way, is one of the tasks of the Human Resources Department. **(3)**

4. **Susan:** Well, it sounds exciting, but *(half sceptical)* does it always work as smoothly as you claim?

5. **Mr Robertson:** Why do you ask, Susan? Have you seen signs that is doesn't?

6. **Susan:** Not here in Milton Keynes, but...

7. **Mr Robertson:** *(Cutting her off)* The key to success is the permanent or quasi-permanent flow of information among departments, whether at staff or line level. **(4)**

KAPITEL 9

Die Wahl des Arbeitsplatzes

Susan hat ihre sechsmonatige Probezeit erfolgreich abgeschlossen. Herr Robertson hat sie gebeten, ihn aufzusuchen, um mit ihr darüber zu sprechen, wo sie nun arbeiten wird. Sie sprechen über die internen Abläufe bei United Chocolate Ltd.

1. **Herr Robertson:** *(Zeigt auf das Organisationsschema von United Chocolate (UK) an der Wand hinter seinem Schreibtisch.)* Wie ich Ihnen in einer unserer ersten Besprechungen sagte – und wie Sie selbst natürlich im Laufe der letzten sechs Monate sehen konnten – ist unsere Unternehmensstruktur relativ einfach: die Betriebs- oder Produktionsabteilungen auf der einen Seite und die Verwaltungsabteilungen auf der anderen.

2. **Susan:** Ist das nicht ein zu strenger oder zu militärischer Ansatz für das Management?

3. **Herr Robertson:** *(Lächelt)* Sie fangen schon an, wie ein erfahrener Manager zu reden! Auf dem Papier vielleicht; aber in der Praxis haben wir durch außergewöhnliche Arbeitsflexibilität und Kooperation zwischen den Abteilungen eine innovative Atmosphäre geschaffen, die die Motivation der Mitarbeiter, von der untersten bis zu obersten Stufe der Hierarchie, sowohl bei Arbeitern als auch bei Angestellten, anregt. Dies ist übrigens eine der Aufgaben der Personalabteilung.

4. **Susan:** Naja, das klingt aufregend, aber *(ein bißchen skeptisch)* funktioniert das immer so reibungslos wie Sie behaupten?

5. **Herr Robertson:** Warum fragen Sie, Susan? Haben Sie Anzeichen dafür gesehen, daß dies nicht so ist?

6. **Susan:** Nicht hier in Milton Keynes, aber...

7. **Herr Robertson:** *(Unterbricht sie)* Der Schlüssel zum Erfolg ist der ständige oder fast ständige Fluß von Informationen zwischen den Abteilungen, egal, ob auf der Verwaltungs- oder Fertigungsebene.

ANMERKUNGEN

(1) **to complete:** "abschließen, beenden"; *to complete a form* "ein Formular ausfüllen".
(2) **staff, line:** Im Militärjargon bezeichnet *staff* das Stabspersonal und *line* die Angehörigen der Kampftruppe.
(3) **blue-collar, white-collar worker(s)** sind die Bezeichnungen für "Arbeiter" (die meistens einen Blaumann tragen; daher *blue-collar* "blauer Kragen") und "Angestellte" (deren Kragen meistens weiß ist).
(4) **information** wird immer im Singular verwendet, auch wenn es mit "Informationen" übersetzt wird. Will man im Englischen den Plural bilden, muß man *pieces of information* oder *elements of information* sagen.

CHAPTER 9

8. **Susan:** Too much information may lead to saturation.

9. **Mr Robertson:** I agree. But then it is up to the respective departments to process what information they deem relevant to their own specific activity, or likely to justify cooperation with other departments. **(5)**

10. **Susan:** From what I saw on my last assignment, I would guess that is particularly true of marketing, research and sales. I can't imagine them working separately in their respective corners.

11. **Mr Robertson:** Obviously our researchers in their labs need constant input from marketing specialists and from our sales force in the field to develop new products. Information on customer reactions is vital to researchers and, conversely, the creativeness of marketing and research will become an essential factor in sales..., and in the improvement of profits. *(After a pause)* Marketing is the area you've chosen to work in, I assume...? **(6)**

12. **Susan:** Oh no! Not for the time being, at least. I'd rather start in human resources.

13. **Mr Robertson:** *(Sounding almost surprised)* I'm very pleased to hear that, Susan! And may I ask what motivated your choice?

14. **Susan:** Well, I was going to say just now, when we were talking about stimulating employees' motivation and you asked me if I'd seen signs that it didn't work... Well, I spoke a lot with the production workers, and sometimes I got the impression that they weren't always motivated...

15. **Mr Robertson:** That's good news, then, isn't it? You'll have plenty of work on your plate! **(7)**

KAPITEL 9

8. **Susan:** Zu viele Informationen können zu einer Art Übersättigung führen.

9. **Herr Robertson:** Da stimme ich Ihnen zu. Aber dann obliegt es den einzelnen Abteilungen, die Informationen zu verarbeiten, die sie für ihre spezifische Aktivität für wichtig erachten oder die geeignet sind, eine Kooperation mit anderen Abteilungen zu rechtfertigen.

10. **Susan:** Demzufolge, was ich auf meinem letzten Posten gesehen habe, würde ich annehmen, daß das besonders für Marketing, Forschung und Vertrieb gilt. Ich kann mir nicht vorstellen, daß da jeder alleine in seiner jeweiligen Ecke arbeitet.

11. **Herr Robertson:** Offensichtlich benötigen unsere Forscher in ihren Labors den permanenten "Input" von Marketing-Spezialisten und von unseren Vertriebskräften vor Ort, um neue Produkte zu entwickeln. Informationen über Kundenreaktionen sind entscheidend für die Forscher, und umgekehrt wird die Kreativität von Marketing und Forschung zu einem wesentlichen Faktor im Vertrieb... und bei der Steigerung der Gewinne. *(Nach einer Pause)* Ich nehme an, Marketing ist der Bereich, den Sie sich für Ihre Arbeit ausgewählt haben...?

12. **Susan:** Oh nein! Zumindest nicht im Moment. Ich würde lieber im Personalwesen anfangen.

13. **Herr Robertson:** *(Klingt fast erstaunt)* Ich freue mich sehr, das zu hören, Susan! Und darf ich fragen, was Sie zu dieser Wahl bewogen hat?

14. **Susan:** Naja, das wollte ich eben schon sagen, als wir über die Anregung der Mitarbeitermotivation sprachen und Sie mich fragten, ob ich Anzeichen dafür gesehen hätte, daß es nicht funktioniert... Also, ich habe mich viel mit den Arbeitern in der Fertigung unterhalten, und manchmal habe ich den Eindruck gewonnen, daß sie nicht immer motiviert waren...

15. **Herr Robertson:** Das ist doch eine gute Nachricht, oder? Dann werden Sie ja eine Menge Arbeit um die Ohren haben!

ANMERKUNGEN (Fortsetzung)

(5) **to process** hat die Grundbedeutung "verarbeiten, bearbeiten, behandeln" und wird sowohl in der Informationstechnik als auch in der Materialbearbeitung verwendet. *Process* "Vorgang, Prozedur, Verfahren"; *real-time processing* "Echtzeitverarbeitung" (in der Informatik).

(6) **input:** "Eingabe, Eingangswert, Einsatzmenge" stammt ursprünglich aus der Datenverarbeitung und bezeichnet alle von außen in ein System eingehenden Informationselemente. Es wird auch in der Produktion verwendet. Heute ist das Wort *input* schon weitgehend in unseren Sprachgebrauch eingegangen. Das Gegenteil, *output*, hat recht unterschiedliche Bedeutungen: "Ausbeute, Förderung" (bei Maschinen); "Ausgabe, Ausgangswert" (in der Informatik); "Produktion, Produktionsleistung, Arbeitsleistung, Ertrag" (in der Produktion).

(7) **to have plenty** (oder **a lot**) ... **on one´s plate:** "viel am Hals/um die Ohren haben".

CHAPTER 9　　　　　　　　　　　　　　　　　　DOCUMENT

Confidential letter from Milton Keynes to Filton

UNITED CHOCOLATE (UK) Ltd
Thornbury House
Arlington Row
MILTON KEYNES
Bucks, MK2 5BQ
Tel: 01908 956384
Fax: 01908 956122

Mr David Evans
Factory Manager
United Chocolate Ltd
Almondsbury Industrial Estate
Filton, Bristol BS9 2TN

10th October 199.

CONFIDENTIAL

Dear Mr Evans,

　　A labour productivity survey, conducted in all UK plants at the request of our Board of Directors by an outside firm of consultants, Redford and Associates, has just been completed.

　　It extends over the first six months of the current year and shows a general increase in absenteeism in each one of our plants.

　　However, that increase appears particularly significant in your plant, at factory worker level.

　　The Board has asked Human Resources to provide detailed information on identifiable causes and suggested remedies.

　　Will you please let me have your personal evaluation of, and appropriate comments on the situation at your plant.

　　A prompt response is expected, to enable us to prepare a full report before the next Board meeting scheduled on 3rd November.

　　Yours sincerely,

　　Alexander Romer-Lee
　　Director of Human Resources

Encl: Labour Productivity Survey (1st January – 30th June 199.) Redford & Associates

KAPITEL 9

Die Geschäftswelt: Ein Schlachtfeld

Schon seit langem haben Unternehmen die Begriffe Wirtschaftskrieg *(economic warfare)* und Schlachtfeld *(battle-field)* in ihrer Organisationsstruktur für sich übernommen: Während die Befehlskette *(chain of command)* die Fertigungsebene *(line)* betrifft, ist es Aufgabe der Verwaltungsebene *(staff)*, die Entscheidungsfindung *(decision making)* zu vereinfachen.

Die Verkaufsmannschaft ist zum Absatzstab *(sales force)* geworden. Sie kämpft an der "Verkaufsfront" in einem ständigen Preiskrieg *(price war* oder *price-cutting war)*.

Ihre Verkaufsziele haben sich zu Ziel- oder Schießscheiben *(targets)* entwickelt. Bei Bedarf wird eine Einsatztruppe *(task force)* gebildet, eine Gruppe, die sich für ein festgesetztes Ziel und eine begrenzte Zeit außerhalb der normalen Strukturen eines Unternehmens konstituiert. Der Ausdruck geht zurück auf den 2. Weltkrieg und bezeichnete damals die zeitweilige Umgruppierung von Einheiten verschiedener Waffengattungen zur Erfüllung einer zeitlich begrenzten Mission.

CHAPTER 9

EXERCISES

Comprehension

Lesen Sie den Dialog aufmerksam durch. Beantworten Sie dann die nachfolgenden Fragen, und zwar immer in ganzen Sätzen:

1. How long has Susan been working for United Chocolate ? **2.** Why has Mr Robertson asked to see her? **3.** Why does Mr Robertson consider that the company structure is relatively simple? **4.** What's Susan's reaction to his description of the company structure? **5.** According to Mr Robertson, why is it important to generate an innovative atmosphere? **6.** According to Susan, what's the risk with too much information? **7.** What sort of input do researchers need in order to develop new products? **8.** Why does Mr Robertson sound surprised by Susan's preference for a job in Human Resources? **9.** Where did Susan get the impression that some workers were not always motivated? **10.** What makes you think that Susan will be very busy in her job?

Translation

1. Herr Robertson hat darum gebeten, Susan am Ende ihrer Probezeit zu sehen. **2.** Susan ist nun in der Lage, für sich selbst die inneren Abläufe des Unternehmens zu erkennen. **3.** Die Einteilung zwischen der Betriebs- und der Verwaltungsebene scheint ihr ein zu militärischer Ansatz für das Management zu sein. **4.** Susan denkt, daß es einfacher ist, die Motivation auf dem Papier zu steigern als in der Praxis. **5.** Sie klingen ziemlich skeptisch, was den Erfolg unserer Aktion angeht. **6.** Egal, ob Sie interessiert sind oder nicht, unterbrechen Sie mich nicht, wenn ich spreche. **7.** Es wird Ihre Aufgabe sein, so schnell wie möglich die Informationen zu bearbeiten, die für unsere Forscher von Nutzen sein könnten. **8.** Es ist schwierig, sich vorzustellen, daß Forschung, Marketing und Vertrieb alleine in ihren jeweiligen Ecken arbeiten. **9.** Eine Untersuchung zur Arbeitsproduktivität hat eine allgemeine Zunahme bei der Abwesenheit [vom Arbeitsplatz] ergeben. **10.** Herr Romer-Lee erwartet eine sofortige Antwort von Herrn Evans, damit er in der Lage ist, seinen Bericht für den Vorstand vorzubereiten.

KAPITEL 9

LÖSUNGSVORSCHLÄGE

Verständnisübung

1. Susan has been working for United Chocolate for six months. 2. He wants to talk about where she is now going to work. 3. He considers it relatively simple because it consists, on the one hand, of operational or line divisions, and of functional or staff divisions on the other. 4. She wonders whether it is not too rigid or too military an approach to management. 5. It stimulates employees' motivation from the bottom to the top of the hierarchy. 6. It may lead to saturation. 7. They need constant input from marketing specialists and from the sales force in the field. 8. He sounds surprised because he assumed she would choose to work in marketing. 9. She got that impression when she visited the United Chocolate factory in Filton. 10. Mr Robertson tells her that she will have plenty of work on her plate.

Übersetzungsübung

1. Mr Robertson has asked to see Susan at the end of her trial period. 2. Susan is now able to see for herself the inner workings of the company. 3. The division between line and staff seems to her too military an approach to management. 4. Susan thinks it is easier to stimulate motivation on paper than in practice. 5. You sound (look) rather sceptical concerning the success of our action. 6. Whether you are interested or not, don't interrupt me (*or* cut me off) when I'm speaking. 7. It will be up to you to process as quickly as possible whatever information is likely to be useful to our researchers. 8. It is difficult to imagine research, marketing and sales working separately in their respective corners. 9. A labour productivity survey has shown a general increase in absenteeism. 10. Mr Romer-Lee expects a prompt reply from Mr Evans to enable him to prepare his report to the Board.

CHAPTER 9

Application

Susan schaut etwas skeptisch drein, als Herr Robertson mit ihr über Innovationen und Mitarbeitermotivation spricht. Lesen Sie noch einmal den Dialog in Kapitel 7 und erläutern Sie die Gründe für Susans Skepsis (80-100 Wörter).

Beachten Sie, daß die Lösung, die wir Ihnen für diese Übung vorschlagen, nur eine Alternative unter vielen sein kann.

DO!

Establish and maintain personal relationships with a few people you can trust in a foreign country: they will be your mentors and as such, they will be able to give you advice and inform you about pitfalls (Klippe, Fallstrick) to avoid.

KAPITEL 9

Praktische Übung

During her conversation with Daphne at the Filton plant, Susan was struck by the following facts:
* she has never met Mr Robertson, who is just a name to her.
* in her 31 years in the plant, she has seen relatively few changes, except that they now use grams and kilos instead of ounces and pounds, and the chocolate is not as good either.
* EC regulations do not make much sense to her, nor do total-quality management, quality circles and the like.
* she does not realise the usefulness of safety and hygiene regulations. She thinks Mr Evans is obsessed about them.
* she loves, though, to go on training courses, but maybe not for the right reason!

DON'T!

You don't need to speak another language perfectly to do business. Don't neglect signals nor the other party's facial expressions and body language.

CHAPTER 10

Managing human resources

Phil and Susan are having lunch together in the company cafeteria.

1. **Phil:** When I joined this company after completing my MBA, I had settled for finance as an initial career.

2. **Susan:** Is that what you had specialised in?

3. **Phil:** Right. But a different opportunity was offered to me. The traditional concept of personnel and labour force had given way to human resources.

4. **Susan:** That's a more sensible approach, isn't it?

5. **Phil:** Definitely. And yet in my obsession with figures, charts and the bottom line, I had never realised that people are a major resource for any type of company or organisation. Ironically, they never appear in the balance sheet, although a few are mentioned in the annual report. **(1) (2) (3)**

6. **Susan:** It must have been a real challenge for you!

7. **Phil:** In that new function for which I had not been thoroughly prepared, I had to learn how human needs are best met, how roles are defined and how formal, as well as informal, interrelationships within the company have to be developed to avoid or reduce possibilities of conflict. *(Questioningly)* I hope I don't sound too pompous in my description of the job? **(4) (5)**

8. **Susan:** Not at all. In such a large company as ours, I suppose you need to work out procedures to achieve so ambitious an objective.

9. **Phil:** We couldn't do without them. People must be recruited, trained, compensated and selected for promotion. That we do by means of individual or team performance evaluations.

10. **Susan:** Are results the basis for reward? **(6)**

KAPITEL 10

Die Personalverwaltung

Phil und Susan essen gemeinsam in der Firmenkantine zu Mittag.

1. **Phil:** Als ich in das Unternehmen eintrat, nachdem ich meinen Abschluß als MBA gemacht hatte, hatte ich mich dafür entschieden, meine Berufslaufbahn in der Finanzwirtschaft zu beginnen.
2. **Susan:** War das das Gebiet, auf das du dich spezialisiert hattest?
3. **Phil:** Stimmt. Aber es wurde mir eine andere Gelegenheit angeboten. Das traditionelle Konzept von Angestellten und Arbeitern hatte der Personalführung Platz gemacht.
4. **Susan:** Das ist ein etwas sinnvollerer Ansatz, nicht wahr?
5. **Phil:** Genau. Und doch hatte ich in meiner Besessenheit für Zahlen, Tabellen und Reingewinn nie erkannt, daß die Menschen eine wichtige Ressource für jede Art von Unternehmen und Organisation sind. Komischerweise tauchen sie niemals in einer Bilanz auf, obwohl einige im Jahresbericht erwähnt werden.
6. **Susan:** Das muß für dich eine echte Herausforderung gewesen sein!
7. **Phil:** In dieser neuen Funktion, auf die ich nicht gründlich vorbereitet worden war, mußte ich lernen, wie man den Bedürfnissen der Menschen am besten gerecht wird, wie Rollen definiert werden und wie, formell wie informell, Beziehungen innerhalb des Unternehmens entwickelt werden müssen, um die Möglichkeit von Konflikten zu vermeiden oder zu reduzieren. *(Fragend)* Ich hoffe, ich klinge nicht zu aufgeblasen in meiner Beschreibung des Jobs?
8. **Susan:** Ganz und gar nicht. In so einer großen Firma wie unserer, nehme ich an, muß man Verfahren ausarbeiten, um ein so ehrgeiziges Ziel zu erreichen.
9. **Phil:** Ohne die könnten wir nicht auskommen. Leute müssen eingestellt, geschult, entlohnt und auf ihre Beförderungswürdigkeit geprüft werden. Das machen wir mit Hilfe von Leistungsbewertungen für Einzelpersonen oder Teams.
10. **Susan:** Wirken sich die Ergebnisse in Form von Belohnungen aus?

ANMERKUNGEN

(1) **bottom line (US):** "Reingewinn". Ein salopper Ausdruck für die letzte Zeile der Gewinn- und Verlustrechnung *(income statement)*, in der der Reingewinn *(net profit, net income)* auftaucht.

(2) **balance sheet:** "Bilanz", der Rechnungsabschluß, der die Aktiva *(assets)* den Passiva *(liabilities)* gegenüberstellt (siehe Kapitel 36, Dokument).

(3) **a few are mentioned in the annual report:** Hiermit bezieht sich Phil auf die Führungskräfte und die Mitglieder des Aufsichtsrates.

(4) **to meet:** "(Bedürfnisse) erfüllen, (Anforderungen) gerecht werden, (Herausforderungen) begegnen".

(5) **interrelationship:** "Wechselbeziehung, Zusammenspiel".

(6) **reward:** "Belohnung, Honorar, Vergütung, Entgelt" umfaßt in diesem Zusammenhang Beförderung *(promotion)*, Gehaltserhöhungen *(salary increase)* und Prämie, Zulage *(bonus)* oder andere Bonusarten.

CHAPTER 10

11. **Phil:** To a large extent, in sectors or activities where they can easily be measured, such as sales.

12. **Susan:** What about staff functions?

13. **Phil:** Other criteria are taken into account, depending on the job: productivity, availability, sense of initiative, etc. **(7)**

14. **Susan:** Deciding who does or doesn't get promoted must be no easy task.

15. **Phil:** There again, we have a system of procedures and in-house recommendations to ensure that we are making the right choice. At that level, we are dealing with human resource strategy.

16. **Susan:** *(Puzzled)* Ah?

17. **Phil:** I'm beginning to sound as if I were delivering a speech! You'll soon realise, though, that labour – ie people – may be the only resource which has the potential to generate almost limitless returns, since it is, in the final analysis, the only creative resource. You will also find out, in due course, that a firm's strategy for managing its employees, executives and workers alike, plays an important part in the business policy. **(8)**

18. **Susan:** You sound so enthusiastic about your job! If I'd had any doubts about where to work, you would have convinced me to opt for human resources.

19. **Phil:** I'm flattered to hear that, and I promise to do my best to help you. Meanwhile, can I get you another cup of this instant coffee – a product of ours, of course?

20. **Susan:** No thanks, Phil. I've had enough! **(9)**

KAPITEL 10

11. **Phil:** Weitgehend in Bereichen oder bei Aktivitäten, die leicht bemessen werden können, z.B. beim Vertrieb.

12. **Susan:** Und auf der Verwaltungsebene?

13. **Phil:** Da werden je nach Tätigkeit andere Kriterien berücksichtigt: Produktivität, Verfügbarkeit, Sinn für Initiative usw.

14. **Susan:** Es muß keine leichte Aufgabe sein, zu entscheiden, wer befördert wird und wer nicht.

15. **Phil:** Auch hier haben wir ein System von Verfahren und internen Empfehlungen, um sicherzustellen, daß wir die richtige Auswahl treffen. Auf dieser Ebene geht es um Strategien der Personalführung.

16. **Susan:** *(Verwirrt)* Ach ja?

17. **Phil:** Klingt schon, als ob ich eine Rede halten würde! Du wirst jedoch bald feststellen, daß Arbeitskräfte – d.h. Menschen – die einzige Ressource sein können, die das Potential besitzt, fast grenzenlose Erträge hervorzubringen, da sie in der Endanalyse die einzig kreative Ressource sind. Du wirst auch mit der Zeit herausfinden, daß die Strategie eines Unternehmens für die Personalführung, sowohl bei den Führungskräften wie auch bei den Arbeitern, eine wichtige Rolle in der Unternehmenspolitik spielt.

18. **Susan:** Du klingst so begeistert, wenn du von deiner Arbeit sprichst. Wenn ich irgendwelche Zweifel hätte, wo ich arbeiten sollte, würdest du mich davon überzeugt haben, in der Personalabteilung zu arbeiten.

19. **Phil:** Es schmeichelt mir, das zu hören, und ich verspreche, ich werde mein Bestes geben, um dir zu helfen. Kann ich dir in der Zwischenzeit noch eine Tasse von diesem Instantkaffee holen – ein Produkt von uns natürlich?

20. **Susan:** Nein, danke, Phil. Ich habe genug gehabt!

ANMERKUNGEN (Fortsetzung)

(7) **criteria:** Achtung! Dies ist der Plural von *criterion* (Kriterium).
(8) **return:** "Gewinn, Ertrag, Einnahmen". *Return on investment (ROI)* "Ertrag des investierten Kapitals".
(9) **I've had enough** kann hier auf zwei Arten interpretiert werden, wörtlich oder ironisch: 1. "Ich habe genug getrunken" und 2. "Ich habe genug gehabt" ("Ich habe schon genug intus").

CHAPTER 10 DOCUMENT

Reply to confidential letter

UNITED CHOCOLATE Ltd
Almondsbury Industrial Estate
Filton, Bristol BS9 2 TN
Tel: 0117 985 4313
Fax: 0117 985 4577

Alexander Romer-Lee, Esq
Director of Human Resources
United Chocolate (UK) Ltd
Thornbury House
MILTON KEYNES
Bucks, MK2 5BQ

15th October 199.

Dear Mr Romer-Lee,
   Thank you for your confidential letter of 10th October.

The Redford survey did not cause much of a surprise here.

We, ourselves, had pointed out to the members of the survey team, on their visit of our plant last July, that we had suffered severe weather conditions in late January. As a consequence, motor traffic was almost totally disrupted for a week. That obviously had an impact on employee absenteeism.

Shortly afterwards, our area was seriously affected by a flu epidemic which aggravated our personnel difficulties.

We have little control over the weather, but we have already planned massive vaccination against the flu in the next four weeks to avoid repetition of last winter's problems.

This being said, I would like to remind you that we have conducted a vigorous and successful campaign to reduce labour injuries by issuing regular warnings to factory personnel and by strictly controlling compliance with hygiene and safety regulations. Our September rate was the lowest ever (detailed statistics enclosed).

Please let me know whether you need further information for your report to the Board.

Yours sincerely,

David Evans
Factory Manager (Filton Plant)

Encl*: Monthly labour injury statistics for the first three quarters of the current year.

* **Encl.: Kurzform für Enclosed, Enclosure(s): "Anlagen"**

KAPITEL 10

Arbeitskräfte oder Personal

Die Strenge des traditionellen Unternehmensmodells mit seiner hierarchischen Struktur (Arbeiter, Büroangestellte, leitende Angestellte, Führungskräfte) hat sich in den letzten Jahren stark abgeschwächt. Auch die Sprache ist dieser Tendenz gefolgt, zuerst in den USA, dann in Japan und dann in Mitteleuropa. Diese Entwicklung wird der Rolle, die dem Einzelnen zugedacht ist, und dem großen Vertrauen, das heute in jede Arbeitskraft gesetzt wird, besser gerecht.
So ist die Sammelbezeichnung Arbeiter *(labour force)* zunächst dem allgemeinen Ausdruck Personal *(personnel)* gewichen, eine Bezeichnung, die politisch und sozial weniger diskriminierend ist. In diesem Zusammenhang sollte man beachten, daß die sozialistische Arbeiterpartei Großbritanniens, die 1906 gegründet wurde, *Labour Party* heißt.
Der Ausdruck *personnel manager* für Personalchef ist mittlerweile durch den Ausdruck *Director of Human Ressources, DHR,* ersetzt worden.

CHAPTER 10

EXERCISES

Comprehension

Lesen Sie den Dialog aufmerksam durch. Beantworten Sie dann die nachfolgenden Fragen, und zwar immer in ganzen Sätzen:

1. What did Phil specialise in during his postgraduate studies? **2.** Why, then, didn't he settle for finance as an initial career? **3.** For what reason had Phil never realised that people are a major resource for the company? **4.** Whose names are mentioned in the annual report? **5.** How can employees be rewarded for their individual performance? **6.** What criteria are taken into account to evaluate staff functions? **7.** Why does Phil think that people have the potential to generate almost limitless returns? **8.** How can Susan's last sentence be understood? **9.** According to Mr Evans, what caused the sudden increase in absenteeism in his factory? **10.** What can Mr Evans do to fight another flu epidemic?

Translation

1. In Phils Laufbahn hat die Finanzwirtschaft der Personalführung Platz gemacht. 2. Ist es sinnvoll, in einem Unternehmen nur den Reingewinn und die materiellen Ressourcen zu berücksichtigen? 3. Sie wurde gründlich vorbereitet, um allen Herausforderungen ihrer Tätigkeit zu begegnen. 4. Ein Computer kann sofort Zahlen und Tabellen liefern, aber er ist nicht in der Lage, die Mitarbeitermotivation anzuregen. 5. Welche Verfahren mußten ausgearbeitet werden, um die Möglichkeit von Konflikten zu reduzieren? 6. Obwohl ihre persönlichen Ergebnisse hervorragend sind, hat sie seit Beginn des Jahres weder eine Gehaltserhöhung noch einen Bonus erhalten. 7. Trotz unseres komplexen Bewertungs- und internen Empfehlungssystems ist es keine leichte Aufgabe sicherzustellen, daß wir die richtige Auswahl treffen. 8. Die Leistung von Führungskräften wie auch von Arbeitern muß auf der Grundlage gut definierter Kriterien bemessen werden. 9. Die Produktivitätsuntersuchung hat im Filton-Werk keine große Überraschung hervorgerufen. 10. Jedermann ist verantwortlich für die Einhaltung von Sicherheits- und Hygienebestimmungen.

KAPITEL 10

LÖSUNGSVORSCHLÄGE

Verständnisübung

1. He specialised in finance. 2. He didn't because a different opportunity was offered to him in human resources. 3. Because of this specialisation in finance, he had an obsession with figures, charts and the bottom line. 4. The names of the top managers and the board members are mentioned. 5. They can be rewarded by means of salary increases, bonuses and/or promotions. 6. It depends on the job: it might be productivity, availability, sense of initiative, etc. 7. He thinks they are the only creative resource in a company. 8. Either she's really had enough coffee so far, or she's drunk too much of it and does not specially enjoy United Chocolate's instant coffee. 9. Motor traffic was interrupted for a week because of weather conditions, and then personnel difficulties were aggravated by a flu epidemic. 10. He has planned massive vaccination in the next four weeks.

Übersetzungsübung

1. Finance has given way to human resources in Phil's career. 2. Is it sensible, in a company, to take into account only the bottom line and material resources? 3. She has been thoroughly prepared to meet all the challenges of her new job. 4. A computer can provide instantly figures and charts, but it is unable to stimulate employee motivation. 5. What procedures have had to be worked out to reduce possibilities of conflict (*or* dispute)? 6. Although her individual results are excellent, she's had neither salary increase nor bonus since the beginning of the year. 7. It is no easy task to ensure that we are making the right choice in spite of our complex system of evaluation and in-house recommendations. 8. The performance of executives and workers alike must be measured according to well-defined criteria. 9. The productivity survey has not caused much of a surprise at the Filton plant. 10. Compliance with safety and hygiene regulations is everybody's responsibility.

CHAPTER 10

Vocabulary revision (Chapters 1-10)

Vervollständigen Sie die untenstehenden Sätze (ein oder mehrere Wörter pro Lücke):

1. The US equivalent of a chartered accountant is a (...).
2. The (...) fees in some private universities are very high.
3. Perks or (...) may add substantially to one's earnings.
4. United Chocolate Ltd is a wholly-owned (...) of the US (...) company.
5. United Chocolate Inc is (...) in Philadelphia.
6. It is sometimes difficult to reconcile the (...) for profit and shareholder satisfaction.
7. Trainee managers are sent to the factory to get some (...) experience.
8. A company may finance itself short term through (...) issued by a bank.
9. In the organisation chart, the sales force is (...) and human resources (...).
10. In an (...) the bottom line shows the net profit earned by the company.

DO!

***Remember that Anglo-Saxons value informality
and equality in human relations.
Be prepared for more simplicity and dispense
with unnecessary formalities.***

KAPITEL 10

Wiederholung des Wortschatzes

1. certified public accountant
2. tuition
3. fringe benefits
4. subsidiary, parent
5. headquartered
6. quest
7. hands-on
8. certificates of deposit (CDs)
9. line (operational), staff (functional)
10. income statement

 DON'T!

Don't assume that Anglo-Saxon familiarity means that private and professional relations are not strictly separate.

CHAPTER 11

Facing a strike

Susan now occupies the position of Junior Manager in the Human Resources Department at Milton Keynes. After barely a fortnight, she gets her first taste of crisis, when a strike breaks out at the Filton plant. She has to drive down to Bristol with Phil Irwin, to whom she reports. **(1)**

1. **Phil:** I hope that when we get off the M25 and onto the M4 there'll be less traffic! **(2) (3)**

2. **Susan:** During the rush hour, I doubt whether it will thin out much until we get past Heathrow airport. **(4)**

3. **Phil:** No. You're probably right. *(A short pause)* I'm sorry to throw you in at the deep end like this, Susan, but I don't want to keep Mr Evans waiting too long. He sounded pretty desperate on the phone.

4. **Susan:** I'm not surprised. I still don't understand why the workers have locked him in his office though.

5. **Phil:** Well after the sacking of that production worker last week... **(5)**

6. **Susan:** For not complying with the hygiene regulations... But it was not the first time, apparently: he'd already had a written warning!

7. **Phil:** Maybe. But it was the first time anyone had actually been fired for that reason. You can be certain that his fellow workers were shocked. They started with a go-slow – a sort of work-to-rule – but the trade union must have picked up the issue... **(6) (7) (8)**

8. **Susan:** And they called a full-scale strike...?

KAPITEL 11

Der Streik

Susan bekleidet nun die Position eines Trainee Managers in der Abteilung für Personalwesen in Milton Keynes. Nach kaum 14 Tagen, als im Werk Filton ein Streik ausbricht, erhält sie einen ersten Vorgeschmack auf eine Krise. Sie muß zusammen mit Phil Irwin, dem sie untersteht, hinunter nach Bristol fahren.

1. **Phil:** Ich hoffe, daß weniger Verkehr sein wird, wenn wir von der M25 runterfahren und auf die M4 kommen.
2. **Susan:** Ich bezweifle, daß der Verkehr während der Stoßzeiten erheblich nachlassen wird, bis wir hinter dem Flughafen Heathrow sind.
3. **Phil:** Nein. Da hast du vermutlich recht. *(Kurze Pause)* Es tut mir leid, daß ich dich so in Schwierigkeiten bringe, Susan, aber ich möchte Herrn Evans nicht zu lange warten lassen. Er klang am Telefon ganz schön verzweifelt.
4. **Susan:** Das überrascht mich nicht. Ich verstehe trotzdem noch nicht, warum die Arbeiter ihn in seinem Büro eingesperrt haben.
5. **Phil:** Naja, nachdem er letzte Woche diesen Produktionsarbeiter rausgeschmissen hat...
6. **Susan:** Weil er sich nicht an die Hygienebestimmungen gehalten hat... Aber das war offensichtlich nicht das erste Mal: er hatte schon eine schriftliche Verwarnung erhalten!
7. **Phil:** Kann sein. Aber es war das erste Mal, daß jemand aus diesem Grund gefeuert wurde. Du kannst sicher sein, daß seine Arbeitskollegen geschockt waren. Sie begannen einen Bummelstreik – eine Art Dienst nach Vorschrift – aber die Gewerkschaft muß das Problem aufgegriffen haben...
8. **Susan:** Und sie haben einen Generalstreik ausgerufen...?

ANMERKUNGEN

(1) **to report to:** "jdm. (in einer Hierarchie) unterstehen", d.h. einer vorgesetzten Person. Bedeutet auch: "sich melden". Man sagt auch *to be responsible to*.

(2) **M25:** Eine Autobahn, die in einer Entfernung von etwa 20 km um London herumführt. Sie wurde im Jahre 1986 fertiggestellt, konnte jedoch schon bald dem hohen Verkehrsaufkommen nicht mehr gerecht werden und ist bekannt für ihre Staus.

(3) **M4:** Eine Autobahn, die London mit Bristol verbindet und die am Flughafen Heathrow vorbeiführt. Auch sie ist für ihre Staus zwischen London und Heathrow bekannt.

(4) **rush hour** bezeichnet die Hauptverkehrs- bzw. Stoßzeiten.

(5) **to sack** ist eine umgangssprachliche Bezeichnung für "jdn. entlassen". Man hört auch oft den Ausdruck *to give somebody the sack*. Andere Ausdrücke sind *to fire* ("feuern"), *to dismiss, to lay off* und *to make redundant* (entlassen nach Rationalisierung). Von diesen Verben wird *sacking, firing, dismissal, lay-off* und *redundancy* abgeleitet).

(6) **go-slow** ist ein Bummelstreik, bei dem durch genaueste Beachtung der Dienstvorschriften der Arbeitsablauf verzögert oder lahmgelegt wird, mit dem Ziel, Gehalts- oder Lohnerhöhungen durchzusetzen.

(7) **work-to-rule** ist ein anderer Ausdruck, der den Bummelstreik, die planmäßige Langsamarbeit bezeichnet, "Dienst nach Vorschrift".

(8) **trade union:** "Gewerkschaft" (für Arbeiter).

CHAPTER 11

9. **Phil:** Well, when Mr Evans got to work at 8 o'clock this morning, there was a picket in front of the factory. **(9)**

10. **Susan:** Poor Mr Evans! I got the impression that he was popular with the workers.

11. **Phil:** Oh, I'm sure he probably is. But he's rather quick-tempered; it doesn't take much to make him flare up.
He said he told the picketers that he wasn't going to tolerate any wildcat strike, and tried to drive past them. **(10)**

12. **Susan:** Mmmm. I can see better, now, how things degenerated. But what are we expected to do when we get down there?

13. **Phil:** Stop the strike of course! Robertson was furious when Evans phoned just now, and Romer-Lee will go through the roof when he finds out. If he hasn't already! He prides himself on the fact that we've had no work stoppages for over two years now. Absenteeism's been abnormally high there, apparently, though Evans blames bad weather and a flu epidemic! **(11)**

14. **Susan:** You'd better explain to me how we go about stopping the strike, Phil.

15. **Phil:** Well, it won't be easy, but we'll have to help Mr Evans negotiate with the shop stewards. They're demanding the immediate reinstatement of the worker. I don't expect you to do much of the talking, of course, but I'd like you to make as many notes as possible. You should also try and talk with as many people as you can down there. Maybe the problem runs deeper! *(Switching on the car radio)* Anyway, let's listen to the news. **(12) (13)**

KAPITEL 11

9. **Phil:** Naja, als Herr Evans heute morgen um 8 Uhr zur Arbeit kam, befand sich ein Streikposten vor der Fabrik.

10. **Susan:** Armer Herr Evans! Ich hatte den Eindruck, daß er bei den Arbeitern beliebt war.

11. **Phil:** Oh, ich bin sicher, daß er das wahrscheinlich ist. Aber er ist ziemlich leicht reizbar; es gehört nicht viel dazu, bei ihm einen Wutausbruch hervorzurufen. Er berichtete, er habe den Streikposten gesagt, er würde keinen wilden Streik tolerieren, und versuchte, mit seinem Auto an ihnen vorbeizufahren.

12. **Susan:** Mmm. Jetzt verstehe ich besser, wie alles ausgeartet ist. Aber was sollen wir machen, wenn wir da hinkommen?

13. **Phil:** Den Streik beenden, natürlich! Robertson war wütend, als Evans eben angerufen hat, und Romer-Lee geht an die Decke, wenn er davon hört. Wenn er es nicht bereits weiß! Er verkündet immer stolz, daß wir seit über zwei Jahren keinerlei Arbeitsunterbrechungen hatten. Die Fälle von unentschuldigtem Nichterscheinen am Arbeitsplatz sind anscheinend sehr zahlreich dort, obwohl Evans schlechtes Wetter und eine Grippeepidemie dafür verantwortlich macht!

14. **Susan:** Du solltest mir besser erklären, wie wir den Streik beenden, Phil.

15. **Phil:** Naja, es wird nicht einfach sein, aber wir müssen Herrn Evans helfen, mit den betrieblichen Vertrauenspersonen zu verhandeln. Sie verlangen die unverzügliche Wiedereinstellung des Arbeiters. Ich erwarte natürlich nicht von dir, daß du den Großteil der Verhandlungen führst, aber ich möchte, daß du so viele Notizen wie möglich machst. Du solltest auch dort mit so vielen Leuten wie möglich sprechen. Vielleicht liegt das Problem tiefer! *(Schaltet das Autoradio ein)* Jetzt hören wir erst mal die Nachrichten.

ANMERKUNGEN (Fortsetzung)

(9) **picket:** "Streikposten"; eine Gruppe streikender Arbeitnehmer, die sich vor dem bestreikten Betrieb versammeln, um zu versuchen, ihre Arbeitskollegen davon abzuhalten, die Arbeit aufzunehmen. Hiervon abgeleitet ist auch *picket-line* und *picketers*.

(10) **wildcat strike:** "wilder Streik". Ein Streik, der ohne die Genehmigung der Gewerkschaft durchgeführt wird und der den Abmachungen der Gewerkschaft mit der Betriebsleitung entgegenläuft.

(11) **(work) stoppage** meint jede längere oder kürzere Arbeitsniederlegung, die auf einen Arbeitskampf zurückgeht.

(12) **shop steward:** Eine Vertrauensperson, die ebenfalls Arbeitnehmer des Betriebs und Mitglied der Gewerkschaft ist, und die von den Arbeitskollegen auf Betriebsebene gewählt wird.

(13) **reinstatement** ist die Wiedereinstellung, z.B. eines entlassenen Arbeiters. Das Verb lautet *to reinstate* "wiedereinstellen".

CHAPTER 11

DOCUMENT

Trade Unions in Great Britain

Trade unions play an important part in what we call industrial relations, ie the relations between employers and employees both at individual and collective level. They negotiate pay and conditions of employment, and provide a number of social services and benefits to their members.

Union membership reached its peak at the end of the seventies and gradually declined throughout the following decade, along with the number of unions. This shrinkage reflects, to a large extent, the changing face of Britain's economy: the shift away from manufacturing and public services, the high unemployment rate and the increasing number of women at work. There remain today, however, about 10 million union members.

The decline in the overall number of trade unions is undoubtedly a result of mergers and the absorption of smaller unions by their larger brothers. Six unions still boast over 500,000 members though, including the largest, the Transport and General Workers' Union (TGWU), with a total membership in excess of a million.

The trade union movement was traditionally very powerful in political life and can still be considered as Britain's leading pressure group. This power was wielded mainly through the Trades Union Congress (TUC), to which the biggest unions, representing about 80% of total union membership, are affiliated. The TUC has long had direct links with the Labour Party.

It is true to say, though, that the power of the trade union movement as a whole is declining, both in political life and in the field of industrial relations. In the eighties, under Margaret Thatcher, successive Conservative governments introduced no fewer than five employment acts aimed at creating a healthier balance in the negotiations between employees and employers.

KAPITEL 11

Der Autofahrer
auf der anderen Seite des Kanals

Wenn wir an den Autoverkehr in Großbritannien denken, fällt uns als erstes ein, daß dort Linksverkehr herrscht. Hieran halten die Engländer eisern fest, auch wenn sie mittlerweile im Zuge der Einführung des metrischen Systems in Großbritannien ihr Benzin wie wir literweise kaufen. Ein weiterer Unterschied zum Kontinent besteht darin, daß die Zahl der Unfälle, der Verkehrstoten und Verletzten in Großbritannien weit unter der Deutschlands liegt, und das bei vergleichbarer Bevölkerungs- und Verkehrsdichte. Dies ist wohl darauf zurückzuführen, daß in Großbritannien im allgemeinen langsamer gefahren wird als bei uns (die Geschwindigkeit auf Autobahnen ist auf etwa 110 km/h begrenzt). Die Engländer achten mehr auf die verschiedenen Verkehrsschilder und es ist – im Gegensatz zur deutschen Gewohnheit – Ehrensache, andere Autofahrer vor- oder vorbeifahren zu lassen. Außerdem genießt der *policeman* in Großbritannien besonders großen Respekt.

Das Straßennetz und vor allem das Autobahnnetz ist modern, gut ausgebaut und kann kostenlos benutzt werden. Dies macht es möglich, das kleine Land schnell und preiswert zu durchfahren – vorausgesetzt, man meidet bestimmte stark übersättigte Verkehrsachsen während der Stoßzeiten! Bekannt ist auch, daß es in Großbritannien sehr viele Baustellen gibt, was einen englischen Humoristen zu dem Ausspruch bewog: "England ist eine dreispurige Autobahn, bei der zwei Spuren geschlossen sind".

CHAPTER 11

EXERCISES

Comprehension

Lesen Sie den Dialog aufmerksam durch. Beantworten Sie dann die nachfolgenden Fragen, und zwar immer in ganzen Sätzen:

1. Why are Phil and Susan progressing rather slowly on their drive down to Bristol? **2.** What does Phil mean when he talks about 'throwing Susan in at the deep end'? **3.** Why do you think Mr Evans might have been pretty desperate? **4.** Why had a worker been fired at Filton? **5.** How did the other workers react to this dismissal? **6.** What probably caused the situation to degenerate? **7.** Why will Mr Romer-Lee be furious when he hears the news? **8.** How does Mr Evans explain the high rate of absenteeism in his factory? **9.** What are Phil and Susan supposed to do when they get to Filton? **10.** What does Phil expect Susan to do?

Translation

1. Wenn Sie einen Blick auf dieses Organisationsschema werfen, dann sehen Sie, daß Susan Phil untersteht. **2.** Während der Hauptverkehrszeiten ist immer viel Verkehr zwischen der M25 und dem Flughafen Gatwick. **3.** Warum haben die Streikenden Herrn Evans in seinem Büro eingesperrt? **4.** Nach dem ersten Mal hat er einfach eine schriftliche Verwarnung bekommen, aber dieses Mal läuft er Gefahr, entlassen zu werden. **5.** Die Gewerkschaft hat beschlossen, einen Streik auszurufen, um die Wiedereinstellung ihres Kollegen zu erreichen. **6.** Herr Evans ist schon immer leicht reizbar gewesen, und er hat versucht, trotz der Streikposten die Fabrik zu betreten. **7.** Romer-Lee ist an die Decke gegangen, als er erfuhr, daß die Dinge so ausgeartet waren. **8.** Ich kann nicht glauben, daß schlechtes Wetter und eine Grippeepidemie der Grund für alles sein sollen. **9.** Du brauchst nicht direkt an den Verhandlungen teilzunehmen, aber hör gut auf alles, was gesagt wird. **10.** In den Nachrichten haben sie heute morgen viel über die große Unruhe gesprochen, die in Frankreich herrscht.

KAPITEL 11

LÖSUNGSVORSCHLÄGE

Verständnisübung

1. Because it's the rush hour and there is a lot of traffic. 2. He means that after very little time in her new position, Susan has to face a crisis in the company. 3. He is probably pretty desperate because he has been locked in his office by the strikers. 4. A worker had been fired because he had not followed the hygiene regulations. 5. His fellow workers were undoubtedly shocked. 6. Mr Evans's quick temper, what he said to the picketers and the fact that he tried to drive through the picket line. 7. Because he is proud of the fact that there have been no work stoppages for over two years. 8. He says it is due to bad weather and a flu epidemic. 9. They are expected to stop the strike. 10. He expects her to take as many notes and speak with as many people as possible.

Übersetzungsübung

1. If you have (*or* take) a look at this organisation chart, you will see that Susan reports to Phil. 2. In the rush hour, there is always a great deal of traffic between the M25 and Gatwick Airport. 3. Why have the strikers locked Mr Evans in his office? 4. After the first incident, he simply received a written warning, but this time he risks being dismissed. 5. The (trade) union (has) decided to call a strike in order to obtain the reinstatement of their colleague. 6. Mr Evans has always been quick-tempered, and he tried to enter the factory in spite of the picket. 7. Romer-Lee went through the roof when he learnt that things had degenerated. 8. I can't believe that bad weather and a flu epidemic can explain everything. 9. You don't need to participate directly in the negotiations, but listen carefully to everything that's said. 10. On the news this morning, they spoke a lot about the deep sense of uneasiness currently affecting France.

CHAPTER 11

Application

Sehen Sie sich noch einmal das Dokument 'Trade Unions in Great Britain' an. Lesen Sie dann die untenstehenden Aussagen und entscheiden Sie, welche wahr und welche falsch sind. Korrigieren Sie die falschen Aussagen.

1. Union membership gradually declined throughout the seventies.
2. The following decade saw a decline in the number of unions.
3. The fall in the number of union members can be explained by several macroeconomic factors.
4. Union membership was traditionally high in manufacturing and public services.
5. There remain today about 10 million women at work.
6. There are now only six unions, but they each boast more than 500,000 members.
7. The largest of the remaining unions is the TGWU.
8. The TUC's links with the Labour Party enabled it to wield considerable power in political life.
9. Margaret Thatcher's governments introduced five employment acts aimed at trying to save the trade union movement.
10. Things are now more evenly balanced between employers and employees in the field of industrial relations.

DO!

Remain optimistic and enthusiastic even when everything seems to be going wrong.

KAPITEL 11

Wahr oder falsch?

1. *Falsch:* It gradually declined throughout the eighties.
2. *Wahr.*
3. *Wahr.*
4. *Wahr.*
5. *Falsch:* This is the figure for total union membership.
6. *Falsch:* There are only six unions which boast more than 500,000 members.
7. *Wahr.*
8. *Wahr.*
9. *Falsch:* The five acts were aimed at reducing the trade union movement's power.
10. *Wahr.*

DON'T!

Don't try to find a chink (Ritze, Spalt, Schlitz) in the armour of the people who are your superiors, but respect them and try to learn from them.

CHAPTER 12

Career development

Susan and Phil Irwin are back in Milton Keynes after a week spent at the Filton plant near Bristol.

1. **Phil:** So, Susan, how was your weekend?

2. **Susan:** Fine. It was very relaxing after last week's tension.

3. **Phil:** No doubt your parents were pleased to see you.

4. **Susan:** You bet they were! My mother is always saying I don't go and see them enough now.

5. **Phil:** *(Smiling)* Anyway, all that tension last week was worthwhile. Mr Romer-Lee gave me a buzz just now to congratulate us on our successful handling of the strike! **(1)**

6. **Susan:** It's true they resumed work very quickly, but we were lucky that the worker who was sacked had found a better-paid job elsewhere. **(2)**

7. **Phil:** OK, Susan. But results are what counts! Anyway, what were you able to glean from your various discussions?

8. **Susan:** Well, I spoke to a lot of people: shop-floor workers, supervisors, some secretaries... After a lot of reflection, I believe that one of the major underlying problems is career development. **(3) (4) (5)**

9. **Phil:** Mmm. That came up in the claims they were making at the beginning of the negotiations. It's strange, because we are constantly organising training courses for production workers... You noticed that when you did a spell on the production line! **(6) (7)**

KAPITEL 12

Karriereausbau

Susan und Phil Irwin sind nach Milton Keynes zurückgekehrt, nachdem sie eine Woche im Werk Filton in der Nähe von Bristol verbracht haben.

1. **Phil:** Na, Susan, wie war dein Wochenende?
2. **Susan:** Schön. Es war sehr ruhig nach der Spannung der letzten Woche.
3. **Phil:** Bestimmt waren deine Eltern froh, dich zu sehen.
4. **Susan:** Darauf kannst du wetten! Meine Mutter sagt immer, daß ich sie nicht mehr oft genug besuche.
5. **Phil:** *(Lächelt)* Jedenfalls hat sich die Spannung letzte Woche gelohnt. Herr Romer-Lee hat mich gerade angerufen, um uns zu unserer erfolgreichen Abwendung des Streiks zu beglückwünschen.
6. **Susan:** Stimmt, sie haben die Arbeit schnell wieder aufgenommen, aber wir hatten Glück, daß der Arbeiter, der entlassen worden war, woanders einen besser bezahlten Job gefunden hatte.
7. **Phil:** OK, Susan, aber es sind die Ergebnisse, die zählen! Was konntest du denn aus deinen verschiedenen Gesprächen erfahren?
8. **Susan:** Also, ich habe mich mit sehr vielen Leuten unterhalten: den Mitarbeitern in der Fertigung, den Vorarbeitern, einigen Sekretärinnen... Nach vielem Nachdenken glaube ich, daß eines der grundlegenden Probleme der Karriereausbau ist.
9. **Phil:** Mmm. Das tauchte auch in den Forderungen auf, die sie zu Beginn der Verhandlungen gestellt haben. Das ist komisch, denn wir organisieren permanent Schulungen für Produktionsarbeiter... Das hast du bemerkt, als du eine Zeitlang in der Fertigung gearbeitet habst!

ANMERKUNGEN

(1) **to give s.o. a buzz**: Umgangssprachlich für "jdn. anrufen".
(2) **to resume work**: "die Arbeit wiederaufnehmen", z.B. nach einem Arbeitskampf.
(3) **shop-floor**: In einer Fabrik oder einem Werk alle Mitarbeiter in der Fertigung, wobei auch Angestellte gemeint sein können (z.B. der "Werksleiter" *shop-manager*).
(4) **supervisor**: Eine Person, der eine gewisse Anzahl Arbeiter unterstellt sind und die deren Arbeit kontrolliert: "Vorarbeiter, (Werk)Meister; Polier (auf dem Bau)".
(5) **carreer development**: Ausbau der Karriere durch Weiter- und Fortbildung.
(6) **claims**: Forderungen oder Ansprüche, die von den Streikenden gestellt werden und auf deren Basis die Verhandlungen mit den Arbeitgebern geführt werden.
(7) **spell**: "(Zeit)Dauer, Zeit". Auch "Zauberspruch, Zauberformel". *To put a spell on someone* "jdn. verzaubern"; *to be under someone's spell* "von jdm. verzaubert, gebannt sein".

CHAPTER 12

10. **Susan:** OK, Phil. But several employees complained that the courses were reserved for people with a lot of seniority, who were already earning more and were sometimes close to retirement. The younger people often said they felt they had a dead-end job. No possibility to develop in their career, to have more challenging work or more responsibility... **(8) (9)**

11. **Phil:** Or earn more money...!

12. **Susan:** Probably, but that was never given as the number one concern. Even the secretaries said that they had no future despite everything they hear about how the secretary's role is changing.

13. **Phil:** But this company has always had a reputation for creating staff loyalty by offering in-company training, by encouraging continuing education. It's part of our corporate culture. Look how well we treat some of our talented junior managers! **(10) (11) (12) (13)**

14. **Susan:** That may be so at executive level, but is it working lower down?

15. **Phil:** I admit we do have a high staff-turnover rate, at Filton at least. *(After a pause)* Listen Susan. I'll have a word with Mr Robertson. He's the one who coordinates questions of career development, draws up the annual corporate training plan, negotiates the budget with the finance department, and so on. I'm going to suggest that you prepare a report for him, recommending what changes need to be made at various levels... **(14)**

16. **Susan:** But it may be a problem peculiar to Filton.

17. **Phil:** Well, let's find out. You can use Filton as a pilot plant. **(15)**

KAPITEL 12

10. **Susan:** In Ordnung, Phil. Aber einige Angestellte haben sich darüber beklagt, daß die Kurse für Leute reserviert sind, die ein hohes Dienstalter haben, die schon mehr verdienen und die manchmal kurz vor der Rente stehen. Die jüngeren Leute haben oft gesagt, sie hätten das Gefühl, einen Arbeitsplatz ohne Aufstiegsmöglichkeit zu haben. Keine Gelegenheit, sich in ihrer Karriere weiterzuentwickeln, eine herausfordernde Arbeit oder mehr Verantwortung zu bekommen.
11. **Phil:** Oder mehr Geld zu verdienen...!
12. **Susan:** Vielleicht, aber das wurde nie als vorrangigste Sorge angegeben. Sogar die Sekretärinnen sagten, sie hätten keine Zukunft, trotz allem, was sie über die sich wandelnde Rolle der Sekretärin hören.
13. **Phil:** Aber diese Firma hat immer den Ruf gehabt, daß sie durch betriebsinterne Schulungen und durch die Förderung von Weiter- und Fortbildung Loyalität bei den Mitarbeitern erzeugt. Das ist Teil unserer Unternehmensphilosophie. Sieh dir nur an, wie gut wir einige unserer Trainee Manager behandeln!
14. **Susan:** Das ist vielleicht auf der Ebene der Führungskräfte so, aber funktioniert es auch weiter unten?
15. **Phil:** Ich gebe zu, daß wir eine hohe Personalfluktuation haben, zumindest in Filton. *(Nach einer Pause)* Hör zu, Susan. Ich spreche mal mit Herrn Robertson. Er ist derjenige, der Fragen des Karriereausbaus koordiniert, der den jährlichen Schulungsplan des Unternehmens ausarbeitet, mit der Finanzabteilung über das Budget verhandelt, usw. Ich werde ihm vorschlagen, daß du einen Bericht für ihn verfaßt und empfiehlst, welche Veränderungen auf den verschiedenen Ebenen gemacht werden müssen...
16. **Susan:** Aber vielleicht ist es ein Problem, das Filton-spezifisch ist.
17. **Phil:** Naja, das können wir ja herausfinden. Du kannst Filton als Pilotwerk verwenden.

ANMERKUNGEN (Fortsetzung)

(8) **retirement**: "Pensionierung, Ruhestand". Man sagt auch *early retirement* "Vorruhestand". Das Substantiv kommt vom Verb *to retire*.
(9) **dead-end (job)**: *dead-end* heißt "Sackgasse". Hier handelt es sich also um eine Arbeitsstelle, die keine Zukunftsaussichten bietet.
(10) **(staff) loyalty**: Loyalität oder Treue eines Angestellten gegenüber seinem Arbeitgeber. Merken Sie sich auch *brand loyalty* "Markentreue".
(11) **in-company (training)**: Weiter- und Fortbildungskurse für Angestellte, die vom Arbeitgeber bezahlt werden.
(12) **continuing education**: "Fort- und Weiterbildung".
(13) **corporate culture**: "Unternehmensphilosophie". Die "Identität" oder "Persönlichkeit" eines Unternehmens.
(14) **staff-turnover**: "Belegschaftswechsel".
(15) **pilot (plant)**: Werk, das in einer Studie oder in einem Versuch als Beispielbetrieb herangezogen wird.

CHAPTER 12 DOCUMENT

Internal Memorandum

UNITED CHOCOLATE (UK) Ltd
MILTON KEYNES

Department of Human Resources

From: Manager, Human Resources

To: Assistant Director of Human Resources   **Date:** 22/10/199.

Re: Career development project

Further to our conversation yesterday morning and your suggestions concerning the procedure to follow, I am requesting your go-ahead for the above project.

As I told you, it is my intention to put my Junior Manager, Susan Edwards, in charge of this project, which will entail an extensive study of personnel at all levels in one of our production units. After the period of field research, she will write a report, analysing the situation and making recommendations on how to improve career development. Susan did remarkably well in the informal discussions she undertook recently during our visit to the Filton plant.

Moreover, given the problems we are currently encountering with this production unit (absenteeism and work stoppage), I suggest that Filton be used as the pilot plant in this project.

Phil Irwin
Manager, Human Resources

cc*: AR-L

* (carbon) copy

KAPITEL 12

 Die Berufsausbildung

Im Jahr 1988 hat die britische Regierung die Grundlagen für ihre neue Strategie in der Berufsausbildung gelegt, indem sie den Arbeitgebern in ihrer Organisation und Finanzierung eine wichtigere Rolle eingeräumt hat und ein Maximum an Dezentralisierung einführte.
Diese Strategie wird auf nationaler Ebene durch die *Training Agency* und auf lokaler Ebene von den *Training and Enterprise Councils (TECs)* durchgeführt, von denen es in England und Wales 82 gibt. Diese *TECs* erlauben es dem öffentlichen und privaten Sektor, partnerschaftlich zusammenzuarbeiten, damit das Angebot an Möglichkeiten für die Berufsausbildung so weit wie möglich den lokalen Erfordernissen entspricht.

CHAPTER 12

EXERCISES

Comprehension

Lesen Sie den Dialog aufmerksam durch. Beantworten Sie dann die nachfolgenden Fragen, und zwar immer in ganzen Sätzen:

1. Where did Susan spend her weekend? 2. Why do you think Phil is smiling? 3. What probably contributed to bringing about a prompt end to the strike? 4. With whom was Susan able to have discussions while in Filton? 5. What is the opinion of certain production workers about the training courses which are organised? 6. What do the younger people mean when they say they have 'a dead-end job'? 7. What is one of the elements of United Chocolate's corporate culture, according to Phil Irwin? 8. Does the company's policy of creating staff loyalty seem to be working? 9. Why is Phil going to have a word with Mr Robertson? 10. How will it be possible to find out whether the problem is peculiar to Filton?

Translation

1. Rufen Sie mich an, wenn Sie nach Milton Keynes zurückkommen. 2. Ich beglückwünsche Sie dazu, daß Sie es geschafft haben, daß sie die Arbeit schnell wiederaufgenommen haben. 3. Letztendlich bin ich froh, daß ich entlassen wurde, da es mir dadurch möglich war, woanders eine besser bezahlte Stelle zu finden. 4. Im Geschäft zählen Ergebnisse mehr als alles andere. 5. Am Beginn der Verhandlungen bezogen sich die Forderungen hauptsächlich auf Gehälter und Arbeitsbedingungen. 6. Wenn Sie nicht wenigstens zehn Jahre in der Firma gearbeitet haben, haben Sie keine Chance, an interessanten Schulungen teilzunehmen. 7. Heutzutage hat sich die Arbeit der Sekretärin sehr verändert: sie ist eine größere Herausforderung, weil man mehr Verantwortung erhält. 8. Es ist selbstverständlich, daß United Chocolate (UK) mehr von einer amerikanischen Unternehmensphilosophie haben sollte. 9. In unserer Fabrik ist die Personalfluktuation viel geringer als in Filton. 10. United Chocolate ist in einem großen Forschungsprojekt, das von der Universität Aston durchgeführt wird, zum Pilotunternehmen ausgewählt worden.

KAPITEL 12

LÖSUNGSVORSCHLÄGE

Verständnisübung

1. Susan spent her weekend at her parents'. 2. Phil is probably smiling because he is pleased with himself. Mr Romer-Lee has just congratulated them. 3. The fact that the worker who was sacked had found a better paid job elsewhere probably contributed. 4. She managed to have discussions with a lot of people: for example, shop-floor workers, supervisors and secretaries. 5. They feel that they are reserved for people with a lot of seniority, earning more and sometimes close to retirement. 6. They mean that they have no possibility to develop in their career, have more challenging work or more responsibility. 7. The fact that United Chocolate tries to create staff loyalty through in-company training and continuing education. 8. It is probably working at executive level, but perhaps not lower down. 9. He's going to suggest to him that Susan do a report on career development. 10. It will be possible by using Filton as a pilot plant.

Übersetzungsübung

1. Give me a buzz when you get back to Milton Keynes. 2. I congratulate you for having got them to resume work quickly. 3. As it turns out, I'm pleased to have been sacked, for it enabled me to find a better-paid job elsewhere. 4. In business, results count above all. 5. At the beginning of the negotiations, the claims concerned mainly salaries and working conditions. 6. If you haven't been with the firm for at least ten years, you have no chance of going on interesting training courses. 7. Nowadays, the work of the secretary has changed a lot: it's more challenging, because you are given more responsibility. 8. It is natural that United Chocolate (UK) should have more of an American corporate culture. 9. In our factory, the staff-turnover rate is much lower than at Filton. 10. United Chocolate has been (was) chosen as a pilot company in a big research project undertaken by Aston University.

CHAPTER 12

Application

Sehen Sie sich noch einmal die Dienstanweisung (siehe Dokument) an, die Phil Irwin an seinen Vorgesetzten, Herrn Robertson, geschrieben hat und die das Projekt des Karriereausbaus betrifft.

Verfassen Sie ebenfalls auf der Basis der Vorlage eine Dienstanweisung, die die folgenden Elemente enthält:

* Herr Robertson antwortet Phil Irwin und gibt grünes Licht für das vorgeschlagene Projekt.
* Er erklärt sich damit einverstanden, Filton als Pilotwerk zu verwenden und fügt hinzu, daß er selbst Herrn Evans schriftlich davon in Kenntnis setzen wird.
* Herr Robertson betont, daß seiner Meinung nach eine solche Studie nicht nur die Arbeiter, sondern auch das Verwaltungspersonal, z.B. die Sekretärinnen, betreffen sollte. Er schlägt vor, Susan solle sich bei Gladys Day, seiner eigenen Sekretärin, die eine der erfahrensten des Unternehmens ist, über die Arbeit der Sekretärinnen informieren.
* Susan soll ihm weiterhin die Fragebögen vorlegen, die sie zu benutzen beabsichtigt, und sie soll ihn über den Fortgang des Projekts informieren.

DO!

Go abroad with an open mind.
Be receptive and learn how business is done,
even if customs are not the same as in your country.

DON'T!

Don't think that familiarity with etiquette and codes
of conduct matters as much as it does in your country.

KAPITEL 12

UNITED CHOCOLATE (UK) Ltd.
MILTON KEYNES

Department of Human Resources

Internal Memorandum

From: Assistant Director of Human Resources

To: Philip Irwin, Manager, Human Resources   **Date:** 23/10/199.

Re: Your memorandum of 10/22/199.

As I already indicated to you during our recent discussion, I view your suggestion of a study on the subject of career development very favourably.
I do not hesitate, therefore, to give the project my official blessing. I am quite happy for Susan Edwards to carry out the study, as I am convinced she is capable of handling it. You will obviously retain overall responsibility for the project.

I agree that Filton would be an ideal pilot plant for the study and I will therefore take the appropriate action to inform David Evans.

It is my belief, however, that such a study should target not merely the production workers but also the administrative staff, particularly secretaries.
It might be useful for Susan to acquaint herself fully with the changes which have taken place in the work of a secretary. This she could do by speaking with Gladys Day, my own assistant and also one of the most experienced in the company.

Susan should show me, in advance, all the questionnaires she intends to use and keep me regularly informed of the project's progress.

Keith Robertson
Assistant Director of Human Resources

cc: AR-L, SE

CHAPTER 13

The work of a secretary

Susan has come down to the Filton plant to start work on her career development project. She is talking to Fiona Cummings, Mr Evans's secretary.

1. **Susan:** So, Fiona, did Mr Evans tell you what this project was all about?

2. **Fiona:** Oh, yes. He explained it very well... I got the impression, though, that he wasn't very enthusiastic about it.

3. **Susan:** *(Smiling)* Our only objective is to try and make things better for UC's employees and perhaps, longer term, to improve the company's performance.

4. **Fiona:** I understand perfectly.

5. **Susan:** Now, what I'd like to do, Fiona, is to have a fairly informal discussion this morning. Then I'll leave you a questionnaire to fill in and send back to me at Head Office. Everything you say, either this morning or in the questionnaire, will be treated confidentially of course. OK?

6. **Fiona:** Fine!

7. **Susan:** Now you told me, last time we met, that you were 25 and that you joined UC about 18 months ago.

8. **Fiona:** That's right. But it wasn't my first job. I worked for a small company, before, which had just started up. I joined them straight after my secretarial course at college in Bristol. **(1) (2)**

9. **Susan:** And how would you compare the two companies – from the point of view of how they used you as a secretary?

KAPITEL 13

Die Arbeit einer Sekretärin

Susan ist ins Werk Filton hinuntergekommen, um die Arbeit für ihr Karriereausbau-Projekt aufzunehmen. Sie unterhält sich mit Fiona Cummings, Herrn Evans Sekretärin.

1. **Susan:** So, Fiona, hat Herr Evans Ihnen gesagt, worum es bei diesem Projekt geht?
2. **Fiona:** Oh, ja. Er hat es sehr gut erklärt... Ich habe allerdings den Eindruck gewonnen, daß er nicht sehr begeistert davon war.
3. **Susan:** *(Lächelt)* Unser einziges Ziel ist es, zu versuchen, die Situation für die Angestellten von UC zu verbessern und vielleicht langfristig die Leistung des Unternehmens zu steigern.
4. **Fiona:** Das verstehe ich gut.
5. **Susan:** Nun, was ich heute morgen gerne tun würde, Fiona, ist, eine relativ ungezwungene Unterhaltung zu führen. Dann lasse ich Ihnen einen Fragebogen hier, den Sie ausfüllen und mir dann in die Zentrale zurücksenden. Alles, was Sie sagen, entweder heute morgen oder auf dem Fragebogen, wird selbstverständlich vertraulich behandelt, OK?
6. **Fiona:** Großartig!
7. **Susan:** Sie haben mir also, als wir uns das letzte Mal trafen, erzählt, Sie seien 25, und Sie hätten vor ungefähr 18 Monaten bei UC angefangen.
8. **Fiona:** Das stimmt! Aber das war nicht meine erste Stelle. Ich habe vorher für ein kleines Unternehmen gearbeitet, das gerade gegründet worden war. Ich habe dort direkt nach meiner Sekretärinnenausbildung an der Handelsschule von Bristol angefangen.
9. **Susan:** Und wie würden Sie die beiden Firmen vergleichen – unter dem Gesichtspunkt, wie Sie bei beiden als Sekretärin eingesetzt wurden?

ANMERKUNGEN

(1) **to start up:** "(ein Unternehmen) gründen"; *(Company/Business) start-up* "Unternehmensgründung"; auch "Inbetriebnahme, Anlauf"; *start-up costs* "Anlaufkosten". Der Plural lautet *start-ups*.
(2) Das **college** (auch "Universitätsinstitut") ist weitgehend mit unserer Handelsschule vergleichbar. *Business/Commercial college* "(höhere) Wirtschaftsschule/ Handelsschule"; *secretarial college* "Sekretärinnenschule".

CHAPTER 13

10. **Fiona:** Oh, completely different. My first post was really a dream situation. Everything was exactly as I'd learned in college. And I'm not only talking about the modern equipment I had at my disposal. I was considered as an assistant, allowed initiative, encouraged to give my opinion, advise, even make decisions.

11. **Susan:** So why did you leave?

12. **Fiona:** I thought that working as a secretary for the Factory Manager of a multinational would be a new challenge for me...

13. **Susan:** ... but it wasn't.

14. **Fiona:** I got the impression I was going back in time. Vera, my predecessor, had been Mr Evans's secretary for over 25 years! I thought I'd be able to change the working methods, but...

15. **Susan:** ... you couldn't.

16. **Fiona:** I've given up trying. I sit behind my desk, with the in-tray on my left, the out-tray on my right and my typewriter – "word-processor", Mr Evans calls it! – in the middle. I have to type everything on it, but not before he's dictated it to me and I've taken it down in shorthand. (3) (4) (5)

17. **Susan:** No more initiative, eh?

18. **Fiona:** None at all! He even tells me sometimes how I should lay letters out. I have to keep duplicates of everything on flimsy, so you can imagine all the time I waste on filing. I seem to spend all my time with staples and paper clips. (6) (7) (8) (9)

19. **Susan:** What other tasks do you find boring or a waste of time?

20. **Fiona:** When Sally, the switchboard operator, gets a call for Mr Evans, she has to put it straight through to his extension, when a lot of the time, I could answer the enquiry myself. And even when he's out of the office, I'm only allowed to take messages!

KAPITEL 13

10. **Fiona:** Oh, völlig unterschiedlich. Meine erste Stelle war wirklich ein Traumposten. Alles war genauso wie ich es auf der Handelsschule gelernt hatte. Und ich spreche nicht nur von der modernen Ausstattung, die mir zur Verfügung stand. Man betrachtete mich als eine Assistentin, ließ mich die Initiative ergreifen, ermunterte mich, meine Meinung zu sagen, Ratschläge zu erteilen, ja sogar Entscheidungen zu treffen.
11. **Susan:** Und warum sind Sie dann da weggegangen?
12. **Fiona:** Ich dachte, daß die Arbeit als Sekretärin für den Fabrikleiter eines multinationalen Unternehmens für mich eine neue Herausforderung darstellen würde...
13. **Susan:** ... aber das war es nicht.
14. **Fiona:** Ich hatte den Eindruck, daß ich einen Rückschritt nach dem anderen machte. Vera, meine Vorgängerin, ist über 25 Jahre lang die Sekretärin von Herrn Evans gewesen! Ich dachte, ich könnte die Arbeitsmethoden ändern, aber...
15. **Susan:** ... Sie konnten nicht.
16. **Fiona:** Ich habe den Versuch aufgegeben. Ich sitze hinter meinem Schreibtisch mit der Eingangspost auf der linken Seite, der Ausgangspost auf der rechten und meiner Schreibmaschine – Herr Evans nennt sie "Textverarbeitungssystem" – in der Mitte. Ich muß alles auf ihr schreiben, aber erst, wenn er es mir diktiert hat und ich es in Steno notiert habe.
17. **Susan:** Keine Initiative mehr, oder?
18. **Fiona:** Überhaupt keine! Er sagt mir sogar manchmal, wie ich die Briefe gestalten soll. Ich muß von allem Kopien auf Durchschlagpapier machen, Sie können sich also vorstellen, wieviel Zeit ich mit der Ablage verschwende. Ich scheine meine gesamte Zeit mit Heft- und Büroklammern zu verbringen.
19. **Susan:** Welche anderen Aufgaben finden Sie langweilig oder halten Sie für eine Zeitverschwendung?
20. **Fiona:** Wenn Sally, die Telefonistin, einen Anruf für Herrn Evans annimmt, muß sie ihn direkt zu ihm durchstellen, wobei es oft so ist, daß ich die Anfrage selbst beantworten könnte. Und selbst wenn er nicht im Büro ist, darf ich nur Nachrichten entgegennehmen.

ANMERKUNGEN (Fortsetzung)

(3) **typewriter:** "Schreibmaschine". *to type* "(auf der Schreibmaschine/dem Computer usw.) schreiben, tippen"; *typist* "Schreibkraft"; *shorthand typist* "Stenotypist(in)" (vgl. Anmerkung 5).

(4) **word-processor:** "Textverarbeitungssystem" wurden die ersten Speicherschreibmaschinen genannt, die heute weitgehend durch Computer ersetzt werden.

(5) **shorthand:** "Stenographie"; daher auch *shorthand typist* "Stenotypist(in)" (vgl. Anmerkung 3).

(6) **to lay out:** "gestalten, planen, anordnen". *Lay-out* "Gestaltung, Plan, Anordnung"; "Layout" (z.B. eines Briefes).

(7) **flimsy:** "dünn, leicht, dürftig" ist ein Adjektiv, das auch als Substantiv verwendet wird: "Durchschlagpapier".

(8) **filing:** "Archivierung, Ablage". *Filing-cabinet* "Aktenschrank"; *to file* "archivieren, ablegen", *file* "Akte", aber auch "Datei" (in der Datenverarbeitung).

(9) **staple:** "Heftklammer". *To staple* "heften"; *stapler* "Heftmaschine".

CHAPTER 13　　　　　　　　　　　　　　DOCUMENT

Stationery Order Form

One of Fiona's jobs is to order, each month, supplies of stationery for the managers and secretaries at the Filton Plant. Here is one of her monthly order forms:

Description of article	Reference	Unit price	Quantity	Total
Self-adhesive tape, magic, Sellotape[1]	110010	.53p	5	
Self-adhesive tape, transparent, Sellotape	110075	.72p	10	
Glue, tube (transparent)	140150	.39p	10	
Glue, stick (small)	140725	.26p	5	
Glue, stick (medium)	140750	.70p		
Correction fluid + thinner	260105	.70p	5	
Eraser, plastic	260830	.14p	2	
Folders, paper - 310x220 mm (packet of 100)	310114	£3.00p	2	
Folders, card - 320x240 mm (packet of 100)	310163	£7.65p	1	
Ruler, plastic - 30 cm (transparent)	420174	.61p		
Pencil-sharpener	512150	.14p		
Pencils - HB (box of 10)	512300	£1.80p	2	
Ball point pens - medium, black (box of 10)	530000	.76p	4	
Ball point pens - medium, blue (box of 10)	530025	.76p	1	
Felt-tip pens - fine, black (box of 10)	540381	£1.05p	4	
Felt-tip pens - fine, blue (box of 10)	540382	£1.05p	1	
Highlighter pen, yellow	541101	.26p	3	
Highlighter pen, pink	541103	.26p	3	
Notepad, lined (A4)	610450	.40p	6	
Notepad, lined (A5)	610475	.22p	2	
Post-it notes (76x127 mm)	611150	.45p	15	
Envelopes, manila[2] - 162x229 mm (box of 500)	641475	£6.58p	1	
Envelopes, manila - 229x324 mm (box of 250)	641500	£5.08p	2	
Carbon paper, A4 (box of 100 sheets)	720505	£7.21p	1	
Stapler	810003	£14.68p		
Staples (box of 5000)	811204	£2.19p	1	
Paper-clips, small - 25 mm (box of 1000)	820375	£1.03p	1	
Paper-clips, large - 50 mm (box of 100)	820400	.76p		
Drawing-pins (box of 20 assorted colours)	820910	.47p	8	
Scissors (16 cm)	850452	£1.20p		
Rubber bands, assorted sizes (box of 100)	860150	.76p	4	

[1] **Sellotape: Eine Schutzmarke, die in Großbritannien etwa wie der "Tesafilm" in Deutschland ein Sammelbegriff für alle Klebebänder geworden ist.**
[2] **manila: Starkes Packpapier.**

KAPITEL 13

Der Tag der Sekretärinnen

In den USA, wo eine weitgehend protestantische Kultur herrscht, haben Geburts- oder Namenstage von Personen keine so große Bedeutung wie bei uns. Wichtig sind dagegen der Sankt-Valentins-Tag *(Valentine's Day)*, der Muttertag *(Mother's Day)* und der Tag der Großmütter *(Grandmother's Day)*. Kürzlich wurde diese Liste um den Tag der Sekretärinnen *(Secretaries' Day)* ergänzt. Er wird am 14. April gefeiert. Anläßlich dieses Datums erhalten in vielen Unternehmen engagierte Sekretärinnen von ihren Vorgesetzten als großzügige und symbolische Geste einen Blumenstrauß. Dieses Fest ist mittlerweile zu einer echten Institution geworden, für die sich auch der Präsident der Vereinigten Staaten offiziell einsetzt.

CHAPTER 13

EXERCISES

Comprehension

Lesen Sie den Dialog aufmerksam durch. Beantworten Sie dann die nachfolgenden Fragen, und zwar immer in ganzen Sätzen:

1. Does Fiona seem to share Mr Evans's lack of enthusiasm for the project?
2. What should Fiona do with the questionnaire which Susan has brought?
3. Can Fiona take the risk of being perfectly frank in her discussion with Susan?
4. How long do you think Fiona spent in her first job? 5. What does Fiona mean by the expression 'a dream situation'? 6. Has working for UC been a challenge for Fiona? 7. Were Vera's working methods any different from those which Fiona has adopted at UC? 8. What must Fiona do before she can type a letter for Mr Evans? 9. Why does Fiona say she seems to spend all her time with staples and paper clips? 10. Can Fiona deal with enquiries when Mr Evans is out of the office?

Translation

1. Bitte füllen Sie diesen Fragebogen für mich aus und senden Sie ihn so schnell wie möglich an meinen Assistenten in Milton Keynes zurück. 2. Was Sie während des informellen Interviews sagen, wird vertraulich behandelt. 3. Wie alt waren Sie, als Sie in unser Unternehmen eintraten? 4. Nach meiner Sekretärinnenausbildung entschloß ich mich, zuerst einmal in einer kleinen Firma zu arbeiten. 5. Diese erste Stelle war eine große Herausforderung für mich, weil ich ermutigt wurde, Eigeninitiative zu zeigen. 6. Der Fabrikleiter hatte mehr als 20 Jahre mit der gleichen Sekretärin gearbeitet. 7. Ich hätte lieber einen richtigen Computer zu meiner Verfügung als meine Briefe auf dieser Speicherschreibmaschine zu tippen. 8. Sie mag es nicht, daß er ihr seine Briefe diktiert, denn sie ist nicht sehr gut in Stenographie. 9. Die Plastikbüroklammern sind billiger, aber warum benutzt man in diesem Fall nicht Heftklammern? 10. Die Telefonistin hat sich geweigert, mich zu ihm (ihr) durchzustellen. Ich mußte ihm (ihr) eine Nachricht hinterlassen.

KAPITEL 13

LÖSUNGSVORSCHLÄGE

Verständnisübung

1. Apparently not. She says she understands the project perfectly. 2. She should send it back to Susan at Head Office, once she has filled it in. 3. She can be perfectly frank, because everything she says will be treated confidentially. 4. She probably spent about 3 or 4 years: she's now 25, she's been with UC for 18 months and she joined her first company straight after her secretarial studies. 5. She means that in her first job, everything was as she'd learnt in college: she had modern equipment and she was considered more as an assistant. 6. No. She finds a lot of what she does boring or a waste of time. 7. No. Fiona says she's given up trying to change them. 8. She must wait until Mr Evans has dictated it and she has taken it down in shorthand. 9. Because she wastes so much time on filing. 10. No she can't. She is only allowed to take messages.

Übersetzungsübung

1. Please fill in this questionnaire for me and send it back as quickly as possible to my assistant in Milton Keynes. 2. What you say during the informal interview will be considered as confidential. 3. How old were you when you joined our company? 4. After my secretarial studies I decided to work first of all in a small company. 5. This first post was a great challenge for me because I was encouraged to take initiatives. 6. The Factory Manager had been working with the same secretary for more than 20 years. 7. I'd rather have a real (*or* proper) computer (at my disposal) rather than having to type my letters on this word-processor. 8. She doesn't like him dictating (*or* to dictate) his letters to her because she's not very good at shorthand. 9. (The) plastic paper clips are cheaper, but in that case, why not use staples? 10. The switchboard operator refused to put me through to his (*or* her) extension. I had to leave him (*or* her) a message.

CHAPTER 13

Application

Sehen Sie sich noch einmal das Dokument, den von Fiona ausgearbeiteten monatlichen Bestellschein über Büromateriallieferungen, an. Lesen Sie dann die untenstehenden Aussagen und entscheiden Sie, welche wahr und welche falsch sind. Korrigieren Sie die falschen Aussagen.

1. The magic Sellotape is more expensive than the transparent self-adhesive tape.
2. The large paper clips are twice as big as the small ones.
3. The dearest item on the order form is the stapler.
4. Felt-tip pens are not as expensive as ball point pens.
5. Folders made of card are not so big as those made of paper.
6. You get as many rubber bands as you do sheets of carbon paper, but the price isn't the same, as you can imagine.
7. Fiona has ordered more than twenty-five different articles this month.
8. Fiona has ordered fewer blue pens than black ones.
9. A box of large paper clips costs less than a box of small ones.
10. Fiona buys pencils and pencil sharpeners every month.

DON'T!

Never leave a letter unanswered. Answer your mail right away, especially if you deal with Germans. If you cannot give an answer right away, inform your customer.

KAPITEL 13

Wahr oder falsch?

1. *Falsch:* On the contrary, the magic Sellotape is cheaper.
2. *Wahr.*
3. *Wahr.*
4. *Falsch:* In fact, ball point pens are cheaper.
5. *Falsch:* It's the other way round: paper folders are smaller than those made of card.
6. *Wahr.*
7. *Falsch:* She's ordered exactly twenty-five.
8. *Wahr.*
9. *Wahr.*
10. *Falsch:* She hasn't bought any pencil sharpeners this month.

DO!

Treat all the people you meet in a company with equal consideration. Whether you're dealing with the chauffeur, the hostess, the secretary or the CEO, be direct, precise and courteous with him (or her).

CHAPTER 14 📼

The high-tech office (1)

Susan is back in Milton Keynes, speaking with Gladys Day, Mr Robertson's secretary. They are discussing what Fiona Cummings said about her work as a secretary.

1. **Gladys:** Well, of course, that's how it used to be here, too. You know, Susan, I've been a secretary in UC's Head Office ever since I left secretarial college. *(Laughing)* That's longer than I care to think. But we've always tried to keep up with the latest innovations.

2. **Susan:** How long have you worked for Mr Robertson?

3. **Gladys:** For about five years.

4. **Susan:** I've noticed that Mr Robertson often refers to you as his assistant...

5. **Gladys:** That's not really my official title, but it's true that he treats me that way.

6. **Susan:** He delegates a certain amount of responsibility, you mean? **(2)**

7. **Gladys:** When he can, yes. For instance, I filter all his phone calls – apart from those he gets on his direct line, of course – and I deal with anything I can. Accepting appointments for him, managing his diary. He does a lot of travelling, too, as you know, but he always phones in, using his cordless telephone, or from his car. If there's a small problem to sort out, he'll usually tell me to decide what to do. I can send him a message on his pager, too, if necessary. **(3) (4) (5)**

8. **Susan:** I suppose you've seen a lot of evolution in communications technology.

9. **Gladys:** Absolutely. Mr Robertson always says that improved technology doesn't make you a better manager. It doesn't help you to motivate your staff or get them involved...

KAPITEL 14

Das High-Tech-Büro

Susan ist zurück in Milton Keynes und unterhält sich mit Gladys Day, Herrn Robertsons Sekretärin. Sie sprechen darüber, was Fiona Cummings über ihre Arbeit als Sekretärin sagte.

1. **Gladys:** Naja, so war das hier natürlich auch. Wissen Sie, Susan, ich bin Sekretärin in der Zentrale von UC, seit ich die Sekretärinnenschule verlassen habe. *(Lacht)* Das ist länger als ich denken kann. Aber wir haben immer versucht, mit den neuesten Innovationen Schritt zu halten.
2. **Susan:** Wie lange haben Sie für Herrn Robertson gearbeitet?
3. **Gladys:** Ungefähr fünf Jahre.
4. **Susan:** Ich habe bemerkt, daß Herr Robertson oft von Ihnen als seiner Assistentin spricht...
5. **Gladys:** Das ist nicht wirklich mein offizieller Titel, aber es stimmt, daß er mich als eine behandelt.
6. **Susan:** Sie meinen, er delegiert einen bestimmten Teil der Verantwortung an Sie?
7. **Gladys:** Wenn er kann, ja. Zum Beispiel filtere ich all seine Telefonanrufe – natürlich abgesehen von denen, die er direkt auf seinem Anschluß erhält – und ich kümmere mich um alles, soweit ich kann. Termine annehmen, seinen Terminkalender führen. Er reist auch viel, wie Sie wissen, aber er ruft immer mit seinem schnurlosen Telefon oder von seinem Wagen aus an. Wenn es ein kleines Problem zu regeln gibt, weist er mich normalerweise an, zu entscheiden, was zu tun ist. Ich kann ihm auch, wenn nötig, auf seinem Piepser eine Nachricht schicken.
8. **Susan:** Ich nehme an, Sie haben viele Entwicklungen in der Kommunikationstechnik miterlebt.
9. **Gladys:** Aber ja. Herr Robertson sagt immer, daß eine verbesserte Technik aus einem keinen besseren Manager macht. Es hilft einem nicht, seine Mitarbeiter zu motivieren oder ihr Engagement zu steigern...

ANMERKUNGEN

(1) **high-tech**: Abkürzung von *high technology* "Hochtechnologie". In den USA wird oft der Ausdruck *state-of-the-art* benutzt.

(2) **to delegate responsibility** "Verantwortung abgeben, Verantwortung delegieren". Vorsicht: Selbst wenn man Verantwortung delegiert, bleibt man trotzdem verantwortlich für die Konsequenzen, die sich aus der getroffenen Entscheidung ergeben.

(3) **diary** ist nicht nur das "Tagebuch", sondern auch der "Terminkalender".

(4) **cordless (telephone):** "Schnurloses Telefon", das sowohl in geschlossenen Räumen als auch im Freien benutzt werden kann. Die bei uns in letzter Zeit so häufig zu findenden Handys nennt man auf englisch *hand portable* oder *mobile telephone*.

(5) Mit einem **pager** "Personenrufgerät" oder "Piepser" können numerische Informationen oder kurze Nachrichten empfangen werden.

CHAPTER 14

10. **Susan:** That's the manager of human resources in him speaking!

11. **Gladys:** ... but it's true that new technology has made the task of communicating both easier and faster.

12. **Susan:** Mr Robertson talks proudly about your work-station... **(6)**

13. **Gladys:** It sounds a little grandiose, but the office really does revolve around the computer now. I use it for all our correspondence, most of which is sent by fax, incidentally, and electronically filed. Our computers are networked, so Mr Robertson can prepare documents or letters on his PC and transfer them to my computer for me to type up the final version. **(7) (8) (9)**

14. **Susan:** You prepare the newsletter, too, don't you?

15. **Gladys:** The house magazine? Yes, I do a lot of it, thanks to our desk-top publishing possibilities. **(10) (11)**

16. **Susan:** And what about communications with the parent company?

17. **Gladys:** Well, Mr Robertson uses E-mail for a short message to one of his colleagues. But the time difference makes communication very convenient. **(12)**

18. **Susan:** Mr McDuff explained how important instant communication is in finance.

KAPITEL 14

10. **Susan:** Aus ihm spricht der Personalchef!

11. **Gladys:** ... aber es ist wahr, daß neue Technik die Kommunikation leichter und schneller gemacht hat.

12. **Susan:** Herr Robertson spricht mit Stolz über Ihren Arbeitsplatzrechner...

13. **Gladys:** Das klingt ein bißchen hochtrabend, aber im Büro dreht sich jetzt wirklich alles um den Computer. Ich benutze ihn für unsere gesamte Korrespondenz, von der übrigens das meiste per Fax gesendet und elektronisch gespeichert wird. Unsere Computer sind über ein Netzwerk miteinander verbunden, so daß Herr Robertson Dokumente oder Briefe auf seinem PC vorbereiten und sie dann an meinen Computer übertragen kann, damit ich dann die Endversion schreibe.

14. **Susan:** Sie bereiten auch das Mitteilungsblatt vor, nicht?

15. **Gladys:** Die Hauszeitung? Ja, ich übernehme einen großen Teil davon, dank unserer DTP-Möglichkeiten.

16. **Susan:** Und die Kommunikation mit der Muttergesellschaft?

17. **Gladys:** Naja, Herr Robertson benutzt die elektronische Post für eine kurze Nachricht an einen seiner Kollegen. Aber durch die Zeitverschiebung wird die Kommunikation sehr praktisch.

18. **Susan:** Herr McDuff erläuterte, wie wichtig schnelle Kommunikation in der Finanzwelt ist.

ANMERKUNGEN (Fortsetzung)

(6) **work-station:** "Arbeitsplatzrechner" umfaßt einen mit einem Computer und den nötigen Peripheriegeräten, z.B. Drucker, ausgestatteten Arbeitsplatz.

(7) **fax:** "Telefax". Im Englischen ist *fax* die Abkürzung von *facsimile*.

(8) **networked:** "in einem Netzwerk verbunden". Die einzelnen Arbeitsplatzrechner sind untereinander und jeder einzelne mit einem sog. Server, einer Zentraleinheit, verbunden. Auf diese Weise können alle Benutzer von Arbeitsplatzrechnern auf die gleichen Daten zugreifen und die gleichen Programme benutzen.

(9) **PC** ist die Abkürzung von *personal computer*, ein von der Firma IBM kreierter Ausdruck für den Mikrocomputer. Man sagt auch *desktop (computer)*.

(10) Ein **house magazine** "Hauszeitung" gibt es in vielen Firmen. Mit ihr werden die Mitarbeiter über betriebsinterne Neuigkeiten informiert. Merken Sie sich auch *in-house training* "betriebsinterne Schulung", *house football team* "Betriebsfußballmannschaft".

(11) Mit den Mitteln des **DTP** (*desktop publishing*) können unter Verwendung spezieller Software Dokumente auf einem Computer erstellt, grafische Elemente in Dokumente eingebunden und das Layout von Dokumenten bearbeitet werden, die anschließend auf dem angeschlossenen Drucker ausgedruckt werden können.

(12) **E-Mail** ist die Kurzform von *electronic mail*. Hierbei werden Daten über die Telefonleitung von einem Computer an einen anderen übertragen.

CHAPTER 14

19. **Gladys:** I often prepare figures and statistics on the computer and we transfer the information in the late afternoon – thanks to the modem. Philadelphia gets the data in what is the late morning for them. They come back to us with their answer or decision and it's waiting for us when we get to work the following day. **(13)**

20. **Susan:** I suppose the fax has replaced the telex... **(14)**

21. **Gladys:** Absolutely. Our commercial people, transport, logistics..., they've now stopped using it altogether.

THE HIGH-TECH OFFICE

DO!

Prejudices are inherent in man. Admit yours and try to correct them when making judgements instead of denying them and thus becoming their lifelong captive.

KAPITEL 14

19. **Gladys:** Ich bereite oft Abbildungen und Statistiken auf dem Computer vor, und wir übertragen die Informationen – dank des Modems – am späten Nachmittag. Philadelphia erhält die Daten, wenn es dort später Vormittag ist. Wir erhalten die Daten mit ihrer Antwort oder ihrer Entscheidung zurück; sie erwarten uns, wenn wir am nächsten Tag zur Arbeit kommen.

20. **Susan:** Ich nehme an, das Faxgerät hat den Fernschreiber ersetzt...

21. **Gladys:** Auf jeden Fall. Unser kaufmännisches Personal, die Leute vom Transportservice, von der Logistik ... sie alle benutzen ihn überhaupt nicht mehr.

ANMERKUNGEN (Fortsetzung)

(13) modem ist im Englischen die Kurzform von *modulator/demodulator*. Hierbei handelt es sich um ein Gerät, das an einen Computer angeschlossen wird und mit dem unter Verwendung spezieller Übertragungssoftware Daten über eine Telefonleitung an ein anderes Modem übertragen werden können (vgl. Anmerkung 12).

(14) telex "Fernschreiber": Ein Textbearbeitungs- und Textübertragungssystem für die Bürokommunikation, bei dem häufig wiederkehrende Texte, z.B. Geschäftsbriefe, in einen Speicher geladen und über öffentliche Nachrichtennetze übertragen werden können.

DON'T!

Avoid sexual jokes with your collaborators.
You might be charged with sexual harassment.

CHAPTER 14 DOCUMENT

The information super highway

The telephone, communication satellites, TV cables, fax machines, the computer, electronic mail, video-conferencing have all, in their way, revolutionised our lives. These communication tools also happen to be the components of global data-exchange networks also known as the 'information super highway'. Our social, cultural and environmental landscapes are likely to be transformed by this electronic future. The challenge taken up by the 'information super highway' (a term coined by US vice-president Al Gore Jr), will be to fit these components together. It should enable users to exchange data, study or work, purchase goods, watch the video movies of their choice, play video games on demand and even invest money on the stock exchange without leaving their home. However, this information super highway still remains something hard to conceptualise. For the time being, technology is not able to meet all these demands at once. Ideally, the information super highway should combine the flexibility of the telephone with the carrying capacity of TV and the command of computers. And this can only be achieved at a staggering price...

Sceptics also wonder what these new techniques are good for and whether they will fulfil a real need. The heart of the matter is that some information is important and some is not. Are data networks, which contain facts by the billion without providing meaning, really progress?

KAPITEL 14

**Die Sekretärin:
Ein aussterbender Berufszweig?**

Die Tatsache, daß der Ausdruck "Assistentin" immer mehr den der "Sekretärin" ersetzt, ist nicht nur in der *political correctness* (siehe Kapitel 18, [i]) begründet. Dies erklärt sich aus der bedeutenden Entwicklung, die die Rolle der Sekretärin durchmacht. Bestimmte "Gurus" (*gurus*) in den Verwaltungen der Betriebe gehen soweit, zu sagen, daß der Posten der Sekretärin, wie man ihn in der Vergangenheit gekannt hat, über kurz oder lang wahrscheinlich nicht mehr existieren wird.

Hierfür gibt es zwei Gründe: Zuerst einmal muß jede Führungskraft, die diesen Namen auch verdient, heute EDV-Kenntnisse, besonders was Bürotechnik *(office automation)* betrifft, besitzen und in der Lage sein, die meisten auch weniger anspruchsvollen Tätigkeiten, die er/sie normalerweise der Sekretärin überlassen würde, selbst auszuführen. Außerdem kann bei den heutigen Bestrebungen zur Einsparung von Personal eine Sekretärin fast zu einem Luxus werden, besonders wenn man in Betracht zieht, wieviel ein Brief von dem Moment an, in dem er verfaßt wird, bis zu dem Moment, in dem er seinen Empfänger erreicht, kostet.

Und außerdem: Könnten Sie sich nicht auch vorstellen, irgendwann Büros zu haben, in denen es kein Papier mehr gibt?

CHAPTER 14

EXERCISES

Comprehension

Lesen Sie den Dialog aufmerksam durch. Beantworten Sie dann die nachfolgenden Fragen, und zwar immer in ganzen Sätzen:

1. For how long has Gladys been working in UC's Head Office? **2.** Why does Mr Robertson often call her his assistant? **3.** What does Gladys mean by 'filtering' Mr Robertson's phone calls? **4.** How can Mr Robertson keep in touch with his secretary even when he's travelling? **5.** Why does Mr Robertson say that improved technology doesn't make you a better manager? **6.** What has new technology helped to achieve? **7.** Quote two of the tasks that Gladys says she does on her computer. **8.** How does the time difference between England and the USA facilitate communications between UC (UK) and the parent company? **9.** Why is instant communication important in the world of finance? **10.** Is it true to say that the telex is gradually disappearing?

Translation

1. Seitdem ich mein Studium abgeschlossen habe, arbeite ich für ein und dieselbe Firma. **2.** Sie müssen wissen, wie Sie mit den neusten technologischen Innovationen Schritt halten, und sie übernehmen, wenn sie nützlich sind. **3.** Gladys hatte schon 20 Jahre für UC gearbeitet, als Herr Robertson in die Firma kam. **4.** Er behandelt mich wie eine wirkliche Assistentin und nicht bloß wie eine Sekretärin. **5.** Nehmen Sie nächstes Mal keine Termine an, ohne vorher in meinen Terminkalender zu schauen. **6.** Wenn es ein Problem zu regeln gibt, rufen Sie mich an. Ich werde mein schnurloses Telefon dabeihaben. **7.** Nur weil man die fortschrittlichste Technologie zur Verfügung hat, kann man die Menschen nicht besser führen. **8.** Diese Woche ist in der Hauszeitung ein Artikel über das neue Computer-Netzwerk. **9.** Komischerweise erleichtert die Zeitverschiebung zwischen Europa und den Vereinigten Staaten sehr die Kommunikation mit unseren Filialen. **10.** Wir vermeiden heute, den Fernschreiber zu benutzen, es sei denn, es ist anders nicht möglich.

KAPITEL 14

LÖSUNGSVORSCHLÄGE

Verständnisübung

1. We don't know exactly; she says longer than she cares to think. But obviously a long time, since she joined UC straight after leaving secretarial college. 2. Probably because that's the way he treats her: he delegates a certain amount of responsibility. 3. She answers all the calls first, and only puts through to him those which she cannot handle herself. 4. He can keep in touch with her because he has a phone in his car as well as a cordless telephone. 5. Because it doesn't help you motivate your staff or get them involved. 6. New technology has made communication easier and quicker. 7. She types letters, files them and works on the house magazine. 8. Because thanks to the modem, people at UC (UK) can send data to Philadelphia in the late afternoon. Their colleagues at the parent company can get an answer or decision back to them for the start of work the following morning. 9. Because financial information is accessible in real time on all markets and decisions can be made more rapidly. 10. Yes, Gladys says it's no longer used by the commercial people, transport and logistics.

Übersetzungsübung

1. I've been working for the same firm ever since I finished my studies (... ever since I left school *or* college). 2. You have to know how (*or* be able) to keep up with the latest technological innovations and to adopt them if they are useful. 3. Gladys had already been working for UC for twenty years when Mr Robertson arrived (*or* joined the company). 4. He treats me like a real assistant and not like a mere secretary. 5. Next time, don't accept appointments without looking in my diary. 6. If there's a problem to sort out, give me a ring (*or* a buzz). I'll have my cordless telephone. 7. It's not because you have the most advanced technology at your disposal that you can manage people better. 8. In the house magazine this week, there's an article about the new computer network. 9. Strangely (enough), the time difference between Europe and the United States makes communicating with our subsidiaries much easier. 10. We avoid using the telex today, except when we can't do otherwise.

CHAPTER 14

Application

Der Fernschreiber hatte den Vorteil, daß die Benutzer lernten, kurze Nachrichten zu verfassen, die eine Vielzahl von Abkürzungen enthielten. Einige dieser Abkürzungen sind zu Standards geworden; andere, individuelle Abkürzungen forderten die Phantasie des Empfängers.
Auf jeden Fall ist es immer nützlich, wenn man weiß, wie man diese Art von Mitteilungen verfaßt und entziffert. Sehen Sie sich nun das erste Telex und die darunterstehende Übersetzung an. Versuchen Sie dann, das auf der gegenüberliegenden Seite abgebildete Telex in "normales" Englisch zu übersetzen.

Telex 1

```
22/10/9.                09.27
ATTN: UNITED CHOCOLATE (UK) LTD, PCHSING DPT

RE ORDER UC010/9./562H.
RGRT DLVRY IMPOSS 31/10. WILL DSPTCH 5 TNNES
TDAY. EXPCT DLVRY 15/11.
5 TNNES ASAP.
DEL DUE STRKE RFNRY WKERS.
PLSE NTE PRCE RSE: + $7.55 PER TNNE CIF. BAD
HRVEST THIS YR. APOLS.

RGDS.
CMMCIAL DPT. IVORY COAST COCOA SHIPPERS,
ABIDJAN.
```

22nd October 199., 9.27 am - for the attention of the Purchasing Department of United Chocolate (UK) Ltd.
With reference to your order No UC 010/9.562H, we regret that it will be impossible to deliver the goods by 31st October – (we are dispatching 5 tonnes today – expect delivery by 15th November) – the other 5 tonnes will be sent as soon as possible – the delay is due to a strike by refinery workers – please note, also, the following price rise, due to the bad harvest this year: + $7.55 per tonne (cost, insurance and freight) – we apologize for these problems.
We send our regards – from the Commercial Department of Ivory Coast Cocoa Shippers, Abidjan.

KAPITEL 14

Telex 2

> 22/11/9.   14.52
> ATTN: UNITED CHOCOLATE, SALES DPT.
>
> RE ORDER NO. 52BG 0028/9. 200 1KG BXES 'AVON'
> ASSTED CHOCS. DEL DUE 19/11.
> RCVD 50 BOXES TDAY. 5 DMGED.
> MUST RCVE REST BY 24/11 LATEST. XMAS RUSH
>
> PLSE QTE ASAP FOR 250 500G BXES 'MIDNIGHT
> BLUE' CHOC MINTS. DEL URGENT. IN SHPS FOR
> XMAS
>
> RGDS.
> PCHSING DPT. THRIFTY THISTLE DISCOUNTERS,
> ABERDEEN.

Lösung

22nd October 199., 2.52 pm - for the attention of the Sales Department United Chocolate.
With reference to our order (No 52BG 0028/9) for 200 lkg boxes of 'Avon' assorted chocolates, which was due to be delivered on 19th November; we received fifty boxes today, of which five were damaged. We must receive the rest of the order by 24th November because of the Christmas rush.
Please quote as soon as possible for two hundred and fifty 500g boxes of 'Midnight Blue' chocolate mints, for urgent delivery. We want them in the shops for Christmas.
Regards, the Purchasing Department, Thrifty Thistle Discounters, Aberdeen.

CHAPTER 15

Supporting the local community

Susan is discussing her progress on the career development project with Phil Irwin.

1. **Phil:** So, Susan, how is your project going along?

2. **Susan:** Fine. I spent several weeks down in Filton, as you know, and I've also been speaking to a lot of people here in Milton Keynes.

3. **Phil:** And is it too early for your tentative conclusions…?

4. **Susan:** A little too early, yes. But I think It's true to say that there is definitely a problem.

5. **Phil:** Specific to Filton, you mean.

6. **Susan:** Absolutely!

7. **Phil:** Evans?

8. **Susan:** *(She nods her head. A pause)* Mmm. What do you think they'll do about it?

9. **Phil:** Appoint some troubleshooter to sort things out. Evans is fairly close to retirement, anyway. You know he used to be in the army? **(1)**

10. **Susan:** The Royal Engineers. Mmm, he told me. He said that's where he learnt to be a manager… **(2)**

11. **Phil:** … never noticed there's a difference between a chocolate factory and a regiment!

12. **Susan:** Things have changed, too, since he left the army. He's really very sweet though. He was awfully excited about the celebrations he's organising.

13. **Phil:** For the 75th anniversary of the Filton plant?

KAPITEL 15

Unterstützung der örtlichen Gemeinde

Susan bespricht mit Phil Irwin den Verlauf ihres Projekts zum Karriereausbau.

1. **Phil:** Na, Susan, wie läuft es mit deinem Projekt?

2. **Susan:** Gut. Wie du weißt, habe ich mehrere Wochen unten in Filton verbracht, und ich habe auch mit vielen Leuten hier in Milton Keynes gesprochen.

3. **Phil:** Und ist es zu früh für vorläufige Schlußfolgerungen...?

4. **Susan:** Ein bißchen zu früh, ja. Aber ich denke, man kann auf jeden Fall sagen, daß es tatsächlich ein Problem gibt.

5. **Phil:** Speziell in Filton, meinst du?

6. **Susan:** Absolut!

7. **Phil:** Evans?

8. **Susan:** *(Nickt mit dem Kopf. Pause)* Mmm. Was denkst du, werden sie in diesem Punkt unternehmen?

9. **Phil:** Einen Schlichter benennen, um die Sache zu klären. Evans geht sowieso bald in Rente. Wußtest du, daß er in der Armee war?

10. **Susan:** Bei den Royal Engineers. Mmm, er hat es mir erzählt. Er sagte, er habe dort gelernt, ein Manager zu sein...

11. **Phil:** ... hat nie bemerkt, daß es einen Unterschied zwischen einer Schokoladenfabrik und einem Regiment gibt!

12. **Susan:** Die Dinge haben sich auch verändert, seit er die Armee verlassen hat. Er ist trotzdem sehr nett. Er war schrecklich aufgeregt wegen der Feiern, die er gerade organisiert.

13. **Phil:** Für das 75. Jubiläum des Filton-Werks?

ANMERKUNGEN

(1) **troubleshooter:** "Schlichter; Sanierer; Krisenmanager". Eine Person, die gerufen wird, um in einem Streit oder Konflikt zwischen den streitenden Parteien zu vermitteln.

(2) Die **Royal Engineers** sind ein besonderes Regiment der britischen Armee. Seine Veteranen tragen mit Stolz die Krawatte des Regiments mit einem leicht erkennbaren Motiv.

CHAPTER 15

14. Susan: Mmm.

15. Phil: Public Relations thought it was a great idea to make it into a huge charity event. They were afraid our image had suffered in the Bristol area after that strike.

16. Susan: Lord Werrett was delighted, too – you can imagine – when it was decided to give all the money to help build a children's wing for Thornbury hospital.

17. Phil: So what has Evans got lined up for the celebrations, then?

18. Susan: Well there's the open day – or weekend, in fact – at the factory, with lots of fund-raising activities there. Then there's the sponsored charity run... **(3)**

19. Phil: How does that work?

20. Susan: Well, virtually all UC's employees in Filton, including Mr Evans, will run as far as they can. They've found friends, etc. to 'sponsor' them – £1 a mile, I believe – and then UC is going to double the total amount they raise. **(4)**

21. Phil: Didn't I hear something about a football match, too?

22. Susan: That's right. On the Saturday evening, there's a charity match between Lord Werrett's XI – which includes some former England internationals, apparently – and Bristol Rovers. Then on the Sunday evening there's a big concert with two or three big stars from the world of opera and rock music.

23. Phil: Very eclectic! When is this, Susan? I must make a note in my diary.

KAPITEL 15

14. **Susan:** Mmm.

15. **Phil:** Die Öffentlichkeitsabteilung meinte, es wäre eine tolle Idee, daraus eine große Wohltätigkeitsveranstaltung zu machen. Sie hatten Angst, unser Image hätte nach diesem Streik im Gebiet von Bristol gelitten.

16. **Susan:** Lord Werret war auch erfreut – du kannst es dir vorstellen – als entschieden wurde, daß das gesamte Geld verwendet werden soll, um einen Gebäudeflügel für die Kinderabteilung des Thornbury-Krankenhauses zu bauen.

17. **Phil:** Was also hat Evans für die Feiern geplant?

18. **Susan:** Naja, da gibt es den Tag – bzw. das Wochenende – der offenen Tür in der Fabrik, an dem viel Geld gesammelt werden soll. Dann ist da das von Sponsoren unterstützte Wohltätigkeitswettrennen...

19. **Phil:** Wie funktioniert das?

20. **Susan:** Naja, fast alle Angestellten von UC in Filton einschließlich Herrn Evans laufen so weit wie sie können. Sie haben Freunde usw. gefunden, die sie 'sponsern' – 1 Pfund pro Meile, glaube ich – und dann verdoppelt UC den gesamten Betrag, der aufgebracht wird.

21. **Phil:** Habe ich nicht auch etwas von einem Fußballspiel gehört?

22. **Susan:** Das ist richtig. Am Samstag abend gibt es ein Wohltätigkeitsspiel zwischen den 'Lord Werrets XI' – zu dem offensichtlich auch einige der ehemaligen Nationalspieler von England gehören – und den 'Bristol Rovers'. Dann ist am Sonntag abend ein großes Konzert mit zwei oder drei großen Stars aus der Welt der Oper und der Rockmusik.

23. **Phil:** Eine bunte Mischung! Wann ist das, Susan? Ich muß mir das in meinem Terminkalender notieren.

ANMERKUNGEN (Fortsetzung)

(3) **sponsered charity run (swim, ride...):** Ein im Rahmen einer Wohltätigkeitsveranstaltung durchgeführter Dauerlauf (oder ein Wettschwimmen oder Radrennen), bei dem für die Teilnehmer pro gelaufenem, geschwommenem oder geradeltem Kilometer ein bestimmter Betrag von Personen aus dem Freundes-, Verwandten- oder Kollegenkreis eingesetzt wird. *To sponsor* "finanzieren, fördern, unterstützen"; "Patenschaft übernehmen". Im Deutschen hat sich auch "sponsern" eingebürgert.

(4) **mile:** Ein in Großbritannien und den USA gebräuchliches Längenmaß. *1 mile* entspricht 1.760 *yards*, was wiederum 1.609 Metern entspricht. *1 yard* (91,44 cm) = *3 feet* (Fuß = 30,48 cm); 1 *foot* = 12 *inches* (Zoll = 2,54 cm).

CHAPTER 15

DOCUMENT

Anniversary Celebrations

UNITED CHOCOLATE (UK) Ltd
Filton Plant 75th Anniversay Celebrations
PROGRAMME

Saturday 23rd April:

9 am - 5 pm: Filton Plant open to visitors
Exhibition: *'UC then and now: 75 years of chocolate-making history'*
(a team of UC workers in period dress[1] will manufacture for you to taste the products of 75 years ago on the original machines)
2 pm: Grand Sponsored Charity Run on Filton Common
Special Guest Star: Olympic Bronze Medalist **Winfield Jackson**
8.30 pm: Charity Football Match
Lord Werrett's XI v. Bristol Rovers
(at the Rovers' Stadium, Bristol)

Sunday 24th April:

10 am - 4 pm: Filton Plant open to visitors
Exhibition (see above)
12 noon - 5 pm: Vintage Car Rally and Exhibition on Filton Common
(all cars were on the roads 75 years ago!)
8.30 pm: Grand Charity Concert starring:
Barbara Hitchcock, Sergio Silvestrelli
Melvyn Jones, The Limestone Cowboys, *etc.*

NB: Throughout the weekend, anniversary tee-shirts, baseball caps, lapel pins[2] and many other gift items will be on sale. All proceeds from this very special weekend will go to the Children's Wing Fund of Thornbury Hospital.

---

[1] *period dress:* "Zeitgenössische Tracht"
[2] *lapel pins:* "Anstecker, Pin"; *lapel:* "Revers"

KAPITEL 15

Die Wohltätigkeitseinrichtungen

In Großbritannien gibt es eine Vielzahl von Wohltätigkeitsorganisationen (*charity organisations*). Viele unter ihnen, z.B. *Oxfam*, der *Save the Children Fund* oder die *British Heart Foundation*, sind berühmt und von jedermann anerkannt.
Aber die Organisationen wissen, daß die Konkurrenz unter ihnen hart ist und daß sie sich nicht mehr damit zufriedengeben können, nur an die Barmherzigkeit zu appellieren. Die Menschen möchten gerne etwas spenden, nur möchten sie dafür auch etwas zurückerhalten. Aus diesem Grund entstanden zahlreiche Geschäfte, in denen Artikel, z.B. Glückwunschkarten, Schallplatten u.ä. verkauft werden, deren Erlös wohltätigen Zwecken zugutekommt. Darüber hinaus werden Konzerte (z.B. *Live Aid* im Wembley-Stadion im Jahr 1985) oder Theaterspiele (ursprünglich auf Initiative von *Comic Relief* im Jahr 1984) veranstaltet. Und immer häufiger gruppieren sich die Organisationen im Rahmen dieser Aktivitäten neu und teilen sich die gesammelten Gelder.
Nicht nur Schauspieler und Sportler stellen gerne ihre Talente zur Verfügung, auch das Publikum möchte bei solchen Veranstaltungen immer öfter aktiv teilnehmen. Hieraus entstanden die *sponsered charity runs* und auch der *Red Nose Day*, der aus *Comic Relief* hervorgegangen ist und bei dem die Teilnehmer sich sponsern lassen und eine Clownsnase aufsetzen, um sich zur Schau zu stellen. Selbstverständlich für einen guten Zweck!

CHAPTER 15

EXERCISES

Comprehension

Lesen Sie den Dialog aufmerksam durch. Beantworten Sie dann die nachfolgenden Fragen, und zwar immer in ganzen Sätzen:

1. Will it be long, now, before Susan starts drawing her conclusions? **2.** Has her study brought to light any general problems among UC employees? **3.** Why is a troubleshooter likely to be sent to the Filton plant? **4.** How much formal management training do you think Mr Evans has had? **5.** Do you get the impression that Phil Irwin thinks the army is a good place to learn how to manage? **6.** Why was Mr Evans very excited when he spoke to Susan? **7.** Why are Public Relations keen to improve UC's image in the Bristol area? **8.** Mention three ways in which UC will raise money for charity. **9.** How much money has UC accepted to give for the sponsored charity run? **10.** Had Phil already made plans to attend the anniversary celebrations?

Translation

1. Phils Projekt läuft gut, aber es ist viel zu früh, um Schlußfolgerungen zu ziehen. **2.** Herr Evans hat 14 Tage in der Unternehmenszentrale verbracht, wo er viel mit Phil und Susan gesprochen hat. **3.** Was denken Sie, werden sie tun, um zu versuchen, das Problem zu lösen? **4.** Er mag Offizier bei den Royal Engineers gewesen sein, aber in der Armee lernt man nicht, eine Keksfabrik zu leiten. **5.** Viele Dinge haben sich verändert, seit die Fabrik vor 75 Jahren gebaut wurde. **6.** Das Image unserer Firma wird leiden, wenn wir dieses Jubiläum nicht feiern. **7.** Das ist eine gute Idee, aber ich fürchte, daß ein einfacher Tag der offenen Tür nicht genug sein wird. **8.** Ich verstehe immer noch nicht genau, wie dieses Wettrennen funktioniert. **9.** Ich bin damit einverstanden, den Gesamtbetrag, den Sie aufbringen können, zu verdoppeln. **10.** Vergessen Sie nicht, in Ihrem Terminkalender die Tage und Uhrzeiten all dieser Sport- und Kulturveranstaltungen zu notieren.

DO!

***Look on the bright side in difficult times:
think positive and cultivate optimism.***

KAPITEL 15

LÖSUNGSVORSCHLÄGE

Verständnisübung

1. No. She says it's a 'little' too early for tentative conclusions. However, she seems to have already identified one problem. 2. Apparently not, because she only mentions the problem specific to Filton. 3. In order to solve the problem which seems to have arisen down there. 4. Probably not very much, because he says that he learnt to manage in the army. 5. No. He insists on the fact that there's a difference between the army and a company. 6. Because he was able to tell her about the 75th anniversary celebrations he's organising. 7. They're afraid that UC's image has been damaged by the recent strike. 8. Various fund-raising activities will be organised during the open weekend: the sponsored charity run, the football match and the concert. 9. They will give an amount identical to that which the runners raise. 10. Apparently not, because he hadn't even noted the dates in his diary.

Übersetzungsübung

1. Phil's project is going along fine, but it's much (*or* far) too early to draw (any) conclusions. 2. Mr Evans spent a fortnight (*or* two weeks) at the company headquarters (*or* registered office) (*or* head office), where he spoke a lot with Phil and Susan. 3. What do you think they'll do to try and sort things out? 4. He may have been an officer in the Royal Engineers, but you don't learn to manage a biscuit factory in the army. 5. A lot of things have changed since the factory was built 75 years ago. 6. Our company's image may suffer if we don't celebrate this anniversary. 7. It's a good idea, but I'm afraid that a mere open day won't be enough. 8. I still don't understand exactly how this run works. 9. I agree to double the total amount you manage to raise. 10. Don't forget to make a note (*or* note down) in your diary the dates and times of all these sporting and cultural activities (*or* events).

DON'T!

Don't be obsessed by the idea of perfection. Be yourself and use your common sense. Don't forget that people are tolerant with foreigners.

CHAPTER 15

Application

Unmittelbar nach seinem Gespräch mit Susan erhält Phil das komplette Veranstaltungsprogramm der Feiern anläßlich des 75jährigen Jubiläums des Filton-Werks (siehe Dokument). Er holt sofort seinen Terminkalender hervor.
*Er hofft, an möglichst vielen Aktivitäten teilnehmen zu können. Aus seinem Lebenslauf (Kapitel 6, Übung 3) wissen wir, daß er ein begeisterter Sportler ist, aber genauso gerne in die Oper geht. Eigentlich liebt er alle Sportarten und alle Musikrichtungen. Er fährt gerne Auto, aber nicht nachts, da er Kontaktlinsen trägt. Sehen Sie sich das Veranstaltungsprogramm und die Seiten in Phils Terminkalender (auf der gegenüberliegenden Seite) aufmerksam an, und lesen Sie dann die folgenden Aussagen. Entscheiden Sie, ob die Aussagen **eher zutreffen** oder **eher falsch** sind. Korrigieren Sie die falschen Aussagen.*

1. Phil, who likes running, will be able to participate in the sponsored charity run. **2.** Phil can go ahead and book his ticket for the charity football match. **3.** It doesn't matter if the Grand Charity Concert finishes quite late, because Phil won't have to get up early the next day. **4.** Phil will have to ask James and Janet to come to lunch another day. **5.** Phil expects the IPM* conference to finish on Saturday afternoon. **6.** The next Department breakfast meeting will take place in May. **7.** Phil meets with the Union representatives nearly every week. **8.** Mr Robertson never misses a milk-round recruiting session. **9.** Phil's daughters often complain that they don't see their daddy enough. **10.** Phil will ask Susan to drive him and his family back to Milton Keynes after the concert.

* IPM : Institute of Personnel Management.

KAPITEL 15

Wahr oder falsch?

1. *Falsch:* Phil can't be in Filton for 2 pm if he only leaves Harrogate at noon.
2. *Wahr.*
3. *Falsch:* Phil has an important meeting at 8.30 am: either he drives back on Sunday night, but he doesn't like doing this, or he has to drive back very early on Monday morning.
4. *Wahr.*
5. *Falsch:* He hopes to depart from Harrogate by noon, if possible.
6. *Wahr.*
7. *Falsch:* These meetings are monthly.
8. *Falsch:* Phil is replacing him in Exeter and Southampton.
9. *Wahr.*
10. *Wahr.*

Auszug aus Phils Terminkalender

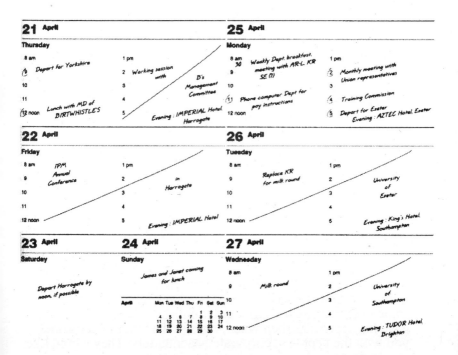

CHAPTER 16

Making the grade

Susan has been with United Chocolate (UK) Ltd for about eighteen months now, nearly twelve of which have been spent working in the Human Resources Department at the head office. Mr Romer-Lee, the DHR, has asked to see her. **(1)**

1. **Mr Romer-Lee:** *(Standing up and coming round his desk as Susan enters)* Hello, Susan. How nice to see you again! I've just got back from Philadelphia.

2. **Susan:** I know; Phil Irwin told me. He's been keeping me pretty busy with that project on staff development.

3. **Mr Romer-Lee:** Well I told you, when you first joined us, that the holiday was over, do you remember?

4. **Susan:** Oh, yes, I remember!

5. **Mr Romer-Lee:** *(He laughs)* Please take a seat. *(After a pause)* And how have you found it? Do you think we've worked you too hard?

6. **Susan:** If I'd wanted a more cosy rhythm, I would have done something else. Joined the Civil Service, for instance, as my mother wanted me to do.

7. **Mr Romer-Lee:** Well, I, for one, am glad you didn't. Everyone in the department is more than satisfied with the work you've done for us. Particularly on that staff development project. Mr Robertson says you're the best trainee manager he's had in the department in a long time.

8. **Susan:** Well, I really enjoy what I'm doing...

9. **Mr Romer-Lee:** That's why I asked you to come and see me this morning. Before I left for the States, I proposed to the Managing Director that we send you back to university for some postgraduate management training. Of course, the MD gave his approval. Then when I was in the US, I talked about you with the people at corporate headquarters. They would like you to do an MBA. **(2)**

KAPITEL 16

Geschafft

Susan ist nun seit etwa 18 Monaten bei United Chocolate (UK) Ltd, von denen sie fast zwölf Monate in der Abteilung für Personalwesen in der Hauptgeschäftsstelle gearbeitet hat. Herr Romer-Lee, der Personalchef, hat sie um ein Treffen gebeten.

1. **Herr Romer-Lee:** *(Steht auf und geht um den Tisch herum, als Susan hereinkommt)* Hallo Susan. Wie schön, Sie wiederzusehen! Ich bin gerade aus Philadelphia zurückgekommen.

2. **Susan:** Ich weiß; Phil Irwin hat es mir erzählt. Er hält mich ganz schön mit diesem Personalentwicklungsprojekt auf Trab.

3. **Herr Romer-Lee:** Naja, ich habe Ihnen ja gesagt, als wir uns das erste Mal trafen, daß die Ferien vorbei sind, erinnern Sie sich?

4. **Susan:** Oh, ja, ich erinnere mich!

5. **Herr Romer-Lee:** *(Lacht)* Nehmen Sie doch Platz. *(Nach einer Pause)* Und wie finden Sie es? Denken Sie, daß wir Sie zu hart rangenommen haben?

6. **Susan:** Wenn ich eine gemütlichere Gangart gewollt hätte, hätte ich etwas anderes gemacht. Ich wäre zum Beispiel in den Staatsdienst gegangen, wie es meine Mutter für mich wollte.

7. **Herr Romer-Lee:** Naja, ich für meinen Teil bin froh, daß Sie das nicht getan haben. Alle in der Abteilung sind mehr als zufrieden mit der Arbeit, die Sie für uns geleistet haben. Besonders was dieses Personalentwicklungsprojekt betrifft. Herr Robertson sagt, Sie sind der beste Trainee Manager, den er seit langem in der Abteilung gehabt hat.

8. **Susan:** Naja, was ich mache, gefällt mir wirklich...

9. **Herr Romer-Lee:** Darum habe ich Sie gebeten, heute morgen zu mir zu kommen. Bevor ich in die Staaten flog, habe ich dem geschäftsführenden Direktor vorgeschlagen, Sie für ein Aufbaustudium an die Universität zurückzuschicken. Selbstverständlich hat er zugestimmt. Als ich dann in den Staaten war, habe ich mit den Leuten von der Zentrale über Sie gesprochen. Sie hätten gerne, daß Sie einen Abschluß als MBA machen.

ANMERKUNGEN

(1) **DHR** ist die Abkürzung für *Director of Human Resources*, was in etwa unserem "Personalchef" entspricht.

(2) **MD** ist die Abkürzung für *Managing Director* "geschäftsführender Direktor", "Geschäftsführer". In einem anderen Kontext bedeutet MD *Doctor of Medicine*, um eine Unterscheidung zum *PhD, Doctor of Philosophy*, zu schaffen.

CHAPTER 16

10. Susan: In Pennsylvania?

11. Mr Romer-Lee: As a matter of fact, no. You know that United Chocolate has a factory down in San Antonio.

12. Susan: Mmm.

13. Mr Romer-Lee: Well, they have contacts with Texas A&M University, has an excellent school of business, incidentally. The people in San Antonio have a project which they want someone to work on. **(3) (4)**

14. Susan: Someone doing an MBA, for example!

15. Mr Romer-Lee: A part-time MBA. How did you guess?! You can't blame us, can you? The company puts up the money for your studies, so it expects something back in return. **(5)**

16. Susan: Absolutely! And is this project in the field of human resources?

17. Mr Romer-Lee: Not at all. It's marketing. About a new product they intend to develop. But I'm sure that won't stop you. Marketing always ends up pinching my best people!

18. Susan: But you told me that as you work your way up in management, whatever you're doing, you always have to manage people…

19. Mr Romer-Lee: … so you need human resource management. Well, do you want to go to Texas?

20. Susan: *(With a Texas accent)* Yes sir!

KAPITEL 16

10. **Susan:** In Pennsylvania?

11. **Herr Romer-Lee:** Nein. Sie wissen, daß United Chocolate eine Fabrik unten in San Antonio hat.

12. **Susan:** Mmm.

13. **Herr Romer-Lee:** Naja, sie haben Kontakte zu der Texas A&M Universität, die zufällig über eine hervorragende Wirtschaftsfakultät verfügt. Die Leute in San Antonio benötigen jemanden, der an einem Projekt mitarbeitet.

14. **Susan:** Beispielsweise jemanden, der den MBA macht!

15. **Herr Romer-Lee:** Einen MBA auf Teilzeitbasis. Wie haben Sie das erraten?! Das können Sie uns nicht zum Vorwurf machen, nicht wahr? Die Firma bringt Geld für Ihr Studium auf, also erwartet sie eine Gegenleistung.

16. **Susan:** Absolut! Und handelt es sich um ein Projekt im Bereich Personalwesen?

17. **Herr Romer-Lee:** Ganz und gar nicht. Im Bereich Marketing. Es geht um ein neues Produkt, das sie entwickeln wollen. Aber ich bin sicher, das kann Sie nicht stoppen. Die vom Marketing nehmen mir letztendlich immer die besten Leute weg!

18. **Susan:** Aber Sie haben mir gesagt, daß man, wenn man sich im Management hinaufarbeitet, schließlich immer Leute führen muß, egal, was man macht...

19. **Herr Romer-Lee:** ... also braucht man Personalmanagement. Na, möchten Sie nach Texas gehen?

20. **Susan:** *(Mit texanischem Akzent)* Ja, Sir!

ANMERKUNGEN (Fortsetzung)

(3) **Texas A&M:** Eine bedeutende Universität des Staates Texas, die im Jahre 1876 gegründet wurde und sich in College Station zwischen Dallas und Houston befindet. Die Initialen bedeuten *agricultural and mechanical*, auch wenn die Universität heute nicht mehr nur auf diese beiden Fachbereiche beschränkt ist.

(4) **school of business:** Bezeichnet an den amerikanischen Universitäten die Fakultät für Unternehmensmanagement, an der man sich unter anderem auf den berühmten MBA vorbereiten kann. (Siehe Dokument.)

(5) **part-time:** "Teilzeit(beschäftigung)". Eine Beschäftigungsform, die es Arbeitnehmern erlaubt, neben der normalen Arbeit ein Studium zu absolvieren. Die Studieninhalte verteilen sich auf einen längeren Zeitraum; die Kurse finden meistens in den Abendstunden statt.

CHAPTER 16　　　　　　　　　　　　　　　　DOCUMENT

The MBA

In Chapter 2, we talked about management education in British universities and the former polytechnics. In the US, graduate management education is often synonymous with the MBA, or Master of Business Administration, even though many other master's degrees exist in this field. Some, like the MBA, are generalist business courses, whereas others concentrate on specific areas of management or careers.

It cannot be denied, however, that the MBA is the business degree most in demand. Over 700 US colleges and universities now offer MBA programmes, producing, today, more than 70,000 graduates, compared with a mere (!) 18,000 in 1968. These programmes are open to students holding a bachelor's degree in any area of study and not only those who majored in business and management subjects.

In the past, the MBA often provided an opportunity to return to college, after several years of career experience, to obtain some specialised management qualification. It is probably true to say, though, that today more and more students embark on these graduate courses immediately after obtaining their bachelor's degree. Three formats exist, however: full time, part time (for students reluctant or unable to give up their job) and executive MBA programmes. The latter are designed for middle managers who would normally be sponsored by their employer.

The MBA concept has proved so popular that it has been copied elsewhere, particularly in Europe. Nearly 500 programmes exist outside of the US, some of which have acquired an aura, equivalent almost to their top US counterparts. With so many courses available, and so many graduates entering the career market each year, it is important to make the right choice. One criterion might be whether or not a school is accredited by the American Assembly of Collegiate Schools of Business (AACSB), the only recognised accrediting agency for bachelors' and masters' degrees in business administration.

KAPITEL 16

Fortbildung

Diejenigen Arbeitnehmer, die nicht wie Susan die Möglichkeit haben, ein von der Firma finanziertes Studium aufzunehmen, müssen andere Mittel finden, um ihre berufliche Situation und damit auch oft ihre soziale Stellung zu verbessern.
In der Regel geht man in sogenannte Abendkurse *(night school)*, die besonders in Großbritannien und in den Vereinigten Staaten stark frequentiert werden. In beiden Ländern herrscht vorwiegend eine protestantische, wenn nicht sogar puritanische Kultur, in der die Arbeitsmoral stark verwurzelt ist.
Noch heute steht jedem Einwohner Großbritanniens dank der *Open University* ("Fernuniversität"), die 1969 gegründet wurde und des *Open College*, das seit 1987 besteht, die Möglichkeit offen, eine Fortbildung *(continuing education)* per Fernunterricht *(distance learning)* zu machen.

CHAPTER 16

EXERCISES

Comprehension

Lesen Sie den Dialog aufmerksam durch. Beantworten Sie dann die nachfolgenden Fragen, und zwar immer in ganzen Sätzen:

1. For how long has Susan been with the Human Resources Department of the Head Office? **2.** Why has Mr Romer-Lee asked to see Susan today? **3.** Do you think that Susan's boss has seen her recently? **4.** Do you think Susan has found working for United Chocolate too hard? **5.** Would you say that Mr Robertson and his colleagues have a good opinion of Susan's work? **6.** Can Mr Romer-Lee decide, himself, who is going to study in the USA? **7.** What connection exists between United Chocolate and the State of Texas? **8.** Why will the company give Susan a project to work on while she's studying? **9.** What do you think Mr Romer-Lee means when he says that Marketing always ends up pinching his best people? **10.** Does Mr Romer-Lee think that human resource management is useful to all managers?

Translation

1. Susan arbeitet schon seit 18 Monaten für UC, aber sie arbeitet erst seit einem Jahr in der Personalabteilung. **2.** Was Herrn Romer-Lee betrifft, so hat er vor etwa 15 Jahren begonnen, bei UC zu arbeiten, aber er ist erst seit 1990 Personalchef. **3.** Herr Romer-Lee war gerade erst von der Muttergesellschaft in Philadelphia zurückgekehrt, als er Susan um ein Treffen bat. **4.** Das Projekt zur Personalentwicklung, das Phil Irwin Susan übergeben hat, beschäftigt sie ganz schön. **5.** Es ist wahr, daß sie einen bei UC hart rannehmen, aber wenn ich eine gemütlichere Gangart gewollt hätte, hätte ich die Stelle nicht angenommen. **6.** Ich für meinen Teil bin froh, daß Sie sich entschieden haben, für uns zu arbeiten, und jeder ist mehr als zufrieden mit Ihrer Arbeit an diesem Projekt. **7.** Herr Romer-Lee muß für seine Entscheidung die Genehmigung des geschäftsführenden Direktors einholen, aber letzterer braucht nicht den Vorstand zu konsultieren. **8.** UC hat sogar eine Fabrik in Texas. Die dortigen Manager arbeiten zusammen mit den Professoren für Marketing der Texas A&M Universität an einem Projekt. **9.** Um den MBA zu machen, ist dies eine der besten Universitäten des Bundesstaates, vielleicht der gesamten USA. **10.** Wenn eine Führungskraft Menschen führen muß, so wird sie immer Personalmanagement benötigen, egal, in welchem Bereich sie arbeitet.

KAPITEL 16

LÖSUNGSVORSCHLÄGE

Verständnisübung

1. Susan has been working in the Human Resources Department of the Head Office for nearly a year now. **2.** In order to offer her the chance to study in the USA. **3.** Probably not. He's been in Philadelphia, and he says that it's nice to see her again. **4.** No, she seems to have welcomed the rhythm. It is what she expected. **5.** Absolutely. Everybody has a very positive opinion, particularly Mr Robertson. **6.** Not by himself. He must get the Managing Director's approval. **7.** UC has a plant in San Antonio, Texas. **8.** Because the company is paying for the studies, so it expects something back in return. **9.** Some of Mr Romer-Lee's best managers have probably ended up working for Marketing. **10.** Certainly. He told Susan that you need it as you make your way up in management, whatever you're doing.

Übersetzungsübung

1. Susan has already worked for UC for eighteen months, but she's only been working in the Human Resources Department for a year. **2.** As for Mr Romer-Lee, he came to work for UC about fifteen years ago, but he's only been DHR since 1990. **3.** Mr Romer-Lee had only just got back from the parent company in Philadelphia, when he asked to meet Susan. **4.** The project concerning staff development which Phil Irwin gave to Susan is keeping her pretty busy. **5.** It's true that they work you hard at UC, but if I'd wanted a more cosy rhythm, I wouldn't have accepted the post. **6.** I, for one, am glad you decided to work for us, and everyone is more than satisfied with your work on this project. **7.** Mr Romer-Lee must get the MD's approval for this decision but the latter doesn't need to consult the Board of Directors. **8.** UC has even got a factory in Texas. The local managers are working on a project with the marketing professors of Texas A&M University. **9.** This is one of the best universities in the State to do an MBA, maybe even in the whole of the USA. **10.** When an executive has to manage people, he will always need human resource management, whatever field he works in.

CHAPTER 16

Application

Lesen Sie sich die folgenden Aussagen aufmerksam durch und entscheiden Sie, welche wahr und welche falsch sind. Korrigieren Sie die falschen Aussagen.

1. The MBA is the only Master's degree which exists in the field of management education in the USA.
2. The MBA always concentrates on specific areas of management or careers.
3. In 1989, 55,000 more MBAs graduated than in 1968.
4. In the USA alone, more than 700 colleges and universities offer MBA programmes.
5. The executive MBA programme is designed for students reluctant or unable to give up their job.
6. A company will always sponsor a student with several years of career experience.
7. Nearly 500 MBA programmes now exist in Europe.
8. Some non-US programmes have a very good reputation.
9. The AACSB offers one of the best MBA programmes in the USA.
10. It is essential for the would-be graduate student to make the right choice.

DO!

Conform to company values in matters of dress:
- *in banking and finance, be unobtrusive* (diskret)
- *in marketing and sales, more extravagance is tolerated or even recommended.*

KAPITEL 16

Wahr oder falsch?

1. *Falsch:* Many Master's degrees exist in this field.
2. *Falsch:* On the contrary, it is a generalist business course.
3. *Wahr.*
4. *Wahr.*
5. *Falsch:* It is designed for middle managers. Students reluctant or unable to give up their job can do a part-time MBA.
6. *Falsch:* A company may sponsor a middle manager.
7. *Falsch:* Nearly 500 exist outside of the US.
8. *Wahr.*
9. *Falsch:* The AACSB is an accrediting agency for degrees in business administration.
10. *Wahr.*

DON'T!

Don't serve tea, coffee, coke or alcohol, to a Mormon. He (or She) considers them all as intoxicating drinks.

CHAPTER 17

Studying in the USA

Susan has been at Texas A&M University for barely a month. She's having lunch at a Mexican restaurant with two fellow graduate students, Glenn and Wade.

1. **Glenn:** *(As they sit down)* Hey Susan, what did you get?

2. **Susan:** 'Chili con carne'. It's my favourite Mexican dish.

3. **Glenn:** You should've gone for the special like us: two beef 'enchiladas', with rice and refried beans. It's a good deal! **(1) (2) (3)**

4. **Wade:** Yeah, Susan. You've got a lot to learn. You should try the 'fajitas', too. They're great! **(4)**

5. **Glenn:** When you're a student, you've got to eat cheap. We often go to the Chinese joint and have the buffet. **(5) (6)**

6. **Susan:** The buffet? Sounds more French to me.

7. **Glenn:** It just means you pay a fixed price and eat as much as you want. Boy, you can really pig out! **(7)**

8. **Wade:** Have you heard that expression, Susan?

9. **Susan:** No, but I can guess what it means! Are you both paying for your own studies?

10. **Wade:** You bet we are! Why Susan, aren't you?

KAPITEL 17

Studium in den Vereinigten Staaten

Susan ist seit knapp einem Monat an der Texas A&M Universität. Sie ißt in einem mexikanischen Restaurant mit Glenn und Wade, zwei Kommilitonen aus dem Aufbaustudium, zu Mittag.

1. **Glenn:** *(Beim Hinsetzen)* He, Susan. Was hast du dir geholt?
2. **Susan:** 'Chili con Carne'. Das ist mein mexikanisches Lieblingsgericht.
3. **Glenn:** Du hättest wie wir das Tagesgericht nehmen sollen: Zwei Rindfleisch-'Enchiladas' mit Reis und gebackenen Bohnen. Das ist 'ne tolle Sache!
4. **Wade:** Ja, Susan. Du mußt noch viel lernen. Du solltest auch die 'Fajitas' probieren. Die sind super!
5. **Glenn:** Als Student mußt du billig essen. Wir gehen oft zum Chinesen und essen vom Buffet.
6. **Susan:** Buffet? Das klingt für mich eher französisch.
7. **Glenn:** Es bedeutet lediglich, daß du einen festen Preis bezahlst und so viel ißt, wie du willst. Mensch, da kann man sich wirklich vollstopfen!
8. **Wade:** Hast du diesen Ausdruck schon gehört, Susan?
9. **Susan:** Nein, aber ich kann erraten, was er bedeutet! Bezahlt ihr beide für euer Studium?
10. **Wade:** Da kannst du drauf wetten! Warum, Susan, du nicht?

ANMERKUNGEN

(1) **special** oder *today's special* ist das Tagesgericht in einem Restaurant, das in der Regel preiswerter ist als die anderen Gerichte.
(2) **'enchilada':** Ein mit Chili gewürztes Gericht der mexikanischen Küche.
(3) **refried beans:** Eine sehr beliebte Beilage der mexikanischen Küche. Die roten Bohnen werden so lange gekocht, bis eine Art Teig entsteht, der anschließend in der Pfanne gebraten *(refried)* wird.
(4) In der mexikanischen Küche sind **'fajitas'** geschnetzelte Fleischstücke (vom Huhn, Rind,...), die auf dem Grill gebraten werden.
(5) **joint** ist ein umgangssprachlicher Ausdruck für ein billiges Restaurant, eine Kneipe o.ä.
(6) Das **buffet** ist besonders in den amerikanischen Restaurants sehr beliebt. Alle Speisen sind auf einem großen Tisch oder einer Theke angeordnet und der Gast bedient sich selbst. Meistens kann man zu einem festen Preis so viel essen, wie man möchte, und sich beliebig oft einen Nachschlag nehmen.
(7) Der Slang-Ausdruck **to pig out** bedeutet "sich vollstopfen", "sich (wie ein Schwein) vollfressen".

CHAPTER 17

11. **Susan:** Actually, no. My MBA is sponsored – part time – by the company I work for. United Chocolate. **(8)**

12. **Glenn:** You don't say! Hey, y'hear that, Wade? When I think that I worked three years for a bank before coming to do an MS in Finance and those guys didn't give me a cent! **(9)**

13. **Wade:** Me neither. I was working for an advertising outfit up in Fort Worth. All the same, having worked for two years, I'm not quite as broke as I was doing my BBA. I was in a really expensive college up in Dallas, too. At least I don't have to work any more, to pay my way through graduate school. **(10) (11)**

14. **Susan:** What's a BBA?

15. **Wade:** It's a bachelor's degree with a major in business administration. That gives me some credits for my MBA. So I get waivers on certain subjects and I don't have to do so many semester hours. My minor was in Spanish incidentally. **(12) (13) (14) (15)**

16. **Susan:** Do most students work to pay for their studies in the USA?

17. **Glenn:** How else are you going to pay for them? Texas A&M isn't an expensive school, but most undergraduates have to work. Christie, my girlfriend, she works in a honky-tonk, most nights. **(16)**

18. **Susan:** A honky-tonk?

KAPITEL 17

11. **Susan:** Eigentlich nicht. Mein MBA auf Teilzeitbasis wird von der Firma gesponsert, für die ich arbeite. United Chocolate.

12. **Glenn:** Sag bloß! He, hast du das gehört, Wade? Wenn ich bedenke, daß ich drei Jahre lang für 'ne Bank gearbeitet habe, bevor ich meinen Magister in Finanzwesen gemacht habe und diese Kerle haben mir nicht einen Pfennig gegeben!

13. **Wade:** Mir auch nicht. Ich habe für so einen Werbeladen oben in Fort Worth gearbeitet. Jedenfalls bin ich, da ich zwei Jahre gearbeitet habe, nicht so abgebrannt wie zu der Zeit, als ich mein BBA [Diplom in Betriebswirtschaft] gemacht habe. Ich war auch an einer richtig teuren Universität oben in Dallas. Wenigstens muß ich nicht mehr arbeiten, um mein Aufbaustudium zu finanzieren.

14. **Susan:** Was ist ein BBA?

15. **Wade:** Das ist ein Diplomabschluß mit Hauptfach Betriebswirtschaft. Dadurch bekomme ich einige Scheine für meinen MBA angerechnet. Ich werde zum Beispiel von bestimmten Kursen freigestellt, und ich muß nicht so viele Semesterwochenstunden absolvieren. Mein Nebenfach war übrigens Spanisch.

16. **Susan:** Arbeiten die meisten Studenten in den USA, um ihr Studium zu finanzieren?

17. **Glenn:** Wie sonst willst du es finanzieren? Die Texas A&M Universität ist keine teure Hochschule, aber die meisten Studenten müssen arbeiten. Christie, meine Freundin, arbeitet meistens nachts in einem "Honky-Tonk".

18. **Susan:** Honky-Tonk?

ANMERKUNGEN (Fortsetzung)

(8) **to sponsor** sagt man, wenn ein Unternehmen die Studiengebühren eines Studenten übernimmt, der während des Studiums oder nach dem Studium in diesem Unternehmen arbeitet.

(9) **MS** ist das amerikanische Äquivalent für *MSc (Master of Science* "Magister einer naturwissenschaftlichen Fakultät").

(10) **outfit** ist ein salopper Ausdruck für "Firma": "Laden, Verein".

(11) **BBA** ist in den USA die Kurzform für *Bachelor of Business Administration* "Diplom in Betriebswirtschaft".

(12) Ein **credit**, "Schein", wird für eine erfolgreich abgelegte Prüfung an der Universität ausgestellt. Er berechtigt zur Teilnahme an weiterführenden Studiengängen.

(13) **waiver:** "Freistellung" von einem Kurs usw.

(14) **semester hour:** Entspricht an amerikanischen Universitäten pro Semester einer Unterrichtsstunde in der Woche.

(15) **minor** "Nebenfach", im Gegensatz zum Hauptfach *(major)*.

(16) **honky-tonk:** In den USA eine Bar, in der man Musik hören und tanzen kann.

CHAPTER 17

19. **Glenn:** Yeah, that's a place where you go to drink beer and dance the Texas two-step! **(17)**

20. **Wade:** Don't you have to pay for your studies in England?

21. **Susan:** Well, actually, your local education authority pays the tuition fees, and then you get a grant to help with your living expenses. **(18) (19)**

22. **Glenn:** Hey, Wade, maybe we ought to have gone to college in England!

23. **Wade:** I don't know. I guess I'd miss the Texas climate. They forecast temperatures of over 100 °F again today. **(20)**

24. **Susan:** I'm sure you'd miss the Mexican restaurants too. You wouldn't find the 'faj...' What did you call them?

25. **Wade:** 'Fajitas'!

KAPITEL 17

19. Glenn: Ja, das ist ein Ort, wo man Bier trinken und den texanischen Twostep tanzen kann!

20. Wade: Müßt ihr in England das Studium nicht bezahlen?

21. Susan: Naja, eigentlich zahlt die kommunale Bildungsbehörde die Studiengebühren, und danach bekommt man eine finanzielle Unterstützung für den Lebensunterhalt.

22. Glenn: He, Wade, vielleicht hätten wir in England auf die Uni gehen sollen!

23. Wade: Ich weiß nicht. Ich denke, ich würde das texanische Klima vermissen. Für heute wurden wieder Temperaturen von über 100° F vorausgesagt.

24. Susan: Ich bin sicher, ihr würdet auch die mexikanischen Restaurants vermissen. Ihr fändet keine 'faj...' Wie habt ihr sie genannt?

25. Wade: 'Fajitas'!

ANMERKUNGEN (Fortsetzung)
- **(17) two-step:** Ein Paartanz zu Country-Musik, der in Texas sehr beliebt ist.
- **(18) local education authority (LEA):** In Großbritannien die lokale Bildungsbehörde, die einer Stadtverwaltung oder einer *county* unterstellt ist und die unter anderem die Stipendien für Studenten verwaltet.
- **(19) grant** kann je nach Kontext ein "Stipendium", eine "Finanzbeihilfe", ein "Zuschuß" oder eine "Subvention" sein.
- **(20) °F** steht für die Temperatureinheit Fahrenheit. 110°F entspricht 37,6°C. 100°C entspricht 212°F.

CHAPTER 17　　　　　　　　　　　　　　　　　　DOCUMENT

Map of Texas

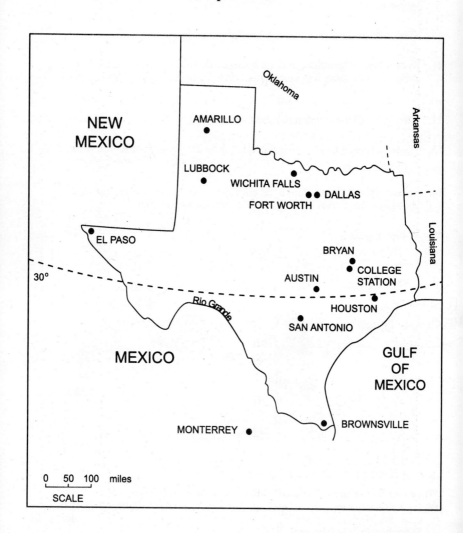

KAPITEL 17

Die Texaner

In jedem Land gibt es eine Region, deren Einwohner in dem Ruf stehen, unter einem Überlegenheitskomplex zu leiden. In den Vereinigten Staaten ist dies ohne Zweifel Texas. Man erzählt sich, daß ein Texaner einmal beim Anblick der Niagara-Fälle gesagt haben soll: *"We've got plumbers in Texas who could fix that for you!"* Tatsächlich ist Texas ein großer Bundesstaat (größer als Deutschland), der bis 1959, als Alaska Teil der Vereinigten Staaten wurde, der größte Staat der USA war. Früher sagte man, wenn man Texas mit dem Auto durchquerte: *"The sun has ris'n and the sun has set and we ain't out of this son of a bitch yet!"*. Man braucht sich nur einmal die unermeßlichen Weiten des texanischen Westens anzusehen, um die Bedeutung des Ausdrucks *big sky* zu verstehen.

Außer der Größe und des wirtschaftlichen Reichtums dieses Bundesstaates hat auch die Geschichte die texanische Persönlichkeit geprägt. Nach der heroischen Erstürmung von Alamo mit der Missionsstation San Antonio durch die Mexikaner unter Santa Ana folgte trotz heftigen Widerstands die Niederlage der Texaner. Den entscheidenden Sieg errang General Sam Houston im Jahr 1836, woraufhin Texas Republik wurde. Die Texaner sind seitdem eifrig bedacht auf diese Unabhängigkeit. Dies symbolisiert vor allem die Bezeichnung ihres Staates, *Lone Star State*.

Der Name Texas entstand ursprünglich aus dem Wort "teysha" *(friend)*. Diese Bezeichnung wurde von den Caddo-Indianern für die spanischen Eroberer benutzt. Aus diesem Wort ging "Tejas" und in der Folge Texas hervor.

CHAPTER 17

EXERCISES

Comprehension

Lesen Sie den Dialog aufmerksam durch. Beantworten Sie dann die nachfolgenden Fragen, und zwar immer in ganzen Sätzen:

1. When did Susan arrive at Texas A&M University? **2.** Glenn and Wade are fellow graduate students. Are they both following the same course as Susan? **3.** Explain what the advantage of the 'special' is. **4.** Explain the system of the 'buffet'. **5.** Say, in your own words, what the expression 'to pig out' means. **6.** Why is Susan not so worried about saving money as Glenn and Wade are? **7.** Explain the advantages to Wade of having done a BBA. **8.** Why do you think Wade no longer has to work to pay for his studies? **9.** Why didn't Susan have to pay for her undergraduate studies? **10.** Why would Wade have been reluctant to go to college in England?

Translation

1. Susan ist seit fast einem Monat in Texas, und sie findet das Klima ein bißchen zu heiß. **2.** Susan hätte das Tagesgericht nehmen sollen; ist es immer preisgünstiger. **3.** Ich habe das Wort 'fajitas' nie gehört, aber ich werde dieses Gericht nächstes Mal probieren. **4.** Mein Lieblingsgericht ist 'Boeuf Bourguignon', aber französische Restaurants sind zu teuer für Studenten. **5.** Ich habe fünf Jahre lang für eine Werbeagentur gearbeitet, aber seit März arbeite ich in einer Bank. **6.** Meine Firma wird mein Studium finanzieren, wenn ich mich damit einverstanden erkläre, acht Jahre für sie zu arbeiten. **7.** Für sein Diplom hatte er als Hauptfach internationale Wirtschaft und als Nebenfach Französisch. **8.** Glenn trinkt gerne Bier und hört gerne Musik, aber er haßt Tanzen. **9.** In England brauchen Studenten ihre Studiengebühren nicht zu bezahlen, und darüber hinaus erhalten sie eine finanzielle Hilfe. **10.** Ich hätte in Texas auf die Universität gehen können, aber möglicherweise hätte mir das englische Klima gefehlt.

KAPITEL 17

LÖSUNGSVORSCHLÄGE

Verständnisübung

1. Susan arrived at Texas A&M University about one month ago. 2. No, they are not. Wade is doing an MBA, but Glenn is doing an MS in finance. 3. The advantage of the 'special' is that you get more food for less money, ie, better value for money. 4. The system of the 'buffet' is that you help yourself to as much as you can eat, all for a fixed price. 5. To 'pig out' means to be like a pig and to eat until you can't eat any more. 6. Because unlike Glenn and Wade, she is having her tuition fees paid by her company. 7. The advantages are that he got some credits for his MBA. He got waivers for some subjects and doesn't have so many semester hours to do. 8. Probably because he has already worked for two years for an advertising agency and has saved some money. 9. Because she went to university in England and her tuition fees were paid by her local education authority. 10. He would have missed the Texas climate and probably the Mexican restaurants, too.

Übersetzungsübung

1. Susan has been in Texas for barely a month, and she is finding the climate a little too hot. 2. Susan should have taken the special; it's always more advantageous. 3. I've never heard the word 'fajitas', but I'll try that dish next time. 4. My favourite dish is 'bœuf bourguignon', but French restaurants are too expensive for students. 5. I worked for an advertising agency for five years, but since March, I've been working in a bank. 6. My company will sponsor my studies if I agree to work for them for eight years. 7. For his bachelor's, he majored in international business and his minor was French. 8. Glenn likes drinking beer and listening to music, but he hates dancing. 9. In England, students don't have to pay their tuition fees and moreover, they are given a grant. 10. I could have gone to university in Texas, but I probably would have missed the English climate.

CHAPTER 17

Application

Sehen Sie sich die Karte von Texas an (Dokument). Lesen Sie sich dann die folgenden Aussagen aufmerksam durch und entscheiden Sie, welche wahr und welche falsch sind. Korrigieren Sie die falschen Aussagen.

1. Texas has frontiers with five other states of the USA.
2. Texas is separated from Mexico by the Rio Grande.
3. The cities of Bryan and College Station are very close together.
4. Texas has no coastline.
5. Fort Worth lies just to the east of Dallas.
6. It's more than 600 miles from Houston to El Paso.
7. Monterrey is in the south of Texas.
8. Brownsville is the most southerly town in Texas.
9. San Antonio is located north of the 30th parallel.
10. Amarillo is a big town in northwest Texas.

 DO!

Pay attention! In the USA, all your purchases are subject to a sales tax of up to 15 % according to the state. Thus, price tags do not correspond to the actual price you pay.

KAPITEL 17

Wahr oder falsch?

1. *Falsch:* Four states only: Louisiana, Arkansas, Oklahoma and New Mexico.
2. *Wahr.*
3. *Wahr.*
4. *Falsch:* It has a coastline in the southeast on the Gulf of Mexico.
5. *Falsch:* It lies just to the west of Dallas.
6. *Wahr.*
7. *Falsch:* Monterrey is in Mexico.
8. *Wahr.*
9. *Falsch:* It's south of the 30th parallel.
10. *Wahr.*

DON'T!

***Don't confuse 'college' (in 'to go to college':
to enter or be in higher education) and high school
(secondary school).***

CHAPTER 18

Studying the market

In compliance with the curriculum of Texas A&M's part-time MBA program, students are required to carry out a major project for a company. Susan has managed to persuade Russ Kingman, United Chocolate Inc's VP, Marketing and Sales, to put her in charge of a market survey for the prospective launch of a new product: a pecan praline bar, aimed at the Hispanic population of the USA. **(1) (2) (3)**

1. **Russ Kingman:** Well, Susan, you'll be in charge of collecting all relevant information to help us make the right decision concerning the launching of the pecan praline chocolate bar we plan to manufacture in our brand new San Antonio plant.

2. **Susan:** Wow! It seems my wildest dreams are coming true! This is the most exciting challenge I've taken up so far.

3. **Russ Kingman:** Mind you, Susan, we're aware of the risks we're taking. You may still be a little soft on the edges... And UC is not at all familiar with the Hispanic market. More than others, Hispanic consumers may be full of surprises. Figuring them out may be awfully tough... UC expects you to design a new method for collecting information, to manage and implement the data-collection process and analyze the results. **(4) (5)**

4. **Susan:** What a program! When would you like me to communicate the findings? **(6)**

5. **Russ Kingman:** The company has agreed to give you a three-month deadline. First, you'll have to define the problem and the research objectives. This step is crucial. Don't hesitate to report to me as often as you feel necessary. You'll be your own boss, but obviously we'll have to work closely together to define the problem and agree on our research objectives. **(7)**

KAPITEL 18

Marktstudien

Als Teil des Lehrplans im Teilzeit-Programm für MBA der Texas A&M Universität müssen die Studenten ein größeres Projekt für eine Firma durchführen. Susan hat es geschafft, Russ Kingman, den Vize-Präsidenten von United Chocolate Inc. von der Abteilung Marketing und Vertrieb, davon zu überzeugen, sie mit einer Marktumfrage für die zukünftige Einführung eines neuen Produkts zu betrauen: ein Schokoriegel mit gebrannten Pecannüssen, dessen Zielkäufergruppe die lateinamerikanische Bevölkerung der USA sein soll.

1. **Russ Kingman:** Gut, Susan, Sie haben die Aufgabe, alle wichtigen Informationen zu sammeln, die uns helfen, die richtige Entscheidung hinsichtlich der Einführung des Pekannuß-Schokoriegels zu treffen, den wir in unserem nagelneuen Werk in San Antonio herstellen wollen.

2. **Susan:** Super! Scheinbar werden meine kühnsten Träume wahr! Das ist die aufregendste Herausforderung, die ich bisher angenommen habe.

3. **Russ Kingman:** Aber passen Sie auf, Susan, wir sind uns der Risiken bewußt, die wir eingehen. Ihnen fehlt vielleicht noch ein wenig Erfahrung... Und UC ist überhaupt nicht vertraut mit dem lateinamerikanischen Markt. Bei lateinamerikanischen Konsumenten ist man möglicherweise noch mehr als bei anderen nicht vor Überraschungen sicher. Es könnte furchtbar schwer sein, sie einzuschätzen... UC möchte, daß Sie ein neues Verfahren für das Sammeln von Informationen entwickeln, das Verfahren der Datenerfassung organisieren und umsetzen und die Ergebnisse analysieren.

4. **Susan:** Was für ein Programm! Wann soll ich Ihnen die Ergebnisse mitteilen?

5. **Russ Kingman:** Die Firma hat sich darauf verständigt, Ihnen eine Frist von drei Monaten zu setzen. Zuerst sollen Sie die Fragestellung und die Forschungsziele definieren. Dieser Schritt ist entscheidend. Zögern Sie nicht, mit mir so oft Sie es für nötig halten, darüber zu sprechen. Sie werden Ihr eigener Chef sein, aber es ist klar, daß wir eng zusammenarbeiten müssen, um das Problem zu definieren und uns über unsere Forschungsziele abzustimmen.

ANMERKUNGEN

(1) **VP** ist die Abkürzung für *Vice-President* "Vizepräsident" (siehe Kapitel 27, Dokument.)
(2) **launch, launching (of a product):** "Einführung" eines Produkts. *To launch* "einführen".
(3) **pecan:** Eine Nußart, die im Süden der USA und besonders in Mexiko geerntet und in Louisiana 'pacane' genannt wird. Auch in Deutschland findet man die Pekannnuß seit einigen Jahren im Handel.
(4) **soft on the edges** ist ein salopper Ausdruck für "unerfahren".
(5) **to implement:** "in die Praxis umsetzen", "in der Praxis anwenden".
(6) **findings:** "Resultate, Ergebnisse".
(7) **deadline:** "Termin, Frist". Verwechseln Sie dies nicht mit *delay*: "Verzögerung, Verspätung".

CHAPTER 18

6. **Susan:** That makes sense!

7. **Russ Kingman:** Marketing is a matter of common sense anyway! I would also like your team to do a survey of the existing data, study periodicals, books and all the commercial data that's to be found in Nielsen's Retail Index. And of course, you'll also have to prepare a questionnaire. **(8)**

8. **Susan:** Yes. At Texas A&M, they taught us how to write a good questionnaire. I'll make sure it's carefully developed and tested before using it on a big scale.

9. **Russ Kingman:** Make the wording as simple, direct and unbiased as possible and ask the questions in a logical order. **(9) (10)**

10. **Susan:** I think I will contact consumers by phone. It's the best method for collecting information quickly.

11. **Russ Kingman:** Maybe. But you may find it difficult to reach young people who are seldom at home. Besides, the Hispanics live more often out of doors than we Anglos do. **(11)**

12. **Susan:** Agreed!

13. **Russ Kingman:** And one more recommendation: don't give me too many statistics. Just present the major findings. Is that OK?

14. **Susan:** Yes. There was just one last point I wanted to make... In the words of the immortal David Ogilvy, many managers 'use research as a drunkard uses a lamppost, not for illumination but for support...' Are you sure you haven't already made up your mind about the launching of the pecan praline bar whatever the results of the survey? **(12)**

15. **Russ Kingman:** Hell, no! A failure would be too expensive! It would cost me my job for one!

16. **Susan:** Not to mention mine!

KAPITEL 18

6. **Susan:** Das versteht sich von selbst!
7. **Russ Kingman:** Marketing ist sowieso eine Sache des gesunden Menschenverstands! Ich möchte außerdem, daß Ihr Team eine Untersuchung der bestehenden Daten, Fachzeitschriften, Bücher und aller Geschäftsdaten vornimmt, die im Nielsen Retail Index zu finden sind. Und selbstverständlich müssen Sie auch einen Fragebogen ausarbeiten.
8. **Susan:** In Ordnung. An der Texas A&M hat man uns beigebracht, wie man einen guten Fragebogen verfaßt. Ich werde mich vergewissern, daß er sorgfältig ausgearbeitet und getestet wird, bevor wir ihn im großen Umfang einsetzen.
9. **Russ Kingman:** Sorgen Sie dafür, daß die Formulierungen so einfach, direkt und neutral wie möglich sind und stellen Sie die Fragen in einer logischen Reihenfolge.
10. **Susan:** Ich denke, ich werde die Verbraucher telefonisch befragen. Das ist die beste Methode, um schnell Informationen zu sammeln.
11. **Russ Kingman:** Vielleicht. Aber es könnte schwierig werden, junge Leute zu erreichen, die selten zu Hause sind. Außerdem findet das Leben der Lateinamerikaner viel mehr im Freien statt als das der Angloamerikaner.
12. **Susan:** Stimmt!
13. **Russ Kingman:** Und noch ein Rat: Geben Sie mir nicht zu viele Statistiken. Präsentieren Sie nur die wichtigsten Ergebnisse. Ist das in Ordnung?
14. **Susan:** Ja. Da ist noch ein letzter Punkt, den ich ansprechen möchte... Um mit den Worten des unsterblichen David Ogilvy zu sprechen, verwenden viele Manager 'die Forschung wie ein Trinker einen Laternenpfahl: nicht zum Zweck der Erleuchtung, sondern als Stütze...'. Sind Sie sicher, daß Sie nicht schon eine Entscheidung über die Einführung des Pekanschokoriegels getroffen haben, egal, wie die Ergebnisse der Untersuchung ausfallen?
15. **Russ Kingman:** Aber nein! Ein Fehlschlag würde uns zu teuer zu stehen kommen! Zuerst einmal würde es mich meinen Job kosten.
16. **Susan:** Von meinem ganz zu schweigen!

ANMERKUNGEN (Fortsetzung)

(8) **Nielsen´s Retail Index:** Eine Sammlung von Informationen, die auf der Basis regelmäßiger Untersuchungen und Umfragen des Einzelhandels an mehr als 2000 Verkaufsstellen in den USA angelegt wird.

(9) **wording:** "Wortlaut, Formulierung".

(10) **unbiased:** "unvoreingenommen, objektiv, neutral".

(11) **Anglo(s):** Amerikaner angelsächsischer Abstammung.

(12) Der Schotte **David Ogilvy** wurde 1911 geboren und ist der Gründer der Agentur *Ogilvy & Mather*, einer der größten Werbeagenturen der Welt. Er ist auch der Autor des bekannten Werkes *Confessions of an Advertising Man*.

CHAPTER 18   DOCUMENT

Market Research Questionnaire
Below is a copy of the questionnaire which Susan gave to UC's pollsters* for the market study.

Hello, I'm conducting a survey with people who eat chocolate.

Do you eat chocolate bars?   Yes. ❑   No. ❑

Do you prefer   plain chocolate? ❑   milk chocolate? ❑

Offer a sample of the new chocolate bar to the respondent.

Does this product taste good?   poor | 1 | 2 | 3 | 4 | 5 | excellent

Does the filling taste good? | 1 | 2 | 3 | 4 | 5 |

Does the coating taste good? | 1 | 2 | 3 | 4 | 5 |

Does this product have a long-lasting flavour? | 1 | 2 | 3 | 4 | 5 |

Is there a harmonious balance between the ingredients? | 1 | 2 | 3 | 4 | 5 |

Do you like the consistency of this product?   Yes. ❑   No. ❑

What characteristics apply to this product?

   1. The taste of chocolate:

not strong enough	just right	too strong
❑	❑	❑

   2. Fat content:

not enough	just right	too much
❑	❑	❑

   3. Sugar content:

not enough	just right	too much
❑	❑	❑

   4. Crispness:

not enough	just right	too much
❑	❑	❑

   5. Softness:

not enough	just right	too much
❑	❑	❑

   6. This product melts in your mouth

too slowly	at the right speed	too fast
❑	❑	❑

Thank you very much for your cooperation. Have a nice day!

---

* **Meinungsforscher(in)**

KAPITEL 18

Die Euphemismen

In den USA sind Euphemismen *(euphemism)*, sprachliche Abschwächungen für zu harte oder schockierende Ausdrücke, heute zu einem wesentlichen Bestandteil des Konzepts der *political correctness (PC)* geworden. Sie haben zum Ziel, rassistische und diskriminierende Bezeichnungen oder Schimpfworte aus dem täglichen Vokabular zu verbannen. Ein Schwarzer wird deshalb als *Afro-American* bezeichnet, ein Indianer als *native American* und statt *chairman* sagt man im Interesse der Gleichberechtigung *chairperson* (fast könnte man so weit gehen, *herstory* statt *history* zu sagen) und eine Person von kleinem Wuchs wird als *vertically challenged person* bezeichnet.

Kritiker bemängeln, daß die PC-Bewegung eine völlig falsch verstandene Gleichmacherei betreibt. Während die Amerikaner einerseits den *self-made man* bewundern, ergreifen sie freimütig Partei für jeden Unterprivilegierten und Unterlegenen *(underdog)*, der von einem Stärkeren *(bully)* schikaniert wird. George Orwell bezeichnete die *political correctness* als neue Sprache *(newspeak)*, die sich durch einen Mangel an Humor auszeichnet.

CHAPTER 18

EXERCISES

Comprehension 🔲

Lesen Sie den Dialog aufmerksam durch. Beantworten Sie dann die nachfolgenden Fragen, und zwar immer in ganzen Sätzen:

1. What is Susan's assignment? **2.** Why is UC running risks by appointing Susan head of the market research team? **3.** What difficulties is the market research team likely to encounter? **4.** What are the different steps in the market survey? **5.** Why should Susan work closely together with Russ Kingman? **6.** According to Russ Kingman, what quality should marketers value? **7.** What desk research work will Susan have to carry out? **8.** Why is the preparation of a questionnaire a difficult task? **9.** In what way do Hispanics differ from Anglos? **10.** Why does Susan have misgivings about the survey?

Vocabulary

Vervollständigen Sie die folgenden Sätze:

1. M...... r...... is the collection, analysis and interpretation of data for guiding marketing decisions. **2.** I'm glad our company has finally realized that the l...... of a new product, without previously studying the market, is most hazardous. **3.** The most common instrument for data collection is the q...... **4.** A researcher who must gather research information quickly is most likely to use the t...... **5.** A c...... is a person who buys goods or services to satisfy his needs. **6.** The major f...... of the market study were taken into account by the marketing department. **7.** A product d...... 5 years ago is now very often obsolete. **8.** Many new products f...... in the market place and new production techniques are often resisted by organized labor. **9.** Different w...... might make the meaning of your letter clearer. **10.** Marketing people are in the business of m...... the needs of other people. 'Find a need and fill it' is the maxim.

🔲 *DO!*

Get down to business straight away. The French are known for their love of broad generalizations and abstraction. Stick to the point you are in the process of negotiating.

KAPITEL 18

LÖSUNGSVORSCHLÄGE

Verständnisübung

1. Susan will be in charge of carrying out a market survey for the prospective launch of UC's new product, a pecan praline bar aimed at the Hispanic population. **2.** Susan somewhat lacks experience. She still has to show her ability. **3.** UC is not at all familiar with the Hispanic market which may prove to be full of surprises. **4.** The different steps are as follows: first, a definition of the problem, then a survey of the existing data, field-research with a questionnaire, the interpretation of responses and finally a presentation of the findings. **5.** He wants to make sure Susan will not divert her attention from the research objectives. **6.** According to him, common sense is very important. **7.** She will have to do a survey of existing data, study periodicals, books and also Nielsen's Retail Index. **8.** Because a good questionnaire must be carefully developed: the wording of the questions must be simple and clear, and the questions must appear in a logical order. **9.** Hispanics are more often away from home than Anglos. **10.** She wonders if her research is not just an alibi and if Russ Kingman has not already made up his mind about the launching of the new product.

Lösungen der Wortschatzübung

1. marketing research. **2.** launching. **3.** questionnaire. **4.** telephone. **5.** consumer. **6.** findings. **7.** designed (*or* developed). **8.** fail. **9.** wording. **10.** meeting.

DON'T!

*Don't arrive late at an appointment.
Instead of having a ready run of plausible excuses
(traffic jams, etc.), turn up on time.*

CHAPTER 18

Application

Kreuzen Sie bei jeder Frage oder Aussage die richtige Antwort bzw. die richtigen Antworten an:

1. What helps a manager make sound business decisions?
    a. a sense of leadership
    b. pertinent information
    c. an MBA from Harvard Business School

2. What should marketing research do?
    a. forecast the future
    b. determine consumer behaviour in the future
    c. reduce the risk of error in the launching of new products

3. How can marketing research costs be reduced?
    a. by studying existing documents
    b. by commissioning business students to do it
    c. by contacting a smaller sample of consumers

4. When there are too many products of the same kind on the market, we can say it has reached:
    a. boiling point
    b. starting point
    c. saturation point

5. Which of the following survey techniques offers the greatest advantages in terms of speed of data collection?
    a. telephone interviews
    b. mail interviews
    c. personal interviews

KAPITEL 18

6. Personal interviews, telephone interviews and mail questionnaires are part of:
    a. field research
    b. desk research
    c. academic research

7. Which of the following data-collection techniques are the most costly?
    a. mail questionnaires
    b. personal interviews
    c. telephone interviews

8. To be effective, the questions of a questionnaire must be:
    a. biased and precise
    b. long and detailed
    c. short and simple

9. When he or she analyzes the research information, the researcher:
    a. divides the respondents into age-groups
    b. treats them as a whole group
    c. divides them into identifiable groups

10. When a firm decides to carry out a market survey, it is in its interest to hire highly-skilled:
    a. investors
    b. investigators
    c. informers

Lösungen
1. b. 2. c. 3. a, b *und* c. 4. c. 5. a. 6. a. 7. b. 8. c. 9. a *und* c. 10. b.

CHAPTER 19

From theory to practice

Mary-Ann, a friendly anthropology student from Australia, is sitting next to Susan in the library. She starts chatting with her.

1. **Mary-Ann:** Susan, we've been working for hours! We've become workaholics! **(1)**

2. **Susan:** Really! I haven't seen the time go by. American libraries are so pleasant to work in that I don't even feel I'm working. They are open every day until midnight, access to books is unrestricted...

3. **Mary-Ann:** Don't you think it's time for a cuppa and a smoke-O? **(2) (3)**

4. **Susan:** I don't smoke, but I could do with a cup of tea!

5. **Mary-Ann:** As a matter of fact, it will have to be a cup of iced tea. Have you forgotten that this is Texas, not Mother England?

6. **Susan:** You're right. I will end up believing I'm overworked.

   In the cafeteria.

7. **Mary-Ann:** Are you satisfied with the progress of your report, Susan?

8. **Susan:** Yes. I'm really doing good work with my portable computer.

9. **Mary-Ann:** You're really into computers, aren't you? **(4)**

10. **Susan:** My portable computer's possibilities are simply fantastic! It's amazing how quickly it can capture, store and retrieve masses of information. I especially appreciate it because it performs tedious, repetitive tasks...

11. **Mary-Ann:** ... that you wouldn't want to do!

KAPITEL 19

Von der Theorie zur Praxis

Mary-Ann, eine sympathische Anthropologiestudentin aus Australien, sitzt in der Bibliothek neben Susan. Sie beginnt, sich mit ihr zu unterhalten.

1. **Mary-Ann:** Susan, wir arbeiten seit Stunden! Wir sind zu 'Workaholics' geworden!
2. **Susan:** Stimmt! Ich habe gar nicht gemerkt, wie die Zeit vergangen ist. In amerikanischen Bibliotheken arbeitet man so angenehm, daß man gar nicht merkt, daß man arbeitet. Sie sind jeden Tag bis Mitternacht geöffnet, es gibt uneingeschränkten Zugang zu den Büchern...
3. **Mary-Ann:** Denkst du nicht, daß es Zeit für eine Kaffee- und Zigarettenpause ist?
4. **Susan:** Ich rauche nicht, aber ich könnte eine Tasse Tee vertragen!
5. **Mary-Ann:** Es wird wohl eine Tasse Eistee sein müssen. Hast du vergessen, daß dies Texas ist und nicht dein Heimatland England?
6. **Susan:** Du hast recht. Irgendwann glaube ich doch noch, daß ich überarbeitet bin.

In der Cafeteria.

7. **Mary-Ann:** Kommst du mit deinem Bericht gut voran, Susan?
8. **Susan:** Ja. Ich leiste wirklich gute Arbeit mit meinem tragbaren Computer.
9. **Mary-Ann:** Du bist ein richtiger Computerfreak, nicht wahr?
10. **Susan:** Die Möglichkeiten meines tragbaren Computers sind wirklich phantastisch! Es ist erstaunlich, wie schnell er Massen von Daten erfassen, speichern und abrufen kann. Ich schätze ihn besonders, weil er mühsame und wiederkehrende Aufgaben ausführt...
11. **Mary-Ann:** ... die du nicht würdest machen wollen!

ANMERKUNGEN

(1) workaholic ist ein amerikanischer Neologismus, der in Anlehnung an das Wort *alcoholic* diejenigen Personen bezeichnet, die ohne Arbeit nicht leben können, also arbeitssüchtig sind. Nach dem gleichen Schema sind die Begriffe *computaholic* (Dialog, Satz 23) und *chocoholic* entstanden.

(2) cuppa ist ein salopper Ausdruck, der oft in Australien und England für *cup of...* benutzt wird.

(3) smoke-O (oder **smoko**): Auch diese phonetische Kreation stammt aus Australien und bezeichnet die Arbeitspausen, die etwa die Dauer einer Zigarettenlänge haben.

(4) to be into something: Umgangssprachliche Version von "sich einer Sache eingehend widmen, begeistert von etwas sein, sich mit etwas auskennen".

CHAPTER 19

12. Susan: That goes without saying! You know, my computer is so good at crunching numbers. I collected a lot of data and kept them in a data base. Then I analyzed all the information using the statistics and models available. When I think I was such a poor mathematics student, I have a big laugh. **(5)**

13. Mary-Ann: So, you used your computer to process your questionnaires?

14. Susan: All the time.

15. Mary-Ann: I can very well picture you toying with spreadsheets, printing nice colored pie-charts and bar-graphs... **(6) (7) (8)**

16. Susan: Don't assume I'm getting carried away. I have no time for that. Besides, Russ, my boss, warned me against too many statistics. 'Stick to the major findings!' is the watchword. **(9) (10)**

17. Mary-Ann: How did you organize your work?

18. Susan: First, I had to define the problem and set my research objective. Then I figured out a plan for collecting data from primary and secondary sources. Afterwards, I managed to collect, process and analyze the information. **(11) (12)**

19. Mary-Ann: In other words, all you have to do now is write 'The End' on your report.

20. Susan: No. I still have to interpret and report the findings, but of course, my brainless computer cannot do it for me!

KAPITEL 19

12. **Susan:** Das versteht sich von selbst! Weißt du, mein Computer ist so gut in der Verarbeitung von Zahlen. Ich habe eine Menge Daten gesammelt und sie in einer Datenbank gespeichert. Dann habe ich alle Informationen unter Verwendung der verfügbaren Statistiken und Modelle analysiert. Wenn ich bedenke, daß ich in Mathematik so eine schlechte Schülerin war, kann ich nur lachen.

13. **Mary-Ann:** Also hast du deinen Computer benutzt, um deine Fragebögen zu bearbeiten?

14. **Susan:** Die ganze Zeit.

15. **Mary-Ann:** Ich kann dich mir sehr gut vorstellen, wie du mit Rechentabellen spielst und hübsche, farbige Tortendiagramme und Balkengrafiken druckst...

16. **Susan:** Glaub nicht, daß ich da nicht zu bremsen bin. Ich habe keine Zeit für so was. Außerdem hat mich Russ, mein Chef, vor zu vielen Statistiken gewarnt. Die Parole lautet: 'Halte dich an die wichtigsten Ergebnisse!'.

17. **Mary-Ann:** Wie hast du deine Arbeit organisiert?

18. **Susan:** Zuerst mußte ich die Fragestellung definieren und meine Forschungsziele abstecken. Dann habe ich einen Plan entworfen, um Daten aus Primär- und Sekundärquellen zu sammeln. Danach konnte ich die Informationen erfassen, verarbeiten und analysieren.

19. **Mary-Ann:** Mit anderen Worten: Alles, was du jetzt noch tun mußt, ist 'Ende' unter deinen Bericht zu schreiben.

20. **Susan:** Nein, ich muß die Ergebnisse noch interpretieren und über sie berichten, aber das kann mein hirnloser Computer natürlich nicht für mich machen!

ANMERKUNGEN (Fortsetzung)

(5) **to crunch numbers:** "Berechnungen anstellen; Zahlen knacken". *crunch* heißt eigentlich "zerfressen, knacken, zerbeißen".

(6) **spreadsheet** ist eine Rechentabelle bzw. ein Rechenblatt, wörtlich: ausgebreitetes Blatt. Für Berechnungen auf einem Computer gibt es spezielle Tabellenkalkulationsprogramme, die *spreadsheet programs* genannt werden.

(7) **pie-chart:** Eine grafische Darstellungsform für statistische Daten, die wie eine in verschieden große Stücke geschnittene Torte *(pie)* aussieht.

(8) **bar-graph** ist eine andere Form der Darstellung für statistische Daten, bei der einzelne Balken verschiedener Länge nebeneinander angeordnet sind.

(9) **to get carried away:** "sich von etwas begeistern bzw. mitreißen lassen".

(10) **to stick to something:** "sich an etwas halten, bei etwas bleiben, etwas treubleiben".

(11) **primary sources:** Primärquellen sind Quellen, bei denen Informationen unmittelbar aus erster Hand stammen bzw. direkt an Ort und Stelle des Geschehens gesammelt wurden.

(12) **secondary sources:** Als Sekundärquellen gelten Bücher und andere gedruckte Dokumentationen; *secondary literature* "Sekundärliteratur".

CHAPTER 19 📼

21. Mary-Ann: Nevertheless, you can't live without your laptop, mate! **(13) (14)**

22. Susan: It's so convenient that it's a pleasure to work with it. It's hardly bigger than a note-pad and I can take it anywhere. I use it in the library, on the train, at home…

23. Mary-Ann: Just what I was thinking! You've become a computaholic. Soon, you won't be able to distinguish between work and leisure.

24. Susan: Never fear!

KAPITEL 19

21. **Mary-Ann:** Trotzdem kannst du nicht ohne dein Laptop leben, meine Liebe!
22. **Susan:** Es ist so bequem, daß es ein Vergnügen ist, damit zu arbeiten. Es ist kaum größer als ein Notizblock, und ich kann es überall mit hinnehmen. Ich kann es in der Bibliothek, im Zug oder zu Hause benutzen...
23. **Mary-Ann:** Genau was ich gedacht habe! Du bist computersüchtig geworden. Bald wirst du nicht mehr in der Lage sein, zwischen Arbeit und Freizeit zu unterscheiden.
24. **Susan:** Keine Bange!

ANMERKUNGEN (Fortsetzung)

(13) laptop: Ein kleiner tragbarer Computer, der meistens wie ein Aktenkoffer aufgeklappt werden kann, wobei sich dann im unteren Teil Tastatur und Systemeinheit und im oberen Teil der Bildschirm befinden. Der Wortbestandteil *lap* "Schoß" impliziert, daß man ihn wie einen Notizblock auf die Oberschenkel legen kann. Das Gegenteil dazu ist der *desktop computer*, der größer ist, meistens aus mehreren Komponenten besteht und auf einem Schreibtisch aufgestellt werden muß.

(14) mate ist ein häufig von den Australiern verwendeter, salopper Ausdruck und bedeutet in etwa "Freund(in), Kamerad(in), Kumpel".

CHAPTER 19   DOCUMENT

Computers in our lives

There is no denying that today, computer science plays a major part in corporate life. Computers are widely used in business management. Thus, accounting, invoicing and pay calculation could not be done without them. Likewise, they have proved to be indispensable in production management, financial management (especially connections with banks) and bureautics (word-processing, internal and external communications).

However, computers do not benefit companies exclusively. They have also revolutionized education (computer-assisted education) by introducing a lot of flexibility. Thus, learners may work at their own pace, which is impossible in a traditional classroom. Moreover, students have the possibility to check their progress.

Computer science has altered employees' life by taking care of repetitive or tedious tasks and by making communications much faster. In no time, managers can know the results and check the evolution of the company. Computers also ensure dynamic interaction between the different departments of the company so that decision-makers may react more quickly.

Computer science keeps evolving towards more miniaturization (portable computers), more power, more speed, stronger integration (one single machine may serve as a telephone, fax machine, videotex, minitel, photocopying machine and computer) and easier use (new models are said to be 'user-friendly'). As a consequence, companies have started recruiting generalists with computer skills and a feel for human relationships rather than just computer-science specialists.

Today, it is becoming possible to work on top of a mountain, in your car, at home, just anywhere...

KAPITEL 19

 Die Tortendiagramme

Die grafische Darstellungsform *pie-chart* wird originalgetreu im Deutschen mit "Tortendiagramm" wiedergegeben. Die Amerikaner verbinden mit dieser Grafik ein typisch amerikanisches Dessert: den Apfelkuchen. Der Ausdruck *'as American as Mom's apple pie'* reflektiert gut die Vorliebe der Amerikaner für Apfelkuchen. Im ganzen Land wird der Apfel als eine überaus sympatische und typisch amerikanische Frucht angesehen. Die Stadt New York trägt beispielsweise den Beinamen *the Big Apple* und ein bekannter Computerhersteller hat sich sogar nach dem Apfel benannt...

CHAPTER 19

EXERCISES

Comprehension

Lesen Sie den Dialog aufmerksam durch. Beantworten Sie dann die nachfolgenden Fragen, und zwar immer in ganzen Sätzen:

1. Why does Susan like working in American libraries? **2.** What shows that Mary-Ann is not so hard-working as Susan? **3.** Why has Susan made so much progress with her report? **4.** In what way did Susan's computer help her in the drafting of her report? **5.** How did Susan cope with the tedious parts of her study? **6.** What makes Susan laugh? **7.** What wrong assumption does Mary-Ann make? **8.** What approach did Russ recommend to Susan? **9.** What advantages does a laptop present? **10.** According to Mary-Ann, what risks do computer-users run?

Vocabulary

Vervollständigen Sie die Sätze, indem Sie jeweils das passende Wort aus der untenstehenden Liste einfügen. Jedes Wort kann nur einmal verwendet werden.

fast, automatic indexing, word-processor, store, check, records, information, file management, production, productivity, printer, computer science

Computers are more and more used because they are efficient and **(1.)**. Firms have invested a lot in automated **(2.)** systems. For instance, a company uses computers to **(3.)** and retrieve customers' files. The **(4.)** manager uses them to **(5.)** the stocks. The personnel manager uses them to keep **(6.)** of the employees. No doubt they have contributed to better **(7.)**.
Hardware and software are unsophisticated terms designating different aspects of **(8.)**. Hardware refers to **(9.)** and **(10.)** for instance whereas software refers to **(11.)** and **(12.)**.

KAPITEL 19

LÖSUNGSVORSCHLÄGE

Verständnisübung

1. She likes working in American libraries because they are pleasant, they have long opening hours and they offer a lot of freedom. **2.** She feels like taking a break. **3.** She has made so much progress because she has used her portable computer very efficiently. **4.** It captured, stored and retrieved the mass of information she had collected. **5.** The computer helped her by performing tedious, repetitive tasks like crunching numbers, calculating statistics, etc. **6.** She laughs at the thought that she was bad at mathematics. **7.** She assumes that Susan is wasting time playing with her computer. **8.** He told Susan to stick to the main findings and not to use too many statistics. **9.** A laptop is very convenient because it is small and it can be used practically anywhere. **10.** A computer user runs the risk of no longer being able to distinguish between work and leisure.

Lösung der Wortschatzübung

1. fast **2.** information **3.** store **4.** production **5.** check **6.** records **7.** productivity **8.** computer science **9.** word-processors **10.** printers **11.** automatic indexing **12.** file management

CHAPTER 19

Application

Sehen Sie sich die untenstehende Abbildung an. Schreiben Sie dann hinter jedes Wort in der Liste die Nummer des dazugehörigen Gegenstandes.

pie-chart
keyboard
diskette
plug
screen
bar-chart
stationery
disk-drive
printer
switch

KAPITEL 19

Lösungen

1. bar-chart
2. pie-chart
3. screen
4. disk-drive
5. plug
6. diskette
7. printer
8. stationery
9. switch
10. keyboard

DO!

Quick deals entail many drawbacks. It is easy to make mistakes that you will regret. Thus, be well prepared when you negotiate with Americans (or anybody else, for that matter). Improvisation is too costly.

DON'T!

Don't get worried if you negotiate with a time-hustled American executive. Americans are impressed by people who are in a hurry. In the USA, success is synonymous with pace. To have little to do is considered a symptom of failure.

CHAPTER 20

Cultural differences

On Saturday afternoon, Susan went to watch the baseball game between UC's team and Comput'X, another corporate team from San Antonio. She sat next to Jaime Maldonado, who works as a foreman in the company.

1. **Jaime:** Do you enjoy watching baseball, Susan?

2. **Susan:** You bet! Besides, it's a good introduction to US culture. **(1)**

3. **Jaime:** And of course, this game reminds you of cricket.

4. **Susan:** 'Cricket with an American accent', as someone said.

5. **Jaime:** And what do you think of corporate life with an American accent?

6. **Susan:** I'm getting used to it, as you must have done in your time. I understand you emigrated from Ecuador ten years ago. **(2)**

7. **Jaime:** Oh, yes! I remember... I didn't speak much English then. And I found it hard to adjust to the American way of life at the beginning.

8. **Susan:** Yet Americans are quite informal and hospitable. I find them very helpful.

9. **Jaime:** They were hospitable to me all right, but they soon disappeared, leaving me on my own.

10. **Susan:** *(Smiling)* I see. You expected them to take you by the hand.

11. **Jaime:** In a way. And I found it hard to adjust to the fast pace of life.

12. **Susan:** I feel Americans work fast in a relaxed way. *(A short pause)* What else did you find hard to adjust to?

KAPITEL 20

Kulturelle Unterschiede

Am Samstag nachmittag sah Susan sich das Baseball-Spiel zwischen dem Team von UC und Comput'X, einer anderen Firmenmannschaft aus San Antonio, an. Sie saß neben Jaime Maldonado, der als Vorarbeiter in der Firma arbeitet.

1. **Jaime:** Sehen Sie sich gerne Baseball an, Susan?

2. **Susan:** Aber sicher! Und es ist eine gute Einführung in die US-amerikanische Kultur.

3. **Jaime:** Und natürlich erinnert Sie dieses Spiel an Cricket.

4. **Susan:** 'Cricket mit einem amerikanischen Akzent', wie jemand sagte.

5. **Jaime:** Und was denken Sie vom Leben in einem Unternehmen mit amerikanischem Akzent?

6. **Susan:** Ich gewöhne mich daran, wie Sie es zu Ihrer Zeit getan haben müssen. Ich habe gehört, daß Sie vor zehn Jahren aus Ecuador eingewandert sind.

7. **Jaime:** Oh, ja! Ich erinnere mich... ich habe zu dieser Zeit nicht viel Englisch gesprochen. Und ich fand es am Anfang schwer, mich an die amerikanische Lebensweise zu gewöhnen.

8. **Susan:** Und dabei sind die Amerikaner ziemlich locker und gastfreundlich. Ich finde sie sehr hilfsbereit.

9. **Jaime:** Sie waren wohl gastfreundlich zu mir, aber sie verschwanden bald und ließen mich allein.

10. **Susan:** *(Lächelt)* Ich verstehe. Sie haben erwartet, daß sie Sie an die Hand nehmen.

11. **Jaime:** In gewisser Weise. Und ich fand es schwer, mich an den schnellen Lebensrhythmus zu gewöhnen.

12. **Susan:** Ich finde, Amerikaner arbeiten auf eine entspannte Art schnell. *(Kurze Pause)* An was konnten Sie sich noch schwer anpassen?

ANMERKUNGEN

(1) **to bet** "wetten", *You bet!* "Aber sicher!, Darauf kannst du wetten!".
(2) **to get used to doing something** "sich an etwas gewöhnen". Nicht zu verwechseln mit dem Verb *used to* + Infinitiv, das man benutzt, wenn von etwas die Rede ist, das man in der Vergangenheit zu tun pflegte, jetzt jedoch nicht mehr tut. Beispiel: *I used to smoke (but I don't any more)* = "Früher habe ich geraucht (aber ich rauche nicht mehr)".

CHAPTER 20

13. **Jaime:** *(Smiling)* What I found hardest to learn was not to trifle with schedules and deadlines. **(3) (4)**

14. **Susan:** Indeed. Here, you soon learn that time is money.

15. **Jaime:** And Americans don't waste time with small talk. They go straight to the point. **(5)**

16. **Susan:** To be sure, here, there's no beating about the bush, whereas in Spanish-speaking countries, people seem to be tolerant of many different things happening at once. I don't think they object to being interrupted by telephone calls or people dropping in with questions. **(6)**

17. **Jaime:** Right. In Ecuador, our attitude to time is more flexible because we live much more in the present and whenever it is possible, we avoid being tied down to specific dates in the future. It has taken me quite some time to understand the way of doing things here.

18. **Susan:** You've got to admit that in San Antonio, people are very straightforward. When an outsider doesn't have a clue about something, it is his responsibility to ask for explanations. People will be glad to answer. **(7)**

19. **Jaime:** And what I found very hard to accept at first, was the fact that family and friends hardly ever influence decisions. In South America, people act quite differently... We are Latins...

20. **Susan:** Come to think of it, I realize there is a lot of wisdom in the old saying 'business and friendship don't mix...'. Oh! Look at that! Wow! Johnny has just scored a run for UC. Isn't that wonderful? **(8)**

KAPITEL 20

13. **Jaime:** *(Lächelt)* Am schwierigsten war für mich, nicht nachlässig mit Zeitplänen und Terminen umzugehen.

14. **Susan:** In der Tat. Hier lernt man schnell, daß Zeit Geld ist.

15. **Jaime:** Und die Amerikaner verschwenden keine Zeit mit Small Talk. Sie kommen sofort auf den Punkt.

16. **Susan:** Sicherlich, hier geht man nicht wie die Katze um den heißen Brei herum, während die Menschen in den spanischsprachigen Ländern viel besser akzeptieren können, daß verschiedene Dinge gleichzeitig passieren. Ich denke nicht, daß sie etwas dagegen haben, durch Anrufe oder von Leuten, die plötzlich mit Fragen hereinschneien, unterbrochen zu werden.

17. **Jaime:** Richtig. In Ecuador ist unsere Einstellung zur Zeit flexibler, weil wir viel mehr in der Gegenwart leben, und wenn immer es möglich ist, vermeiden wir es, uns auf bestimmte Termine in der Zukunft festnageln zu lassen. Es hat eine ganze Zeit gedauert, bis ich verstand, wie die Dinge hier laufen.

18. **Susan:** Sie müssen zugeben, daß die Leute in San Antonio sehr direkt sind. Wenn ein Außenseiter keine Ahnung von etwas hat, ist er dafür verantwortlich, nach einer Erklärung zu fragen. Man wird ihm gerne antworten.

19. **Jaime:** Und was für mich anfangs nur schwer zu akzeptieren war, war die Tatsache, daß die Familie und die Freunde fast niemals Entscheidungen beeinflussen. In Südamerika handeln die Leute ganz anders... Wir sind eben Südländer...

20. **Susan:** Wenn ich darüber nachdenke, wird mir klar, daß eine Menge Weisheit in dem Spruch 'Geschäft und Freundschaft soll man nicht vermischen' liegt... Oh! Sehen Sie! He! Johnny hat soeben einen Punkt für UC errungen. Ist das nicht klasse?

ANMERKUNGEN (Fortsetzung)

(3) **trifle:** "Kleinigkeit, Belanglosigkeit". *To trifle with something* "mit etwas spielen, nachlässig mit etwas umgehen".

(4) **schedule:** "Zeitplan, Programm"; auch "Stundenplan, Fahrplan". *To schedule* "planen, ansetzen"; *scheduling* "Planung"; *scheduled flight* "planmäßiger Flug".

(5) **small talk:** "leichte Unterhaltung; über`s Wetter reden". Der Begriff *Small Talk* ist mittlerweile in den deutschen Sprachgebrauch eingegangen.

(6) **to beat about the bush:** "wie die Katze um den heißen Brei herumgehen" = nicht aussprechen, was man wirklich sagen will.

(7) **not to have a clue:** "keine Ahnung von etwas haben". *Clue* "Anhaltpunkt, Schlüssel". *I haven't got a clue* "Ich habe keine Ahnung". *I'll give you a clue* "Ich werde dir einen Anhaltspunkt geben".

(8) **to score a run:** "(beim Baseball oder Cricket) einen Punkt erringen".

CHAPTER 20 DOCUMENT

A student's first impressions of the USA

Susan has kept in touch with Dr Alwyn Hewitt who was her tutor* at the University of Leeds. She sends him a letter to give him an account of her first impressions of corporate life in the USA.

4 B Alamo Apartments
970 Bowie Street
College Station, TX 77843

Dr Alwyn Hewitt
Department of Modern Languages
University of Leeds
LEEDS LS2 9JT

March 8th, 199.

Dear Dr Hewitt,

    I know how eager you are to read my impressions of corporate life in America. Because I still have a lot of work to do on my report, I'll just write you a quick note.

    Well, I remember you always gave me credit for my buoyancy. This is probably why I am so nicely getting used to working in an American company. As a matter of fact, I enjoy corporate life very much and Americans are very kind to me.

    Although I try not to be ethnocentric, ie not to judge them by using English standards, I am tempted to consider that people here get their priorities mixed up. They seem very materialistic, work-oriented and they tend to equate anything new with best.

    I also find them time-motivated and for them, success is synonymous with pace. A waste of time is considered 'un-American'. An interesting comparison between England and America is the contrast between our football (soccer) and their football. In American football, which I don't find as spectacular as our soccer, matches are divided into sessions where every second, including the last one, counts. The play often stops. During the breaks, the players devise a strategy while spectators nervously watch the clock.

    In the USA, there appears to be a real obsession with clocks. 'Rock around the clock', which was the first rock n'roll song, could only have been written by an American...

    Anyway, I feel I'm learning a lot here. For one thing, I'm already making better use of my time and I'm more efficient at work. In my opinion, cultural differences are a resource, not a barrier to overcome.

    I promise to send you a more thorough analysis of my observations in my next letter. I hope you are well and your students don't give you too much trouble.

    Best regards,

    Susan Edwards

---

* Tutor "Tutor": An englischen Universitäten ein Dozent, dessen Aufgabe es ist, eine bestimmte Anzahl von Studenten (seine *tutees*) zu betreuen, um einen reibungslosen Ablauf des Studiums zu gewährleisten. Er kann ein *academic tutor* oder ein *personal tutor* sein. Der *academic tutor* trifft seine Studenten regelmäßig in den *tutorials* (Kurse, an denen nur eine kleine Anzahl von Studenten teilnimmt).

KAPITEL 20

Die Entspanntheit der Amerikaner

Das puritanische Erbe der USA hat der Arbeit einen moralischen Wert *(ethics of work)* verliehen. Aus Pflichtgefühl sich selbst gegenüber bemüht sich jeder Amerikaner, seine eigenen Talente bestmöglich zu entwickeln. Da die Arbeit einen Wert darstellt, ist es wichtig, schnell und gut zu arbeiten und, wenn möglich, gleichzeitig eine gewisse Entspanntheit an den Tag zu legen. Besonders im Vertrieb liegt der Akzent auf dem Lächeln *(the voice with a smile, smile behind the counter, the smile that wins* usw.) Ausdruck der Geringschätzung, die die Amerikaner denjenigen gegenüber empfinden, die sie als Faulpelze betrachten, ist der Ausspruch *'People who don't believe in hard work.'*

CHAPTER 20

EXERCISES

Comprehension

Lesen Sie den Dialog aufmerksam durch. Beantworten Sie dann die nachfolgenden Fragen, und zwar immer in ganzen Sätzen:

1. Why did Susan go and watch the baseball game? **2.** Why should a baseball game not be too 'exotic' for an English person? **3.** What attitude to US corporate life has Susan taken? **4.** What adjustment difficulties did Jaime encounter at the beginning? **5.** According to Susan, how do Americans behave with strangers? **6.** When he arrived in the USA, what did Jaime expect from Americans? **7.** What do Americans value in a worker's performance? **8.** What different South American conception of time does Susan allude to? **9.** How much time do Americans devote to the preliminaries of a negotiation? **10.** What role do family and friends play in American business deals?

Conversational English

Wie antwortet man einer anderen Person in korrekter Weise? In der Geschäftswelt ist es sehr nützlich, wenn man die Ausdrücke kennt, die in informellen Situationen benutzt werden. Suchen Sie für jede im folgenden Abschnitt aufgeführte Aussage und Frage, die in einer Unterhaltung vorkommen könnte, aus dem darunterstehenden Absatz die passende Entgegnung bzw. Antwort.

1. It was very kind of you to invite me to a baseball game. **2.** Would you happen to know Mr Robertson's phone number? **3.** Tomorrow at 8:00 a.m. would suit me fine. **4.** I've decided to take sabbatical leave. **5.** How was the baseball game? **6.** I'm afraid I haven't got the findings yet. **7.** Would you like me to give you a lift to the office? **8.** How is their advertising campaign going? **9.** Do you know San Antonio at all, Susan? **10.** Good luck with your test! **11.** What line of work are you in? **12.** Are they likely to be home at this time of day?

a. Accountancy. **b.** Smart move! **c.** Much better than they expected! **d.** It's very kind of you but I prefer to go on foot. **e.** Not a chance! They'll be working. **f.** No. In fact, this is my first visit. **g.** It's been a pleasure to be with you. **h.** Thank you. I'll need it! **i.** See you tomorrow morning, then! **j.** Never mind! But be sure to give them to me as soon as you have them. **k.** Quite spectacular! **l.** I might have it in my diary.

KAPITEL 20

LÖSUNGSVORSCHLÄGE

Verständnisübung

1. She went and watched the baseball game because she likes this sport, she is loyal to the company's team and she considers baseball is part of American culture. **2.** Baseball was derived from cricket and there are some similarities between these two sports. **3.** She has decided to accept it thoroughly. **4.** At the beginning, he spoke little English and had difficulties coping with the American way of life. **5.** Americans are unaffected, they have a genuine sense of hospitality and they help strangers. **6.** He expected Americans to take him by the hand. **7.** They like a worker to be punctual in his assignments. **8.** In South America, people have a more casual approach to time. Schedules and deadlines are not always met and tasks may be postponed. **9.** Americans devote as little time as possible to preliminaries. **10.** Family and friends exert practically no influence on business decisions.

Lösungen

1. g. **2.** l. **3.** i. **4.** b. **5.** k. **6.** j. **7.** d. **8.** c. **9.** f. **10.** h. **11.** a. **12.** e.

CHAPTER 20

Vocabulary revision (Chapters 11-20)

Vervollständigen Sie die folgenden Sätze (ein oder mehrere Wörter pro Lücke):

1. A (...) strike is an unofficial strike. **2.** The staff (...) in this company is 25%, which means they replace 25% of their staff every year! **3.** I like the (...) of this poster, ie the arrangement of the words and pictures. **4.** (...) enables any skilled computer user to create his own magazine. **5.** A (...) is a person employed specially to discover and remedy the causes of trouble. **6.** This student is currently studying towards an MBA on a (...) basis: his employer has put up money for his studies but he must also carry out some tasks for the company. **7.** As John has already taken some business courses, which he feels would be redundant, he hopes to get a (...) on some subjects. **8.** The (...) for submitting your project is June 1st. After that date, it will no longer be accepted. **9.** Instead of paying attention to the (...) of the market study, the manager was carried away by his enthusiasm and the new product failed. **10.** If you don't want to miss your train, you'd better look at the (...) in the hall of the station.

DO!

Just because Americans work in a relaxed way, don't assume you can be self-indulgent. Dress correctly and wait until they tell you to loosen your tie or take off your jacket.

KAPITEL 20

Lösungen der Wortschatzübung

1. wildcat
2. turnover
3. layout
4. desk-top publishing
5. troubleshooter
6. part-time
7. waiver
8. deadline
9. findings
10. schedule

DON'T!

Don't waste time on preliminaries.
Wasting time is considered un-American.

CHAPTER 21

Modifying the product

Susan meets George Ray McEachern, Director of UC's Research and Development Department, at the San Antonio plant. They discuss his work on the pecan praline bar.

1. **George Ray:** As you remember, Susan, our research team devised five product concepts. Each was tested on five groups of consumers who tasted them under the observation of your market research team. Out of the five concepts, four were discounted. **(1) (2)**

2. **Susan:** Yes. And we all agreed to give the go-ahead to Amigo, the fifth one, because it showed a great deal of potential.

3. **George Ray:** We are currently devoting all our efforts to Amigo...

4. **Susan:** '... a real treat the consumer can indulge in without too much caloric guilt.'

5. **George Ray:** We developed it in our laboratory according to these specifications. Of course, we had to alter the prototype in order to accommodate the requirements of the sensorial evaluation tests. Believe me Susan, we now have a blockbuster! **(3) (4)**

6. **Susan:** I'm pleased to see you so enthusiastic, George Ray. Yet, I'm a little concerned...

7. **George Ray:** You're not going to tell me that you've thought up more modifications!

8. **Susan:** Well, you know, in these times of growing consumer awareness...

9. **George Ray:** Do you think Hispanics worry a lot about consumerism? **(5)**

KAPITEL 21

Produktänderungen

Susan trifft George Ray McEachern, den Direktor der Forschungs- und Entwicklungsabteilung von UC, im Werk von San Antonio. Sie sprechen über seine Arbeit an dem Pekannußriegel.

1. **George Ray:** Wie Sie sich erinnern, Susan, hat unser Forschungsteam fünf Produktkonzepte ausgearbeitet. Jedes wurde an fünf Verbrauchergruppen getestet, die die Produkte unter der Aufsicht Ihres Marktforschungsteams probiert haben. Von den fünf Konzepten sind vier aus dem Rennen.
2. **Susan:** Ja. Und wir haben uns alle darauf verständigt, Amigo, dem fünften Konzept, grünes Licht zu geben, da es eine Menge Potential aufwies.
3. **George Ray:** All unsere Bemühungen konzentrieren sich gegenwärtig auf Amigo...
4. **Susan:** '... ein echter Leckerbissen, mit dem der Verbraucher sich verwöhnen kann, ohne ein schlechtes Gewissen wegen zu vieler Kalorien haben zu müssen.'
5. **George Ray:** Wir haben ihn auf der Grundlage dieser Vorgaben in unserem Labor entwickelt. Natürlich mußten wir den Prototyp ändern, um den Anforderungen der Geschmacksprüfung gerecht zu werden. Glauben Sie mir, Susan, wir haben hier einen Knüller!
6. **Susan:** Es freut mich, Sie so begeistert zu sehen, George Ray. Dennoch bin ich ein bißchen beunruhigt...
7. **George Ray:** Sie wollen mir doch jetzt nicht sagen, daß Sie sich weitere Änderungen ausgedacht haben!
8. **Susan:** Naja, Sie wissen, in diesen Zeiten des wachsenden Käuferbewußtseins...
9. **George Ray:** Denken Sie, die Lateinamerikaner machen sich viele Sorgen um Konsumerismus?

ANMERKUNGEN

(1) **product concept:** "Produktkonzept". Eine Beschreibung der objektiven und subjektiven Eigenschaften, die das Endprodukt aufweisen sollte.

(2) **to discount** stammt eigentlich aus einem kommerziellen Kontext: "diskontieren, Rabatt gewähren"; *discount* "Rabatt, Diskont"; *discount rate* "Diskontsatz".

(3) **sensorial evaluation:** "sensorische Prüfung, Geschmacksprüfung". Hierbei müssen Probanden ein Produkt mittels ihres Geschmackssinns beurteilen.

(4) **blockbuster:** Eigentlich "große Fliegerbombe", im übertragenen Sinn "Knüller, Kassenschlager", also ein Produkt, das außergewöhnlich gut ankommt.

(5) **consumerism:** "Konsumerismus; organisierter Schutz der Verbraucherinteressen". Eine von den Bürgern initiierte Bewegung, die zum Ziel hat, die Rechte der Konsumenten gegenüber den Händlern zu schützen (siehe Kapitel 32, Dokument).

CHAPTER 21

10. **Susan:** It would be a big mistake to underestimate them! They appreciate top-quality natural products too!

11. **George Ray:** Can you think of anything more natural than pecan praline bars? Even if the FDA people came to snoop around here, they could find nothing wrong with Amigo bars. We are using 100 % natural ingredients. **(6) (7)**

12. **Susan:** My point is, studies have shown that the use of cocoa butter instead of vegetable fat in the making of chocolate bars is appreciated by Hispanic consumers.

13. **George Ray:** But we have carried out all our research with vegetable fat and the results are very positive.

14. **Susan:** Yet, vegetable fat is banned in France for instance. Who knows? Some day, the FDA might do the same in this country. The use of cocoa butter could give us an additional edge over our competitors.

15. **George Ray:** It's also more expensive than vegetable fat. Besides, additional research will cost us time and money. When he sees the bill, Ol' Dan Bush, our dear Finance Manager, is gonna wail like Uncle Scrooge after the loss of his first dollar. **(8)**

16. **Susan:** Let him wail!... But believe me, I'm very much against flinging money out of the window. As a matter of fact, I have Scottish ancestors! But I'd rather UC spent a lot of time and money on the front-end stage of the new product process than risked a flop because of insufficient product planning. In today's world, the odds weigh heavily against success. **(9) (10)**

KAPITEL 21

10. **Susan:** Es wäre ein großer Fehler, sie zu unterschätzen. Auch sie mögen qualitativ hochwertige Naturprodukte!

11. **George Ray:** Können Sie sich etwas natürlicheres vorstellen als Pekanschokoriegel? Selbst wenn die Leute von der Lebensmittelbehörde kämen, um hier rumzuschnüffeln, hätten sie nichts an den Amigo-Riegeln auszusetzen. Wir verwenden zu 100% natürliche Zutaten.

12. **Susan:** Worauf ich hinweisen wollte, ist: Studien haben gezeigt, daß die lateinamerikanischen Verbraucher es schätzen, wenn bei der Herstellung von Schokoladenriegeln Kakaobutter anstelle von Pflanzenfett verwendet wird.

13. **George Ray:** Wir haben aber all unsere Forschungen mit Pflanzenfett durchgeführt und die Ergebnisse sind sehr positiv.

14. **Susan:** Dennoch ist Pflanzenfett beispielsweise in Frankreich verboten. Wer weiß? Möglicherweise macht die Lebensmittelbehörde dies eines Tages auch in diesem Land. Die Verwendung von Kakaobutter könnte uns einen zusätzlichen Vorteil gegenüber unseren Konkurrenten verschaffen.

15. **George Ray:** Sie ist auch teurer als Pflanzenfett. Darüber hinaus wird uns die zusätzliche Forschung Zeit und Geld kosten. Wenn der alte Dan Bush, unser Finanzmanager, die Rechnung sieht, wird er jammern wie Onkel Dagobert nach dem Verlust seines ersten Dollars.

16. **Susan:** Lassen Sie ihn jammern!... Aber glauben Sie mir, ich bin entschieden dagegen, Geld aus dem Fenster zu werfen. Schließlich habe ich schottische Vorfahren! Aber ich hätte es lieber, UC würde im Anfangsstadium des neuen Produktverfahrens viel Zeit und Geld investieren, anstatt wegen unzureichender Produktplanung einen Flop zu riskieren. In der heutigen Welt sind die Chancen, mit einem neuen Produkt einen Flop zu riskieren, sehr hoch.

ANMERKUNGEN (Fortsetzung)

(6) **FDA** ist die Abkürzung für *Food and Drug Administration*, die etwa unserer Lebensmittelbehörde entspricht.

(7) **to snoop around:** "schnüffeln". *To snoop on somebody* "jemanden ausspionieren". *to have a snoop around* "sich (ein bißchen) umsehen". Von diesem Verb ist auch *Snoopy* abgeleitet, der Name des Hundes in den Comics von Charles M. Schulz.

(8) **Uncle Scrooge** ist der englische Name für Onkel Dagobert, den geizigen Onkel in den Donald-Duck-Geschichten von Walt Disney.

(9) **flop:** "Reinfall". Mittlerweile sagt man auch im Deutschen "Flop". Im Kontext des Dialogs ist Flop das Gegenstück zu *blockbuster* (Anmerkung 4).

(10) **odds:** "Chancen, Aussichten". *Odd* "ungerade; überzählig", auch "merkwürdig, seltsam". (Siehe auch *odd pricing* in Kapitel 22, Dokument).

210

CHAPTER 21

17. **George Ray:** OK. I'll work on this cocoa butter problem. Still, I'll bet a case of Texas Chardonnay that within a year of the launching, copycats will show up with knock-offs of Amigo. **(11) (12)**

18. **Susan:** Texas Chardonnay?! What next?

19. **George Ray:** Well, Susan, as you said a while back, it would be a big mistake to underestimate it!

KAPITEL 21

17. **George Ray:** In Ordnung. Ich kümmere mich um diese Kakaobuttersache. Aber ich wette eine Kiste Texas Chardonnay, daß innerhalb eines Jahres nach der Einführung erste Imitationen des Amigo auftauchen werden.

18. **Susan:** Texas Chardonnay? Haben Sie sonst noch was auf Lager?

19. **George Ray:** Naja, Susan, wie Sie vor einer Weile sagten: es wäre ein großer Fehler, die Dinge zu unterschätzen!

ANMERKUNGEN (Fortsetzung)

(11) copycat: Bezeichnung für eine Person oder ein Unternehmen, die bzw. das Duplikate eines Produkts auf den Markt bringt. Man sagt auch *copycat product*.

(12) knock-off: "Kopie, Imitation".

CHAPTER 21

Product development

The design and development of new products are an essential function of the marketing department. In most companies, a product executive is in charge of new projects.

A product's lifespan is more or less limited and newer products must be launched on the market. The failure rate of new products is high, but the key factors of success are the intrinsic quality of the product and the company's marketing know-how.

If a firm decides to develop a new product, it must pay special attention to planning and organization.

Product development consists of five stages:

1. **Idea generation and assessment.** The approach to generating new ideas may be intuitive (idea-boxes, brainstorming sessions, contacts with independent inventors, etc.) or rational (analysis of environment trends, of the market structure, of competing products, etc.). Afterwards, a screening takes place: good ideas are selected and poor ones dropped.

2. **Concept development.** The company defines the way it wishes its product to be perceived by consumers. In order to protect the innovation, the company takes out a patent.

3. **Testing.** The prototype of the new product is submitted to a test aimed at checking that it is consistent with the objectives of the company, and the expectations of consumers. Particular care is given to the choice of the brand name and packaging. Afterwards, the psychological price (optimal sales price) is determined and advertising can get under way.

4. **Sales forecast.** In this stage, management evaluates the business attractiveness of the new product. Such an exercise is difficult because the product has no history. If the sales, costs and projections satisfy the company's objectives, the product can move to the development stage. Test marketing may enable the company to test the novelty in realistic market settings.

5. **Product launching plan.** This is the final phase. The launching plan becomes operational once the product has been presented to the sales force.

KAPITEL 21

Brainstorming

In vielen Firmen wird schon länger eine bestimmte Methode praktiziert, um neue Produktideen zutage zu fördern: das *Brainstorming*. Hierbei setzen sich die Mitarbeiter zu einer Gruppe zusammen und versuchen, wie ein "Wind, der durch die Gehirne bläst", neue und originelle Ideen zu entwickeln, indem jeder zu einem bestimmten Thema oder einer Fragestellung spontan die Gedanken ausspricht, die ihm im Moment durch den Kopf gehen.

Daß bei solchen Sitzungen tatsächlich auf ganz unerwartete Weise neue Ideen entstehen, zeigt die Geschichte der Manager, die im Anschluß an eine solche Brainstorming-Sitzung im Rahmen eines Arbeitsfrühstücks damit begannen, Pappteller umherzuwerfen, um sich etwas abzureagieren. Aus diesem für Manager wahrhaft unwürdigen Spiel entstand das *Frisbee*!

CHAPTER 21

EXERCISES

Comprehension

Lesen Sie den Dialog aufmerksam durch. Beantworten Sie dann die nachfolgenden Fragen, und zwar immer in ganzen Sätzen:
1. What methodology did UC's research team adopt in its work on the new chocolate bar? **2.** Why was the Amigo concept adopted? **3.** Why did the research team alter the prototype? **4.** Is Susan as enthusiastic as George Ray? Why? **5.** According to Susan, what mistake should George Ray avoid making? **6.** Why is George Ray quite confident? **7.** Why is George Ray not too keen on modifying the product? **8.** According to Susan, what is a wise research and development policy? **9.** What shows George Ray's confidence in the new product? **10.** How would you characterize Susan's attitude in this scene?

Vocabulary

Die zehn untenstehenden Wörter kommen im Dialog dieser Lektion vor. Suchen Sie unter den drei angegebenen Synonymen dasjenige heraus, das nicht in die Liste paßt.

1. discounted
    a. reduced   b. cast away   c. discarded
2. alter
    a. deteriorate   b. change   c. modify
3. blockbuster
    a. tremendous success   b. best-selling product   c. big risk
4. think up
    a. invent   b. devise   c. remember
5. bother
    a. give trouble   b. worry   c. contribute
6. wail
    a. expect   b. lament   c. complain
7. flop
    a. failure   b. frustration   c. fiasco
8. the odds
    a. chances   b. strange things   c. auspices
9. copycats
    a. counterfeiters   b. flatterers   c. forgers
10. knock-off
    a. blow   b. clone   c. fake

215

KAPITEL 21

LÖSUNGSVORSCHLÄGE

Verständnisübung

1. It devised five product concepts, tested them on five groups of consumers and chose the one which was considered best. **2.** This chocolate bar showed the best potential. **3.** Researchers had to take the sensorial evaluation team's observations into account. **4.** No. She is thinking of the difficulties of the market whereas George Ray is only thinking of the quality of the product. **5.** He should refrain from underestimating Hispanic consumers' tastes. **6.** He is quite confident because Amigo bars are made with 100 % natural ingredients. **7.** He thinks the prototype is a good product and he also fears the finance manager's opposition. **8.** It is to devote a lot of time and money to the preparation of the launching of a new product. **9.** He is prepared to bet a case of Texas Chardonnay the new bar will be successful and he forecasts that knock-offs of Amigo bars will soon appear on the market. **10.** She tries and does everything to limit failure risks, she is firm with George Ray (she gently orders him to use cocoa butter instead of vegetable fat), and she anticipates the future (possible new decisions by the FDA).

Lösungen zur Wortschatzübung

1. a. **2.** a. **3.** c. **4.** c. **5.** c. **6.** a. **7.** b. **8.** b. **9.** b. **10.** a.

CHAPTER 21

Application

Ordnen Sie die in Spalte A stehenden Wörter oder Begriffe denen in Spalte B zu.

A	B
1. product executive	a. counterfeit goods
2. idea screening	b. brainstorming session
3. idea generation	c. blind tasting
4. FDA	d. selection of 'good ideas'
5. patent	e. new product testing
6. prototype	f. health regulations
7. sensorial evaluation team	g. protection of the innovation
8. copycat	h. new product management

DO!

Be very cautious when you write out a contract in America if you don't want to end up with a lawsuit.
There are many more lawyers in the USA than in Europe and these people are keen to work! As for US negotiators, they operate in a world of prepared contracts.

KAPITEL 21

Lösungen

1. h. **2.** d. **3.** b. **4.** f. **5.** g. **6.** e. **7.** c. **8.** a.

DON'T!

*Don't be afraid if American negotiators talk quickly, shout or utter threats.
Many Americans consider that shouting is a sign of firmness.*

CHAPTER 22

Getting the marketing mix right (1)

It's 8.30 pm at UC headquarters in Philadelphia. Susan and Russ have been working after hours. Before leaving the office, Russ produces a bottle of Bourbon which was stashed away in the bottom drawer of his desk.

1. **Russ:** How about a glass of whisky, Susan?

2. **Susan:** A small one then. And it's not for the sake of drink...

3. **Russ:** ... but for the sake of company! Well, Susan, we now have a difficult decision to make concerning the price of our Amigo bars.

4. **Susan:** I'm all in favour of cost-oriented pricing. Our costs must set the floor for the price UC can ask for Amigo bars. We want to charge a price that covers all the costs for producing, distributing and selling the product plus a fair rate of return for our effort and risk. It's only fair to add a mark-up to our costs! **(2) (3)**

5. **Russ:** It's not as simple as that, though.

6. **Susan:** Agreed. We cannot avoid setting our prices on the basis of our competitors' prices...

7. **Russ:** ... rather than our costs and revenues!

8. **Susan:** Indeed, our main competitors set the tone for price decisions in the entire industry. Nevertheless, I hope we'll do better than break even. **(4) (5)**

9. **Russ:** Of course, it's always difficult to know what prices our competitors charge.

10. **Susan:** Although their price lists are closely guarded, I managed to get a look at their prices.

KAPITEL 22

Der richtige Marketing-Mix

Es ist 20.30 Uhr im Hauptgeschäftssitz von UC in Philadelphia. Susan und Russ haben über die normale Bürozeit hinaus gearbeitet. Bevor sie das Büro verlassen, holt Russ eine Flasche Bourbon heraus, die er in der unteren Schublade seines Schreibtischs verborgen hatte.

1. **Russ:** Ein Glas Whisky, Susan?
2. **Susan:** Aber ein kleines. Und nicht um des Trinkens willen...
3. **Russ:** ... aber um der Gesellschaft willen! Also, Susan, wir müssen nun eine schwierige Entscheidung bezüglich des Preises unserer Amigo-Riegel treffen.
4. **Susan:** Ich bin durchaus für eine kostenorientierte Preisgestaltung. Unsere Kosten müssen die Untergrenze für den Preis darstellen, zu dem UC seine Amigo-Riegel verkauft. Wir wollen einen Preis verlangen, der alle Kosten für die Produktion, die Verteilung und den Vertrieb des Produkts deckt, und eine angemessene Ertragssumme für unsere Bemühungen und unser Risiko miteinschließt. Es ist nur fair, unseren Kosten eine Gewinnspanne hinzuzufügen.
5. **Russ:** Das ist aber nicht so einfach.
6. **Susan:** Einverstanden. Wir können nicht umhin, unsere Preise auf der Basis der Preise unserer Mitbewerber festzusetzen...
7. **Russ:** ... und nicht auf der Basis unserer Kosten und Einnahmen!
8. **Susan:** Tatsächlich geben unsere Hauptmitbewerber die Richtung für Preisentscheidungen in der gesamten Branche vor. Trotzdem hoffe ich, daß wir besser als plus minus null abschneiden.
9. **Russ:** Es ist natürlich immer schwer zu wissen, welche Preise unsere Mitbewerber verlangen.
10. **Susan:** Obwohl sie ihre Preislisten streng bewachen, konnte ich mir einen Überblick über ihre Preise verschaffen.

ANMERKUNGEN

(1) Unter **marketing mix** "Marketing-Mix" versteht man die Variation verschiedener Marketing-Instrumente, die die vier "P"s genannt werden: Price, Packaging, Product, Promotion.
(2) **to set the floor:** "Mindestpreis ansetzen". *Floor* bezeichnet die unterste Grenze, die Schwelle. Gegenteil: *ceiling* "oberste Grenze".
(3) **mark-up:** "Preisaufschlag, Gewinnaufschlag". Man sagt auch *profit margin*.
(4) **to set the tone:** "die Richtung angeben, die allgemeine Tendenz bestimmen".
(5) **to break even:** "mit plus minus null abschneiden, kostendeckend arbeiten". *Break-even point*: "Rentabilitätsgrenze".

CHAPTER 22

11. **Russ:** They may not be informative, though, because the actual prices are established through negotiation.

12. **Susan:** Indeed, I see what you mean when you say that the task of setting a price is not easily tackled. I realize that! But allow me to repeat myself. We must also try to offer competitive prices whilst making some profit. I'm fairly confident. Don't we pay a lot of attention to cost control? Of course, we could still do better. We still have to streamline and simplify operations. **(6) (7)**

13. **Russ:** *(Laughing)* That sounds very much like ol' Dan Bush!

14. **Susan:** Come on Russ. Be serious for a while! You know that UC is a thrifty shopper and our buyers certainly know how to ferret out cheap pecan nuts and squeeze suppliers for extra savings. NAFTA is good for us. Pecan nuts are cheaper in Mexico and now, we have no more customs duties to pay on them. **(8) (9) (10)**

15. **Russ:** Texas and Louisiana pecan producers would surely be delighted to hear you. By the way, are you sure you want to make a career in marketing? If I were ol' Dan Bush, I would get worried.

16. **Susan:** Stop kidding me, Russ! You know it would be foolish to overlook chances to economize. Lower costs mean lower prices and lower prices mean greater sales profits. **(11)**

17. **Russ:** Of course Susan. I was just teasing you! Where did you leave your sense of humor?

KAPITEL 22

11. **Russ:** Sie sind jedoch möglicherweise nicht sehr aufschlußreich, denn die eigentlichen Preise werden durch Verhandlungen festgesetzt.

12. **Susan:** Tatsächlich verstehe ich, was Sie meinen, wenn Sie sagen, daß die Aufgabe, die Preise festzusetzen, nicht leicht anzupacken ist. Ich sehe das ein! Aber erlauben Sie mir, mich zu wiederholen. Wir müssen auch versuchen, konkurrenzfähige Preise anzubieten und gleichzeitig Gewinn zu machen. Ich bin ziemlich zuversichtlich. Legen wir nicht sehr viel Augenmerk auf die Kostenkontrolle? Natürlich könnten wir es immer noch besser machen. Wir müssen nach wie vor rationalisieren und die Abläufe vereinfachen.

13. **Russ:** *(Lacht)* Das klingt mir sehr nach dem alten Dan Bush!

14. **Susan:** Na kommen Sie, Russ. Seien Sie mal eine Weile ernst! Sie wissen, daß UC sparsam einkauft und daß unsere Einkäufer bestimmt wissen, wie man preiswerte Pekannüsse aufspürt und die Preise der Lieferanten drückt, um zusätzliche Einsparungen zu erreichen. Die NAFTA ist gut für uns. Pekannüsse sind in Mexiko billiger, und jetzt müssen wir keine Zollgebühren mehr für sie bezahlen.

15. **Russ:** Die Anbauer von Pekannüssen in Texas und Louisiana wären bestimmt erfreut, Sie so reden zu hören. Sind Sie eigentlich sicher, daß Sie eine Karriere im Marketing machen wollen? Wenn ich der alte Dan Bush wäre, wäre ich beunruhigt.

16. **Susan:** Hören Sie auf, mich auf den Arm zu nehmen, Russ! Sie wissen, es wäre dumm, Chancen für Einsparungen zu übersehen. Niedrigere Kosten bedeuten niedrigere Preise, und niedrigere Preise bedeuten höhere Verkaufserlöse.

17. **Russ:** Natürlich, Susan. Ich habe Sie nur ein bißchen aufgezogen! Wo haben Sie Ihren Sinn für Humor gelassen?

ANMERKUNGEN (Fortsetzung)

(6) **to tackle**: Dieses Wort stammt ursprünglich aus dem Bereich des Sports, wo es die Bedeutung "angreifen" oder "fassen" (beim Football oder Rugby) hat. *To tackle a problem* "ein Problem angehen, in Angriff nehmen".

(7) Die Grundbedeutung von **to streamline** ist: "etwas eine aerodynamische Form verleihen". Hier jedoch bedeutet es "rationalisieren, modernisieren".

(8) **thrifty**: "sparsam". Thrift "Sparsamkeit". In den Vereinigten Staaten ist *thrift* ebenfalls die Bezeichnung für eine *savings and loan institution (S&L)*, eine Art Sparkasse oder Bausparkasse (ungefähr das Äquivalent zur *building society* in Großbritannien).

(9) **to ferret out**: "aufspüren, aufstöbern". Dieses Wort stammt von *ferret* "Frettchen".

(10) **NAFTA** ist die Abkürzung für *North American Free Trade Agreement*, ein Wirtschaftsbündnis zwischen den USA, Kanada und Mexiko. Dieser gemeinsame nordamerikanische Markt trat 1994 in Kraft.

(11) **Stop kidding me!** "Machen Sie sich nicht über mich lustig". Vergleichen Sie: *No kidding!* "Ohne Witz!"; *You can't kid me* "Sie können mich nicht auf den Arm nehmen"; *to kid* "Witze machen, scherzen".

CHAPTER 22 DOCUMENT

Marketing mix and pricing

Marketing mix is the combination of marketing variables used to achieve objectives and satisfy the target market. It consists of four major factors: product, distribution, promotion and price.

Price is the 'something of value' in an exchange. A buyer exchanges purchasing power for satisfaction from a product. The pricing policy is the course of action for achieving pricing objectives.

Promotional pricing - In order to increase sales, companies may temporarily price their products below the list price. Promotional pricing, which is viewed as an incentive to customers, takes several forms:
Trade discounts - They are offered by the manufacturer to wholesalers and retailers.
Cash discounts - A rebate is offered to buyers who pay their bills promptly.
Quantity discounts - A reduction is offered to buyers who buy large volumes.
Seasonal discounts - Price reductions are offered to buyers who buy a product or service out of season, eg winter rates in hotels.
Trade-in allowances - Reductions given for turning in an old item when buying a new one, eg automobiles or small appliances.

Discriminatory pricing - This is to allow for differences in customers, products and locations. Movie theaters, for example, may offer discounts for children and senior citizens, groups, early performances or Wednesday performances.
Companies may also offer discounts from normal prices to increase sales and reduce inventories. Some manufacturers prefer to make an effort in other directions by offering low-interest financing, longer warranties or free maintenance.

Psychological pricing - This is a pricing policy designed to encourage purchases that are based on emotional rather than rational responses. Among possible policies, prestige and odd pricing may be considered.
Prestige pricing consists in setting artificially high prices to convey a prestigious image. Luxury products such as fast cars, high-fashion clothes or perfume tend to be prestige-priced.
Odd pricing consists in ending a price with an odd number so as to influence customers' perceptions. Odd pricing assumes that consumers will buy more of a product at $99.99 than at $100.00 because they will perceive the product to be a bargain.

KAPITEL 22

Die Rolle des Marketing in unserem Leben

Das Marketing, das in den 20er Jahren in den USA seinen Einzug hielt, betrifft heute alle Bereiche des täglichen Lebens. Es ist für die Unternehmen zu einem Schlüsselfaktor des Erfolgs geworden, weil es ihnen ermöglicht, ihre Ergebnisse auf eine sehr sensible Art zu verbessern. Das Marketing ist jedoch nicht nur den großen Unternehmen in den Industriestaaten vorbehalten. Seit der Wahl von J.F. Kennedy hat man auch in der Politik die Bedeutung des Marketing erkannt. Staatsbetriebe wie z.B. *Amtrack* (das amerikanische Äquivalent zur ehemaligen Deutschen Bundesbahn), der *US Postal Service* oder auch die Armee greifen auf Marketingstrategien zurück. Das gleiche gilt für nicht auf Gewinn ausgerichtete Organisationen *(non-profit organizations)* wie Schulen, Krankenhäuser, Wohlfahrtseinrichtungen *(charities)* und sogar Kirchen.

CHAPTER 22

EXERCISES

Comprehension

Lesen Sie den Dialog aufmerksam durch. Beantworten Sie dann die nachfolgenden Fragen, und zwar immer in ganzen Sätzen:

1. Do Russ and Susan work according to a strict schedule at UC? **2.** What is Susan's first idea about a pricing policy for Amigo bars? **3.** How does she justify her opinion? **4.** What other pricing-policy factors should be taken into account? **5.** What type of information about the competition does Russ Kingman find difficult to obtain? **6.** Why do price lists provide unreliable information? **7.** Why is Susan hopeful that UC will do better than break even with Amigo bars? **8.** What does Susan reveal about UC's buying policy? **9.** Why does NAFTA offer interesting opportunities for UC? **10.** Why would Texas and Louisiana pecan producers not be pleased to hear Susan?

Vocabulary

Wählen Sie in jedem Satz aus den kursiv gedruckten Wörtern das passende Wort aus.

1. Susan studied *economy* (or *economics*) at the university. **2.** Melanie is normally a very *conscious* (or *conscientious*) secretary. **3.** Jaime Maldonado has found a *job* (or *work*) as a foreman. **4.** UC plans to *rise* (or *raise*) its prices by 5 % next year. **5.** Will the plummeting price of pecan nuts *effect* (or *affect*) our sales? **6.** We have just received an *advice* (or *advisory*) note informing us that the pecan order has been dispatched. **7.** The cost of *life* (or *living*) keeps going up. **8.** Keep in mind that this is only an *incentive* (or *estimate*). The final price could be higher. **9.** As it is a *buyer's* (or *seller's*) market for the time being, you should manage to find the items you need at a very reasonable price. **10.** UC's workers did not complain because their salaries kept *pace* (or *place*) with inflation.

KAPITEL 22

LÖSUNGSVORSCHLÄGE

Verständnisübung

1. No. They seem to be used to working after hours. 2. She would like the price of Amigo bars to do better than cover the cost of producing them. 3. She thinks it is only fair for UC to be rewarded for its efforts in the field of research, production, promotion and distribution. 4. Competitors' prices cannot be ignored in the highly competitive environment of chocolate bars. 5. Information about competitors' prices is very difficult to obtain. 6. Actual prices, which are determined through negotiation, are different from the prices mentioned in price lists. 7. Because UC has managed to reduce costs to a minimum. 8. UC buyers seem to have a knack for buying products cheaply. 9. Because the cost of pecan nuts is lower in Mexico and UC will be able to import them without having to pay duties. 10. As the prices they charge are higher than those charged by their Mexican competitors, they are likely to lose market shares.

Lösungen zur Wortschatzübung

1. economics
2. conscientious
3. job
4. raise
5. affect
6. advice
7. living
8. estimate
9. buyer's
10. pace

CHAPTER 22

Application

Alle Unternehmen setzen Preise für ihre Produkte oder ihre Dienstleistungen fest. Ordnen Sie die Preisbezeichnungen in Spalte B dem jeweiligen Produkt oder der jeweiligen Dienstleistung in Spalte A zu.

A
1. Executive
2. Salesperson
3. Worker
4. Dentist
5. Bank
6. Motorway
7. Apartment
8. Insurance
9. Dishonest politician
10. Aboriginal tribe

B
a. barter
b. interest
c. rent
d. premium
e. salary
f. fee
g. commission
h. bribe
i. toll
j. wage

DO!

Take as many testimonials (pressbook, letters of commendation from your best-known customers, etc.) when you negotiate with Americans. They will identify you as a serious, honest person.

KAPITEL 22

Lösungen

1. e. **2.** g. **3.** j. **4.** f. **5.** b. **6.** i. **7.** c. **8.** d. **9.** h. **10.** a.

DON'T!

Don't split hairs when a problem calls for a quick decision.

CHAPTER 23

Contacting an advertising agency

Susan has invited Alan Carr, the Customer Service Manager of a leading advertising firm, for a brief in the course of which she defines the product, the objectives, the means and the deadlines of the Amigo bar advertising campaign. **(1) (2)**

1. **Alan Carr:** Needless to say, I hope we'll become true partners.

2. **Susan:** I must admit it is quite interesting to develop an advertising campaign with an agency. We pretty much know what we want and we'd rely on you for ad writing, artwork, technical production and formulation of the media plan. **(3)**

3. **Alan Carr:** First, we would have to define our advertising objectives in clear, precise and measurable terms.

4. **Susan:** As far as we at UC are concerned, we want to break into the Hispanic market with our Amigo bars. We would like to sell 30 million of them within a year.

5. **Alan Carr:** That is an ambitious goal!

6. **Susan:** We wouldn't have considered working with you if we hadn't thought you were able to help us meet that goal.

7. **Alan Carr:** Success has a price...

8. **Susan:** We don't want to squander our financial resources... Conversely, we are willing to make every effort to allocate enough money so that our program can achieve its advertising and marketing objectives. As a matter of fact, instead of paying the traditional 15 % commission on media and production billings, we prefer to lower the commission down to 13 %, and we'd pay bonuses of up to 5 % if you do outstanding work. **(4) (5)**

KAPITEL 23

Kontaktaufnahme mit einer Werbeagentur

Susan hat Alan Carr, den Großkundenmanager einer führenden Werbeagentur, zu einer Besprechung eingeladen, in deren Verlauf sie das Produkt, die Zielsetzungen, die Mittel und die Fristen der Werbekampagne für den Amigo-Riegel beschreibt.

1. **Alan Carr:** Ich brauche wohl nicht zu betonen, daß ich hoffe, daß wir echte Partner werden.

2. **Susan:** Ich muß zugeben, daß es ziemlich interessant ist, eine Werbekampagne mit einer Agentur auszuarbeiten. Wir wissen sehr genau, was wir wollen, und wir würden uns auf Sie verlassen, was das Verfassen der Werbeanzeigen, di künstlerische Gestaltung, die technische Produktion und die Formulierung des Mediaplans angeht.

3. **Alan Carr:** Zuerst müßten wir unsere Werbeziele in klaren, präzisen und meßbaren Begriffen definieren.

4. **Susan:** Was uns hier bei UC betrifft, so möchten wir mit unseren Amigo-Riegeln auf den Markt der lateinamerikanischen Verbraucher. Wir würden gerne innerhalb eines Jahres 30 Millionen Riegel verkaufen.

5. **Alan Carr:** Das ist ein ehrgeiziges Ziel!

6. **Susan:** Wir hätten keine Zusammenarbeit mit Ihnen in Betracht gezogen, wenn wir nicht gedacht hätten, daß Sie uns helfen können, dieses Ziel zu erreichen.

7. **Alan Carr:** Erfolg hat einen Preis...

8. **Susan:** Wir möchten unsere finanziellen Ressourcen nicht vergeuden... Auf der anderen Seite sind wir bereit, alles zu tun, um genug Geld bereitzustellen, so daß unser Programm seine Werbe- und Marketingziele erreichen kann. Und anstatt die üblichen 15% Kommission auf Media- und Produktionsrechnungen zu zahlen, würden wir lieber die Kommission auf 13% reduzieren und bis zu 5% Bonus zahlen, wenn Sie außergewöhnliche Arbeit leisten.

ANMERKUNGEN

(1) **Customer Service Manager:** "Kundendienstmanager". Der Hauptunterhändler einer Werbeagentur. Er bestimmt die Kommunikationsstrategie.

(2) **brief:** Hier: mündliche und/oder schriftliche Präsentation eines kaufmännischen Problems.

(3) **media plan:** "Mediaplan". Das Konzept, in dem die Medien aufgeführt sind, die nötig sind, um die Zielgruppe eines Produkts zu erreichen. *Media* "Medien, Werbeträger, Reklamemittel".

(4) **billing(s):** "Fakturierung, Rechnungsstellung, Rechnungserteilung" (Synonym: *invoicing*); *billing (invoicing) department*: Rechnungsabteilung.

(5) **bonus:** "Bonus, Prämie, Zulage"; *performance-related bonus* "leistungsabhängige Zulage"; *productivity bonus* "Produktivitätsbonus".

CHAPTER 23

9. **Alan Carr:** I'm not surprised by your proposal. More and more clients are tying their ad agencies' compensation to performance... This point is negotiable. If we work together, we'll create the message we will communicate to the target market. **(6) (7)**

10. **Susan:** *(Handing a report to him)* This report contains the selling features of pecan praline bars to be stressed in the program.

11. **Alan Carr:** Have you mentioned the important features that the competitors' products don't have?

12. **Susan:** Of course. We expect the agency to find words, symbols and illustrations that are meaningful, familiar and attractive to those persons, mostly Hispanics, who make up our target market.

13. **Alan Carr:** Obviously, we would have to work on a concise, simple message for outdoor displays, you know: billboards, advertisements on buses, etc. And short broadcast announcements for radio stations. **(8) (9)**

14. **Susan:** What about magazine and newspaper advertisements?

15. **Alan Carr:** They can include just a little more detail and longer explanations, as long as they grab the reader's attention.

16. **Susan:** Does your agency work fast?

17. **Alan Carr:** We are known for our efficiency. Our artistic director and our creative writers are all very competent. They could come up with roughs very soon. I could submit first drafts to you within a week. **(10) (11)**

18. **Susan:** All right! I suggest we meet again to examine them and possibly discuss the media plan.

KAPITEL 23

9. **Alan Carr:** Ich bin nicht überrascht über Ihren Vorschlag. Immer mehr Kunden knüpfen die Vergütung der Werbeagentur an die Leistung... Über diesen Punkt läßt sich reden. Wenn wir zusammenarbeiten, werden wir die Werbebotschaft erstellen, die wir dem Zielmarkt übermitteln.

10. **Susan:** *(Gibt ihm einen Bericht)* Dieser Bericht enthält die Verkaufseigenschaften des Pekannußriegels, die in dem Programm hervorgehoben werden sollten.

11. **Alan Carr:** Haben Sie die wichtigen Eigenheiten erwähnt, über die die Konkurrenzprodukte nicht verfügen?

12. **Susan:** Selbstverständlich. Wir erwarten von der Agentur, daß sie Begriffe, Symbole und Illustrationen findet, die sinntragend, vertraut und attraktiv für die Leute sind, die unseren Zielmarkt ausmachen, speziell also für Lateinamerikaner.

13. **Alan Carr:** Offensichtlich müssen wir an einer prägnanten, einfachen Werbeaussage arbeiten, die auf Außenwerbungen erscheint, sie wissen schon: Plakattafeln, Werbung auf Bussen usw. Und kurze Werbespots für Radiosender.

14. **Susan:** Wie ist es mit Zeitschriften- und Zeitungsanzeigen?

15. **Alan Carr:** Sie können etwas mehr Details und längere Beschreibungen enthalten, solange sie nur die Aufmerksamkeit des Lesers erregen.

16. **Susan:** Arbeitet Ihre Agentur schnell?

17. **Alan Carr:** Wir sind für unsere Effizienz bekannt. Unser Art Director und unsere Texter sind alle sehr kompetent. Sie könnten schon bald Skizzen liefern. Ich könnte Ihnen innerhalb einer Woche die ersten Entwürfe übermitteln.

18. **Susan:** In Ordnung! Ich schlage vor, wir treffen uns wieder, um sie zu überprüfen und möglicherweise den Mediaplan zu besprechen.

ANMERKUNGEN (Fortsetzung)

(6) **client:** "Kunde". Dieser Ausdruck wird vor allem bei den freien Berufen und den Anbietern von Dienstleistungen, z.B. Anwälten, Bankiers, Rechnungsprüfern, Werbefachleuten usw. und in allen kaufmännischen Bereichen dem Ausdruck *customer* vorgezogen, vor allem, wenn es sich um einen wichtigen Kunden handelt.

(7) **target market:** "Zielmarkt". Der Markt, den ein Unternehmen durch eine Kommunikationsmaßnahme zu erreichen hofft.

(8) **outdoor displays:** "Außenwerbung". Große Werbetafeln an Wänden, auf Straßenbahnen, Bussen, Zügen usw.

(9) **billboard:** "Plakattafel". In Großbritannien verwendet man eher den Begriff *hoarding*.

(10) **creative writer:** "Texter". *Creative department* "Kreativabteilung (Texter und Grafiker)".

(11) **rough:** "Skizze, Entwurf" (Vorentwurf für eine Werbeanzeige).

CHAPTER 23 DOCUMENT

Advertising and society

Youngsters, farmers, teachers, old people, ecologists, political radicals, slum dwellers, the deaf and the blind, none of these audiences is totally insensitive to advertising. Whether it is considered the new opium of the people, a form of art, a reflection of society, a trivial game, a form of waste or hidden persuasion, advertising is part of today's life.

Apart from businesses, many organizations such as governments, environmental groups and even church groups rely on advertising to reach a variety of target markets or make the public aware of their activities.

In fact, advertising goes back to the dawn of times. But it was the launching of the first newspapers which really boosted advertising. In the USA, Benjamin Franklin, who founded a newspaper, is considered the father of American advertising. The USA took an interest in this communication means because the industrial revolution involved the mass-production of items which had to be sold. Later, radio and television contributed to the spread of advertising. In France, André Citroën is often considered a pioneer because he used the Eiffel Tower for neon-sign advertising.

The main criticisms levelled at this form of communication are that it makes people buy products they do not need, that it takes unfair advantage of children and that it makes people too materialistic. Although there is no denying that advertising has been misused, today abuses are more the exception than the rule. Governments and consumer organizations try to curb its misuse. But it is true that people are exposed to as many as 1,600 messages a day! At worst, advertisements are misleading. At best, they only show the bright side of products. To some extent, they highjack* people's quest for happiness by convincing them that they will indeed be happy if they buy this or that product.

Advertising has become a valuable communication tool in our society. As it is a tool, it is neither good nor bad. It all depends on the use advertisers make of it. Actually, it seldom initiates new trends or offers unconventional images of people or lifestyles, because in most cases, it merely reflects attitudes and changes present in our society. In the best case, advertising informs consumers. It also persuades them to buy a company's product rather than the competitor's and it reminds them they may need the product again.

---

* Hier: "betrügen"

KAPITEL 23

Die Werbeslogans

Das Wort Slogan stammt ursprünglich aus dem Gälischen und bezeichnete das Kriegsgeschrei *(sluaghghairm)* der schottischen Stämme. Heute versteht man darunter ein prägnantes Werbeschlagwort, das durch seinen bildreichen und originellen Charakter überzeugt. Diese Werbesprüche prägen sich meistens leicht ein und passen sich vor allem gut an die amerikanische Mentalität an, die sich durch eine Vorliebe für Prägnanz und Schnelligkeit auszeichnet. Es ist also normal, daß Werbeslogans sich im Ursprungsland des *Reader's Digest* ausbreiten. Slogans werden auch weitgehend in der Politik eingesetzt: *I like Ike* war beispielsweise der Slogan zur Wahl von Eisenhower.

Um einen guten Slogan zu finden, empfahl bereits David Ogilvy (siehe Kapitel 18, Anmerkung 12) das *Kiss*-Prinzip (***Keep it simple, stupid!***). Vor allem einfache Slogans sind und waren meist in aller Munde: *"A diamond is for ever"*, *"Don't be vague, ask for Haig (whisky)"*; *"Coke is it!"*, *"Guinness is good for you"* oder der Slogan der amerikanischen Telefongesellschaft AT&T: *"Reach out and touch someone"*.

CHAPTER 23

EXERCISES

Comprehension

Lesen Sie den Dialog aufmerksam durch. Beantworten Sie dann die nachfolgenden Fragen, und zwar immer in ganzen Sätzen:

1. Why does Alan Carr hope to become UC's true partner? **2.** What does Susan expect from an advertising agency? **3.** What is a major advantage of working on the Amigo bar campaign? **4.** What shows that Susan has a lot of confidence in Alan Carr's company? **5.** Why does Susan suggest lowering the commission and offering a bonus for outstanding work? **6.** What is the use of the report prepared by Susan? **7.** What aspect of the report is Alan Carr especially interested in? **8.** What media have Alan Carr and Susan considered? **9.** What media have they failed to consider? **10.** What is the process used by UC in order to select an advertising agency?

Vocabulary

Welche Elemente findet man auf einem Werbeplakat? Ordnen Sie den einzelnen Bestandteilen des unten gezeigten Werbeplakats jeweils einen der folgenden Begriffe zu:
signature, body copy, headline, illustration, subheadline.

1. ....

2. ....

3. ....

4. ....

5. ....

SAVOR

A Delicious Treat!

Our bars are made with 100 %
natural products.
We use only the freshest,
most delicious ingredients:
chewy golden caramel, hearty
pecan nuts, real Vermont maple
sugar and dark chocolate.

AMIGO
pecan praline bars
A new UC product.

KAPITEL 23

LÖSUNGSVORSCHLÄGE

Verständnisübung

1. Because it would mean his agency would get the contract and develop a program with UC. **2.** She expects the advertising agency to take care of the advertising campaign and the media plan. **3.** The objective, however ambitious it may seem, is clearly defined. **4.** She would not have got in touch with him if she had not thought his agency was able to take up the challenge. **5.** She thinks it will motivate the agency more. **6.** As the agency selected will work with UC, it is important to communicate a lot of information. The advertising campaign must be consistent with UC's strategy. **7.** He is interested in the competitive advantages of Amigo bars. **8.** They have considered outdoor displays, radio, magazines and newspapers. **9.** They have failed to consider television. **10.** UC must have studied the performances of different companies and selected those whose creative approach it thinks is suited to Amigo bars. It has invited them for a brief. The agencies interested will submit their proposals to UC, who will decide whom the project will be assigned to.

Lösungen zur Wortschatzübung

1. Illustration.
2. Headline.
3. Subheadline.
4. Body copy.
5. Signature.

CHAPTER 23

Application

Ordnen Sie die in der linken Spalte stehenden Slogans den in der rechten Spalte aufgeführten Produkten zu:

Catchphrases

a. Give a little tenderness.
b. A better career begins with our diploma.
c. Let us make the journey worthy of your destination.
d. You are looking at the reason why a lot of our competitors don't build wagons any more.
e. The Cabernet that fooled the French.
f. Announcing several closeness improvements. Our closest shave. Ever.
g. Doomed... Doomed... Doomed?
h. Sleep better on air.
i. Perhaps the one thing worse than dying is outliving your money.
j. The message is in the bottle.

Products

1. Tour operator
2. Mattress
3. Save the bears
4. Beer
5. Razor
6. Automobile
7. Bank
8. Charolais beef
9. South African wine
10. Business school

> **DO!**
>
> ***There is more than just one market in the USA. In fact, the country consists of a number of regional markets reflecting the geographical diversity of the USA (New England, the MidWest, the South, etc.).***

KAPITEL 23

Lösungen

1. c.
2. h.
3. g.
4. j.
5. f.
6. d.
7. i.
8. a.
9. e.
10. b.

DON'T!

***Don't expect transitions in the USA.
You will be in charge almost immediately.***

CHAPTER 24

Quality control

Susan has an appointment with Torleiv Bilstad, UC's Norwegian-born Quality Control Manager, to take stock of the Amigo production process. He shows her round the production line. **(1)**

1. **Susan:** Torleiv, the production workers seem satisfied.

2. **Torleiv Bilstad:** They don't complain. This brand new plant gives all of us an ideal opportunity to take a clean sheet. Our facilities encourage greater efficiency in a pleasant working environment. **(2) (3)**

3. **Susan:** Management wanted the workers to be well catered for with nice offices, laboratories, locker and laundry rooms, canteen facilities for all... Torleiv, is the quality of Amigo bars up to standard? **(4)**

4. **Torleiv Bilstad:** Yes. It meets our expectations.

5. **Susan:** That is a compliment from the gods! I have often heard about your Viking perfectionism...

6. **Torleiv Bilstad:** You know, in Norway, people consider that every detail is of the utmost importance.

7. **Susan:** I agree with you..., up to a point. I mean, in so far as it doesn't hamper operating efficiency.

8. **Torleiv Bilstad:** As the latest technology is incorporated in a logical sequence in this plant, economy of operation is ensured. This production line represents a carefully scheduled combination of human skill and experience with high technology and automation.

9. **Susan:** *(Pointing at a machine)* What task does this machine perform?

10. **Torleiv Bilstad:** This five-roller grinder ensures that the refining will give the cocoa its sharpness. **(5)**

11. **Susan:** How fine is the powder?

KAPITEL 24

Qualitätskontrolle

Susan hat eine Verabredung mit Torleiv Bilstad, dem aus Norwegen stammenden Manager für die Qualitätskontrolle bei UC, um eine Bestandsaufnahme des Amigo-Produktionsprozesses vorzunehmen. Er zeigt ihr die Fertigungsstraße.

1. **Susan:** Torleiv, die Fertigungsarbeiter scheinen zufrieden zu sein.
2. **Torleiv Bilstad:** Sie beklagen sich nicht. Dieses brandneue Werk gibt uns allen eine ideale Gelegenheit, wieder bei Null anzufangen. Unsere Einrichtungen fördern eine größere Effizienz in einer angenehmen Arbeitsumgebung.
3. **Susan:** Die Unternehmensleitung wollte, daß die Arbeiter gut ausgestattet sind mit schönen Büros, Laboratorien, Umkleideräumen und Wäschereien, Kantinen für alle... Torleiv, entspricht die Qualität des Amigo-Riegels der Norm?
4. **Tovleiv Bilstad:** Ja. Sie erfüllt unsere Erwartungen.
5. **Susan:** Das ist ein himmlisches Kompliment! Ich habe oft von Ihrem Wikinger-Perfektionismus gehört...
6. **Torleiv Bilstad:** Wissen Sie, in Norwegen finden die Leute, daß jede Kleinigkeit von höchster Bedeutung ist.
7. **Susan:** Ich stimme mit Ihnen überein... bis zu einem gewissen Punkt. Ich meine, soweit dies nicht die Arbeitseffizienz behindert.
8. **Torleiv Bilstad:** Da in diesem Werk die neueste Technologie in einer logischen Abfolge integriert wurde, ist die Wirtschaftlichkeit der Betriebsabläufe sichergestellt. Diese Fertigungsstraße stellt eine sorgfältig geplante Kombination von menschlichem Know-how und Erfahrungen mit Hochtechnologie und Automation dar.
9. **Susan:** *(Zeigt auf eine Maschine)* Welche Aufgabe führt diese Maschine aus?
10. **Torleiv Bildstad:** Diese Wälzmühle sorgt dafür, daß der Kakao beim Raffinieren seine Feinheit erhält.
11. **Susan:** Wie fein ist das Pulver?

ANMERKUNGEN

(1) **to take stock of:** "Inventur, Bestandsaufnahme machen"; auch: "Bilanz ziehen".

(2) **a clean sheet** stammt aus der Juristensprache und bezeichnet ein unbelastetes Strafregister, eine "reine Weste". Im übertragenen Sinne: "wieder bei Null anfangen, ganz von vorne anfangen".

(3) **facilities:** Dieses Wort wird oft im Plural benutzt und bedeutet "Ein-, Vorrichtung, Installation, Anlage". *Facilities* kann außerdem die Bedeutungen "Möglichkeit" und "Leichtigkeit, Gewandtheit" haben: *shopping facilities* "Einkaufsmöglichkeiten"; *facilities in speech* "Redegewandtheit".

(4) **to cater for:** "bereitstellen, beliefern". *caterer* "Partyservice", *catering* "Gastronomie, Lieferung von Speisen und Getränken".

(5) **grinder** kann eine "Mühle" und eine "Schleifmaschine" sein. Die Hauptbedeutungen von *to grind* sind "(zer)mahlen; schleifen", weitere Bedeutungen sind "auspressen, "knirschen, sich festfahren" und "hart arbeiten", daher das Substantiv *grind* "Plackerei, harte Arbeit".

CHAPTER 24

12. **Torleiv Bilstad:** The ideal diameter of particles is 15 to 25 microns.

13. **Susan:** What happens if you don't obtain that size?

14. **Torleiv Bilstad:** If it's bigger, the chocolate has a sandy texture; if it's smaller, the chocolate sticks to the palate.

15. **Susan:** Is it the only quality control problem you have to cope with? **(6)**

16. **Torleiv Bilstad:** Crystallization is no easy matter either. We heat the chocolate to a temperature of 160 °F for 72 hours and let it cool down in very gradual stages so as to obtain fine, stable crystals. The process has to be long drawn out. Failing this, the chocolate blanches.

17. **Susan:** *(Smiling)* Too bad! We should have developed a white chocolate bar! It would have been easier to manufacture!

18. **Torleiv Bilstad:** *(Taking an Amigo bar on the line)* Susan, would you care for an Amigo?

19. **Susan:** I'm craving for an Amigo! *(Savouring it)* Mmm! It's delicious. But what is the expert's verdict? **(7)**

20. **Torleiv Bilstad:** *(Tongue in cheek)* Nice blackberry color... Good aromas determined by a judicious selection of cocoa beans... Cocoa beans roasted at the optimum temperature... The cooling process went smoothly... Harmonious blend of chocolate and pecan nuts... No doubt, this vintage bar should satisfy the most demanding consumer. **(8) (9)**

21. **Susan:** I've already developed a strong liking for Amigo bars. If I don't pay attention, it will turn into an addiction. How will I manage to keep a slim figure?

KAPITEL 24

12. **Torleiv Bilstad:** Der ideale Partikeldurchmesser liegt bei 15 bis 25 Mikrometern.

13. **Susan:** Was geschieht, wenn Sie diese Größe nicht erreichen?

14. **Torleiv Bilstad:** Sind die Partikel größer, hat die Schokolade eine sandige Konsistenz; sind sie kleiner, klebt sie am Gaumen.

15. **Susan:** Ist das das einzige Problem bei der Qualitätskontrolle, mit dem Sie sich befassen müssen?

16. **Torleiv Bilstad:** Auch die Kristallisation ist keine einfache Sache. Wir erhitzen die Schokolade 72 Stunden lang auf eine Temperatur von 160°F und lassen sie dann ganz langsam abkühlen, um feine, solide Kristalle zu erhalten. Der Prozeß muß sehr in die Länge gezogen werden. Wenn das nicht gelingt, wird die Schokolade weiß.

17. **Susan:** *(Lächelt)* Schade! Wir hätten einen weißen Schokoladenriegel entwickeln sollen! Er wäre einfacher zu produzieren gewesen!

18. **Torleiv Bilstad:** *(Nimmt einen Amigo-Riegel vom Fließband)* Hätten Sie gerne einen Amigo, Susan?

19. **Susan:** Ich bin ganz wild auf einen Amigo! *(Sie probiert ihn)* Mmm! Er ist köstlich. Aber wie lautet das Urteil des Experten?

20. **Torleiv Bilstad:** *(Ironisch)* Hübsche Brombeerfarbe... Gutes Aroma durch sorgfältige Auswahl der Kakaobohnen... Bei optimaler Temperatur geröstete Kakaobohnen... Sorgfältiger Abkühlungsprozeß... Ausgewogene Mischung aus Schokolade und Pekannüssen... Kein Zweifel, dieser Jahrgangsriegel sollte die anspruchsvollsten Verbraucher zufriedenstellen.

21. **Susan:** Ich habe schon eine große Vorliebe für Amigo-Riegel entwickelt. Wenn ich nicht aufpasse, wird es zu einer Sucht. Wie werde ich es schaffen, eine schlanke Figur zu behalten?

ANMERKUNGEN (Fortsetzung)

(6) **to cope with:** "sich befassen mit". *To cope with a situation* "mit einer Situation fertigwerden"; *to cope* "zurechtkommen mit"; *he just can't cope any more* "er wird einfach nicht mehr damit fertig".

(7) **to crave for:** "sich wünschen, sich sehnen nach" wird verwendet, wenn man ein starkes physiologisches oder auch krankhaftes Verlangen nach etwas hat (Zigaretten, Alkohol, usw). Es kann auch "erflehen, erbitten" bedeuten. *Craving* "(dringendes) Verlangen".

(8) **bean:** "Bohne". *French beans* oder *green beans* "grüne Bohnen". *Cocoa beans, coffee beans, soya beans* "Kakaobohnen", "Kaffeebohnen", "Sojabohnen". *To be full of beans* "putzmunter, quietschlebendig sein"; *he hasn't (got) a bean* "er hat keinen roten Heller".

(9) **vintage** hat zwei Bedeutungen: "Weinlese, Traubenernte" und "Jahrgang". *A vintage Corton* "ein Corton aus einem großen Jahrgang". *We had an early vintage in 1994* "1994 war die Traubenlese früh". Das Wort bedeutet auch "alt, antik, altmodisch": *vintage car* "Oldtimer".

CHAPTER 24 DOCUMENT

Quality, quality control and accreditation

Quality is a very subjective concept. A possible definition could be "what satisfies consumer needs". However, consumer needs keep changing. Whereas yesterday, a customer expressed a simple need by purchasing
a product he desired, today, his desires have become more complex. What's more, he does not necessarily express them. Some of his desires are implicit.

Quality is also crucial for a company's competitiveness which depends on the values perceived by its customers, but also by its supervisors, its staff, its bank, its shareholders, its neighbours, etc.
In a competitive business world, a system of references to standards proves to be necessary. As a matter of fact, there is a proliferation of standards today.

The ISO (International Standard Organization), which has existed for a long time, is a world federation of national standard organizations belonging to 90 countries.
In France, NF (Normes françaises) guarantees the quality of a product.
EN (European norms) performs the same function at a European level.
In the 1980s, quality improvement was sought through the setting-up of quality circles consisting of employees and supervisors who met regularly with a view to suggesting and implementing improvements.
In the 1990s, companies wish to go further. They aim at total quality or zero defect. Total quality is not just concerned with the quality of a specific product but also with all the various stages and aspects of a process.

Accreditation gives consumers a sense of trust in a product or company. Likewise, a company's staff may feel more motivated.
Standards are regularly reviewed because the notion of quality keeps changing. Although accreditation by ISO 9000 is not compulsory, it is in a firm's best interest to obtain it.

KAPITEL 24

Weinverkostung

Obwohl bereits im letzten Jahrhundert in Kalifornien Weinberge angelegt wurden, haben die Amerikaner erst in den letzten Jahren den Wein für sich entdeckt. Es waren die *Yuppies (Young Urban Professional People)*, die in den 80er Jahren damit begannen, einen guten Tropfen zum Essen zu schätzen.
Viele Weintrinker sind sich, was das Thema Wein betrifft, ihrer Unwissenheit bewußt und versuchen, sich durch das Lesen von Büchern oder Fachzeitschriften über Wein zu informieren. Jede Woche widmen Zeitungen wie *The New York Times* oder *The Los Angeles Times* diesem Thema eine Kolumne *(column)*. Die Zeitschrift *The Wine Spectator* ist mittlerweile weltweit bekannt.
Der ehemalige Rechtsanwalt Robert Parker ist ohne Zweifel der bekannteste und angesehenste Journalist für Weine *(wine writer)*. Die Weine, die in seiner Zeitschrift *The Wine Advocat* mit guten Noten beurteilt werden, finden reißenden Absatz, während die Weine, die eine schlechte Note erhalten, in den *wine shops* zu Ladenhütern werden. Robert Parker genießt so viel Ansehen, daß alle Winzer nervös werden, wenn er in ihre Weinkeller hinabsteigt!

CHAPTER 24

EXERCISES

Comprehension

Lesen Sie den Dialog aufmerksam durch. Beantworten Sie dann die nachfolgenden Fragen, und zwar immer in ganzen Sätzen:

1. What shows that UC does not trifle with quality? 2. What were UC's objectives when it built its San Antonio plant? 3. Why does Susan give a lot of credit to Torleiv Bilstad's opinion? 4. According to Susan, what is the danger of perfectionism? 5. Why does Torleiv Bilstad think the dangers of perfectionism are limited in the plant? 6. What important quality factor has not been overlooked? 7. Why does the refining quality matter a lot? 8. Why must the cooling process be closely monitored? 9. What do Torleiv Bilstad's comments on the Amigo bar make you think of? 10. What is Susan concerned about?

Vocabulary

Jede der untenstehenden Aussagen ist die Beschreibung zu einer der 10 im folgenden genannten Berufsbezeichnungen. Ordnen Sie jeder Berufsbezeichnung die passende Beschreibung zu. **Apprentice, production manager, foreman, quality-control manager, maintenance engineer, shift worker, director of human resources, shop steward, product executive, trainee.**

1. This member of a local branch committee of a trade union has been chosen by his fellow workers to represent them. 2. This workman has authority over the others in the workshop. 3. He deals with relationships between individual employees, their problems, their grievances. 4. He has agreed to work for a number of years in return for being taught a trade. 5. This student is acquiring valuable experience by working under the supervision of an engineer. 6. He is responsible for implementing plans for a product, monitoring results and taking corrective action. 7. He starts work as soon as another group of workers finishes. 8. He is in charge of production in the plant. 9. He is responsible for the upkeep of the assembly line. 10. He checks that the product is up to standard.

DO!

Leave no avenue unexplored in negotiations or problem resolution: there must always be a way out.

KAPITEL 24

LÖSUNGSVORSCHLÄGE

Verständnisübung

1. UC has appointed a quality control manager who is known for his perfectionism. **2.** It wanted to build a functional, brand new plant which could provide a pleasant working environment for the workers. It also wanted to improve quality by making good use of human resources. **3.** Because Torleiv Bilstad is not known for being complacent. **4.** If too much attention is paid to detail, operating efficiency may be forgotten, which would be detrimental to the company. **5.** Torleiv Bilstad thinks that UC can pay attention to detail because economy of operation is ensured by the latest technology. **6.** The human factor (human skill and experience) plays a big part in UC's San Antonio plant. **7.** Because, if the size of particles is not up to standard, it affects the taste of chocolate bars. **8.** If it is not gradual, the chocolate blanches. **9.** They make us think of wine-tasting comments. **10.** Susan is afraid of putting on weight.

Lösungen zur Wortschatzübung

1. Shop steward.
2. Foreman.
3. Director of human resources.
4. Apprentice.
5. Trainee.
6. Product executive.
7. Shift worker.
8. Production manager.
9. Maintenance engineer.
10. Quality control manager.

DON'T!

Don't think that your own culture is necessarily considered the best by everybody.

CHAPTER 24

Application

In der linken Spalte finden Sie eine Liste mit Merkmalen, die auf die in der rechten Spalte aufgeführten Produkte zutreffen. Ordnen Sie jedem Produkt die passenden Merkmale zu. Es ist nicht nötig, daß Sie jedes einzelne Wort kennen und verstehen; Werbebotschaften werden global erfaßt.

Characteristics

a. Inside the case beats a movement that has taken a year to make, from the very first operation on the first tiny part through the final assembly by our craftsmen in Geneva.

b. Genuine textured cowhide, pocket for airline tickets, two full-length pockets, opening across entire width with separate snap-on travel cheque-holder, six credit-card pockets, ID pocket and passport compartment.

c. Rich blending of up to six varieties of fine Arabica beans from the world's greatest plantations. Precision roasting process.

d. Rich tan color. Black metal hardware. Roomy 14" x 17" x 6" cargo compartment plus three handy expandable outside pockets. Two 2" adjustable shoulder straps.

Products

1. Oranges

2. Backpack

3. Sleepcap

4. Teddy bear

KAPITEL 24

e. Special knit "gives" naturally to fit any head (man's or woman's); never constricts or binds…, caresses your scalp with gentle warmth.

f. Real lamb, an ingredient not often found in this type of product, brewer's rice and other wholesome ingredients. It's naturally preserved with vitamin E. It has no added artificial colors or preservatives.

g. Genuine premium-quality calf leather is hand-stitched. Inside three compartments plus a card and pen-holder. Outside, two expandable pockets and a zipper section.

h. Plush and huggable, full-jointed reproduction of the 1903 original version offered to Theodore Roosevelt.

i. This item made of silk twill features a contemporary pattern of computer parts, chips and circuitry on a black background.

j. Plump and juicy, tree-ripened, extra-good taste. Shipped directly from our groves since 1948.

5. Tie

6. Watch

7. Wallet

8. Dog food

9. Coffee

10. School bag

Lösungen

1. j. **2.** d. **3.** e. **4.** h. **5.** i. **6.** a. **7.** b. **8.** f. **9.** c. **10.** g.

CHAPTER 25

Promoting the product

Susan and Dr Clifford Cutler, who was her adviser at Texas A&M, are having an open discussion about some issues raised by the impending launching of Amigo bars. **(1) (2)**

1. **Dr Cutler:** So, UC wishes to communicate to its target market positive, persuasive information about its products. You must also present the message in a language it can grasp. **(3)**

2. **Susan:** I've seen to that!

3. **Dr Cutler:** *(Chuckling)* That's a girl!... *(Serious again)* From what I gather, you've been doing a really good job so far! Thanks to your thorough market study, UC has collected useful data which will be critical in successfully communicating with its target market.

4. **Susan:** We know what type of information will persuade consumers to buy Amigo bars. We know who our customers are. We know what information they use when making purchase decisions.

5. **Dr Cutler:** Which means that UC can now plan, implement, coordinate and control all communications. Advertising, sales promotion, personal selling and public relations will of course be the four major elements of your promotion mix. **(4) (5)**

KAPITEL 25

Produktwerbung

Susan und Dr. Clifford Cutler, der an der Texas A&M ihr Studienberater war, führen ein offenes Gespräch über einige Probleme, die durch die bevorstehende Einführung der Amigo-Riegel aufgetaucht sind.

1. **Dr. Cutler:** UC will also den Zielmärkten positive, überzeugende Informationen über seine Produkte vermitteln. Sie müssen die Werbebotschaft auch in einer Sprache präsentieren, die die Leute verstehen können.
2. **Susan:** Dafür habe ich gesorgt!
3. **Dr. Cutler:** *(Lacht leise vor sich hin)* Dieses Mädchen!... *(Wird wieder ernst)* Demnach zu urteilen, was ich mitbekommen habe, haben Sie bis jetzt wirklich gute Arbeit geleistet! Dank Ihrer gründlichen Marktstudie hat UC nützliche Daten gesammelt, die für eine erfolgreiche Kommunikation mit seinem Zielmarkt wichtig sein werden.
4. **Susan:** Wir wissen, welche Art von Information die Verbraucher überzeugt, Amigo-Riegel zu kaufen. Wir wissen, wer unsere Kunden sind. Wir wissen, welche Informationen die Kunden verwenden, wenn sie Kaufentscheidungen treffen.
5. **Dr. Cutler:** Was bedeutet, daß UC nun alle Kommunikationsmaßnahmen planen, in die Praxis umsetzen, koordinieren und steuern kann. Werbung, Verkaufsförderung, Direktverkauf an den Kunden und Public Relations werden natürlich die vier wichtigsten Hauptelemente Ihrer Werbekampagne sein.

ANMERKUNGEN

(1) **Dr (Clifford Cutler):** Siehe Kapitel 1, Anmerkung 9.
(2) **issue** kann viele verschiedene Bedeutungen haben: "Thema, Problem, Streitfrage, Frage, Ausgang" (Synonym: *exit*), "Ausgabe" und "Auflage". *Issue (of a magazine)* "Ausgabe einer Zeitschrift". *Back issue* "eine alte Ausgabe". *To issue* "herausgeben, veröffentlichen"; "ausgeben, ausstellen, erteilen".
(3) **to grasp** heißt konkret "erfassen, ergreifen", im übertragenen Sinne auch "erfassen, verstehen, begreifen". *Something is within/beyond somebody's grasp* "etwas ist in/außer jemandes Reichweite".
(4) **advertising:** "Werbung". Nicht zu verwechseln mit *publicity* "Reklamewesen, (Kunden)Werbung, Publizität; Publicity": Zwar ist das Ziel, das ein Unternehmen mit diesen beiden Formen der Kommunikation verfolgt, das gleiche, jedoch sind die beiden Wörter nicht synonym. *Advertising* ist eine vom Inserenten bezahlte Werbung, *Publicity* ist kostenlos (und oft unbezahlbar); sie kann das Ergebnis von PR sein, kann positiv wie negativ sein und wird von den Medien in Eigenregie verbreitet. In den USA war der Begriff *publicity* früher synonym mit "Public Relations (PR = Öffentlichkeitsarbeit)". *In the full glare of publicity* "im grellen Licht der Öffentlichkeit".
(5) **promotion mix** bezeichnet die Auswahl und das Aufeinanderabstimmen verschiedener Werbemittel: Anzeigenwerbung, Public Relations, Verkaufsförderung usw.

CHAPTER 25

6. **Susan:** Although feedback from advertising is generally slow, if it occurs at all, we intend to direct TV commercials at children on their Saturday morning programs. Thus, we can hope to establish brand loyalty during the early years. **(6) (7) (8)**

7. **Dr Cutler:** Advertising normally has less persuasive power over customers than other forms of promotion.

8. **Susan:** I'm aware of that. Face-to-face communication with potential buyers such as supermarkets would be another element of our promotional mix. Because of its one-to-one nature, personal selling can be very effective.

9. **Dr Cutler:** (*Ironically*) Because it is communication with only one individual, it costs a lot, too.

10. **Susan:** Which is why we will privilege sales promotion. We will offer retailers, salespersons and consumers various inducements such as coupons, sweepstakes, refunds, displays for purchasing Amigo bars... Just think of the thrill of a sweepstake in which consumers could win trips to Cape Kennedy or Disneyland Paris! **(9) (10) (11)**

11. **Dr Cutler:** What about public relations?

12. **Susan:** It will be planned and implemented so that it is compatible with and supportive of the other elements in the promotion mix. I have prepared news releases and encouraged media people to broadcast and print them. Quite a few journalists have been invited to visit our San Antonio plant. We should have magazine, newspaper, radio and TV news stories about our new facilities.

KAPITEL 25

6. **Susan:** Obwohl die Resonanz aus Werbeaktionen in der Regel langsam ist, wenn es überhaupt eine Reaktion gibt, haben wir vor, TV-Werbespots für Kinder in den Samstagmorgen-Programmen zu bringen. Auf diese Weise können wir hoffen, schon bei den Jüngeren Markentreue zu erreichen.

7. **Dr. Cutler:** Werbung besitzt normalerweise weniger Überzeugungskraft bei Kunden als andere Formen der Verkaufsförderung.

8. **Susan:** Ich bin mir dessen bewußt. Die unmittelbare Kommunikation mit potentiellen Kunden wie z.B. Supermärkten wäre ein weiteres Element unserer Werbekampagne. Aufgrund seiner Von-Mensch-zu-Mensch-Eigenschaft kann der Direktverkauf an den Kunden sehr effizient sein.

9. **Dr. Cutler:** *(Ironisch)* Da es Kommunikation mit nur einer Person ist, kostet es auch viel Geld.

10. **Susan:** Das ist der Grund, warum wir der Verkaufsförderung Vorrang einräumen. Wir werden den Einzelhändlern, Verkäufern und Verbrauchern verschiedene Anreize wie z.B. Coupons, Preisausschreiben, Rabatte und Displays beim Kauf von Amigo-Riegeln anbieten... Denken Sie doch nur daran, wie aufregend ein Preisausschreiben sein kann, bei dem die Konsumenten Reisen nach Cape Kennedy oder Disneyland in Paris gewinnen können!

11. **Dr. Cutler:** Was ist mit Public Relations?

12. **Susan:** Das wird so geplant und in die Praxis umgesetzt, daß es kompatibel mit den anderen Elementen der Werbekampagne ist und diese unterstützt. Ich habe Pressemitteilungen vorbereitet und Medienleute ermuntert, sie zu senden und zu drucken. Es sind eine ganze Menge Journalisten eingeladen worden, um unser Werk in San Antonio zu besichtigen. Man sollte in Zeitschriften, Zeitungen, im Radio und im Fernsehen von unseren neuen Einrichtungen sprechen.

ANMERKUNGEN (Fortsetzung)

(6) **feedback:** "Reaktion, Resonanz, Feedback, Rückmeldung".
(7) **commercial:** "Werbespot, Werbung" im Fernsehen, Radio usw.
(8) **loyalty:** "Treue"; *brand loyalty* "Markentreue": Die Bindung eines Kunden an ein Produkt einer bestimmten Marke, um zu erreichen, daß der Kunde nicht das Produkt einer anderen Marke kauft; *customer loyalty* "Kundentreue"; *loyalty card* "Kundenkarte".
(9) **(money-off) coupons:** "Gutscheine" für Kunden.
(10) **sweepstake** "Verlosung, Preisausschreiben". *He "sweeps in" all the stakes.*
(11) **thrill:** "Aufregung, Faszination, Nervenkitzel". Daher auch *thriller* "spannender Roman, Film" o.ä.

CHAPTER 25

13. **Dr Cutler:** Will you be ready on time for the launching?

14. **Susan:** We'd better be! We have to launch Amigo bars in early September when children go back to school and consumers acquire new habits.

15. **Dr Cutler:** By the way, Susan, I have also heard about a flashy idea of yours, on the grapevine... **(12) (13)**

16. **Susan:** What flashy idea?

17. **Dr Cutler:** Hot-air balloons shaped like Amigo bars.

18. **Susan:** *(Laughing)* It is not a flashy idea but a high-visibility promotional tool. As my marketing professor would have said!

KAPITEL 25

13. **Dr. Cutler:** Werden Sie rechtzeitig für die Produkteinführung fertig sein?

14. **Susan:** Das sollten wir! Wir müssen die Amigo-Riegel Anfang September einführen, wenn die Kinder wieder in die Schule gehen und die Verbraucher neue Gewohnheiten annehmen.

15. **Dr. Cutler:** Nebenbei bemerkt, Susan, man hat mir von Ihrer tollen Idee erzählt...

16. **Susan:** Was für eine tolle Idee?

17. **Dr. Cutler:** Heißluftballons in Form von Amigo-Riegeln.

18. **Susan:** *(Lacht)* Das ist keine tolle Idee, sondern ein gut sichtbares Instrument für die Verkaufsförderung. Wie mein Professor in Marketing sagen würde!

ANMERKUNGEN (Fortsetzung)

(12) flashy: "auffällig, auffallend".

(13) grapevine bedeutet wörtlich "Wein". *To hear* oder *to learn something on the grapevine* "etwas durch Mund-zu-Mund-Propaganda erfahren". Man verwendet auch den Begriff *bush telephone*.

CHAPTER 25 — DOCUMENT

Public relations

Public relations is designed to establish, maintain or improve mutual understanding, acceptance and trust between an organization and the various publics with whom it has contact.

It is used to inform people about a firm's products, brands and activities, to enhance its image, to maintain it if it is favorable or to overcome a negative image (eg in the case of an environmental disaster).

Among the tools which are at a public relations officer's disposal, we can mention news releases, audio-visual material, speeches by a charismatic manager, special events such as competitions, anniversaries, exhibits, grand openings, etc.

Public relations privileges press relations by placing newsworthy information in the news media, lobbying, ie dealing with lawmakers to promote or defeat regulations and counseling, ie advising management about public issues and company image. It must also be pointed out that organizations usually do not neglect internal communications to promote understanding within the firm.

Among the most famous public relations operations, we can mention the *I love New York* campaign which attracted millions of tourists to the depressed US city.

As a communication tool, public relations is more credible than advertising because a company's message is perceived by the buyer not so much as sales-directed communication as news. As it is informative without attempting to be persuasive (the message is not repeated), it appears to be objective.

For marketers, public relations can be a very effective and fairly inexpensive tool, but today, companies must be very imaginative and innovative
in this field. For instance, most company news releases are ignored by the press, which explains why many PR officers try to develop personal relationships with media editors.

A taste for communication is critical for success in a PR job. A college or business-school education combined with writing skills appears to be the best preparation for a PR career but many employees also learn on the job.

KAPITEL 25

 Wettbewerbe, Spiele und Lotterien

Wettbewerbe, Spiele und Lotterien, die sich an bestimmte Artikel knüpfen, sind bei den amerikanischen Konsumenten sehr beliebt. Bei allen drei Methoden der Verkaufsförderung winken dem glücklichen Gewinner Preise in Form von Geld, Reisen oder Waren, wobei hier entweder der Zufall entscheidet oder der Konsument selbst seines Glückes Schmied ist, indem er beispielsweise den Namen eines Produkts erraten, eine Werbemelodie *(jingle)* wiedererkennen oder einen Slogan erfinden muß. Der Gewinner wird jeweils von einer Jury ermittelt. Bei Spielen erhält der Konsument jedesmal, wenn er einen bestimmten Artikel erwirbt, Buchstaben, Bilder oder Bingo-Nummern, die er sammeln muß. Mit jedem Buchstaben, jedem Bild und jeder Nummer erhöht sich die Chance für einen Preisgewinn. Bei Lotterien wird der Name des Gewinners ausgelost.

CHAPTER 25

EXERCISES

Comprehension

Lesen Sie den Dialog aufmerksam durch. Beantworten Sie dann die nachfolgenden Fragen, und zwar immer in ganzen Sätzen:

1. What useful effects has the market study had? **2.** How does UC intend to use the data collected? **3.** What is the combination of advertising, sales promotion, personal promotion and public relations called? **4.** What does Susan expect from TV commercials? **5.** What is the drawback of TV commercials? **6.** Why is face-to-face communication with potential buyers usually effective? **7.** Why will Susan privilege sales promotion, however? **8.** What is a necessary condition to make public relations effective? **9.** What public relations action has Susan prepared? **10.** What advantage does Susan see in Amigo-bar-shaped hot-air balloons?

DO!

**Be sure to buy dollars before leaving for America.
Very few banks will accept foreign currency.
Even Canadian dollars are not always accepted.**

KAPITEL 25

LÖSUNGSVORSCHLÄGE

Verständnisübung

1. It has enabled UC to know prospective customers' personality and purchasing behavior and thus to communicate with this target market successfully. **2.** UC intends to plan, implement, coordinate and control the various aspects of communication. **3.** It is called the promotion mix. **4.** She hopes to establish brand loyalty among children. She expects them to keep buying Amigo bars when they are older. **5.** They have less persuasive power than people commonly believe. **6.** Because personal relationships are established between seller and buyer. **7.** Because it is cheaper. **8.** Public relations must be well integrated into the promotion mix. **9.** She has prepared news releases for media people and organized guided tours of the San Antonio plant for newspaper, radio and TV journalists. **10.** Many people can see them.

DON'T!

Don't forget to buy an adapter for your shaver when you go to the USA. The plugs there are flat and the tension is 110 volts.

CHAPTER 25

Vocabulary

Setzen Sie das passende Wort in die Kästchen ein. Die jeweiligen Auswahlmöglichkeiten finden Sie unter jedem Satz:

1. Public relations is designed to create or maintain a favorable ⬜ for an organization.
   a. portrayal; **b.** picture; **c.** image; **d.** drawing.

2. When Amigo bars were launched, UC issued a press ⬜ to all news agencies.
   a. release; **b.** warning; **c.** item; **d.** advertisement.

3. A ⬜ seems more real and believable to readers than ads do.
   a. lie; **b.** cartoon; **c.** hoax; **d.** news story.

4. The ⬜ under the photograph was very witty.
   a. legend; **b.** caption; **c.** print; **d.** issue.

5. This dishonest firm lost its case because it was proven guilty of ⬜
   a. wrong information; **b.** sensational news; **c.** lying publicity; **d.** misleading advertising.

6. UC ⬜ $2,000,000 for the launching of Amigo bars.
   a. invested; **b.** squandered; **c.** withdrew; **d.** allocated.

7. Russ Kingman feels sponsorship is the most effective way of promoting ⬜ towards UC in this town.
   a. civility; **b.** goodness; **c.** good times; **d.** goodwill.

8. This clever Advertising Manager knows how to ⬜ the strengths of a firm successfully.
   a. play up; **b.** show off; **c.** turn on; **d.** hijack.

9. The journalists were entertained at a convenient ⬜ with good transport and parking facilities.
   a. location; **b.** spell; **c.** stage; **d.** course.

10. Susan used all available ⬜ of communication to get her message across.
    a. canals; **b.** charts; **c.** flows; **d.** channels.

Lösungen zur Wortschatzübung: 1. c. 2. a. 3. d. 4. b. 5. d. 6. d. 7. d. 8. a. 9. a. 10. d.

KAPITEL 25

Praktische Übung

Ordnen Sie den Wörtern in der linken Spalte, die alle aus dem PR-Vokabular stammen, die passende Definition aus der rechten Spalte zu.

Begriff

Definition

1. Public relations

    a. A film distributed to TV stations and newspapers in the hope that its content will be used in news stories.

2. Feature article

    b. A 3,000-word article prepared for a specific publication.

3. Editorial film

    c. A meeting held for media representatives.

4. News release

    d. A tape distributed to radio stations and newspapers in the hope that its content will be used for publication.

5. Captioned photograph

    e. Communication activities aimed at creating and maintaining a favorable image of the organization.

6. Editorial tape

    f. A picture with a brief description of the event pictured.

7. Press conference

    g. A one-page typewritten copy about the purchase of brand new high-tech equipment.

Lösungen: 1. e. 2. b. 3. a. 4. g. 5. f. 6. d. 7. c.

CHAPTER 26

A salesperson's life (1)

Susan is pleased to have a chat with Jerry Dixon, one of UC's new star salesmen. She meets him in his office after he has completed his report.

1. **Susan:** The organization has devoted substantial resources to training the sales force.

2. **Jerry Dixon:** Indeed, it has. We have been given crash courses by sales managers and the technical specialists from within the organization, not to mention various motivational speakers, including a well-known football coach! **(2) (3)**

3. **Susan:** Really! Well, football coaches are good at pumping up their team but can they really motivate a sales force?

4. **Jerry Dixon:** A famous sports figure is in a good position to help salespeople improve their performance through motivation.

5. **Susan:** UC has plenty of good ideas. Still, I'm a bit sceptical about that one. After all, coaches usually lack business experience and savvy. **(4)**

6. **Jerry Dixon:** But they leave a sales force excited and hungry to win a sale. In the short run, a good motivational speaker can create an enthusiastic sales atmosphere for a company.

7. **Susan:** What training methods and materials did the company use?

8. **Jerry Dixon:** Very varied ones: lectures, video-films, texts, simulation exercises, case studies, on-the-job training... **(5)**

9. **Susan:** What's the key to success in sales, Jerry?

10. **Jerry Dixon:** In my opinion, in order to succeed, a salesman must communicate with customers and not change them into objects. Like Lieutenant Columbo, he is a good listener. He must solve problems and not bluff his way out of situations or place blame...

KAPITEL 26

Das Leben eines Verkäufers

Susan freut sich, eine Unterhaltung mit Jerry Dixon führen zu können, einer Spitzenkraft unter den neuen Verkäufern bei UC. Sie trifft ihn in seinem Büro, nachdem er seinen Bericht fertiggestellt hat.

1. **Susan:** Das Unternehmen hat beträchtliche Ressourcen für die Schulung der Verkaufsmannschaft vorgesehen.
2. **Jerry Dixon:** In der Tat. Wir haben Schnellkurse von den Verkaufsleitern und den technischen Experten aus dem Unternehmen erhalten, ganz zu schweigen von verschiedenen Motivationstrainern, darunter ein bekannter Football-Trainer!
3. **Susan:** Tatsächlich?! Naja, Football-Trainer sind gut, wenn es darum geht, ihr Team anzuspornen, aber können sie wirklich das Verkaufspersonal motivieren?
4. **Jerry Dixon:** Eine berühmte Person aus der Welt des Sports ist gut in der Lage, dem Verkaufspersonal zu helfen, seine Leistungen durch Motivation zu steigern.
5. **Susan:** UC hat viele gute Ideen. Aber ich bin doch etwas skeptisch, was diese betrifft. Vor allem fehlt Trainern normalerweise die Geschäftserfahrung und der Durchblick.
6. **Jerry Dixon:** Aber hinterher ist die Verkaufsmannschaft begeistert und brennt darauf, Verkäufe zu tätigen. Kurzfristig kann ein guter Motivationstrainer eine enthusiastische Verkaufsatmosphäre für ein Unternehmen schaffen.
7. **Susan:** Welche Schulungsmethoden und -materialien hat die Firma benutzt?
8. **Jerry Dixon:** Sehr unterschiedliche: Vorträge, Videos, Texte, Simulationsübungen, Fallstudien, Fortbildung...
9. **Susan:** Worin liegt beim Verkauf der Schlüssel zum Erfolg, Jerry?
10. **Jerry Dixon:** Meiner Meinung nach muß ein Verkäufer, um erfolgreich zu sein, mit den Kunden kommunizieren und sie nicht zu Objekten machen. Wie Inspektor Colombo ist er ein guter Zuhörer. Er muß Lösungen für Probleme finden und darf sich nicht durchmogeln oder anderen die Schuld in die Schuhe schieben...

ANMERKUNGEN

(1) Der Begriff **salesperson** umfaßt die unterschiedlichsten Tätigkeiten: *sales rep(resentative), travel(l)ing salesman, commercial travel(l)er, area manager, sales manager, technical salesman, sales engineer...*
Verschiedene Berufsbezeichnungen können sich dabei auf gleiche Verantwortungsbereiche beziehen, genau wie eine einzige Berufsbezeichnung verschiedene Verantwortungsbereiche abdecken kann. Deshalb sollte sich ein Bewerber für eine Stelle immer darüber informieren, welche Tätigkeitsbereiche die jeweilige Stelle genau umfaßt.

(2) **crash course:** "Intensiv-, Schnellkurs".

(3) **football** meint hier den *American football.* Unser europäischer "Fußball" wird in Amerika *soccer* genannt.

(4) **savvy** bedeutet als Verb "kapieren", als Nomen "Durchblick" und als Adjektiv "ausgebufft".

(5) **on-the-job training** "Schulung vor Ort, Fortbildung an der Arbeitsstelle"; "Praktikum". *On-the-job accident* "Betriebs-, Arbeitsunfall".

CHAPTER 26

11. Susan: How do you react when you face a refusal?

12. Jerry Dixon: I try not to personalize rejection. I try to take it as information I can learn from. You see, a salesman must always upgrade his skills. **(6)**

13. Susan: It's good to meet someone who is so positive!

14. Jerry Dixon: I love my work. UC leaves its sales force an adequate degree of freedom. It provides a good income and incentives. **(7)**

15. Susan: What sales compensation program are you offered? **(8)**

16. Jerry Dixon: An adequate income combination of salary and commission. Besides, UC offers a certain number of fringe benefits. And, of course, it reimburses expenses.

17. Susan: In such conditions, you're bound to work efficiently.

18. Jerry Dixon: Wes Coyner, the Sales Manager, has seen to it. He has managed to maximize the sales force's sales time and to minimize time and expenses spent on traveling and waiting.

19. Susan: I also know that Wes insists a lot on the sales force being able to enjoy all kinds of perks.

20. Jerry Dixon: It means a lot to me to have a telephone credit-card, sickness benefits, paid vacations, etc. And I was forgetting, membership of a health-club. *(Smiling)* Might come in handy to lose a bit of this paunch! **(9)**

KAPITEL 26

11. **Susan:** Wie reagieren Sie, wenn Sie eine ablehnende Antwort erhalten?

12. **Jerry Dixon:** Ich versuche, eine Ablehnung nicht persönlich zu nehmen. Ich versuche, sie als eine Information zu akzeptieren, aus der ich lernen kann. Sehen Sie, ein Verkäufer muß immer seine Fähigkeiten erweitern.

13. **Susan:** Es ist gut, jemanden zu treffen, der so positiv denkt!

14. **Jerry Dixon:** Ich liebe meine Arbeit. UC läßt seinen Verkäufern ein ausreichendes Maß an Freiheit. Die Firma bietet ein korrektes Einkommen und Leistungsanreize.

15. **Susan:** Wie sieht es mit Ihrer Bezahlung aus?

16. **Jerry Dixon:** Eine angemessene Einkommenskombination aus Gehalt und Provision. Darüber hinaus bietet UC eine bestimmte Anzahl von Sonderleistungen. Und natürlich werden die Spesen erstattet.

17. **Susan:** Unter solchen Bedingungen müssen Sie effizient arbeiten.

18. **Jerry Dixon:** Dafür hat Wes Coyner, der Verkaufsleiter, gesorgt. Er hat es geschafft, die Verkaufszeiten der Mannschaft zu maximieren und die Reise- und Wartezeiten auf ein Minimum zu reduzieren.

19. **Susan:** Ich weiß auch, daß Wes sehr darauf besteht, daß die Verkaufsmannschaft in den Genuß aller möglichen Sondervergünstigungen kommt.

20. **Jerry Dixon:** Es bedeutet mir viel, eine Telefonkarte, Leistungen im Krankheitsfall, bezahlten Urlaub usw. zu haben. Und was ich vergessen habe: die Mitgliedschaft in einem Fitness-Club. *(Lächelt)* Könnte sich als ganz nützlich erweisen, um den dicken Bauch ein bißchen wegzukriegen!

ANMERKUNGEN (Fortsetzung)

(6) **to upgrade:** Eigentlich "befördern, höherstufen". *He has been upgraded to senior management level* "Er wurde in die obere Managementetage befördert".

(7) **incentive** "(Leistungs)Anreiz". *Incentive bonus/payment* "Anreizprämie", *incentive scheme* "(Leistungs-)Anreizsystem".

(8) **compensation:** "Lohn; Gehalt, Vergütung", auch "Entschädigung".

(9) **sickness benefits** "Leistungen im Krankheitsfall, Krankengeld", *sickness insurance* "Krankenversicherung".

CHAPTER 26   DOCUMENT

A salesperson's report

Every salesperson at UC has been assigned a sales territory. Jerry Dixon has based his business on three platforms:
- *a buying platform consisting of regular, loyal customers.*
- *a working platform consisting of customers he has approached but who are not yet buyers.*
- *a market platform consisting of customers he has identified but not yet approached.*

After each call on his customers, Jerry Dixon fills out the following form:

Analysis of Results

Customer's name and address: ....

Type of customer: ....

Business potential: ....

Purpose of call: ....

Date of call: ....

Person met: ....

Function in the company: ....

Nature of the message conveyed: ....

How did the customer respond to this message? ....

What argument interested him most? ....

Have all our services been put forward? ....

Has an order been placed? ....

Follow-up date: ....

KAPITEL 26

Der Sport und die Firma

Ausdruck der enormen Popularität des Sports in den USA ist die Anzahl der Sportseiten und -schlagzeilen in den regionalen und überregionalen Zeitungen. Ebenso gehören Sportübertragungen zu den beliebtesten und am meisten gesehenen Fernsehprogrammen.
Die Unternehmen fördern die Ausübung verschiedener Sportarten wie Baseball, Basketball, Volleyball usw. in Sport- und Fitness-Clubs und stellen interessierten Mitarbeitern Trainingsmöglichkeiten zur Verfügung. Für die Unternehmensleitung liegt der Nutzen des Sports darin, daß er die Moral der Angestellten hebt und darüber hinaus das Image des Unternehmens stärkt. Diejenigen Mitarbeiter, die nicht Mitglied in einer Sportmannschaft des Unternehmens sind, sehen es als ihre Pflicht an, bei der Organisation der Wettkämpfe mitzuhelfen und – ungeachtet der Außentemperaturen – ihre in einem Team engagierten Kollegen anzufeuern.

CHAPTER 26

EXERCISES

Comprehension

Lesen Sie den Dialog aufmerksam durch. Beantworten Sie dann die nachfolgenden Fragen, und zwar immer in ganzen Sätzen:

1. Why is Susan pleased to have a chat with Jerry Dixon? 2. What appears to be a priority at UC? 3. What kind of training has UC provided for its sales force? 4. Why was a football coach hired to train the sales force? 5. What does Jerry Dixon think of the coach's talk? 6. According to Jerry Dixon, what are the qualities of a good salesperson? 7. What effect should rejection have on a salesperson? 8. What kind of pay does Jerry Dixon receive? 9. What characterizes Wes Coyner's approach to salesmanship? 10. What problem can a health-club membership help Jerry Dixon solve?

Translation

1. Unsere Politik besteht darin, die Verkaufsmannschaft gut zu schulen. 2. Unsere Verkäufer haben Schnellkurse an der Handelskammer besucht. 3. Warum, denken Sie, fehlt Trainern der Geschäftssinn? 4. Im Gegensatz zum Personalleiter glaubt der Leiter der Verkaufsabteilung an die Ausbildung vor Ort. 5. Junge Verkäufer denken, daß sie über das Verkaufsgeschäft genau Bescheid wissen, da sie auf der Schule an vielen Fallstudien gearbeitet haben. 6. Es ist ein Fehler zu denken, daß ein Verkäufer sich durchmogeln kann. 7. Einige Großhändler beklagten sich darüber, daß der Vertreter unserer Firma zu viel redet und sie zu wenig informiert. 8. Wenn Handelsvertreter doch nur auf das, was sie sagen, so sehr achten würden wie auf die Art und Weise, wie sie sich kleiden! 9. Dieser Verkäufer ist nicht einmal in der Lage, ein Preisangebot zu machen, ohne in seine Preisliste zu sehen. 10. Bei einem erfolgreichen Verkauf gibt es weder Gewinner noch Verlierer, sondern zwei Gewinner.

KAPITEL 26

LÖSUNGSVORSCHLÄGE

Verständnisübung

1. Because she is interested in discussing sales with one of the company's best salespeople. 2. The training of the sales force appears to be a priority at UC. 3. It has provided commercial as well as technical training to its sales force. 4. Because UC thought he could motivate the sales force effectively. 5. He thinks it has positive effects in the short run. 6. A good salesperson is a good communicator who respects the customers, considers them as partners, listens to them and tries to solve their problems. 7. A good salesperson should not consider it as a personal failure but as an opportunity to learn. 8. He receives a fixed salary and a commission. Besides, he is entitled to some fringe benefits. 9. Wes Coyner insists on efficient work by making sure salespeople devote as much time as possible to the sales act. 10. It can help him solve his weight problem.

Übersetzungsübung

1. Our policy is to train the sales force well. 2. Our salespeople have followed crash courses at the Chamber of Commerce. 3. Why do you think coaches lack business sense? 4. Unlike the Director of Human Resources, the Head of the Sales Department believes in on-the-job training. 5. Young salespersons think that they know the ins and outs of sales because they worked on many case studies at school. 6. It's a mistake to think that a salesperson can bluff his way out of situations. 7. Some wholesalers complained that our company's rep(resentative) talked too much and informed them too little. 8. If only sales representatives were as careful about what they say as they are about the way they dress! 9. This salesman is not even able to quote a price without looking at his price list. 10. In a successful sale, there is neither winner nor loser, but two winners.

CHAPTER 26

Application

Donald Gonnerman versucht, Wes Coyner, den Leiter der Verkaufsabteilung bei UC, in San Antonio wegen einer Bestellung, die er kürzlich aufgegeben hat, anzurufen. Er erreicht zunächst die Telefonzentrale.

Bringen Sie die folgenden Sätze in die richtige Reihenfolge.

1. Good morning. This is Don Gonnerman, a wholesaler from Springfield, Missouri. I would like to speak to Mr Wes Coyner about the order I placed the day before yesterday.

2. I'd like to know whether the 250,000 Amigo bars I ordered the day before yesterday have been sent off.

3. United Chocolate at San Antonio. Good morning.

4. I will, indeed.

5. You're welcome. Good bye.

6. Thank you very much, Mr Coyner.

7. Wes Coyner speaking. Hello, Mr Gonnerman. What can I do for you?

8. In that case, could you please add an extra 50,000 bars to my order. I'm sending a fax for confirmation right away.

9. I'll put you through to him. Could you hang on a second, please?

10. Not yet. They will be despatched by truck tomorrow morning and they should arrive in Springfield the following day.

DO!

When you go to the USA, take copies of your résumé (CV) and photographs of your family. Americans like to know who they are dealing with.

KAPITEL 26

Lösung

3.
1.
9.
7.
2.
10.
8.
4.
6.
5.

DON'T!

***Don't forget what German businessmen say:
'When I want to sell something to you,
I will speak your language.
If you want to sell something to me,
you will have to speak German.'***

CHAPTER 27

In charge of exporting

In her luxurious office and suite on the 30th floor of a business building on Pasadena Boulevard, Susan is planning her agenda for the next four weeks with her young assistant Greg Jimenez. **(1) (2)**

1. **Susan:** The dates of my trip are now more or less final. I will leave immediately after our monthly executive meeting, next week. You will find in the computer a tentative itinerary.
   My first stop will be Sydney, to attend the International Food Packaging Conference. Will you please book me onto a non-stop flight – business class – and confirm hotel reservations there.

2. **Greg:** I've already sent a fax to all our area representatives to let them know that you would hold an informal briefing session there.

3. **Susan:** That reminds me that we will need a seminar room.

4. **Greg:** That has been attended to. We've reserved space to hold about twenty-five, with overhead projector and all the other audio-visual equipment.

5. **Susan:** I would like you to draft a memorandum, for my signature, addressed to all Sales Managers, explaining the purpose of my trip: to get to know our local staff and to pay courtesy calls to our important clients so as to establish a personal
   relationship with them. **(3)**

6. **Greg:** Did you have time to look at my recap of sales figures for the first two quarters, broken down by area? **(4) (5)**

7. **Susan:** Yes, that was a neat job and great help. Thanks a lot. We seem to be doing well everywhere except in Japan.

8. **Greg:** Our market share there has remained stagnant for the last three years. Our advertising campaigns haven't been much of a success.

9. **Susan:** This is where we will have to concentrate our efforts in the next few months... By the way, who is that Mr Tanabe with whom I have an appointment on Friday morning?

KAPITEL 27

Verantwortlich für den Export

In ihrem luxuriösen Büro mit Suite in der 30. Etage eines Geschäftsgebäudes am Pasadena Boulevard plant Susan zusammen mit ihrem jungen Assistenten Greg Jimenez ihr Programm für die nächsten vier Wochen.

1. **Susan:** Die Daten meiner Reise stehen nun mehr oder weniger fest. Ich werde sofort nach unserer monatlichen Sitzung der Unternehmensleitung nächste Woche aufbrechen. Sie werden im Computer eine vorläufige Reiseroute finden. Mein erster Stopp wird in Sydney sein, wo ich an der Internationalen Konferenz für Lebensmittelverpackung teilnehmen werde. Würden Sie bitte einen Non-Stop-Flug – Business Class – für mich buchen und die Hotelreservierungen dort bestätigen.
2. **Greg:** Ich habe bereits ein Fax an all unsere Gebietsvertreter geschickt, um sie darüber zu informieren, daß Sie dort eine informelle Besprechung abhalten.
3. **Susan:** Das erinnert mich daran, daß wir einen Seminarraum benötigen werden.
4. **Greg:** Darum haben wir uns schon gekümmert. Wir haben Platz für etwa 25 Personen reserviert, mit Overhead-Projektor und der ganzen anderen audiovisuellen Ausstattung.
5. **Susan:** Ich hätte gerne, daß Sie ein Memorandum ausarbeiten, das ich unterschreiben werde, das sich an alle Verkaufsleiter richtet und in dem der Zweck meiner Reise dargelegt wird: ich möchte unsere Mitarbeiter vor Ort kennenlernen und unseren wichtigen Kunden Höflichkeitsbesuche abstatten, um eine persönliche Beziehung zu ihnen aufzubauen.
6. **Greg:** Hatten Sie Zeit, sich meine nach Verkaufsgebieten aufgegliederte Zusammenfassung der Verkaufszahlen der ersten beiden Quartale anzusehen?
7. **Susan:** Ja, das war eine ordentliche Arbeit und hat mir sehr geholfen. Danke vielmals. Scheinbar läuft es für uns überall gut, nur nicht in Japan.
8. **Greg:** Unser Marktanteil dort stagniert seit drei Jahren. Unsere Werbekampagnen sind nicht sehr erfolgreich gewesen.
9. **Susan:** Genau dort müssen wir in den nächsten Monaten unsere Bemühungen konzentrieren... Übrigens, wer ist dieser Herr Tanabe, mit dem ich Freitag morgen eine Verabredung habe?

ANMERKUNGEN

(1) **floor:** "Stockwerk, Etage". Vorsicht: In den USA werden die Stockwerke anders gezählt als in Großbritannien! Während das "Erdgeschoß" in Großbritannien *ground floor* heißt, ist es in den USA der *first floor*. Daher ist in den USA jedes Stockwerk um eine Nummer höher als das gleiche Stockwerk in Großbritannien.

(2) **agenda:** "Programm; Tagesordnung" (einer Versammlung usw.) Merken Sie sich in diesem Zusammenhang auch *diary* "Terminkalender"; *pocket diary* "Taschenkalender"; *desk diary* "Tischkalender".

(3) **to draft:** "(Schriftstück) aufsetzen, entwerfen, verfassen"; *rough first draft* "erster Entwurf, Rohentwurf"; *draft contract* "Vertragsentwurf".

(4) **recap:** Kurz für **recapitulation** "Zusammenfassung". *To recap* "zusammenfassen"; *recapitulation sheet* "Sammelbogen (für Materialausgabe oder Löhne)".

(5) **to break down:** "aufgliedern, aufschlüsseln". Achtung: *to break down* kann auch "ausfallen, Defekt haben, abbrechen; scheitern" heißen! *breakdown* heißt "Aufgliederung, Aufschlüsselung", aber auch "Zusammenbruch".

CHAPTER 27

10. **Greg:** He is Purchasing Manager for a large chain of Japanese retail stores, touring the country in search of new products. We haven't done any business with them yet. **(6)**

11. **Susan:** It would be appropriate to take him out to lunch. Could you find out whether he is free and if so, what sort of food he likes. Healthy American or ethnic?

12. **Greg:** May I suggest you invite Yoshi Kyoto, a banker at Barclays who handles our accounts and the financing of our export trade? I am sure Mr Tanabe will appreciate the presence of a fellow countryman. You'll enjoy his company, too. He's the perfect blend of oriental refinement and American pragmatism.
    The former by birth, the latter by training – he studied for two years at Wharton. **(7)**

13. **Susan:** Thanks for the suggestion. That'll be a nice way of combining business and social obligations. As a matter of fact, I was scheduled to meet Mr Kyoto before my departure. This will help create a congenial relationship at once. Make sure you choose a nice place for lunch!

KAPITEL 27

10. Greg: Er ist Einkaufsleiter einer bedeutenden Kette japanischer Einzelhandelsgeschäfte und durchreist das Land auf der Suche nach neuen Produkten. Wir haben zu ihnen bis jetzt noch keine Geschäftsbeziehungen.

11. Susan: Es wäre angebracht, ihn zum Essen einzuladen. Könnten Sie herausfinden, ob er Zeit hat und wenn ja, was er gerne ißt. Gesunde amerikanische Küche oder "ethnisch"?

12. Greg: Dürfte ich vorschlagen, Yoshi Kyoto, einen Bankier bei Barclays, der unsere Konten und die Finanzierung unseres Exporthandels bearbeitet, ebenfalls einzuladen? Ich bin sicher, Herr Tanabe freut sich über die Anwesenheit eines Landsmanns. Auch Sie werden seine Gesellschaft schätzen. Er ist eine perfekte Mischung aus orientalischer Finesse und amerikanischem Pragmatismus. Ersteres ist angeboren, letzteres hat er sich angeeignet – er hat zwei Jahre in Wharton studiert.

13. Susan: Danke für die Anregung. Das wird eine nette Art sein, Geschäft und soziale Verpflichtungen zu kombinieren. Es war sowieso geplant, daß ich Herrn Kyoto vor meiner Abreise treffe. Das wird dazu beitragen, daß sofort ein angenehmes Verhältnis entsteht. Suchen Sie einen schönen Platz zum Essen aus!

ANMERKUNGEN (Fortsetzung)

(6) **retail store:** "Einzelhandelsgeschäft"; *retailer* "Einzelhändler". Im Gegensatz dazu: *wholesale* "Großhandel"; *wholesaler* "Großhändler".

(7) **Wharton** ist eine Wirtschaftsfakultät *(Graduate School of Business)* der Universität von Pennsylvania in Philadelphia. Diese Fakultät, die als Spezialfach unter anderem Finanzwirtschaft anbietet, ist eine der angesehensten in den USA.

CHAPTER 27　　　　　　　　　　　　　　　　DOCUMENT

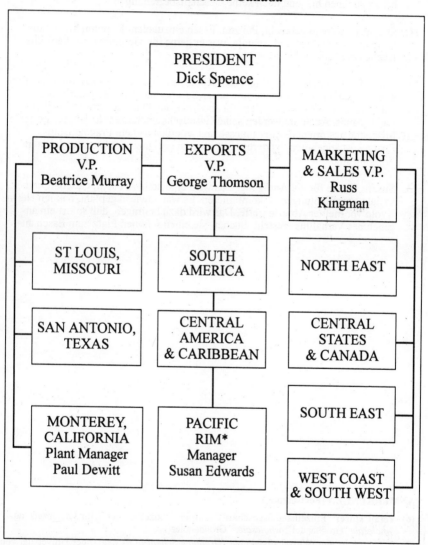

Organization chart: North America domestic and Canada

* Anrainerstaaten des pazifischen Ozeans (*rim*: Rand)

KAPITEL 27

 Das Geschäftsessen

Wenn das Geschäftsessen in den USA unter den anderen Werbungskosten *(entertainment expenses)* auch nicht den gleichen Platz einnimmt wie in Deutschland, so hat es doch eine besondere Bedeutung in allen geschäftlichen Verhandlungen. Davon profitieren zum größten Teil die "Spesenkonto-Restaurants" *(expense-account restaurants)*. Man trinkt hier zwar weniger Wein, dafür fallen aber die Cocktails bei den Amerikanern stark ins Gewicht. Die amerikanische Finanzverwaltung *(IRS, Internal Revenue Service)* erlaubt in der Regel einen Steuerabzug *(tax reduction)* für bis zu zwei Cocktails pro Person.

Jimmy Carter, der 1977 das Amt des Präsidenten übernahm, hatte vor, nicht nur die Inflation zu bekämpfen, sondern auch das *three-Martini business lunch* abzuschaffen.

CHAPTER 27

EXERCISES

Comprehension

Lesen Sie den Dialog aufmerksam durch. Beantworten Sie dann die nachfolgenden Fragen, und zwar immer in ganzen Sätzen:

1. What shows that Susan does not take the monthly executive meeting lightly?
2. Why does she fly to Sydney first?
3. What details show that Greg has prepared Susan's stay in Sydney carefully?
4. How will the seminar room be equipped?
5. What does Susan expect from her trip?
6. What made Greg's recap of sales for the first two years clear and useful?
7. What country poses a problem for UC? Why?
8. Why is Mr Tanabe touring the US?
9. Why does Greg suggest inviting Yoshi Kyoto too?
10. What is a major difference between Yoshi and Mr Tanabe?

Vocabulary

Es gibt Fälle, in denen zwei englische Wörter einen zusammengesetzten Ausdruck bilden, wobei die beiden Elemente entweder zusammengeschrieben werden oder voneinander getrennt stehen, wie z.B. "credit card". Bilden Sie mit den Wörtern der linken und rechten Spalte solche Komposita. Jedes Wort darf nur einmal verwendet werden.

1. word	a. flow
2. cash	b. trust
3. fringe	c. sale
4. field	d. mark
5. unit	e. exchange
6. stock	f. sheet
7. delivery	g. processor
8. balance	h. date
9. trade	i. benefits
10. bargain	j. work

KAPITEL 27

LÖSUNGSVORSCHLÄGE

Verständnisübung

1. She makes a point of attending it before leaving. **2.** Because she wants to attend the International Food Packaging Conference. **3.** He has already informed the area representatives about Susan's briefing session and reserved a seminar room. **4.** There will be an overhead projector and audio-visual equipment. **5.** She expects to get to know UC's local staff as well as the company's major clients. **6.** It was broken down by area. **7.** Japan poses a problem because its market share has been stagnant for three years and advertising campaigns have not been very successful there. **8.** He is in search of new products for his company. **9.** Because he thinks Mr Tanabe will appreciate the presence of a fellow countryman. **10.** Yoshi is more familiar with the American way of life because he studied two years at Wharton.

Lösungen zur Wortschatzübung

1. g.
2. a.
3. i.
4. j.
5. b.
6. e.
7. h.
8. f.
9. d.
10. c.

CHAPTER 27

Jeder der untenstehenden Sätze ist die Beschreibung einer betrügerischen Praxis, mit der Käufer getäuscht werden ('to cheat the buyer'). Wählen Sie unter den fünf angegebenen Wörtern für jeden Satz dasjenige aus, das den Sachverhalt richtig bezeichnet.

false clearance sale, misleading information, repair fraud, switching products, unwanted goods

1. A housewife, attracted by an ad at an unusually low price, finds out the advertised model is used. The salesman then tries to sell her a much more expensive item.
2. A service shop (garage or TV) charges for work that is not needed.
3. Books and magazines, never ordered, are sent through the mail, followed by letters demanding payment.
4. Goods may be advertised at 50 % off the regular price, when, in fact, they were never sold at the higher price.
5. A retailer claims, incorrectly, that goods were made by a nationally advertised company.

DO!

When you are abroad, be sensitive to the atmosphere around you instead of being sensitive only to your own feelings.

KAPITEL 27

Lösungen

1. switching products.
2. repair fraud.
3. unwanted goods.
4. false clearance sale.
5. misleading information.

 DON'T!

***Don't consider that intelligence is the ultimate value.
In America, kindness is more highly valued than intelligence.***

CHAPTER 28

Financing exports

A couple of days later in Yoshi Kyoto's office in Beverley Hills.

1. **Yoshi Kyoto:** I am delighted to see you again, Ms Edwards, if only for business reasons.

2. **Susan:** Please call me Susan.

3. **Yoshi Kyoto:** Thank you. That's nice. I am Yoshi... You know, the luncheon with Mr Tanabe, last week, was very pleasant and will, I hope, prove fruitful.

4. **Susan:** It's too early to tell, but I did enjoy the company: Mr Tanabe has a rather peculiar sense of humor and you were most helpful in every respect... And now to business! **(1)**

5. **Yoshi Kyoto:** *(Smiling)* Of course. Go ahead!

6. **Susan:** One of the important things I learnt during my training at United Chocolate (UK) is that our company – like any other, for that matter – cannot do without the services of a bank, and that's even more evident in the export trade. **(2)**

7. **Yoshi Kyoto:** I like to hear that...

8. **Susan:** *(Sounding very serious)* And I was not only thinking of traditional services, like issuing letters of credit, banker's drafts or the discounting of commercial paper. We are also impressed by the efficiency of your electronic banking system, which ensures speedy transfers and settlements – both ways – with our clients and suppliers to everyone's satisfaction. **(3) (4)**

9. **Yoshi Kyoto:** The bank takes pride in handling your business worldwide through its various divisions or affiliated companies... **(5)**

10. **Susan:** *(Same serious tone)* I looked into our files and realised that bank charges for the above services were quite sizeable! **(6)**

11. **Yoshi Kyoto:** *(Rather taken aback)* Hum, hum!

KAPITEL 28

Exportfinanzierung

Einige Tage später in Yoshi Kyotos Büro in Beverley Hills.

1. **Yoshi Kyoto:** Ich bin hocherfreut, Sie wiederzusehen, Fräulein Edwards, wenn auch nur aus geschäftlichen Gründen.
2. **Susan:** Bitte nennen Sie mich Susan.
3. **Yoshi Kyoto:** Danke. Das ist nett. Ich bin Yoshi... Wissen Sie, das Mittagessen mit Herrn Tanabe letzte Woche war sehr nett und wird, so hoffe ich, Früchte tragen.
4. **Susan:** Es ist zu früh, um das zu sagen, aber ich habe seine Gesellschaft genossen: Herr Tanabe hat einen ziemlich eigenartigen Sinn für Humor, und Sie waren mir in jeder Hinsicht eine große Hilfe.... Und nun zum Geschäft!
5. **Yoshi Kyoto:** *(Lächelt)* Natürlich. Beginnen Sie!
6. **Susan:** Eines der wichtigen Dinge, die ich während meiner Ausbildung bei United Chocolate (UK) gelernt habe, ist, daß unsere Firma – eigentlich wie jede andere – nicht ohne die Dienste einer Bank auskommen kann, und das ist im Exporthandel sogar noch offensichtlicher.
7. **Yoshi Kyoto:** Das höre ich gerne...
8. **Susan:** *(Klingt sehr ernst)* Und ich habe nicht nur an die traditionellen Dienstleistungen gedacht, wie die Ausgabe von Akkreditiven, Bankschecks oder das Diskontieren von Handelspapieren. Wir sind auch von der Effizienz Ihres elektronischen Banksystems beeindruckt, das schnelle Überweisungen und Abrechnungen für unsere Kunden und Lieferanten – in beide Richtungen – zu jedermanns Zufriedenheit gewährleistet.
9. **Yoshi Kyoto:** Die Bank ist stolz darauf, Ihre Geschäfte weltweit durch ihre verschiedenen Abteilungen oder Tochtergesellschaften abzuwickeln...
10. **Susan:** *(Im gleichen ernsten Ton)* Ich habe in unsere Akten gesehen und festgestellt, daß die Bankgebühren für die vorgenannten Dienste ganz beträchtlich sind!
11. **Yoshi Kyoto:** *(Ziemlich erstaunt)* Hmm, hmm!

ANMERKUNGEN

(1) **peculiar:** "seltsam, eigenartig, sonderbar". *What a peculiar person he is!* "Was für ein komischer Kauz er ist!". Eine andere Bedeutung ist "besonders": *To be of peculiar interest* "von besonderem Interesse sein".

(2) **for that matter:** "eigentlich".

(3) **letter of credit:** Eine Anweisung an eine oder mehrere Banken, einem Zahlungsempfänger *(payee)* innerhalb einer bestimmten Frist einen bestimmten Betrag oder einen Betrag bis zu einer bestimmten Höhe auszuzahlen. *Irrevocable letter of credit* "unwiderrufliches Akkreditiv".

(4) **banker's draft:** "Bankwechsel" oder "Bankscheck". Ein Auftrag einer Bank an eine andere Bank (die sich normalierweise in einem anderen Land befindet), einen bestimmten Geldbetrag auszuzahlen.

(5) **affiliated company, affiliate (US):** "Konzern-, Tochtergesellschaft". Bei diesen Firmen kontrolliert die Muttergesellschaft 20-50% des Kapitals. Synonym: *subsidiary*.

(6) **bank charges:** "Bankgebühren, Bankspesen". Sämtliche von einer Bank erhobenen Gebühren für die Abwicklung aller den Kunden betreffenden Bankgeschäfte.

CHAPTER 28

12. **Susan:** I didn't mean excessive!

13. **Yoshi Kyoto:** *(Relieved)* You reassure me! Our ultimate aim is a mutually beneficial cooperation. We are not philanthropists!

14. **Susan:** *(Smiling at last)* We are agreed on that!... You are already aware that headquarters have requested that we negotiate directly with you the extension of our credit line to face contingencies on some of our markets. **(7) (8)**

15. **Yoshi Kyoto:** No problem for us. *(Humorously)* More income, at no risk! UC's credit rating is excellent. **(9)**

16. **Susan:** Good. Then our assistants can work out the details. I will ask Greg to get in touch with your office.

17. **Yoshi Kyoto:** That's fine. *(Changing the subject)* Have you had time to look at our latest newsletter?

18. **Susan:** I've barely glanced at it.

19. **Yoshi Kyoto:** You will see that we are now making available the services of a credit agency especially oriented to the Asian market, and connected to our central data bank in London. We are in a position to provide instantly confidential information on the financial situation of potential clients of yours and on their credit risk to you. **(10)**

20. **Susan:** That's wonderful! It should reduce the tedious task of collecting bad debts. We'll certainly plug into it... You're a first-class salesman, Yoshi! **(11) (12)**

21. **Yoshi Kyoto:** And I have a feeling, Susan, that you are a tough bargainer! Could we now move to the last item...? I would like to reciprocate your invitation. How about a non-business dinner?

22. **Susan:** With pleasure! When I come back from my trip to the Pacific.

KAPITEL 28

12. **Susan:** Ich meinte nicht überhöht!
13. **Yoshi Kyoto:** *(Erleichtert)* Das beruhigt mich! Unser Endziel ist eine für beide Seiten vorteilhafte Zusammenarbeit. Wir sind keine Philanthropen!
14. **Susan:** *(Lächelt schließlich)* Darüber sind wir uns einig!... Sie wissen bereits, daß unsere Zentrale uns gebeten hat, für den Fall unvorhergesehener Ereignisse auf einigen unserer Märkte mit Ihnen direkt über die Erweiterung unseres Kreditrahmens zu verhandeln.
15. **Yoshi Kyoto:** Das ist kein Problem für uns. *(Belustigt)* Mehr Einkünfte bei null Risiko! Die Bonitätsbeurteilung von UC ist hervorragend.
16. **Susan:** Gut. Dann können unsere Assistenten die Einzelheiten ausarbeiten. Ich werde Greg bitten, mit Ihrem Büro Kontakt aufzunehmen.
17. **Yoshi Kyoto:** Das ist prima. *(Wechselt das Thema)* Hatten Sie Zeit, sich unser neustes Mitteilungsblatt anzusehen?
18. **Susan:** Ich konnte kaum einen Blick hineinwerfen.
19. **Yoshi Kyoto:** Sie werden feststellen, daß wir nun die Dienstleistungen einer Kreditauskunftei zur Verfügung stellen, die speziell auf den asiatischen Markt ausgerichtet und mit unserer zentralen Datenbank in London verbunden ist. Wir befinden uns in der Lage, sofort vertrauliche Informationen über die Finanzlage potentieller Kunden und über deren Kreditrisiko für Sie bereitzustellen.
20. **Susan:** Das ist wundervoll! Es sollte uns die mühsame Aufgabe abnehmen, schwer einbringliche Forderungen einzuziehen. Da schließen wir uns bestimmt an... Sie sind ein erstklassiger Verkäufer, Yoshi!
21. **Yoshi Kyoto:** Und ich habe das Gefühl, Susan, daß Sie eine zähe Unterhändlerin sind! Könnten wir nun zum letzten Punkt kommen...? Ich würde mich gerne für Ihre Einladung revanchieren. Was denken Sie über ein Abendessen, bei dem es nicht ums Geschäft geht?
22. **Susan:** Mit Vergnügen! Wenn ich von meiner Reise an die Pazifikküste zurück bin.

ANMERKUNGEN (Fortsetzung)

(7) **credit line:** Die maximale Summe, um die ein Bankkonto überzogen werden darf. "Überziehung" *overdraft*.

(8) **contingency:** "Eventualität, Eventualfall; unvorhergesehenes Ereignis". *Contingency fund/contingency reserve* "Fonds für außerordentliche Rückstellungen"; *contingency plan* "Krisenplan".

(9) **credit rating:** "Bonitätsbeurteilung". Der Betrag, über den ein Kunde nach Einschätzung einer Kreditauskunftei einen Kredit aufnehmen kann. Die beste Beurteilung, AAA *(triple A)*, bedeutet, daß das Kreditrisiko *(credit risk)* minimal ist. B *(bankruptcy)* bedeutet, daß die Wahrscheinlichkeit eines Konkurses erhöht ist. Die Noten werden von spezialisierten Organisationen wie z.B. **Standard and Poor's** oder **Moody's** vergeben.

(10) **credit agency** *(credit bureau)*: Ein Unternehmen, das die Kreditwürdigkeit bzw. Zahlungsfähigkeit *(solvency)* von Personen oder Unternehmen untersucht, das Kreditrisiko ermittelt und entscheidet, ob diese einen Kredit aufnehmen dürfen oder nicht.

(11) **bad debts:** "uneinbringliche Forderung, schwer einziehbare Außenstände". Eine Schuld, die nicht bezahlt wird und die buchhalterisch abgeschrieben werden muß.

(12) **to plug into:** "sich einer Sache anschließen". *Plug* "Steckdose".

CHAPTER 28   DOCUMENT

Draft Memo

United Chocolate Inc

Exports, Pacific Rim

Los Angeles

Internal Memorandum

From: Export Manager

To: Sales Managers, Pacific Rim   **Date:** 10/21/199...*

Re: Export Manager's trip to Sydney and Pacific Rim countries

I wish to take advantage of this first visit to my zone of responsibility to meet all of you in Sydney.

I will also be available for breakfast discussions in smaller groups, during the conference. It is essential that we use every opportunity to get to know each other quickly.

Since I am new to the job, I will have much to learn from your individual and collective actions in the field and from your experience of the market.

Another objective of mine is to pay courtesy calls to our important clients in your respective areas. I count on you to make the necessary appointments and to fax back a tentative schedule for each one of my stops.

Please note that I will be visiting personal friends the weekend following the conference. Leave that period free of engagement.

Looking forward to a fruitful get-together,

                                       Susan Edwards
                                       Export Manager

Encl: itinerary, dates and flight numbers

---

* Beachten Sie hier die amerikanische Schreibregel für das Datum: Monat/Tag/Jahr

KAPITEL 28

Frank und frei

Wir haben bereits in Kapitel 4 gesehen, daß in angelsächsischen Unternehmen die hierarchischen Strukturen durch eine größere Direktheit *(directness)* und einen informelleren Umgang untereinander geprägt sind. Dies gilt in noch stärkerem Maße für gleichrangige Mitarbeiter, wie in unserem Dialog Susan und Yoshi. Überhaupt gehen die Mitarbeiter von Firmen in geschäftlichen Beziehungen viel lockerer miteinander um als bei uns. Man kommt viel schneller auf den Punkt *(straight to the point)* als in Deutschland, ohne daß die äußeren Umstände viel anders wären. Der folgende, für uns Deutsche vielleicht extrem anmutende Dialog ist in angelsächsischen Unternehmen keine Ausnahme:

Auf dem Flur

– Hallo, Tom, ich bin Bob, Ihr neuer Vorsitzender und Generaldirektor.
(Sie tauschen einen Händedruck.)
– Hallo, Bob, ich bin Produktionsleiter...
(Einige Monate später in Bob's Büro.)
– Danke, daß Sie so schnell gekommen sind, Tom.
– Wo ist das Problem, Bob?
– Sie sind entlassen!

Dialog overheard in a corridor

– *Hi, Tom. I'm Bob, your new Chairman and CEO.*
(They shake hands)
– *Hi, Bob. I'm Product Manager...*
(Some months later in Bob's office)
– *Thanks for coming so quickly, Tom.*
– *What's the problem?*
– *You're fired!*

CHAPTER 28

EXERCISES

Comprehension

Lesen Sie den Dialog aufmerksam durch. Beantworten Sie dann die nachfolgenden Fragen, und zwar immer in ganzen Sätzen:

1. Why is Yoshi genuinely pleased to see Susan again? **2.** Has Susan managed to induce Mr Tanabe to do business with UC? **3.** What major fact did Susan learn about banks during her training? **4.** What was Susan also impressed by? **5.** Why can a bank handle a client's business practically anywhere in the world? **6.** What reservations does Susan have about the services offered by Yoshi's Bank? **7.** How does Yoshi justify the bank's sizeable charges? **8.** What task will Susan delegate to Greg? **9.** What interesting new service does the bank offer? **10.** Why should this service be very interesting for UC?

Vocabulary

In der Geschäftssprache werden häufig aus Substantiv und Adjektiv zusammengesetzte Ausdrücke benutzt, die es ermöglichen, Ideen auf eine prägnante Art auszudrücken. Beispiel: **A plant for reprocessing water is a water-reprocessing plant.** *Achten Sie auf die Position des Bindestrichs. Bilden Sie nun auf der Grundlage der untenstehenden Definitionen solche zusammengesetzten Wörter:*

1. Reference books for self-study. **2.** The production of cocoa in the world. **3.** A survey of children who have only one parent. **4.** The stocks of oil in the Western world. **5.** A service specialized in the reservation of tickets. **6.** A convention which lasts three days. **7.** Shortages which last for two weeks. **8.** People who produce sugar from cane. **9.** A budget for marketing of which the total cost is $100,000. **10.** A chemical which is a hazard to health.

DO!

Always know when to sugar the pill (beschönigen) by making unpleasant or painful things appear less so.

KAPITEL 28

LÖSUNGSVORSCHLÄGE

Verständnisübung

1. Because he has excellent memories of the luncheon he had with her and Mr Tanabe. 2. Although the luncheon was pleasant, it's still too early to tell. 3. She learnt that a company, especially an exporting one, needs the services of a bank. 4. She was also impressed by the efficiency of the electronic banking system. 5. Because it has a network of divisions and affiliated companies. 6. She has reservations about the high cost of the bank's services. 7. He states that although the bank is no philanthropic organization, its services also benefit companies. 8. She will delegate to him the task of negotiating the extension of UC's credit line with the bank. 9. The bank offers the possibility of getting confidential information on the financial situation of a firm's prospective client. 10. It should reduce the number of bad debts to be collected.

Lösungen zur Wortschatzübung

1. Self-study reference books 2. World cocoa production 3. A one-parent child survey 4. Western-world oil stocks 5. A ticket-reservation service 6. A three-day convention 7. Two-week shortages 8. Cane-sugar producers 9. A $100,000 marketing budget 10. A health-hazard chemical

 DON'T!

Don't stand too close to an Anglo-Saxon negotiator. Don't put your hand on his shoulder. However, this attitude is acceptable when you talk to Latin Americans.

CHAPTER 28

Application

In dieser Übung geht es um Dienstleistungen einer Bank. Ordnen Sie den in der linken Spalte aufgeführten Bitten und Anfragen des Kunden jeweils aus der rechten Spalte die passende Empfehlung des Bankiers zu.

What the client wants

1. To get cash any time of day or night.

2. To be informed about the risks of exporting electronic equipment to Brazil.

3. To have a smaller but more regular and totally safe income.

4. Not to worry about regular payments to be made (phone bill, electricity bill, gas bill…).

5. To be able to spend more than one pays in.

6. To put a little money aside, but to be able to withdraw it whenever one likes.

7. To travel abroad without taking too much cash.

8. To buy a car although one does not have the cash.

9. To have money available on one's account and make payments by cheque.

10. To invest a large amount of money for a long period.

What the banker recommends

a. Have money transferred by standing orders.

b. Open a savings account.

c. Invest it on the stock exchange.

d. Leave money on one's current account.

e. Buy traveller's cheques.

f. Apply for a loan.

g. Get a cashpoint credit card.

h. Apply for permission to run an overdraft.

i. See our services specialized in the export field.

j. Buy government bonds.

KAPITEL 28

Lösungen

1. g.
2. i.
3. j.
4. a.
5. h.
6. b.
7. e.
8. f.
9. d.
10. c.

CHAPTER 29

A business negotiation

Upon her friend Mary-Ann's suggestion, Susan has made arrangements to meet Bruce Paterson, Mary-Ann's uncle, while she is in Australia. He also happens to be the manager of Black Swan Traders, a major wholesaling company distributing foodstuffs in Western Australia. **(1)**

1. **Bruce Paterson:** *(Shaking her hand)* Good day Susan! Pleased to meet you. Do take a seat! Mary-Ann thinks highly of you. **(2)**

2. **Susan:** I'm certainly happy to hear that. Mary-Ann is very sweet.

3. **Bruce Paterson:** How do you like it here in Oz? **(3)**

4. **Susan:** It's great! Visiting Australia has always been one of my dearest dreams. But let's get down to business..., and hopefully talk about Australia later.

5. **Bruce Paterson:** Good on you! Mary-Ann told me you are an effective businessperson. Well, I have studied your proposal for a distribution agreement of UC's chocolate bars in Western Australia. You'd like our state to be a test market. **(4) (5) (6)**

6. **Susan:** Yes. Needless to say, we at UC hope this will be the beginning of a fruitful business relationship between our companies.

7. **Bruce Paterson:** I share that view.

8. **Susan:** Good. Can we now agree on an overall procedure for our negotiation?

9. **Bruce Paterson:** What outline do you suggest?

10. **Susan:** I would like to begin by asking you some questions about Black Swan Traders and the kind of services you offer. Then we could move on to a definition of UC's objectives in Western Australia. If it appears that we have broad agreement, we could talk about possible pricing, delivery and support arrangements.

KAPITEL 29

Eine Geschäftsverhandlung

Auf Anregung ihrer Freundin Mary-Ann hat Susan ein Treffen mit Bruce Paterson, Mary-Anns Onkel, arrangiert, während sie sich in Australien aufhält. Er ist zufällig auch der Geschäftsführer von Black Swan Traders, einer bedeutenden Großhandelsfirma, die Nahrungsmittel in West-Australien vertreibt.

1. **Bruce Paterson:** *(Schüttelt ihr die Hand)* Guten Tag, Susan! Es freut mich, Sie kennenzulernen. Nehmen Sie Platz! Mary-Ann hält viel von Ihnen.
2. **Susan:** Ich freue mich natürlich, das zu hören. Mary-Ann ist sehr nett.
3. **Bruce Paterson:** Wie gefällt es Ihnen hier in Australien?
4. **Susan:** Es ist großartig! Es war immer einer meiner liebsten Träume, Australien zu besuchen. Aber lassen Sie uns über's Geschäft reden, ... ich hoffe, daß wir später über Australien sprechen können.
5. **Bruce Paterson:** Bravo! Mary-Ann hat mir erzählt, daß Sie eine tatkräftige Geschäftsfrau sind. Also, ich habe Ihren Vorschlag über ein Vertriebsabkommen für die UC-Schokoladenriegel in West-Australien studiert. Sie möchten, daß unser Staat ein Testmarkt ist.
6. **Susan:** Ja. Ich brauche nicht zu betonen, daß wir bei UC hoffen, daß dies der Beginn einer fruchtbaren Geschäftsbeziehung zwischen unseren Firmen sein wird.
7. **Bruce Paterson:** Ich teile diese Auffassung.
8. **Susan:** Gut. Können wir uns nun über eine allgemeine Vorgehensweise für unsere Verhandlungen einigen?
9. **Bruce Paterson:** Welchen Plan schlagen Sie vor?
10. **Susan:** Ich würde gerne mit einigen Fragen über Black Swan Traders und die Art der Dienstleistungen, die Sie anbieten, beginnen. Als nächstes könnten wir die Zielsetzungen von UC in West-Australien definieren. Wenn sich herausstellt, daß wir im großen und ganzen übereinstimmen, könnten wir über mögliche Vereinbarungen hinsichtlich Preisgestaltung, Warenlieferung und Unterstützung sprechen.

ANMERKUNGEN

(1) **Western Australia:** "West-Australien" ist einer der sechs Bundesstaaten Australiens, dessen Hauptstadt Perth ist. Das Wappenzeichen des Staates ist der schwarze Schwan.
(2) **good day:** (sprich: *g'day*) ist anstelle von *good morning, good afternoon, good evening* in Australien die gebräuchliche Begrüßungsformel.
(3) **Oz** "Land der Wunder" ist der Name, der gelegentlich anstelle von "Australien" verwendet wird (in Anlehnung an den Film *"The Wizard of Oz"*).
(4) **good on you:** Australisches Äquivalent für *well done*.
(5) Der Ausdruck **businessperson** anstelle von *businessman* trägt der Tatsache Rechnung, daß auch Frauen Geschäftsleute sein können, und ist somit weniger diskriminierend.
(6) **test-market:** "Testmarkt". Ein auf ein bestimmtes Gebiet beschränkter Markt, auf dem man die Einführung eines Produkts und dessen Akzeptanz testet.

CHAPTER 29

11. **Bruce Paterson:** By that time, we will probably be very hungry! We could go to a BYO restaurant. I have a great bottle of Chardonnay from Margaret River that I'd like you to taste! **(7) (8) (9)**

12. **Susan:** That sounds good. Mary-Ann is very rhapsodic about Australian wines, Mr Paterson.

13. **Bruce Paterson:** Call me Bruce, please!

14. **Susan:** Well, Bruce, where does your company distribute foodstuffs?

15. **Bruce Paterson:** We distribute them in all available outlets in Western Australia. Our well-designed distribution system gives us a competitive edge. **(10)**

16. **Susan:** What kind of business relationships do you have with supermarkets?

17. **Bruce Paterson:** I don't think I'll surprise you much if I tell you that supermarkets are becoming powerful and influential. It used to be that manufacturers had all the cards...

18. **Susan:** ... whereas now, supermarkets own the arena. Would our chocolate bars also be present on the market through vending machines?

19. **Bruce Paterson:** Yes. Virtually everywhere, even beyond the rabbit-proof fence. **(11)**

20. **Susan:** I beg your pardon?

KAPITEL 29

11. **Bruce Paterson:** Bis dahin werden wir wahrscheinlich großen Hunger haben. Wir könnten in ein BYO-Restaurant gehen. Ich habe eine tolle Flasche Chardonnay vom Margaret River, den ich Sie gerne kosten lassen würde!

12. **Susan:** Das klingt gut. Mary-Ann schwärmt sehr für australische Weine, Herr Paterson.

13. **Bruce Paterson:** Sagen Sie bitte Bruce zu mir!

14. **Susan:** Also, Bruce, wo vertreibt Ihre Firma Nahrungsmittel?

15. **Bruce Paterson:** Wir vertreiben sie in allen uns zur Verfügung stehenden Verkaufsstellen in West-Australien. Unser gut ausgebautes Vertriebssystem liefert uns einen Wettbewerbsvorteil.

16. **Susan:** Welche Art von Geschäftsbeziehungen haben Sie mit Supermärkten?

17. **Bruce Paterson:** Ich denke, es überrascht Sie nicht, wenn ich Ihnen sage, daß Supermärkte immer stärker und einflußreicher werden. Die Zeiten, in denen die Hersteller alle Trümpfe in der Hand hielten, sind vorbei...

18. **Susan:** ... wogegen jetzt die Supermärkte die Gangart bestimmen. Würden unsere Schokoladenriegel auch in Verkaufsautomaten auf dem Markt präsent sein?

19. **Bruce Paterson:** Ja. Fast überall, sogar jenseits des Kaninchenzauns.

20. **Susan:** Wie bitte?

ANMERKUNGEN (Fortsetzung)

(7) **BYO** ist die Abkürzung für *bring your own*. In diesen Restaurants können die Gäste ihren eigenen Wein von zu Hause mitbringen.

(8) **Chardonnay:** Eine Rebenart aus Burgund, aus der ein rassiger Weißwein gewonnen wird, der momentan in Australien sehr gefragt ist.

(9) **Margaret River:** Eine Region im Süden West-Australiens, in der ein sehr gemäßigtes und somit für den Weinanbau geeignetes Klima herrscht.

(10) **competitive edge:** "Wettbewerbsvorteil". Vgl. *to have an edge on* (oder *over*) *one's competitor* "der Konkurrenz überlegen sein".

(11) **beyond the rabbit-proof fence** ist eine Anspielung auf die Zäune, die in Australien gegen Kaninchen gezogen werden, die dort als besonders schädlich gelten. *At the back of beyond* "am Ende der Welt". Darüber hinaus wird die westliche und die östliche Hälfte von Australien durch einen riesigen Zaun getrennt, der verhindern soll, daß die in der Westhälfte lebenden Dingos (eine Art wilder Hunde) nicht nach Ost-Australien gelangt.

CHAPTER 29

21. **Bruce Paterson:** The outback if you prefer, the bush, the wilderness. I keep forgetting we are divided by a common language ! At Black Swan Traders, we realize that chocolate bars must be sold in as many outlets as possible to provide maximum brand exposure and consumer convenience. **(12) (13)**

22. **Susan:** You're right! However good a product may be, the truly important questions revolve around the consumer. By the way, let me assure you that at UC, we don't mean to distribute our products *through* you but *to* you. We are quite prepared to discuss interesting margins, special deals, premiums, cooperative advertising, sales contests... **(14)**

23. **Bruce Paterson:** Beaut! **(15)**

KAPITEL 29

21. Bruce Paterson: Das Hinterland, wenn Sie so wollen, der Busch, die Wildnis. Ich vergesse andauernd, daß wir durch eine gemeinsame Sprache getrennt sind! Bei Black Swan Traders stellen wir fest, daß Schokoladenriegel in so vielen Vertriebsstellen wie möglich verkauft werden müssen, um dem Verbraucher ein Höchstmaß an Markenpräsenz und Kaufkomfort zu bieten.

22. Susan: Sie haben recht! Wie gut ein Produkt auch sein mag, die wirklich wichtigen Fragen drehen sich um den Konsumenten. A propos, ich möchte Ihnen versichern, daß wir bei UC unsere Produkte nicht *durch* Sie, sondern *an* Sie vertreiben möchten. Wir sind gerne bereit, über interessante Margen, Sondervereinbarungen, Prämien, kooperative Werbung, Verkaufswettbewerbe usw. zu sprechen.

23. Bruce Paterson: Wunderbar!

ANMERKUNGEN (Fortsetzung)

(12) **outback** bezeichnet das australische Buschland.
(13) **brand exposure:** *exposure* bedeutet "Ausstellung, Enthüllung". Im vorliegenden Kontext bezieht sich dieser Ausdruck auf die Idee, dem Verbraucher das Produkt so oft wie möglich vor Augen zu halten, damit er mit der Marke vertraut wird.
(14) **cooperative advertising:** "kooperative Werbung". Eine Werbung, die vom Hersteller und vom Vertreiber auf gemeinsame Rechnung betrieben wird.
(15) **beaut**, die Abkürzung von *beautiful*, ist in Australien ein umgangssprachlicher Ausdruck, der Begeisterung ausdrückt und ein Synonym für *great, marvellous* ist.

CHAPTER 29   DOCUMENT

Understanding Australia (ns)

Susan prepared her trip to Australia very seriously.
She asked her good friend Mary-Ann from Perth, to give her a few tips about the ways of Australians.

As you know, I am not a business specialist! However, here are a few indications about my country.

Many outsiders have a romantic view of Australia which they see as a land of opportunity at a time when opportunity, especially in the business world, is declining. But what is the reality?

Today, Australia is keen to integrate its economy into Asia because it feels a little isolated in the face of such big economic entities as the EU or NAFTA, but this does not mean it is turning its back on the rest of the world. On the contrary! Although it claims to be an Asian country, it is firmly committed to Western ideas and values.

You will find that Australians are easy to live with. They are generally helpful, tolerant but revolted by injustice. In their worship of equality, they tend to suspect power, side with the underdog[1] and believe that authority is automatically wrong. Such an attitude may be viewed as an inheritance from the time when Australia was a penal colony. This anti-authoritarian attitude is summed up by the expression 'cutting down all poppies to size'.[2] As Australians worship equality, you will understand that they worship few heroes. However, they respect talented sportsmen, scientists and artists provided they don't have an inflated ego. What people **are** matters more than what their social origins are.

You asked me what Australians looked like. Well, there are all kinds, including a sizeable number of fat ones. As my countrymen are known to drink a lot of beer, there are beer bellies! But of course, you'll find plenty of good-looking surfers on beaches.

As far as the language is concerned, the Australian accent is quite noticeable. It may even be unintelligible to untrained ears! For example a 'bison' (basin) is something an 'Ors-trayl-yan' washes his hands in. 'Save' rhymes with 'five' and 'soak' with 'how'.

Anyway, I hope you won't feel 'crook' (ill) in Perth. You should find that 'Aussies' (Australians) are 'fair dinkum' (honest). Oh, just one more thing, some nasty character may call you a 'pom' or 'pommie'. This is not too flattering a word to designate a Briton. But just ignore him. 'Goodoh' (O.K.)?

---

[1] underdog: "Unterprivilegierter, Unterlegener, Benachteiligter".
[2] cutting all poppies down to size: wörtlich "alle Mohnblumen auf die gleiche Höhe zurechtschneiden". Entspricht in etwa unserem "alle über einen Kamm scheren".

KAPITEL 29

Australien

Der kleinste der fünf Erdteile hat eine Fläche von 7,682 Milliarden km² (20 mal größer als die BRD und 90 mal größer als Österreich). Von den insgesamt 17,5 Millionen Einwohnern sind 1% "Aborigines", die Ureinwohner Australiens. Die Bevölkerungsdichte liegt bei 2,1 Einwohner pro km2. Australien besteht aus sechs Bundesstaaten: Western Australia, South Australia, Victoria, Tasmania, New South Wales und Queensland. Außerdem zählen zwei territories zu Australien: das Australian Capital Territory (Canberra) und das Northern Territory.

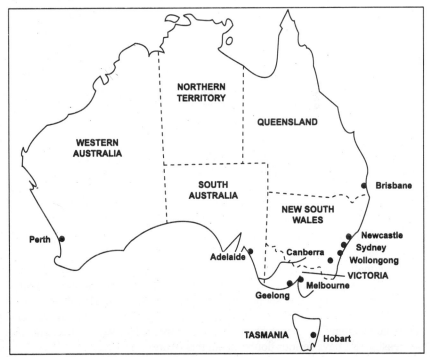

CHAPTER 29

EXERCISES

Comprehension

Lesen Sie den Dialog aufmerksam durch. Beantworten Sie dann die nachfolgenden Fragen, und zwar immer in ganzen Sätzen:

1. What activity is Black Swan Traders involved in? **2.** Why is Bruce Paterson happy to meet Susan? **3.** Why does Bruce Paterson say that Susan is an effective businessperson? **4.** What deal would Susan like to negotiate with Bruce Paterson? **5.** What shows that Susan has prepared the negotiation carefully? **6.** How would you characterize the atmosphere of the negotiation between Susan and Bruce Paterson? **7.** Is Susan impressed when Bruce Paterson speaks about the efficiency of Black Swan Traders' distribution system? **8.** With what form of distribution is UC likely to encounter difficulties in Western Australia? **9.** What other form of distribution does Susan want to discuss? **10.** Why is it important for UC's chocolate bars to be present in as many retail outlets as possible?

Conversational English

In der folgenden Übung sollen Sie trainieren, wie Sie in geschäftlichen Verhandlungen ablehnend antworten. Versuchen Sie, zu jeder der nachfolgend aufgeführten Aussagen die passende Erwiderung zu finden.

1. The crisis is over. **2.** American films are childish. **3.** Marketing is not important. **4.** We're moving towards freer trade. **5.** The weather is mild today. **6.** Ninety per cent of our customers don't like chocolate. **7.** Australia is a backward country. **8.** Smoking is no real health hazard. **9.** The independent small trader is doomed to extinction. **10.** It's a pity the hypermarket is in such an out-of-the-way place.

a. Nevertheless, you often drive there. **b.** I don't agree. I think it is. **c.** Medical research has proved the contrary. **d.** Rubbish! It's a very modern country. **e.** Nonsense! Quite a few shopkeepers are thriving today. **f.** This is not always true. There are some excellent ones. **g.** It is not as warm as yesterday. **h.** Come on! The economy has never been in worse shape. **i.** No way! Protectionism is increasing. **j.** I have serious doubts about this figure.

KAPITEL 29

LÖSUNGSVORSCHLÄGE

Verständnisübung

1. Black Swan Traders is a wholesaling company which distributes foodstuffs all over Western Australia. **2.** Apart from the prospect of doing business with her, he is pleased to meet a person whom his niece regards highly. **3.** She does not waste time on small talk, however much she would like to speak about Australia. **4.** She would like him to sign a distribution agreement for UC's chocolate bars in Western Australia. **5.** She submits an outline of the negotiation for Bruce Paterson's approval. **6.** It is informal. For instance, they discuss things on a first-name basis. **7.** No, she isn't. She almost interrupts him to move on to her next question. **8.** Distribution to supermarkets is likely to be a major challenge for UC because today's market is no longer a seller's market. Buyers can dictate their law much more easily than in the past. **9.** She also wishes to discuss vending machines. **10.** Because consumers must be given plenty of opportunities to see them. They should also have easy access to them.

Lösungen

1. h. **2.** f. **3.** b. **4.** i. **5.** g. **6.** j. **7.** d. **8.** c. **9.** e. **10.** a.

CHAPTER 29

Application

Wie antwortet man korrekt und höflich auf Englisch? Nur mit "Ja" oder "Nein" zu antworten, würde in einer konkreten Gesprächssituation als unhöflich angesehen. Suchen Sie zu jeder Frage die passende höfliche Antwort aus dem zweiten Absatz.

1. Would you like another glass of wine? Yes. **2.** Has the plane taken off? Yes. **3.** Is this the right tube for Victoria Station? Yes. **4.** Do you offer a rebate? No. **5.** Do you speak German? No. **6.** Did you have a pleasant trip? Yes. **7.** Will you be flying to New Zealand? No. **8.** Are you interested in our chocolate bars? Perhaps. **9.** You haven't got their phone number by any chance? Perhaps. **10.** Do you think our competitors will get the contract? No.

a. Yes it is. **b.** Yes I would. Thank you. **c.** Unfortunately, we don't. **d.** I might have. I'll look in my diary. **e.** We might consider buying them. **f.** I don't think they've got a chance. **g.** I'm sorry. It has. **h.** I'm not planning to do so. **i.** I did indeed. Thank you. **j.** I'm afraid I don't.

KAPITEL 29

Lösung

1. b. **2.** g. **3.** a. **4.** c. **5.** j. **6.** i. **7.** h. **8.** e. **9.** d. **10.** f.

DO!

When you travel in the USA, make sure you take travellers' cheques. Regular cheques are practically never accepted. On the other hand, your travellers' cheques will be accepted by shops, restaurants and motels.

DON'T!

Don't speed on a US or Canadian road; don't park in front of a fire hydrant; don't cross a street when the light is red. The police in the USA and Canada are very efficient and very strict.

CHAPTER 30

Reducing the risks

Two months later on a non-stop flight from Tokyo to Los Angeles International. Susan is returning from her second trip to Asia. The passenger on her left is Yoshi Kyoto who has attended a bankers' seminar in Osaka, as guest speaker. They both look happy and relaxed. **(1)**

1. **Susan:** I can't say my visit to Japan was altogether successful. Mr Tanabe is hard to persuade, but the invitation to take part in your workshop on currency fluctuations made up for it!

2. **Yoshi:** I like to hear you say that.

3. **Susan:** The futures markets seem to have no secret for you. Buying spot or forward becomes a matter of routine. **(2) (3)**

4. **Yoshi:** I wish that were true. Managing prospective risks, and especially financial risks, is a risky business and I don't mean that as a joke!

5. **Susan:** I can easily believe you. I heard one of your fellow bankers say that if a trader in currency exchange contracts was successful over too long a period, he or she should be fired or removed to a safer position because his or her luck could not last. **(4) (5) (6)**

6. **Yoshi:** That's a clever way of putting it. What you have to bear in mind, however, is that risk reduction is a business. Whether you deal in commodities, currencies or the various forms of insurance, the deal is always with someone else, a kind of opponent if you consider things realistically. **(7)**

KAPITEL 30

Risikobegrenzung

Deux Zwei Monate später auf einem Non-Stop-Flug von Tokio nach Los Angeles International. Susan kehrt von ihrer zweiten Asienreise zurück. Der Fluggast links neben ihr ist Yoshi Kyoto, der als Gastredner an einem Seminar für Bankiers in Osaka teilgenommen hat. Sie sehen beide zufrieden und entspannt aus.

1. **Susan:** Ich kann nicht behaupten, daß mein Besuch in Japan ein voller Erfolg war. Herr Tanabe ist schwer zu überzeugen, aber die Einladung zur Teilnahme an Ihrem Workshop über Währungsfluktuation hat mich dafür entschädigt!
2. **Yoshi:** Ich freue mich, das von Ihnen zu hören.
3. **Susan:** Die Terminmärkte scheinen für Sie keinerlei Geheimnisse mehr zu bergen. Es wird zu einer Routinefrage, ob man zum Kassapreis oder zum Terminpreis kauft.
4. **Yoshi:** Ich wünschte, das wäre wahr. Künftige Risiken und speziell finanzielle Risiken zu steuern, ist ein heikles Geschäft, und ich meine das nicht als Witz!
5. **Susan:** Ich glaube Ihnen das gerne. Ich hörte, wie einer Ihrer Bankkollegen sagte, daß, wenn ein Devisenmakler über einen zu langen Zeitraum erfolgreich ist, er bzw. sie gefeuert oder in eine sicherere Position versetzt werden sollte, da sein bzw. ihr Glück nicht ewig andauern könne.
6. **Yoshi:** Das ist eine kluge Art, es auszudrücken. Was Sie jedoch im Gedächtnis behalten müssen, ist, daß Risikobegrenzung ein Geschäft ist. Egal, ob Sie mit Waren, Währungen oder den verschiedenen Formen von Versicherungen handeln: der Handel erfolgt immer mit jemand anderem, einer Art Gegner, wenn Sie die Dinge realistisch betrachten.

ANMERKUNGEN

(1) **Los Angeles International:** Der größte Flughafen von Los Angeles und Knotenpunkt für die meisten internationalen Flüge.

(2) **futures market:** "Terminmarkt" im Gegensatz zum *spot market* "Kassamarkt, Lokomarkt". Beispiele: *commodity/commodities futures market* "Warenterminmarkt" (für Grundnahrungsmittel wie Getreide, Kakao, Zucker usw.); *financial futures market* "Finanzterminmarkt".

(3) **spot/forward:** "Sofort-/Voraus-". *Spot price* "Sofortpreis" (... und nicht "Spottpreis"!). Dies ist der Preis für eine Ware, die sofort geliefert wird. *Forward price:* Preis für eine Lieferung an einem festgesetzten Zeitpunkt in der Zukunft, auf den sich Käufer und Verkäufer geeinigt haben (siehe Anmerkung 9).

(4) **fellow:** "Kollege, Kamerad"; "Bursche, Kerl, Freund". Folgt diesem Ausdruck ein weiteres Substantiv, so bezeichnet diese Kombination eine Person, die ähnlich ist, mit der man etwas gemeinsam hat. Ein *fellow being* ist beispielsweise ein "Mitmensch", ein *fellow citizen* ein "Mitbürger", ein *fellow sufferer* ein "Leidensgenosse" und ein *fellow student* ein "Kommilitone".

(5) **trader:** "Händler, -in", "Kaufmann, -frau". Hier: "Devisenhändler".

(6) **currency exchange:** "Devisenbörse, Wechselstube". *Exchange* "Wechselverkehr, Umtausch, Devisen", aber auch "Börse" *(stock exchange)* oder jeder andere organisierte Markt *(labor exchange* "Arbeitsamt"). *Foreign exchange* "fremde Währung, Devisen", *futures exchange* "Devisenterminhandel".

(7) **commodity:** "Handelsware; Erzeugnis" oder alle anderen Gebrauchsgüter, die – normalerweise im Terminhandel – auf dem Markt gehandelt werden.

CHAPTER 30

7. **Susan:** That's obvious. The insurance company, in exchange for its protection or coverage against damage, will compute the premium for its comprehensive policy on the likelihood or unlikelihood of risk, hoping to gain by it. That's *their* way of reducing risk. **(8)**

8. **Yoshi:** The same holds true in currencies or commodities. The two sides involved in any transaction expect a profit or an advantage. For instance, United Chocolate will buy cocoa futures to secure a regular supply at a given price. For the same reason it will buy or sell currency futures to guarantee its production or sales prices, or to maximize its profit on export transactions, thanks to a favorable foreign currency conversion. **(9)**

9. **Susan:** But you can't totally eliminate loss or gain?

10. **Yoshi:** That's where you resort to more sophisticated techniques like hedging. To offset possible losses due to unanticipated price changes, one may enter into a contract in the opposite direction. Let's take again the example of United Chocolate and suppose it has just bought sugar on a long-term contract. It may protect itself against possible variations during the term of the contract by selling the same quantity of sugar on the futures market... **(10)**

11. **Susan:** Then, if prices fall, the profit made on the future the sale will offset the loss incurred on the purchase price. It sounds like an endless chain!

12. **Yoshi:** Yes, something like that. Basically, the purpose of hedging is not to make a profit but to avoid or reduce a loss.

(Voice off)
Ladies and gentlemen, we are now beginning our descent to Los Angeles International. Will you please return to your seats and fasten your seat-belts. Thank you for your cooperation.

13. **Susan:** I am glad you're around to help me in these sensitive matters.

14. **Yoshi:** *(With special emphasis)* Please remember, Susan, I am available whenever you need me!

KAPITEL 30

7. **Susan:** Das ist offensichtlich. Die Versicherungsgesellschaft wird im Austausch für den von ihr gebotenen Versicherungsschutz gegen Schaden die Prämie für ihre Universalversicherung nach der Wahrscheinlichkeit oder Unwahrscheinlichkeit des Risikos berechnen, in der Hoffnung, daran zu verdienen. Das ist *ihre* Art der Risikobegrenzung.
8. **Yoshi:** Das gleiche gilt für Währungen oder Waren. Die beiden an einer Transaktion beteiligten Seiten erwarten einen Gewinn oder einen Vorteil. United Chocolate beispielsweise wird per Termingeschäft Kakao kaufen, um eine gleichmäßige Versorgung zu einem bestimmten Preis zu garantieren. Aus dem gleichen Grund wird das Unternehmen Termindevisen kaufen oder verkaufen, um seine Produktions- oder Verkaufspreise zu garantieren, oder um seinen Gewinn bei Exporttransaktionen dank eines günstigen Wechselkurses zu maximieren.
9. **Susan:** Aber Sie können Verlust oder Gewinn nicht völlig ausschließen!?
10. **Yoshi:** Das ist der Punkt, wo man auf kompliziertere Techniken wie z.B. Kurssicherungsgeschäfte zurückgreift. Um mögliche Verluste aufgrund unerwarteter Preisänderungen auszugleichen, kann man in der entgegengesetzten Richtung einen Vertrag abschließen. Um noch einmal das Beispiel von United Chocolate zu nehmen: Nehmen wir an, die Firma hat soeben auf der Basis eines langfristigen Vertrags Zucker gekauft. Sie kann sich während der Vertragsdauer gegen mögliche Schwankungen schützen, indem sie die gleiche Menge Zucker auf dem Terminmarkt verkauft...
11. **Susan:** Dann gleichen, falls die Preise fallen, die beim Terminverkauf gemachten Gewinne die Verluste aus dem Kaufpreis aus. Das klingt wie eine endlose Kette!
12. **Yoshi:** Ja, etwas in dieser Richtung. Im Grunde genommen ist der Zweck des Hedging nicht, Gewinn zu machen, sondern einen Verlust zu vermeiden oder zu begrenzen.

(Im Hintergrund)

Sehr geehrte Damen und Herren, wir beginnen nun unseren Landeanflug auf Los Angeles International. Bitte kehren Sie zu Ihren Sitzplätzen zurück und legen Sie die Sicherheitsgurte an. Vielen Dank.

13. **Susan:** Ich bin froh, daß Sie da sind, um mir bei diesen heiklen Fragen zu helfen.
14. **Yoshi:** *(Mit besonderem Nachdruck)* Denken Sie bitte immer daran, Susan, ich stehe zu Ihrer Verfügung, wann immer Sie mich brauchen!

ANMERKUNGEN (Fortsetzung)

(8) **coverage:** "Versicherungsschutz" gegen Zahlung einer Prämie *(premium)*. To cover "abdecken, zudecken".

(9) **futures (contract):** Ein standardisierter "Terminkontrakt" auf einem organisierten Markt, der dazu berechtigt, eine Ware in einer bestimmten Menge, an einem bestimmten Datum und zu einem im voraus abgemachten Preis zu kaufen. Es handelt sich hier um ein Spekulationsinstrument auf dem Terminmarkt. Im Gegensatz zum *forward contract* geht es hier nicht unbedingt um die tatsächliche Lieferung der Ware am Fälligkeitsdatum *(maturity date)*, sondern lediglich um die Abrechnung der Differenz zwischen dem ausgemachten Preis und dem Preis bei Fälligkeit.

(10) **hedging:** "Kurssicherungsgeschäft, Hedging". Eine besondere Art des Warentermingeschäfts (z.B. Rohstoffeinkauf), das zur Absicherung gegen Preisschwankungen mit einem anderen, auf den gleichen Zeitpunkt terminierten Geschäft (z.B. Produktverkauf) gekoppelt wird.

CHAPTER 30 DOCUMENT

Futures

1. Main futures markets and specialization

Chicago Board of Trade (CBOT): grains.

Chicago Mercantile Exchange (CMER): currencies.

London Commodity Exchange (LCE): coffee, cocoa.

London International Financial Futures and Options Exchange (LIFFE): currencies and financial products (equivalent to MATIF, Paris).

New York Coffee and Sugar Exchange (NCSE): coffee, cocoa, sugar.

New York Commodity Exchange (NCMX): metals.

2. Commodity futures (Extracts from the financial press, 15th January 199...)

a. Cocoa (NCSE) minimum volume 10 metric tonnes − $ per tonne

Maturity	Open	High	Low	Close	Change
March	1169	1173	1160	1165	− 4
June	1186	1195	1181	1182	− 4
Sept.	1230	1232	1225	1227	− 3
Dec.	1262	1265	1253	1254	− 8

b. Yen (CMER) minimum amount $1 million − $ per yen

Maturity	Open	High	Low	Close	Change
March	0.009473	0.009510	0.009443	0.009492	− 19
June	0.009514	0.009549	0.009498	0.009531	− 17
Sept.	0.009587	0.009595	0.009580	0.009580	+ 7
Dec.	0.009600	0.009616	0.009603	0.009606	− 7

3. Spot and Forward Rates $ per Australian dollar (AUD)

Spot	1.4043
1 month	1.4022
3 months	1.4011
6 months	1.4020
12 months	1.401

KAPITEL 30

Risiko-Management

Beim Risiko-Management *(risk management)* sind alle erdenklichen Arten von Wagnissen *(hazards, risks)* oder unvorhergesehenen Ereignissen *(contingencies)* in Betracht zu ziehen, die den reibungslosen Betrieb eines Unternehmens negativ beeinflussen können.
Das Risiko-Management betrifft nicht nur Währungsfluktuation und Rohstoffe.
Andere potentielle Risiken müssen vorausgesehen und bewertet werden, um in Form verschiedenster Versicherungen eine Risikobegrenzung vorzunehmen:
- Schadenersatz *(damages)*
- Haftpflicht *(liability)*
- Schutz gegen die Risiken eines Betrugs durch Firmenangehörige *(bonding)*, wie z.B. die Veruntreuung von Geldern *(embezzlement)*
- höhere Gewalt *(acts of God)*.
Für die nationalen und internationalen Unternehmen gibt es außerdem das politische Risiko, das noch schwieriger einzuschätzen und zu handhaben ist. Dennoch ist es für jede Art von Aktion unumgänglich, Risiken – auch kalkulierte *(calculated)* – einzugehen.

CHAPTER 30

EXERCISES

Comprehension

Lesen Sie den Dialog aufmerksam durch. Beantworten Sie dann die nachfolgenden Fragen, und zwar immer in ganzen Sätzen:

1. Why was Susan not too happy with her visit to Japan? **2.** What aspect of her visit did she enjoy, though? **3.** Is the futures market as simple for Yoshi as Susan seems to believe? **4.** According to Yoshi's fellow banker, what factor also accounts for success in the futures market? **5.** But in fact, what approach should characterize risk reduction? **6.** On what basis does an insurance company calculate the premiums? **7.** What is UC's goal when it buys cocoa futures? **8.** How can UC manage to maximize its profit on export transactions? **9.** What advantages can UC draw from a technique like hedging? **10.** Is the basic purpose of hedging to enable a company to make a big profit?

Vocabulary

Bilden Sie zusammengesetzte Ausdrücke (wie in Kapitel 27, Übung 2):

1. work   a. order
2. hire   b. made
3. credit   c. accounts
4. custom   d. standards
5. bar   e. purchase
6. living   f. tax
7. income   g. maintenance
8. file   h. station
9. bank   i. code
10. mail   j. worthiness

KAPITEL 30

LÖSUNGSVORSCHLÄGE

Verständnisübung

1. Because Mr Tanabe proved to be hard to persuade (*or* a tough customer). **2.** She enjoyed her participation in Yoshi's workshop on currency fluctuations. **3.** No. According to Yoshi, it is a risky business. **4.** According to the banker, luck is also a factor of success. **5.** A strict business approach should characterize risk reduction. **6.** It takes the likelihood or unlikelihood of risk into account and hopes to make a profit. **7.** Its goal is to secure a regular supply at a given price for a given date. **8.** By converting the foreign currency when the exchange rate is good. **9.** It can protect itself from possible losses due to unanticipated price changes. **10.** No. It just enables a company to avoid or reduce a loss.

Lösungen zur Wortschatzübung

1. h. **2.** e. **3.** j. **4.** b. **5.** i. **6.** d. **7.** f. **8.** g. **9.** c. **10.** a.

CHAPTER 30

Vocabulary revision (Chapters 21-30)

Vervollständigen Sie die folgenden Sätze (ein oder mehrere Wörter pro Lücke):

1. These knock-offs of luxury watches have been sold by clever (…). **2.** The (…) is the rate of profit made in selling an article or commodity. **3.** Posters on walls, billboards, advertisements on buses or taxis, etc., all make up (…). **4.** When you take a client for a tour of the factory, you (…) him (…) the facilities. **5.** (…) is the information about a product given by the user to the supplier. **6.** A (…) is an intensive course given on a specific subject. **7.** The (…) is the list of items to be considered or decided at a meeting. **8.** A (…) is a letter from one bank to another bank by which a customer mentioned in the letter is given the right to obtain the credit he may need. **9.** A (…) is a machine enabling the buyer to obtain delivery of small items such as sweets or cigarettes by putting a coin into a slot. **10.** A trader in (…) contracts to buy or sell a standardized class of commodity at a standard price in the future, thus hedging the risks of price changes.

DO!

Avoid the 'hard-sell' approach when you negotiate with the Japanese.

KAPITEL 30

Lösungen zur Wortschatzübung

1. copycats
2. mark-up
3. outdoor displays
4. show, round
5. feedback
6. crash course
7. agenda
8. letter of credit
9. vending machine
10. futures

DON'T!

Don't confuse the 'collectivist' business approach in which group harmony takes precedence over individual performance and the 'individualist' business approach in which the individual's performance matters. Japan belongs to the first; the USA and Britain to the second.

CHAPTER 31

Facing political problems

Another few weeks have gone by. Susan is on the phone with her friend Mary-Ann.

1. **Susan:** Hi Mary-Ann! This is Susan. I apologize for not calling earlier. Mine is a hectic life with not enough time to devote to my friends.

2. **Mary-Ann:** Look Susan, you don't need to apologize.

3. **Susan:** I am just back from my third trip to Asia in five months. I should have called to tell you how pleasant my visit to your uncle was.

4. **Mary-Ann:** I already know. He called after your departure and said you had great charm and a remarkable aptitude for business.

5. **Susan:** He is very entrepreneurial himself! We think he will provide interesting outlets for several of our products. The follow-up is being taken care of by one of our representatives in Australia. In the meantime, I have had to face serious problems. **(1)**

6. **Mary-Ann:** Nothing personal I hope.

7. **Susan:** No, from that point of view things are going beautifully. I'll tell you later. Unfortunately, we are caught in the current turmoil between the US and Japan over the enforcement of the GATT agreements. **(2) (3) (4)**

8. **Mary-Ann:** I thought the matter had been settled with the formal signing of the Treaty. **(5)**

9. **Susan:** Alas not! Washington and Tokyo do not read the same meaning into the Treaty. The President wants Japan to shrink its massive trade surplus with the US and the rest of the world by pledging to buy not only more foreign cars, but also services like computer software or insurance, **and** food products. **(6)**

10. **Mary-Ann:** That's good for you!

KAPITEL 31

Politische Probleme

Wieder sind einige Wochen vergangen. Susan telefoniert mit ihrer Freundin Mary-Ann.

1. **Susan:** Hallo Mary-Ann! Susan hier. Entschuldige, daß ich nicht früher angerufen habe. Ich führe ein hektisches Leben, in dem nicht genug Zeit für meine Freunde bleibt.
2. **Mary-Ann:** Ist gut, Susan, du brauchst dich nicht zu entschuldigen.
3. **Susan:** Ich komme gerade von meiner dritten Asienreise innerhalb von fünf Monaten zurück. Ich hätte dich anrufen sollen, um dir zu sagen, wie nett mein Besuch bei deinem Onkel war.
4. **Mary-Ann:** Ich weiß es schon. Er rief nach deiner Abfahrt an und sagte, daß du viel Charme und eine bemerkenswerte Begabung für's Geschäft hast.
5. **Susan:** Er hat selbst sehr viel Unternehmergeist! Wir denken, er wird interessante Vertriebsstellen für einige unserer Produkte finden. Einer unserer Vertreter in Australien wird dafür sorgen, daß die Sache weiterverfolgt wird. In der Zwischenzeit hatte ich ernste Probleme.
6. **Mary-Ann:** Ich hoffe, nichts Persönliches.
7. **Susan:** Nein, in dieser Hinsicht läuft alles wunderbar. Ich erzähle es dir später. Leider sind wir in den aktuellen Aufruhr zwischen den USA und Japan über die Durchsetzung der GATT-Vereinbarungen verstrickt.
8. **Mary-Ann:** Ich dachte, die Sache sei mit der formellen Unterzeichnung des Vertrags beigelegt worden.
9. **Susan:** Oh nein! Washington und Tokio interpretieren den Vertrag nicht auf die gleiche Weise. Der Präsident möchte, daß Japan seinen enormen Handelsbilanzüberschuß gegenüber den Vereinigten Staaten und der restlichen Welt vermindert, indem es zusichert, nicht nur mehr ausländische Autos, sondern auch Dienstleistungen wie Computer-Software oder Versicherungen **und** Lebensmittelerzeugnisse zu kaufen.
10. **Mary-Ann:** Das ist gut für dich!

ANMERKUNGEN

(1) **entrepreneurial:** "dynamisch, unternehmerisch, mit Unternehmergeist und Risikobereitschaft". *Entrepreneur* "Unternehmer/in"; *Entrepreneurial association* "Unternehmerverband"; *entrepreneurial management* "Unternehmertum"; *entrepreneurial risk* "Unternehmerrisiko".

(2) **turmoil:** "Aufruhr, Durcheinander".

(3) **enforcement:** "Durchsetzung; Vollstreckung, Erzwingung". *Enforcement of a right* "Durchsetzung eines Rechtsanspruchs"; *to enforce* "durchsetzen; vollziehen"; *to enforce one's claims by suit* "seine Ansprüche gerichtlich geltend machen".

(4) **GATT** *(General Agreement on Tariffs and Trade):* "Allgemeines Zoll- und Handelsabkommen".

(5) **Treaty:** Die Unterzeichnung des GATT-Abkommens fand am 15. April 1994 in Marakesch statt. Das GATT hat sich danach in die *World Trade Organization (WTO)* "Welthandelsorganisation" umgewandelt.

(6) **trade surplus:** Überschuß in der Handelsbilanz *(balance of trade).* (Für den Unterschied zur Zahlungsbilanz *(balance of payments)* siehe Dokument.)

CHAPTER 31

11. **Susan:** It certainly is. The problem is that public opinion in this country is divided. You have the hard-liners who want to crack down on Japan by raising customs duties on products threatening our manufacturing industry, and those who believe that the door should not be slammed to negotiation. **(7) (8)**

12. **Mary-Ann:** Although I am by no means an expert in business, I would be inclined to think you side with the latter.

13. **Susan:** You've guessed right! Trade sanctions, in whatever form, would harm us at a time when we are trying hard to expand our sales there. Another option would be to manufacture our products in Japan. But the rub is that their labour costs are high compared to other Asian countries. **(9)**

14. **Mary-Ann:** You've got a tough job. I sympathize!

15. **Susan:** Some economic advisors in the present administration are not adverse to currency manipulation and to forcing the yen up against the dollar. **(10)**

16. **Mary-Ann:** That's one way of making imported Japanese goods more expensive, and our own cheaper in Japan.

17. **Susan:** Of course. But, in the long run, disrupting normal exchange mechanisms only brings short-lived relief. **(11)**

18. **Mary-Ann:** You're beginning to speak like an expert yourself... Now, tell me more about your personal life. You always sound so mysterious!

19. **Susan:** Here's the big news! I have been dating a banker associate for several weeks and, honestly, I have never felt so happy before. We have even started making plans for the future... **(12) (13)**

KAPITEL 31

11. **Susan:** Das ist es bestimmt. Das Problem ist, daß die öffentliche Meinung in diesem Land geteilt ist. Da sind die Hardliner, die hart gegen Japan durchgreifen wollen, indem sie die Zollsätze auf Produkte, die unsere verarbeitende Industrie bedrohen, anheben wollen, und da sind diejenigen, die denken, daß man die Tür, die zu Verhandlungen führt, nicht zuschlagen sollte.
12. **Mary-Ann:** Obwohl ich absolut kein kaufmännischer Experte bin, würde ich dazu neigen, zu sagen, daß du auf der Seite der letzteren stehst.
13. **Susan:** Richtig geraten! Handelssanktionen, in welcher Form auch immer, würden uns zu einer Zeit, in der wir versuchen, unseren Absatz dort zu erhöhen, schaden. Eine andere Möglichkeit wäre, unsere Produkte in Japan herzustellen. Der Haken dabei ist jedoch, daß die dortigen Lohnkosten im Vergleich zu anderen asiatischen Ländern hoch sind.
14. **Mary-Ann:** Du hast einen harten Job. Du tust mir wirklich leid!
15. **Susan:** Einige Wirtschaftsberater in der gegenwärtigen Regierung lehnen eine Währungsmanipulation und ein Hochtreiben des Yen gegenüber dem Dollar nicht ab.
16. **Mary-Ann:** Das ist eine Art, importierte japanische Güter teurer und unsere eigenen in Japan billiger zu machen.
17. **Susan:** Natürlich. Aber langfristig gesehen bringt die Unterbrechung normaler Wechselkursmechanismen nur eine kurzlebige Atempause.
18. **Mary-Ann:** Du beginnst selbst wie ein Experte zu reden... Jetzt erzähl mir mal mehr über dein Privatleben. Du klingst immer so geheimnisvoll!
19. **Susan:** Hier kommen die großen Neuigkeiten! Ich treffe mich seit einigen Wochen mit einem Geschäftspartner von einer Bank und, ehrlich gesagt, ich habe mich nie zuvor so glücklich gefühlt. Wir haben sogar begonnen, Pläne für die Zukunft zu schmieden...

ANMERKUNGEN (Fortsetzung)

(7) **hard-liner:** Befürworter einer harten Linie *(hard line)* in der Politik.
(8) **to crack down on:** "hart durchgreifen, drastische Maßnahmen ergreifen". *To crack a whip* "mit einer Peitsche knallen".
(9) **rub** bedeutet "reiben, streichen". *There's the rub* "Da liegt der Haken".
(10) **administration** bezeichnet in den USA die "Regierung" und gleichzeitig die Gesamtheit der Mitarbeiter, deren Nominierung vom jeweils gewählten Präsidenten abhängt.
(11) **relief:** "Erleichterung; Ruhe, Atempause". *tax relief* "Steuererleichterung, -vergünstigung".
(12) **to date each other/somebody:** "mit jemandem gehen". *Date* ist nicht nur die "Verabredung", sondern auch die Person, mit der man sich verabredet. Eine besondere Form ist das *blind date*, bei dem man den Partner, mit dem man sich verabredet, vorher nicht kennt. Eine andere Form ist das *computer date*, bei dem die Zusammenführung der Partner dem Computer überlassen wird!
(13) **associate:** "Partner(in), Kollege, Kollegin", aber auch "Gefährte, Kamerad, Komplize".

CHAPTER 31 DOCUMENT

International trade

A free trade economy is one in which there are few or no restrictions to exchanges (or trade barriers) in the form of customs duties (tariffs), currency controls or quotas on imported goods, thus reducing competition for domestic products.

Balance of trade (trade balance)

Difference of value between imported and exported goods.
If imports exceed exports: trade deficit.
If exports exceed imports: trade surplus.

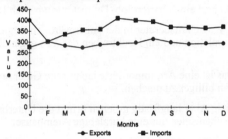

January shows a surplus (S); the following months show a deficit (D).

Balance of payments

Payments include: imports/exports of goods (visibles) plus tourist spending, shipping charges, capital transactions, investments and various services (invisibles).
Inflow: total value of visibles (exports) and invisibles (credited).
Outflow: total value of visibles (imports) and invisibles (debited).

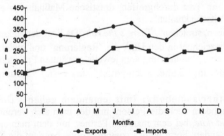

The balance of payments shows a net surplus over 12 consecutive months.

KAPITEL 31

 Die Multis, Unternehmen ohne Grenzen

Multinationale Unternehmen *(worldwide corporations)* beschränken sich heute nicht mehr nur darauf, Rohstoffe zu importieren oder fertige Produkte *(manufactured goods, finished goods)* zu exportieren, also Warenhandel zu betreiben *(to trade)*.
Wenn sich ihre Erzeugnisse in einem anderen Land gut verkaufen, können sie in diesem Land eine Produktionseinheit *(production unit)* errichten, d.h. sie fertigen an Ort und Stelle für den Konsum im betreffenden Land oder für den Export in die angrenzenden Gebiete *(proximity zone)*.
Die nächste Etappe besteht darin, neue Produkte herzustellen, die besser auf den lokalen oder regionalen Markt abgestimmt sind. Diese neue industrielle Aktivität mit seinen von der Zentrale unabhängigen Entscheidungszentren *(decision centres)* entwickelt dann ihre eigene Marktlogik, die nicht mehr mit der der Nationalstaaten *(nation states)* übereinstimmt.

CHAPTER 31

EXERCISES

Comprehension

Lesen Sie den Dialog aufmerksam durch. Beantworten Sie dann die nachfolgenden Fragen, und zwar immer in ganzen Sätzen:

1. What is Susan's excuse for not calling her friend Mary-Ann? **2.** Why should she have called Mary-Ann earlier? **3.** Is Susan in charge of the follow-up to her Australian business trip? **4.** What serious problems did Susan have to face? **5.** Why did the formal signing of the Treaty fail to settle the matter? **6.** What does the US President expect from the Japanese? **7.** What is the position taken by hard-liners? **8.** What solution does Susan favour? **9.** What is the drawback of having UC's products manufactured in Japan? **10.** Why is the idea of forcing the yen up against the dollar tempting in the short run but risky in the long run?

Vocabulary

The colour of business. *In der Wirtschaftssprache gibt es eine Reihe von Ausdrücken, die Farbbezeichnungen in Form von Adjektiven enthalten. Setzen Sie in die Lücken jeweils den Namen der passenden Farbe ein. Sie können eine Farbe in mehreren Ausdrücken benutzen.*

1. When you buy goods unofficially, you buy them on the .... market. **2.** In a plant, workers who work with their hands are called ....-collar workers. **3.** The Marketing Manager was given the .... light (ie, he was given permission to go ahead with his project). **4.** Many managers get angry about .... tape (ie, official regulations and papers). **5.** As this customer is considered unreliable, he has been .... -listed. **6.** This company has lost a great deal of money. It is in the .... for the first time in its history. **7.** The trainee is ....: he is totally inexperienced. **8.** The shares of companies listed on the Stock Exchange and offering reliable investment opportunities are called .... chips. **9.** Today, most companies rely on .... matter (ie, their staff's brain intelligence). **10.** Our company is afraid of being taken over by this well-known raider. It hopes a .... knight will show up before it's too late.

KAPITEL 31

LÖSUNGSVORSCHLÄGE

Verständnisübung

1. She is too busy to devote much time to her friends. 2. Because she was pleasantly entertained by Mary-Ann's uncle in Australia. 3. No. This task is performed by one of UC's representatives in Australia. 4. She had to face the problems raised by the disputes between the US and Japan over the GATT Treaty. 5. Because the Americans and the Japanese interpret the Treaty differently. 6. He expects them to increase their imports of goods and services. 7. They are in favour of raising customs duties on Japanese products threatening the US manufacturing industry. 8. She is in favour of keeping the door to negotiation open. 9. Labour costs are higher in Japan than in other Asian countries. 10. In the short run, US products would be cheaper in Japan and Japanese products more expensive in the USA, but in the long run, exchanges would be disrupted and new problems would arise.

Lösungen zur Wortschatzübung

1. black. 2. blue. 3. green. 4. red. 5. black. 6. red. 7. green. 8. blue. 9. grey. 10. white.

CHAPTER 31

Application

*Geben Sie an, in welche Kategorie **(a=visibles, b=invisibles)** die folgenden Transaktionen bei der Erstellung einer Bilanz für ein bestimmtes Jahr fallen:*

1. imported automobiles
2. exported software
3. transfers of investment funds
4. imported aircraft
5. air-freight charges
6. imported microprocessors
7. international travel expenses
8. collection of insurance premiums
9. sales of military equipment
10. maintenance contracts

DO!

Speak in a down-to-earth way and give examples.

KAPITEL 31

Lösungen

1. a. **2.** b. **3.** b. **4.** a. **5.** b. **6.** a. **7.** b. **8.** b. **9.** a. **10.** b.

 DON'T!

Don't use meaningless clichés like:
- *all Englishmen are tea-drinkers.*
- *America is a nation of cowboys or of grown-up children* **(große Kinder).**
- *Chicago is a city of gangsters.*

CHAPTER 32

Mind the market (1)

Several months have gone by. Susan has been summoned to Philadelphia for discussions on problems concerning her export zone. She is now in the office of her boss, Mr George Thomson, VP North American Exports. **(2) (3)**

1. **Mr Thomson:** I have read with interest the detailed report on your latest trip to the Far East. I like your approach. You don't beat about the bush. You go straight to the point.

2. **Susan:** Thanks! I found out early that the Export Manager has to wage war on several fronts at the same time. The individual consumer is our target. And yet our main dealings are with the various distribution networks in each country of the zone.

3. **Mr Thomson:** Do you find their preoccupations so different from an ordinary consumer's?

4. **Susan:** I wouldn't put it like that. As a matter of fact, both expect the best possible product at the lowest price.

5. **Mr Thomson:** *(Slightly pompous)* That's exactly what we try to achieve. At production level, our quality control tests are extremely rigorous while we constantly seek to improve productivity. Our goal: total quality management. **(4)**

6. **Susan:** No doubt...

7. **Mr Thomson:** On the other hand, our supply of raw materials is guaranteed at stable prices by long-term contracts on the different commodity markets. Our own financial resources and income are safeguarded by means of futures contracts in the various operating currencies. **(5) (6)**

8. **Susan:** Our competitors do the same...

9. **Mr Thomson:** Yes, and it's up to us to do better!

KAPITEL 32

Den Markt beachten

Mehrere Monate sind vergangen. Susan ist zu einer Besprechung über die Probleme ihres Exportgebietes nach Philadelphia gerufen worden. Sie befindet sich nun im Büro ihres Chefs, George Thomson, Vize-Präsident für den Export in Nordamerika.

1. **Herr Thomson:** Ich habe mit Interesse Ihren detaillierten Bericht über Ihre letzte Reise in den Fernen Osten gelesen. Ich mag Ihren Ansatz. Sie gehen nicht um den heißen Brei herum. Sie kommen direkt auf den Punkt.

2. **Susan:** Danke! Ich habe früh herausgefunden, daß der Exportleiter zur gleichen Zeit an mehreren Fronten kämpfen muß. Der einzelne Verbraucher ist unser Ziel. Und dennoch erfolgen unsere wichtigsten Geschäftsabschlüsse mit den verschiedenen Vertriebsnetzen in jedem Land des Verkaufsgebiets.

3. **Herr Thomson:** Finden Sie, daß deren Anliegen sich so sehr von denen des gewöhnlichen Verbrauchers unterscheiden?

4. **Susan:** So würde ich es nicht ausdrücken. Eigentlich erwarten beide das bestmögliche Produkt zum niedrigsten Preis.

5. **Herr Thomson:** *(Ein bißchen großspurig)* Das ist genau das, was wir erreichen wollen. Auf der Produktionsebene sind unsere Qualitätskontrollen extrem streng, während wir gleichzeitig permanent versuchen, die Produktivität zu verbessern. Unser Ziel: Total Quality Management.

6. **Susan:** Zweifellos...

7. **Herr Thomson:** Auf der anderen Seite wird unsere Versorgung mit Rohmaterialien zu stabilen Preisen durch langfristige Verträge auf den verschiedenen Warenmärkten garantiert. Unsere eigenen finanziellen Ressourcen und Gewinne werden durch Warentermingeschäfte in den unterschiedlichen Währungen geschützt.

8. **Susan:** Unsere Mitbewerber machen das Gleiche...

9. **Herr Thomson:** Ja, und es liegt an uns, es besser zu machen!

ANMERKUNGEN

(1) **to mind:** "auf etw. achten, auf etw. achtgeben". *Mind the step* "Vorsicht Stufe".
(2) **to summon:** "rufen zu, holen, zusammenrufen". *To summon a shareholders' meeting* "Aktionärsversammlung einberufen", *summons* "Ruf, Berufung; gerichtliche Vorladung".
(3) **VP** ist die Abkürzung von *vice president*.
(4) **total quality management:** Siehe Kapitel 7, Anmerkung 9.
(5) **income:** hier: "Gewinne". Synonym: *profit*. *Gross income* "Brutto-, Gesamteinkommen"; *net income* "Nettoeinkommen, Reinertrag"; *income tax* "Einkommensteuer".
(6) **operating:** "Betreiben, Betrieb; in Betrieb befindlich, betrieblich". *Operating income* "Betriebseinnahmen, Geschäftserträge"; *operating loss* "Betriebsverlust".

CHAPTER 32

10. **Susan:** You will agree with me that the Australian farmer or the Japanese suburbanite doesn't care a hang about the rise and fall of futures markets. What the distributors want is prompt and punctual delivery of goods. **(7) (8)**

11. **Mr Thomson:** Well, Susan, that's the Export Manager's job. Corporate headquarters can't be held responsible for everything!

12. **Susan:** Definitely. But defective or ill-conceived packaging is my main worry right now. This is where we get most complaints. I know, some of the gripes have to do with minor points, like tabs that don't pull easily enough, or wrapping paper with cutting edges. **(9) (10) (11)**

13. **Mr Thomson:** But, you did mention such mishaps in your report. And I have already passed on the information to our specialists. They promised they would provide satisfactory solutions to problems you were not the only one to raise.

14. **Susan:** I am grateful for your support. I am, perhaps, getting obsessed by our brand image and anxious about any incident, even unimportant, that might affect it.

15. **Mr Thomson:** I can't blame you for that. On the contrary. Some of our brands are renowned all over the world, although they are not necessarily associated with the name of our company in the consumers' minds. I would say those brands are our most precious intangible assets... By the way, the protection of brand image will be the theme of the Food Retailers' Conference to be held in New Orleans two weeks from now. I presume I will see you there. **(12)**

16. **Susan:** I am sorry. I am getting married that weekend. I'm sure you've heard that Yoshi Kyoto and I had got engaged. After the wedding, we will fly to Honolulu for a short honeymoon and a much deserved rest. I am sending my assistant, Greg Jimenez, to attend in my place. It will give him a chance to make personal contacts.

17. **Mr Thomson:** We'll miss you! My warm wishes to you and Yoshi!

KAPITEL 32

10. **Susan:** Sie werden mit mir darin übereinstimmen, daß der australische Landwirt oder der japanische Vorstädter sich nicht um das Auf und Ab der Warenterminmärkte schert. Was die Vertriebsstellen wollen, ist eine schnelle und pünktliche Anlieferung der Waren.
11. **Herr Thomson:** Naja, Susan, das ist der Job des Exportleiters. Die Unternehmenszentrale kann nicht für alles verantwortlich gemacht werden!
12. **Susan:** Sicher. Aber meine Hauptsorge gilt im Moment defekter oder schlecht durchdachter Verpackung. Das ist der Punkt, wo wir die meisten Beschwerden erhalten. Ich weiß, einiges von dem Gemecker hat mit Nebensächlichkeiten zu tun, wie beispielsweise Laschen, die sich nicht leicht genug herausziehen lassen oder Verpackungspapier mit scharfen Kanten.
13. **Herr Thomson:** Aber Sie haben solche Mißgeschicke bereits in Ihrem Bericht erwähnt. Und ich habe die Informationen schon an unsere Experten weitergegeben. Die haben versprochen, zufriedenstellende Lösungen für diese Probleme zu finden, Probleme, die nicht nur Sie angesprochen haben.
14. **Susan:** Ich bin dankbar für Ihre Unterstützung. Vielleicht werde ich langsam besessen von unserem Markenimage und bin besorgt um jeden noch so unwichtigen Zwischenfall, der ihm schaden könnte.
15. **Herr Thomson:** Ich kann Ihnen daraus keinen Vorwurf machen. Im Gegenteil. Einige unserer Marken sind in der ganzen Welt berühmt, obwohl sie in den Köpfen der Verbraucher nicht unbedingt mit dem Namen unserer Firma verbunden sind. Ich würde sagen, solche Marken sind unsere wertvollsten immateriellen Vermögenswerte... Ach, übrigens, der Schutz des Markenimage wird das Thema der Konferenz der Lebensmitteleinzelhändler sein, die in zwei Wochen in New Orleans abgehalten wird. Ich nehme an, daß ich Sie dort treffen werde.
16. **Susan:** Es tut mir leid. Ich werde an dem betreffenden Wochenende heiraten. Sicher haben Sie gehört, daß Yoshi Kyoto und ich uns verlobt haben. Nach der Hochzeit werden wir für kurze Flitterwochen und eine wohlverdiente Verschnaufpause nach Honolulu fliegen. Ich schicke meinen Assistenten, Greg Jimenez, der mich vertreten soll. Das wird ihm die Gelegenheit geben, persönliche Kontakte zu knüpfen.
17. **Herr Thomson:** Sie werden uns fehlen! Meine herzlichsten Glückwünsche für Sie und Yoshi!

ANMERKUNGEN (Fortsetzung)

(7) **suburbanite:** "Vorstädter(in)" kommt von *suburb* "Vorstadt".

(8) **don´t care a hang** ist ein sehr salopper Ausdruck, wobei *hang* hier ein Euphemismus für *damn* ist.

(9) **packaging:** "Verpackung", bei der es auch auf die äußere Aufmachung ankommt. Das Verb lautet *to package*. Eine andere Form der Verpackung ist *packing* (Verb: *to pack*); hier steht der Schutz des verpackten Gutes im Vordergrund.

(10) **gripes:** "Gemecker, Meckern" ist ein abwertender Ausdruck für *complaint* "Beschwerde".

(11) **tab** kann im technischen Kontext sehr viele Bedeutungen haben: "Metallspitze, Dorn, Lappen, Lasche, Zunge"...

(12) **intangible assets**: In der Bilanz *(balance sheet)* die immateriellen Güter bzw. Aktivposten, die nicht physisch existieren: Marken *(brands)*, Warenzeichen *(trademarks*; eingetragene *registered)*, Patente *(patents)*, Fertigungsverfahren *(manufacturing processes)*. Gegenteil von *tangible assets* "Sachanlagen, Sachvermögen", also die Gesamtheit aller physischen Güter, die zur Produktionsausrüstung gehören.

CHAPTER 32 DOCUMENT

Protecting the consumer and the environment

> Never before have consumers been offered so many products, gadgets and services meant to make life easier.
>
> This is one of the familiar facets of affluence. But it is felt by more and more people that the forces of technology, combined with marketing oriented towards growth at any cost, have developed a 'consumption' culture, which, in the final analysis, may be detrimental to the individual and to the natural environment. In most countries, government agencies and private organizations are actively promoting legislation, or programs to maintain, the quality of life.
>
> Consumerism is the name currently used to describe this new approach to the satisfaction of human needs and desires. It covers every problem of pollution, from cleaning up air and water to waste disposal, calls for the preservation of limited natural resources, the elimination of unsafe products, clearer labels on packages and legal protection of the buyer's rights.

KAPITEL 32

Die Marktbeherrschung

Soll man es dem Markt überlassen, sich selbst zu regulieren *(to be self-regulating)*, geführt von der berühmten unsichtbaren Hand *(the invisible hand)*, wie es der schottische Volkswirt Adam Smith Ende des 18. Jahrhunderts forderte? Dieser Doktrin des Laisser-faire *(non-interference, laisser-faire)* steht gewöhnlich die Planwirtschaft des Staates *(state* oder *government interventionism)* gegenüber.

Die meisten Industriestaaten haben sich aus der Furcht vor Monopolen *(monopolies)* heraus eine umfassende Kartellgesetzgebung *(antitrust legislation)* zugelegt, um den freien Wettbewerb *(free competition)* aufrechtzuerhalten und unerlaubte Preisabsprachen *(price-fixing)* zu unterbinden.

CHAPTER 32

EXERCISES

Comprehension

Lesen Sie den Dialog aufmerksam durch. Beantworten Sie dann die nachfolgenden Fragen, und zwar immer in ganzen Sätzen:

1. Why has Susan been summoned to Philadelphia? **2.** What does Mr Thomson like about her approach? **3.** What has Susan found out about being an Export Manager? **4.** What preoccupation do individual consumers and distribution networks share? **5.** How is product quality achieved at United Chocolate? **6.** Why does the company buy futures contracts in its various operating currencies? **7.** According to Mr Thomson, are corporate headquarters responsible for the delivery of goods to foreign clients? **8.** What does Susan worry about, right now? **9.** How does Mr Thomson reassure her about those problems? **10.** Will Susan be able to attend the Food Retailers' Conference in New Orleans?

Translation

1. Einige Monate sind vergangen, seit Susan zum Exportleiter für den Pazifikraum ernannt wurde. **2.** Als Exportleiter hat Susan weniger mit dem einzelnen Verbraucher als mit Vertriebsnetzen zu tun. **3.** Langfristige Verträge garantieren die Versorgung mit Rohstoffen zu stabilen Preisen. **4.** Es liegt an Ihnen, es in allen Bereichen besser zu machen als Ihre Konkurrenten. **5.** Der australische Landwirt schert sich nicht um Währungsfluktuationen. **6.** Wer muß für die schlechte Qualität eines Produkts verantwortlich gemacht werden? **7.** Die meisten Beschwerden drehen sich um Nebensächlichkeiten. **8.** Achten Sie auf die scharfen Kanten bei Einpackpapier. **9.** Das Markenimage eines Unternehmens muß ebenso geschützt werden wie seine finanziellen Ressourcen. **10.** Marken und Patente gehören zu dem, was man immaterielle Vermögenswerte nennt. Fabrikanlagen sind materielle Vermögenswerte.

KAPITEL 32

LÖSUNGSVORSCHLÄGE

Verständnisübung

1. She's been summoned to Philadelphia for discussions on problems concerning her export zone. **2.** Susan doesn't beat about the bush, but goes straight to the point. **3.** She has to wage war on several fronts at the same time. **4.** Both expect the best possible product at the lowest price. **5.** Extremely rigorous quality control tests are used at production level. **6.** It does so to protect its income and financial resources from currency fluctuations. **7.** No, it's the Export Manager's job. **8.** She worries about defective or ill-conceived packaging. **9.** He tells her that the company specialists have promised they would provide satisfactory solutions. **10.** No, she won't, because she will be on her honeymoon; she is sending Greg Jimenez in her place.

Übersetzungsübung

1. Several months have gone by since Susan was appointed Export Manager for the Pacific rim. **2.** As Export Manager, Susan has fewer dealings with the individual consumer than with distribution networks. **3.** Long-term contracts guarantee the supply of raw materials at stable prices. **4.** It is up to you to do better than your competitors in every area. **5.** The Australian farmer doesn't care a hang about currency (*ou* exchange) fluctuations. **6.** Who must be held responsible for the poor quality of a product? **7.** Most complaints have to do with minor points. **8.** Mind the cutting edge(s) of wrapping paper. **9.** The brand image of a company must be safeguarded as much as its financial resources. **10.** Brands and patents are part of what are called intangible assets. Plants are tangible assets.

CHAPTER 32

*Lesen Sie den Dialog des Kapitels 30, das Dokument und die **ANMERKUNGEN** aufmerksam durch. Lassen Sie sich nicht durch diesen neuen Übungstyp verunsichern. Bei jeder Frage wird als Hilfestellung auf ein Dokument aus einem anderen Kapitel verwiesen.*

Question 1

In June of last year, United Chocolate purchased 1,000 tonnes of cocoa futures on NCSE at $1,200 per tonne, maturity December.
In early January, UC receives information from confidential but reliable sources on the likelihood of overproduction, due to exceptional weather conditions in some of the producing countries.
On January 15, the decision is made to hedge, by selling the same volume, December futures, rate at close $1,254.
In December, the information proves true. The price of cocoa has fallen by over 10 %. UC buys 1,000 tonnes spot at $1,120 per tonne.
Give detailed figures showing how UC has benefited from these successive transactions *(consult Document, Chapter 30, paragraph 2)*.

Question 2

(a) Compute the value in yen of 1 million US dollars futures sold, maturity December, rate at close 0.009606 *(consult Document, Chapter 30, paragraph 2)*.

(b) Compute the US dollar value of 1 million Australian dollars, sold forward 6 months (July) *(consult Document, Chapter 30, paragraph 3)*.

DO!

Do some research to find out who your competitors are, but never criticize them.

KAPITEL 32

Lösungen

Frage 1

Purchase of 1,000 tonnes of cocoa futures in June,
   maturity December of following year: $1,200 x 1,000 = $1,200,000
Sale of 1,000 tonnes of cocoa futures in January,
   maturity December of the same year: $1,254 x 1,000 = $1,254,000
Profit for UC: **$54,000**

Spot purchase of 1,000 tonnes in December at $1,120 per tonne:
   $1,120 x 1,000 = $1,120,000
Since UC had originally contracted to buy at $1,200, the saving per tonne is:
   $1,200 – $1,120 = $80
Total saving for UC: **$80,000**

Frage 2

(a) December futures Yen, close:

Yen 1.00   0.009606

US $1.00 = $\dfrac{1.00}{0.0009606}$ = Yen 104,1016

US $1 million = **Yen 104 million 101,600**

(b) AUD 1 million, sold forward 6 months (July):

US $1.00   AUD 1.4020

AUD 1.00 = $\dfrac{1.00}{1.4020}$ = US $0.713667

AUD 1 million = **US $713,266.00**

DON'T!

*Don't refuse to answer questions about your salary.
It's an accepted way of assessing yourself in the USA.*

CHAPTER 33

The threat of a boycott

To meet the needs of its expanding Pacific markets, UC has decided to increase capacity by enlarging its Monterey production unit. The local conservationist association is up in arms against the project and threatens a boycott of UC products. Paul DeWitt, the plant manager, is discussing the situation with George Thomson. (1) (2)

1. **Paul DeWitt:** Thanks for coming at such short notice, George. The situation has become so critical I couldn't handle it myself. (3) (4)

2. **George Th'son:** I took the first available flight after I got your message. Apparently, our project does not break any zoning regulation. (5)

3. **Paul DeWitt:** Certainly not! But in the process of enlarging our facilities, we will have to cut into about two acres of wooded land. Although our extension will create badly needed jobs,
it has triggered passionate reactions from the ecologists, not only locally, but throughout the state. They have set up a 'Fighters for Ozone' committee and are calling upon lobbies for major environmental organizations to endorse their campaign. (6) (7) (8) (9)

KAPITEL 33

Ein Boykott droht

Um die Anforderungen seines expandierenden pazifischen Marktes zu befriedigen, hat UC beschlossen, seine Kapazität durch den Ausbau der Produktionseinheit Monterey zu erweitern. Die örtliche Naturschutzvereinigung lehnt sich gegen das Projekt auf und droht mit einem Boykott der UC-Produkte. Paul DeWitt, der Werksleiter, bespricht die Situation mit George Thomson.

1. **Paul DeWitt:** Danke, daß Sie so kurzfristig gekommen sind, George. Die Situation ist so kritisch geworden, daß ich sie alleine nicht bewältigen konnte.

2. **George Th´son:** Ich habe den ersten verfügbaren Flug genommen, nachdem ich Ihre Nachricht erhalten habe. Anscheinend verletzt unser Projekt keinerlei Bebauungsbestimmungen.

3. **Paul DeWitt:** Sicherlich nicht! Aber die Vergrößerung unserer Einrichtungen erfordert die Abholzung von etwa zwei Morgen Waldgebiet. Obwohl unser Ausbau dringend benötigte Arbeitsplätze schafft, hat er leidenschaftliche Reaktionen von seiten der Umweltschützer ausgelöst, nicht nur im Umkreis, sondern im gesamten Bundesstaat. Sie haben ein Komitee mit dem Namen "Kämpfer für Ozon" eingerichtet und appellieren an die Interessenvertretungen bedeutender Umweltschutzorganisationen, ihre Kampagne zu unterstützen.

ANMERKUNGEN

(1) **conservationist association:** Die Vereinigung zum Schutz der Natur hat sich den Erhalt der Ressourcen in Natur und Tierwelt und den Schutz der Landschaft auf die Fahne geschrieben. Sie kam zu Beginn des 20. Jahrhunderts unter Präsident Theodor Roosevelt auf, der die ersten Nationalparks *(National parks)* gründete.

(2) **to be up in arms:** "kampfbereit sein"; *to be up in arms about something* "wegen etwas aufgebracht sein".

(3) **at short notice:** "kurzfristig". *Notice* "Benachrichtigung"; *advance notice* "vorherige Benachrichtigung, Vorankündigung".

(4) **to handle:** "umgehen mit, fertigwerden mit, zurechtkommen mit".

(5) **zoning regulation:** Bestimmungen für die Stadtplanung, die die Standortnormen festlegen.

(6) Ein **acre** entspricht 0,4 Hektar.

(7) **to trigger:** "auslösen, hervorrufen". *Trigger* "Auslöser".

(8) **lobby:** "Lobby", auch *pressure group*, bezeichnet eine Interessenvertretung, die sich bildet, um in einer bestimmten Sache Druck auf die Staatsgewalt oder den Behörden auszuüben. Der Name Lobbyisten *(lobbyists)* stammt aus der Anfangszeit der Unabhängigkeit, in der Lobbyisten sich Zutritt zu den Fluren *(lobbies)* des Kongresses in Washington verschafften, um dort die Abgeordneten abzufangen und zu überreden, bei politischen Entscheidungen im Sinne der Lobbyisten zu votieren. Die Existenz der *lobbies* und des *lobbying* wird vom Gesetz anerkannt (siehe Kapitel 25, Dokument).

(9) **to endorse:** "billigen, gutheißen, unterstützen". Auch "einen Scheck indossieren". *Endorsement* "Indossament; Billigung, Unterstützung"; *celebrity endorsement:* Werbung für ein bestimmtes Produkt durch einen Prominenten.

CHAPTER 33

4. **George Th'son:** I am not surprised. Ecology has become a political issue. We had to face the same problem in Germany on a new construction site. The green vote, as they call it, carries real weight there.

5. **Paul DeWitt:** The trouble is that our opponents have struck a sensitive chord in California. They are no longer content with marching past our plant calling us names. They are now threatening a state boycott of our products. **(10)**

6. **George Th'son:** Gosh! It's as if we were rejecting toxic waste into the city sewage system! Do you think there might be serious repercussions for us?

7. **Paul DeWitt:** Well, I am not so much concerned by its effect on sales. We manufacture a variety of products, some of which are sold under the distributors' own brand names.

8. **George Th'son:** That's true. What we should fear most is the damage inflicted upon our reputation. Until recently, opinion polls on corporate image have placed us top in our category, not merely in terms of quality, but also of community service. The UC Foundation has been active in public health and humanitarian actions. **(11)**

9. **Paul DeWitt:** The Foundation financed an exhibition of local arts and crafts less than a year ago.

10. **George Th'son:** Right! I remember. Our President attended the opening! Look, we must act promptly before the whole thing gets out of control. Have your secretary call LA and put us through to Susan Edwards. Her record shows that she displayed real talent in conflict resolution when she worked in Human Resources at UC (UK)... **(12)**
(A few minutes later)

11. **George Th'son:** Hi, Susan! George Thomson speaking from Monterey.

12. **Susan:** Hi! Enjoying your visit to sunny California?

13. **George Th'son:** So, so. We have a problem here, and your skills as a negotiator are needed. Can you come right away? We'll take care of hotel reservations. Plan on staying a few days.

14. **Susan:** I'll drive, to save time. Yoshi won't be happy. We had tickets for the opera tomorrow night...

KAPITEL 33

4. **George Th´son:** Das überrascht mich nicht. Umweltschutz ist zu einem politischen Thema geworden. Wir hatten das gleiche Problem in Deutschland auf einer neuen Baustelle. Die grüne Stimme, wie sie das nennen, hat dort echtes Gewicht.

5. **Paul DeWitt:** Der Ärger ist, daß unsere Gegner in Kalifornien einen wunden Punkt getroffen haben. Sie begnügen sich nicht mehr damit, vor unserem Werk auf- und abzulaufen und uns zu beschimpfen. Sie drohen nun mit einem staatsweiten Boykott unserer Produkte.

6. **George Th´son:** Gott! Es ist, als würden wir giftige Abfälle in die städtische Kanalisation leiten! Denken Sie, daß sich ernste Konsequenzen für uns ergeben werden?

7. **Paul DeWitt:** Naja, ich mache mir nicht so viele Sorgen um die Auswirkungen auf den Verkauf. Wir stellen eine Vielzahl von Produkten her, von denen einige unter den eigenen Markennamen der Vertreiber verkauft werden.

8. **George Th´son:** Das ist wahr. Was wir am meisten fürchten sollten, ist der Schaden, den unser Ruf nehmen könnte. Bis vor kurzem haben wir bei Meinungsumfragen über das Firmenimage an erster Stelle in unserer Kategorie gelegen, nicht nur was die Qualität betrifft, sondern auch den Dienst für die Allgemeinheit. Die UC-Stiftung hat sich immer für das öffentliche Gesundheitswesen und humanitäre Aktionen engagiert.

9. **Paul DeWitt:** Vor weniger als einem Jahr hat die Stiftung eine Ausstellung über das hiesige Kunsthandwerk finanziert.

10. **George Th´son:** Richtig! Ich erinnere mich. Unser Generaldirektor ist zur Eröffnung dagewesen! Sehen Sie, wir müssen schnell handeln, bevor die ganze Sache außer Kontrolle gerät. Lassen Sie Ihre Sekretärin in Los Angeles anrufen und uns zu Susan Edwards durchstellen. Aus ihrer bisherigen Berufslaufbahn geht hervor, daß sie echtes Talent zur Konfliktlösung gezeigt hat, als sie bei UC (UK) im Personalwesen gearbeitet hat...
(Einige Minuten später)

11. **George Th´son:** Hallo, Susan! Hier ist George Thomson. Ich rufe von Monterey aus an.

12. **Susan:** Hallo! Genießen Sie Ihren Besuch im sonnigen Kalifornien?

13. **George Th´son:** So la-la. Wir haben hier ein Problem und Ihre Vermittlerfähigkeiten sind gefragt. Können Sie sofort kommen? Wir kümmern uns um die Hotelreservierung. Rechnen Sie mit ein paar Tagen.

14. **Susan:** Ich fahre mit dem Auto, um Zeit zu sparen. Yoshi wird das nicht gefallen. Wir hatten Karten für die Oper morgen abend...

ANMERKUNGEN (Fortsetzung)

(10) **to call somebody names:** "jdn. beschimpfen".
(11) **corporate image:** Bild, das die Öffentlichkeit von einem Unternehmen hat.
(12) **record:** hier: "Werdegang, Vorleben". Bezeichnet ansonsten in der Buchhaltung *(accounting)* ein Dokument, ein Aktenstück, ein Register, eine Liste. *To record* "registrieren, aufzeichnen".

CHAPTER 33   DOCUMENT

Congratulatory letter

United Chocolate, North America
(Domestic and Canada)
Philadelphia, PA

May 13, 199.

Office of the President

Susan Edwards
Manager
UC Exports
Los Angeles, CA

Dear Susan:

    I have just received George Thomson's report on your splendid work at Monterey. It was clever of George to capitalize on your former experience, and generous of you to respond at once.

    Everybody, on both sides of the negotiation table, was impressed by your calm assurance, and your opening statement that you had come to find a solution agreeable to all, without loss of face.

    Your suggestion to call upon an outside landscape architect*, to draw up a new plan integrating a greater number of trees into our site, cleared the road to the resolution of the conflict.

    Following your recommendation, I have informed the Chairman of FFO that we will pay for the plantation of as many trees as won't be saved, in areas of the city of their own choosing, subject to acceptance by the city authorities.

    We are all most grateful to you, and I personally look forward to seeing you on your next trip to Philadelphia.

    Sincerely yours,

Dick Spence
President, UC, North America (Domestic and Canada)

---

* **Landschaftsarchitekt**

KAPITEL 33

Wirtschaft und Unternehmen
(Einige historische Zitate)

The business of the United States is business sagte Calvin Coolidge, von 1923 bis 1928 Präsident der USA.
Dieser Einstellung steht die Vorstellung des Wohlfahrtsstaates *(welfare state)* gegenüber, in dem es dem Staat obliegt, sich um das Wohl *(welfare)* seiner Bürger zu kümmern.
"Alles, was für General Motors gut ist, ist gut für die Vereinigten Staaten und umgekehrt" *(Everything good for General Motors is good for the United States and vice versa)* ist ein Ausspruch von Charles E. Wilson, Präsident von General Motors und später Verteidigungsminister *(Secretary of Defense)* unter Präsident Eisenhower. Und der Ausspruch "Wenn Amerika niest, bekommt Europa eine Erkältung" *(When Amerika sneezes, Europe catches (a) cold)* soll die Verschachtelung *(interlocking)* der amerikanischen und europäischen Wirtschaft verdeutlichen.

CHAPTER 33

EXERCISES

Comprehension

Lesen Sie den Dialog aufmerksam durch. Beantworten Sie dann die nachfolgenden Fragen, und zwar immer in ganzen Sätzen:

1. Why has UC decided to enlarge its Monterey production unit? **2.** What measure does the local conservationist association consider to stop the project? **3.** Can Paul DeWitt handle the situation himself? **4.** What is the exact cause of the conflict? **5.** Is the conflict strictly local? **6.** Why does George Thomson say he is not surprised? **7.** Is Paul really concerned by the effect of the boycott on sales? **8.** Does UC have a good corporate image? **9.** What criteria are taken into account by opinion polls? **10.** Give an example of what the UC foundation has done for the Monterey community.

Translation

1. Um den Anforderungen seines expandierenden Marktes gerecht zu werden, muß UC sein Werk erweitern. **2.** Die Naturschutzvereinigung lehnte sich sofort gegen dieses Projekt auf. **3.** Danke, daß Sie so kurzfristig einen Flug genommen haben, nachdem Sie meine Nachricht erhielten. **4.** Wir dachten nicht, daß die Vergrößerung unserer Anlagen die Bebauungsbestimmungen verletzen könnte. **5.** Die Entscheidung, etwa zwei Hektar Waldgebiet abzuholzen, wird leidenschaftliche Reaktionen von seiten der Umweltschützer auslösen. **6.** Ihr Komitee hat andere Interessenvertretungen aufgefordert, dieser Kampagne zuzustimmen. **7.** Der Ärger ist, daß sie nun mit einem Boykott unserer Produkte drohen, nachdem sie vor unserem Werk auf- und abgelaufen sind und uns beschimpft haben. **8.** Ich würde unsere Gegner verstehen, wenn wir giftige Abfälle in die städtische Kanalisation leiten würden. **9.** Sie müssen schnell reagieren, bevor die ganze Sache außer Kontrolle gerät. **10.** Susan Edwards hat wahres Talent als Vermittlerin gezeigt. Bitten Sie sie, sofort zu kommen.

KAPITEL 33

LÖSUNGSVORSCHLÄGE

Verständnisübung

1. UC wants to increase its production capacity. 2. It threatens a boycott of UC products. 3. No, the situation has become so critical he has called George Thomson for help (*or* asked George Thomson to come and help him). 4. In the process of enlarging its production unit, UC will have to cut into about two acres of wooded land. 5. No, it is beginning to have repercussions throughout the state because it has triggered passionate reactions from the ecologists. 6. It's because UC has had to face the same problem on a new construction site in Germany. 7. No, he's not, because UC manufactures a variety of products, some of which are sold under the distributors' own brand name. 8. Yes, indeed. Opinion polls have placed it top in its category. 9. The criteria taken into account are product quality and community service. 10. It has financed an exhibition of local arts and crafts.

Übersetzungsübung

1. To meet the needs of its expanding markets, UC must enlarge its plant. 2. The conservationist association was immediately up in arms against that project. 3. Thanks for taking a flight at such short notice after getting my message. 4. We did not think that the process of enlarging our facilities was likely to break the zoning regulations. 5. The decision to cut into about two acres of wooded land is going to trigger passionate reactions from the ecologists. 6. Their committee has called upon other lobbies to endorse that campaign. 7. The trouble is that they are now threatening a boycott of our products, after marching past our plant calling us names. 8. I would understand our opponents if we were rejecting toxic waste into the city sewage system. 9. You must act promptly before the whole thing gets out of (your) control. 10. Susan Edwards has displayed real talent as a negotiator. Ask her to come right away.

CHAPTER 33

Application

Finden Sie heraus, welche Wörter in den folgenden Sätzen fehlen.

1. New products are developed by researchers according to .... based on consumer tests. 2. The pricing of a new product must take into account a fair .... for investment, effort and risk. 3. The .... of the product will be stressed in the advertising campaign. 4. .... is an essential component of the production process. 5. By ...., we were able to offset losses due to a brutal decline in the price of cocoa. 6. Changes in packaging are one way of prolonging the .... 7. The .... in Asia shows that our market share in Japan has remained stagnant. 8. The company's .... is excellent because its credit risk is minimal. 9. Buying currency on the .... means buying at the current rate of exchange. 10. Don't forget to .... the check before cashing it.

DO!

Call a colored American Afro-American instead of black or negro which are not considered politically correct.

KAPITEL 33

Lösungen zur Wortschatzübung

Versuchen Sie nun, als zusätzliche Übung, jeweils in ganzen Sätzen die Bedeutung der nachfolgenden Wörter oder Ausdrücke zu erklären.

1. specifications.
2. rate of return.
3. selling features.
4. quality control.
5. hedging.
6. lifespan of a product.
7. breakdown of sales.
8. credit rating.
9. spot market.
10. (to) endorse.

DON'T!

Don't forget that humor is often a real source of division.
Avoid telling your favorite jokes to foreigners.
Humor is not universal.

CHAPTER 34

Living in the fast lane (1)

At times, Susan finds it hard to cope with her hectic life. In a rare downbeat moment, she telephones her mother to share her difficulties. (2)

1. **Susan:** Hello, Mum. It's Susan.
2. **Mrs Edwards:** Oh! Hello, Susan. How are you?
3. **Susan:** Well,... I suppose.
4. **Mrs Edwards:** Oh dear, what's wrong with you? You don't sound your usual self.
5. **Susan:** I guess I'm all right.
6. **Mrs Edwards:** Come on, Susan. You're all tuckered out. (3) Did you have an argument with Yoshi?
7. **Susan:** Not exactly. It's just a case of 'welcome to the great two-career family and pass the aspirin, please'!
8. **Mrs Edwards:** I don't like to hear you speak so bitterly, like that. Try and see the bright side of things!
9. **Susan:** Sometimes, I'm at my wits' end and I wonder how to reconcile the often conflicting demands of Yoshi's job, my job and our relationship. Sometimes, I feel our marriage is becoming as much a business merger as it is an emotional commitment. (4) (5) (6)
10. **Mrs Edwards:** Be more sensible, Susan! You only have so much energy, emotion and time to go round.
11. **Susan:** Right Mum! When Yoshi and I meet at home, we are usually exhausted and often our conversation is confined to work. Sometimes, boredom sets in, I'm afraid.
12. **Mrs Edwards:** You mustn't allow your career to disrupt your private life. There's more to life than production, output, competition and excellence!

KAPITEL 34

Leben auf vollen Touren

Gelegentlich findet Susan es schwer, mit ihrem hektischen Leben fertigzuwerden. In einem der seltenen ruhigen Momente ruft sie ihre Mutter an, um ihr von ihren Schwierigkeiten zu erzählen.

1. **Susan:** Hallo Mami. Ich bin's, Susan.
2. **Frau Edwards:** Oh! Hallo Susan. Wie geht's?
3. **Susan:** Naja, es geht so...
4. **Frau Edwards:** Oje, was stimmt nicht mit dir? Du klingst nicht wie sonst.
5. **Susan:** Ach was, mir geht's gut.
6. **Frau Edwards:** Komm, Susan. Du bist fix und fertig. Hast du dich mit Yoshi gestritten?
7. **Susan:** Nicht gerade das. Es ist nur ein Fall von 'Willkommen in der großen Familie der Doppelverdiener, und reich mir bitte das Aspirin'!
8. **Frau Edwards:** Ich mag es nicht, dich so verbittert reden zu hören. Versuch, die Dinge von der schönen Seite zu sehen!
9. **Susan:** Manchmal weiß ich mir keinen Rat mehr und ich frage mich, wie ich die sich oft widersprechenden Anforderungen von Yoshis Job, meinem Job und unserer Beziehung miteinander vereinbaren soll. Manchmal habe ich das Gefühl, daß unsere Ehe mehr auf Geschäfts- als auf Gefühlsebene stattfindet.
10. **Frau Edwards:** Sei vernünftiger, Susan! Du hast nur ein begrenztes Maß an Energie, Gefühl und Zeit.
11. **Susan:** Stimmt, Mami! Wenn Yoshi und ich nach Hause kommen, sind wir normalerweise erschöpft, und oft beschränken sich unsere Gespräche auf die Arbeit. Manchmal, fürchte ich, kommt Langeweile auf.
12. **Frau Edwards:** Du darfst nicht zulassen, daß dein Privatleben unter deiner Karriere leidet. Es gibt mehr Dinge im Leben als Produktion, Ertrag, Wettbewerb und hervorragende Leistungen!

ANMERKUNGEN

(1) **fast lane**: "Überholspur". *Lane* ist ein "Landsträßchen" bzw. eine "Fahrspur". *Air lane* "Luftkorridor". *Ad lane* bezeichnet die Madison Avenue in New York, in der sich zahlreiche Werbeagenturen befinden.
(2) **downbeat** stammt aus der Musik und bezeichnet den betonten Taktteil. Im vorliegenden Kontext hat es jedoch die Bedeutung "ungezwungen, entspannt".
(3) **tuckered out**: "fix und fertig, groggy".
(4) **to be at one's wits' end**: "nicht mehr weiter wissen, mit seinem Latein am Ende sein". *Wit* "Witz; Geist, Verstand".
(5) **merger**: "Fusion, Zusammenschluß".
(6) **commitment**: "Verpflichtung, Engagement". *To commit oneself* "sich verpflichten".

CHAPTER 34

13. **Susan:** There is something else, Mum.

14. **Mrs Edwards:** What?

15. **Susan:** It's rather difficult to explain... *(she hesitates)*. You see, it's that Yoshi is more Japanese than I thought at the beginning. He's very kind, but sometimes I feel he has these feudal notions. He'd be happy if I stayed home surrounded by labor-saving gadgets galore. **(7)**

16. **Mrs Edwards:** Come on, Susan. You're exaggerating.

17. **Susan:** Perhaps... But anyway, it might be easier if I took second billing instead of being the principal wage-earner in the couple. I suspect Yoshi feels secretly humiliated by such a situation and I feel guilty about it. **(8)**

18. **Mrs Edwards:** It's a thorny question indeed. Yoshi mustn't start doubting his professional success. Why couldn't he also take a diversionary interest in sport or music? **(9)**

19. **Susan:** Before we got married, he enjoyed playing golf. I don't know why he quit. Perhaps I should encourage him to practise that sport again. I could even start practising it myself!

20. **Mrs Edwards:** Be that as it may, I don't see the point of your striving to be a superwoman. You can't hope to be a fast-tracker **and** have the quality of marriage you would like at the same time. You must learn to temper your expectations. Anyway, there are some lovely golf-courses in England... **(10)**

21. **Susan:** Well actually, Mum, I wasn't going to tell you yet, but I've been offered a **position** at Birtwhistle's, up in Halifax... We still haven't **decided,** but we're thinking about it.

KAPITEL 34

13. **Susan:** Da ist noch etwas anderes, Mami.

14. **Frau Edwards:** Was?

15. **Susan:** Es ist ziemlich schwierig zu erklären... *(Sie zögert)* Siehst du, Yoshi ist japanischer als ich am Anfang dachte. Er ist sehr nett, aber manchmal merke ich, daß er diese altmodischen Vorstellungen hat. Er wäre glücklich, wenn ich zu Hause bleiben würde, umgeben von jeder Menge arbeitseinsparendem Krimskrams.

16. **Frau Edwards:** Komm, Susan. Du übertreibst.

17. **Susan:** Kann sein... Naja, aber es wäre vielleicht einfacher, wenn ich die zweite Geige spielen würde, anstatt der Hauptverdiener in unserer Ehe zu sein. Ich habe den Verdacht, daß Yoshi sich im geheimen durch eine solche Situation erniedrigt fühlt, und ich habe deswegen ein schlechtes Gewissen.

18. **Frau Edwards:** Das ist wirklich eine heikle Frage. Yoshi darf nicht anfangen, seinen beruflichen Erfolg in Zweifel zu ziehen. Warum könnte er sich nicht auch als Ablenkung für Sport oder Musik interessieren?

19. **Susan:** Bevor wir geheiratet haben, hat er gerne Golf gespielt. Ich weiß nicht, warum er aufgehört hat. Vielleicht sollte ich ihn dazu ermuntern, diese Sportart wieder auszuüben. Ich könnte sogar selbst damit beginnen!

20. **Frau Edwards:** Wie dem auch sei, ich sehe nicht, warum es dir so wichtig ist, eine Superfrau zu sein. Du kannst nicht darauf hoffen, eine steile Karriere zu machen **und** gleichzeitig die gute Ehe zu führen, die du dir wünschst. Du mußt lernen, deine Erwartungen zu mäßigen. Jedenfalls gibt es einige hübsche Golfplätze in England...

21. **Susan:** Naja, Mami, eigentlich wollte ich es dir noch nicht sagen, aber ich habe eine Stelle bei Birtwhistle oben in Halifax angeboten bekommen... Wir haben uns noch nicht entschlossen, aber wir denken darüber nach.

ANMERKUNGEN (Fortsetzung)
- (7) **galore:** "in Hülle und Fülle".
- (8) **to take second billing:** wörtlich "auf dem Plakat an zweiter Stelle erscheinen". *To be top of the bill* "der Star [des Abends] sein".
- (9) **diversionary:** "Ablenkungs-". *Diversion* "Unterhaltung, Zerstreuung, Abwechslung".
- (10) **fast-tracker:** "Karrierist". Bezeichnung für jemanden, der unbedingt und schnell Karriere machen will (*to be on the fast track*).

CHAPTER 34 — DOCUMENT

Working abroad

Lorraine Standish, one of Susan's English friends, has been offered the opportunity to work for the foreign-based subsidiary of a British company, but she has some misgivings. She wrote to Susan to ask her for some advice. Below are excerpts from Susan's answer:

(...) You asked me what I feel about holding a position abroad. As far as I am concerned, I can honestly consider myself a contented expatriate. When I received my first overseas posting, it seemed that my wildest dreams were coming true! My work abroad has really been beneficial to my career.

You also told me that you would like to work abroad because you like to travel, but I must warn you that it takes more than the love of travel to succeed in one's career. Overseas assignments should be an act of faith.

Trust between the employee and the company must prevail. Should an employee be treated unfairly while abroad or upon return, he/she'll be tempted to look for a job elsewhere and, afterwards, few staff members will volunteer for positions abroad.

On the other hand, I feel deeply that an expatriate employee has a responsibility to "repay" the cost and the trust placed in him / her by diffusing an international spirit. This can only work when he/she is happy and the recipient company helps to establish a culture of openness to foreign ideas.

Expatriate employees who accept to adjust to foreign cultures can contribute to giving their company a competitive advantage...

KAPITEL 34

Statussymbole

Auf der Führungsebene *(at executive level)* eines Unternehmens sind geldwerte Vorteile wie Statussymbole *(status symbols)*, denn sie dienen dazu, eine Unterscheidung zwischen den Spitzenmanagern *(top managers, senior managers)* und den anderen, den Managern der mittleren Führungsebene *(middle managers)* und der unteren Unternehmensführung *(junior managers)* vorzunehmen. Zu diesen Vorteilen zählen:
- Firmenwagen *(company cars)*,
- ein Spesenkonto *(expense account)*, dessen Höchstgrenze sich nach der Position im Unternehmen richtet,
- ein Aktienbezugsrecht für Betriebsangehörige *(stock options)*,
- Zutritt zu den reservierten Zuschauertribünen *(reserved boxes)* bei großen Kultur- oder Sportveranstaltungen,
- und – in den Vereinigten Staaten – das ultimative Privileg für die obersten Stufen der Hierarchie: eigene Toiletten *(private restrooms)*!

CHAPTER 34

EXERCISES

Comprehension

Lesen Sie den Dialog aufmerksam durch. Beantworten Sie dann die nachfolgenden Fragen, und zwar immer in ganzen Sätzen:

1. Why did Susan's mother guess her daughter had a problem? 2. What was Mrs Edwards's first assumption? 3. What causes a strain in Susan and Yoshi's marriage? 4. What was Mrs Edwards's diagnosis? 5. What do Susan and Yoshi discuss when they are at home together? 6. What does Mrs Edwards reproach Susan with? 7. What other factor accounts for Susan's problem? 8. Why does Yoshi feel secretly humiliated? 9. What suggestion did Mrs Edwards make? 10. What is Mrs Edwards's final recommendation?

Application – 1) *Wie kommuniziert man effizient?*

Der vorliegende Dialog ist ein Telefongespräch zwischen Susan und ihrer Mutter. Aber es gibt auch noch andere Kommunikationsmittel. In der folgenden Übung sollen Sie zu jedem der in der rechten Spalte aufgeführten Problem die passende Kommunikationsmethode aus der linken Spalte auswählen:

Means of communication

1. Write a memo to all the staff.
2. Write a letter.
3. Hold a meeting.
4. Put a notice on the bulletin board.
5. Ask him her to come for an interview.
6. Stick a handwritten note on your door.
7. Pick up your phone.
8. Arrange an appointment.
9. Talk to the person face to face.
10. Send a telex or fax.

Problem

a. A visitor may come whilst you are away. You inform him her that you will be back soon.
b. You want to meet a manager in another firm to discuss a licensing agreement.
c. You want to tell an employee his her work is not up to standard.
d. You want to talk briefly to a supplier.
e. You want to inform a customer of a policy change.
f. You want to communicate something important to all the firm's employees.
g. You want to discuss the company's strategy with three other managers.
h. You urgently need to contact a firm abroad.
i. You want to see a student who has applied for a placement.
j. You want to inform everyone about the corporate team's soccer game.

KAPITEL 34

LÖSUNGSVORSCHLÄGE

Verständnisübung

1. Because Susan was not as cheerful as usual. Her answer 'Well, ... I suppose' betrayed a lack of enthusiasm. 2. She assumed Susan and Yoshi had been quarrelling. 3. The conflicting demands of Susan's and Yoshi's respective jobs and their relationship cause a strain in their marriage. 4. Mrs Edwards felt that Susan was too much committed to her work. 5. They usually speak about their work. 6. She reproaches Susan with focusing her life too much on work-related values such as production, output, competition and excellence. 7. Cultural differences between Yoshi and Susan also account for her problem. 8. Because Susan earns more money than Yoshi does. 9. She suggested that Yoshi took his mind off things by practising a sport or playing music. 10. She advises Susan not to play superwoman and to temper her expectations.

Lösungen – 1) *Wie kommuniziert man effizient?*

1. f.
2. e.
3. g.
4. j.
5. i.
6. a.
7. d.
8. b.
9. c.
10. h.

CHAPTER 34

Application – 2) *Akronyme*

Bei ihrer täglichen Arbeit kommen Susan wie jedem Angestellten eines Unternehmens permanent Dokumente in die Hand, die Akronyme enthalten. Es wird erwartet, daß sie die Bedeutung dieser Akronyme kennt.
Ordnen Sie jedem in der linken Spalte aufgeführten Akronym die passende Definition aus der rechten Spalte zu.

Acronyms

1. ASEAN
2. CEO
3. CIF
4. COD
5. GDP
6. IOU
7. LIBOR
8. PAYE
9. ROI
10. VIP

Definition

a. Total incomes received by a country.

b. Profitability of an investment.

c. Acknowledgement of a debt.

d. Method of collecting income tax by requiring employers to deduct it from earnings.

e. A big shot.

f. Managing Director.

g. Regional organization formed by Malaysia, Thailand, Indonesia, the Philippines and Singapore.

h. The seller's price includes all charges and risks up to the moment when the ship carrying the goods arrives at the port of destination.

i. Rate of European currencies.

j. The customer pays the postman the full price of the goods and any delivery charges.

KAPITEL 34

Lösungen -2) *Akronyme*

1. g (Association of South East Asian Nations).
2. f (Chief Executive Officer).
3. h (Cost, Insurance and Freight).
4. j (Cash On Delivery).
5. a (Gross Domestic Product).
6. c (I Owe U [you]).
7. i (London InterBank Offered Rate).
8. d (Pay As You Earn).
9. b (Return On Investment).
10. e (Very Important Person).

DO!

**Check out the attitude to gifts,
before entering into negotiations in a foreign country.
In the USA, for instance, gifts may be interpreted as bribery.**

DON'T!

**Don't blame cultural differences for failed deals.
In most cases, business reasons
are the cause of failure.**

CHAPTER 35

Back in the UK

Susan and Yoshi are on a plane, somewhere over the Atlantic. They are returning to the UK, where Susan has just been appointed Acting Managing Director of Birtwhistle's, a subsidiary of United Chocolate.

1. **Yoshi:** So, how does it feel to be going back home after all these years in the US?

2. **Susan:** (*With mixed feelings*) OK, I suppose. It's true I was getting tired of that crazy yuppie existence we were leading in LA. **(1)**

3. **Yoshi:** Me too. No time to enjoy life!

4. **Susan:** But I don't look on England as home now, anyway. Not since I first went to Texas.

5. **Yoshi:** Don't let your mother hear you say that!

6. **Susan:** 'Home is where the heart is'. That's what she always used to say! (*They laugh*) And how do you feel about giving up a good job?

7. **Yoshi:** It doesn't matter. I might have lost it anyway. The banking sector is cutting back heavily on jobs. It was good of UC to ask me to act as an independent consultant for Birtwhistle's. I'd never even heard of the company till then! **(2)**

8. **Susan:** Birtwhistle's Yorkshire fudge is a household name in the UK. I remember when I was at university in Leeds, I used to buy it all the time! **(3) (4)**

9. **Yoshi:** I'm still not sure I know what it is, though. In the States, fudge is a sort of chocolate sauce you put on ice cream, right?

10. **Susan:** Yes. But in England it's a sort of soft toffee, flavoured with chocolate, coffee or coconut... Mmm, delicious. It melts in your mouth!

KAPITEL 35

Zurück in Großbritannien

Susan und Yoshi befinden sich in einem Flugzeug irgendwo über dem Atlantik. Sie kehren nach Großbritannien zurück, wo Susan soeben zur geschäftsführenden Generaldirektorin von Birtwhistle ernannt wurde, einer Tochtergesellschaft von United Chocolate.

1. **Yoshi:** Na, was ist es für ein Gefühl, nach all diesen Jahren in den Vereinigten Staaten nach Hause zurückzukehren?

2. **Susan:** *(Mit gemischten Gefühlen)* Gut eigentlich. Es stimmt, daß mich dieses verrückte Yuppie-Leben, das wir in LA geführt haben, müde gemacht hat.

3: **Yoshi:** Mich auch. Keine Zeit, um das Leben zu genießen!

4. **Susan:** Ich betrachte England sowieso jetzt nicht mehr als mein Zuhause. Und das, seitdem ich zum ersten Mal nach Texas ging.

5. **Yoshi:** Laß das nicht deine Mutter hören!

6. **Susan:** 'Zu Hause ist da, wo das Herz ist'. Das hat sie immer gesagt! *(Sie lachen)* Und was ist es für dich für ein Gefühl, einen guten Job aufzugeben?

7. **Yoshi:** Das ist nicht wichtig. Möglicherweise hätte ich ihn sowieso verloren. Auf dem Banksektor werden eine Menge Stellen abgebaut. Es war gut von UC, mich zu bitten, als unabhängiger Berater für Birtwhistle tätig zu werden. Ich hatte bis dahin noch nicht einmal was von dieser Firma gehört!

8. **Susan:** In Großbritannien kennt jeder 'Birtwhistle Yorkshire Fudge'. Ich erinnere mich, als ich in Leeds studiert habe, habe ich es immer gekauft!

9. **Yoshi:** Ich bin immer noch nicht sicher, ob ich weiß, was es ist. In den Staaten ist "fudge" eine Art Schokoladensauce, die man auf Eis gibt, nicht wahr?

10. **Susan:** Ja. Aber in England ist es eine Art weiches Karamel mit Schokoladen-, Kaffee- oder Kokosnußgeschmack... Mmmm, lecker. Es zergeht dir auf der Zunge!

ANMERKUNGEN

(1) **yuppie:** Ein von Marketingspezialisten kreierter Neologismus der 80er Jahre. Der Ausdruck steht für *Young Urban Professional People* und bezeichnet junge, beruflich erfolgreiche Leute, die sich aufgrund ihres guten Einkommens einen relativ hohen Lebensstandard leisten können.

(2) **to cut back on:** "einschränken, kürzen"; *cutback* "Arbeitskräfteabbau; Reduzierung, Kürzung (von Ausgaben, Personal usw.)".

(3) **fudge** ist in den Vereinigten Staaten eine Art Schmelz oder Schokoladensauce, in Großbritannien bezeichnet es ein Weichkaramel.

(4) **household name:** Ein Markenname, der allgemein bekannt ist. Die Grundbedeutung von *household* ist natürlich "Haushalt"; *household appliance* "Haushaltsgerät"; *household economics* "Hauswirtschaftslehre"; *household insurance* "Hausratversicherung".

CHAPTER 35

11. **Yoshi:** I look forward to tasting it. *(A pause)* What are your conclusions about Birtwhistle's problems, by the way? I see you've been reading up on them a lot already.

12. **Susan:** I'm not certain, yet, but it must be linked to all the rumours that were going around during the takeover five years ago. Things got off to a bad start... **(5)**

13. **Yoshi:** Mmm. No doubt you're right. But aren't you overlooking something important? You said, yourself, that Birtwhistle's Yorkshire fudge is a household name...

14. **Susan:** So?...

15. **Yoshi:** Surely that's what UC wanted. Getting its hands on that trademark meant a lot more to them than the company itself. Can you really believe they didn't intend to close down the factory in Halifax, sooner or later? **(6)**

16. **Susan:** You don't seem to have a very high opinion of my company, do you?

17. **Yoshi:** Oh, come now, Susan. Don't be so righteous! You know all companies are the same. Business is business.

18. **Susan:** Look, Yoshi, let's not talk shop. Otherwise we'll start arguing again. *(A pause)* My mother reminded me that there are lovely golf-courses up in Yorkshire... **(7)**

19. **Yoshi:** Yes, I intend to start playing golf again. It's very important in England for building up business relations, so I'm told. Just what I need if I decide to set up as a consultant. I intend to take things easier, and I hope you will too. After all, we'll have the baby to think about...

KAPITEL 35

11. **Yoshi:** Ich freue mich darauf, es zu probieren. *(Pause)* Was sind übrigens deine Schlußfolgerungen über die Probleme bei Birtwhistle? Ich habe gesehen, daß du dich schon viel darüber informiert hast.

12. **Susan:** Ich bin noch nicht sicher, aber es muß mit all den Gerüchten in Zusammenhang stehen, die zum Zeitpunkt der Übernahme vor fünf Jahren herumgingen. Die Dinge haben schlecht angefangen...

13. **Yoshi:** Mmm. Sicher hast du recht. Aber übersiehst du nicht etwas wichtiges? Du hast selbst gesagt, daß 'Birtwhistle Yorkshire Fudge' sehr bekannt ist...

14. **Susan:** Und?

15. **Yoshi:** Sicher ist es das, was UC wollte. Dieses Warenzeichen in die Finger zu bekommen, bedeutete für sie viel mehr als das Unternehmen selbst. Glaubst du wirklich, sie hatten nicht vor, die Fabrik in Halifax früher oder später zu schließen?

16. **Susan:** Du scheinst von meiner Firma keine allzu gute Meinung zu haben, oder?

17. **Yoshi:** Oh, komm, Susan, tu nicht so betroffen! Du weißt, daß alle Unternehmen gleich sind. Geschäft ist Geschäft.

18. **Susan:** Ach, Yoshi, laß uns nicht fachsimpeln. Sonst fangen wir wieder an, uns zu streiten. *(Pause)* Meine Mutter hat mich daran erinnert, daß es oben in Yorkshire hübsche Golfplätze gibt...

19. **Yoshi:** Ja, ich habe vor, wieder Golf zu spielen. Wie man mir sagte, ist das in England sehr wichtig, um Geschäftsbeziehungen zu knüpfen. Genau das, was ich brauche, wenn ich mich entschließe, mich als Berater selbständig zu machen. Ich habe vor, die Dinge leichter zu nehmen und ich hoffe, du wirst das auch tun. Wir müssen doch auch an das Baby denken...

ANMERKUNGEN (Fortsetzung)

(5) **takeover:** Aufkauf eines Unternehmens durch ein anderes. *Takeover bid* "Übernahmeangebot" (vgl. Kapitel 37, Anmerkung 3).

(6) **trademark:** "Warenzeichen". *Registered trademark* "eingetragenes Warenzeichen". Synonym: *brand* (vgl. Kapitel 32, Anmerkung 12).

(7) **to talk shop** ist ein sehr umgangssprachlicher Ausdruck: "fachsimpeln". *No talking shop, please!* "Keine Fachsimpelei, bitte!"

CHAPTER 35 — DOCUMENT

How to run a meeting

Executives usually devote a large amount of their time to meetings. Susan is fully aware that meetings are quite expensive for a company, but she does not view them as time-wasters. On the contrary, she feels that meetings do matter because:
– employees tend to support decisions they have helped to make,
– group discussion is a powerful tool for persuading employees and developing creativity,
– debates contribute to unfreezing fixed ways of thinking. In her desire to make future meetings as effective as possible, she has decided to take advantage of her transatlantic flight to draft this memo to the managers of Birtwhistle's.

Birtwhistle's

Internal Memorandum
From: Acting Managing Director
To: All managers   Date: 26th June 199.

Subject: Guidelines for successful meetings

– Pre-meeting planning must include agenda management. The agenda must be constructed with care: easy items should be tackled first, difficult ones in the middle and non-controversial ones at the end so that people leave the meeting on an 'up' note.

– No meeting should last beyond 90 minutes.

– Investigate who attends meetings and why. Eliminate 'passengers'.

– If possible, hold more small and informal meetings. Likewise, promote face-to-face meetings.

– The meeting chairperson is responsible for making the meeting effective. He/she calls the meeting, holds it together and devises an effective way of working.
He/she must retain a clear view of the task.

– The chairperson must make sure that all decisions are summarised and recorded right away.

Susan Edwards
Acting Managing Director

KAPITEL 35

Golf

Das Golfspiel, von dem man zum ersten Mal im 15. Jahrhundert in Schottland sprach, ist für die geschäftlichen Beziehungen mittlerweile ebenso wichtig wie das Geschäftsessen (vgl. Kapitel 27, [i]). Dies gilt im besonderen für das Vereinigte Königreich, die USA und Japan.

Hat man nicht schon oft gehört, daß viele geschäftliche Besprechungen und selbst Geschäftsabschlüsse bei einer Partie Golf oder anschließend im *clubhouse* getätigt wurden, bei dem, was die Golfer *the nineteenth hole* nennen?

Auch wenn die japanischen Führungskräfte erst seit kurzem Opfer dieses Virus geworden sind, so sind sie doch nicht weniger davon betroffen. Für eine ganze Reihe japanischer Unternehmen sind die englischen Golfplätze mit ihren leuchtenden *greens* und ihren erschwinglichen *green fees* ein schlagkräftiges Argument, wenn es darum geht, in Großbritannien ein Werk zu bauen.

CHAPTER 35

EXERCISES

Comprehension

Lesen Sie den Dialog aufmerksam durch. Beantworten Sie dann die nachfolgenden Fragen, und zwar immer in ganzen Sätzen:

1. Is Susan pleased to be going back to the UK? **2.** Is Yoshi sorry to have given up a good job? **3.** What has UC done to help Yoshi? **4.** Is Birtwhistle's Yorkshire fudge a household name in the US as well? **5.** Does Yoshi agree with his wife's conclusions about Birtwhistle's problems? **6.** According to Yoshi, why did UC want to buy Birtwhistle's? **7.** Why does Susan say that Yoshi doesn't have a high opinion of UC? **8.** Why does Yoshi call Susan righteous? **9.** What seems to happen whenever Susan and Yoshi start talking shop? **10.** Why does Yoshi intend to take up golf again?

Translation

1. Yoshi ist gerade zum geschäftsführenden Finanzdirektor der britischen Tochtergesellschaft von Nikkai Electronics Inc. ernannt worden. **2.** Was ist es für ein Gefühl, nach Japan zurückzukehren, nachdem man mehr als vierzehn Jahre in Europa verbracht hat? **3.** Die Yuppies an der Wall Street führen ein verrücktes Leben. **4.** In Frankreich ist das Warenzeichen *Gervais* ein sehr bekannter Name. **5.** Ich freue mich darauf, ihre neue Eiscreme mit Kokosnußgeschmack zu probieren. **6.** Diese Übernahme bedeutete uns viel, und glücklicherweise haben die Dinge einen guten Anfang genommen. **7.** Als die Firma übernommen wurde, dachten die Arbeiter, daß die Fabrik früher oder später geschlossen würde. **8.** Gut, hören wir auf zu fachsimpeln, aber Geschäft ist halt Geschäft. **9.** Ich habe keine sehr gute Meinung von Golfspielern, die nur ihre Beziehungen ausbauen wollen. **10.** Wenn du ein Baby hast, hoffe ich, daß du die Dinge etwas leichter nehmen wirst.

KAPITEL 35

LÖSUNGSVORSCHLÄGE

Verständnisübung

1. Yes and no. She seems to have mixed feelings. **2.** Probably not, because he says it doesn't matter. **3.** They have asked him to act as an independent consultant for Birtwhistle's. **4.** No, it's not. For Americans the word 'fudge' does not have the same meaning. **5.** To a certain extent, perhaps, but he thinks that she's forgotten something important. **6.** According to Yoshi, UC wanted to buy Birtwhistle's in order to get hold of the trademark, which is a household name. **7.** Because he suggests that UC had ulterior motives when it took Birtwhistle's over. **8.** He thinks she is suggesting that UC is somehow less ruthless than other companies. **9.** It seems that they always argue when they talk shop. **10.** Apparently for two reasons: he wants to take things easier but also to build up business relations.

Übersetzungsübung

1. Yoshi has just been appointed Acting Financial Manager of the British subsidiary of Nikkai Electronics Inc. **2.** How does it feel to be going back to Japan after more than fourteen years spent in Europe? **3.** The yuppies on Wall Street lead a crazy existence. **4.** In France, the *Gervais* trademark is a household name. **5.** I'm looking forward to tasting their new coconut-flavoured ice-cream. **6.** That takeover meant a lot to us and fortunately things have got off to a good start. **7.** When the firm was taken over, the workers thought that, sooner or later, the factory would be closed. **8.** OK, let's stop talking shop, but may I remind you that business will always be business. **9.** I don't have a very high opinion of golfers who only want to build up (their) relations. **10.** When you have a baby, I hope you will take things a little easier.

CHAPTER 35

Application

Eine gute Rede zu halten, will gelernt sein. Untenstehend finden Sie einige Auszüge aus einer Rede. Setzen Sie in die Lücken jeweils das passende Wort oder den passenden Ausdruck aus der folgenden Liste ein.

a. first of all. **b.** may I begin **c.** sum up **d.** priorities **e.** purpose **f.** up to date **g.** motion **h.** call on **i.** move on **j.** feel free **k.** next **l.** as you all know **m.** review **n.** object **o.** finally **p.** at such short notice.

Ladies and gentlemen, **1.** _____ by welcoming you all, especially as this meeting had to be called **2.** _____ .

We have lots of things to discuss today and I would like to begin by stating the specific **3.** _____ it is to achieve. **4.** _____ , the launching of our new chocolate bar has been the target of intense speculation in the media. The **5.** _____ of this meeting is to bring you **6.** _____ on what has been happening.

7. _____ , I'd like to give you, briefly, the historical background to the project. **8.** _____ , I'll inform you about what has been achieved so far. At that stage, I'd like to **9.** _____ Mr George Ray McEachern, Director of UC's R & D, to present his view. **10.** _____ , I'll tell you what our **11.** _____ will be over the next few months.

If anyone has anything further they wish to say before we **12.** _____ to each new item, they should **13.** _____ to interrupt. Once everybody who wishes to bring up a point has had their say, I'll **14.** _____ the position. At that point, I'll **15.** _____ the points raised. If we are all agreed, we'll vote a **16.** _____ .

DO!

In Japan, it's critical to avoid making the other party lose face. Choices are made on the basis of saving someone from embarrassment.

KAPITEL 35

Lösungen

1. b. 2. p. 3. n. 4. l. 5. e. 6. f. 7. a. 8. k. 9. h. 10. o. 11. d. 12. i. 13. j. 14. c. 15. m. 16. g.

DON'T!

Don't consider that silence is a bad sign when you negotiate with the Japanese. They consider it unnecessary to talk during the thinking process.

CHAPTER 36

Analysing company accounting

Susan, with Yoshi's help, has gone over the company books from the time Birtwhistle's was taken over by UC (UK). She is now in her office overlooking the plant and grounds, discussing her findings with George Howard, Financial Manager.

1. **George H.:** You must have become familiar, now, with the way we present financial documents in Britain.

2. **Susan:** Well, you know, the principles are very much the same. It's mostly a question of vocabulary. I was more used to income statements, but profit and loss account makes as much sense. I noticed one major difference: the statement of movement of reserves – which the Americans call retained earnings – is left out. (1) (2) (3) (4)

3. **George H.:** It is to be found in the Notes to the Financial Statements.

4. **Susan:** The US format provides a more global view of the year's financial situation.

5. **George H.:** I agree.

6. **Susan:** Correct me if I am wrong, but I assume the decline in last year's turnover, compared to the previous year – over £2 million – is the direct consequence of labour disputes.

7. **George H.:** That's unfortunately true.

8. **Susan:** And the decrease in net profits is even more spectacular – over 60 %.

9. **George H.:** UC's decision to restructure its British operations didn't go unnoticed. The unions considered there had been no hint of negotiation before the management announced the plans for restructuring the company. Their call for a warning strike was successful and caused near stoppage of production for almost three weeks. There is still persistent unrest.

10. **Susan:** Couldn't we have caught up with target production through overtime?

11. **George H.:** Not with demotivated workers and staff!

KAPITEL 36

Analyse der Firmenbuchhaltung

Susan hat mit Yoshis Hilfe die Geschäftsbücher aus der Zeit, in der Birtwhistle von UC (UK) übernommen wurde, durchgesehen. Sie befindet sich nun in ihrem Büro, von dem aus sie das Werk und das Gelände überblicken kann, und bespricht ihre Erkenntnisse mit George Howard, dem Finanzdirektor.

1. **George H.**: Sie müßten mittlerweile mit der Art und Weise vertraut sein, wie wir in Großbritannien Finanzdokumente vorlegen.
2. **Susan**: Naja, wissen Sie, die Prinzipien sind sehr ähnlich. Es ist hauptsächlich eine Frage des Vokabulars. Ich war mehr an Ertragsrechnungen gewöhnt, aber Gewinn- und Verlustrechnung macht genauso viel Sinn. Ich habe einen bedeutenden Unterschied bemerkt: Die Aufstellung des unverteilten Reingewinns – was die Amerikaner "nicht ausgeschüttete Gewinne" nennen – erscheint nicht.
3. **George H.**: Man findet sie im Anhang zum Jahresabschluß.
4. **Susan**: Die amerikanische Form bietet einen globaleren Überblick über die jährliche Finanzsituation.
5. **George H.**: Da stimme ich zu.
6. **Susan**: Korrigieren Sie mich, falls ich mich irre, aber ich nehme an, daß der Umsatzrückgang des letzten Jahres, verglichen mit dem Vorjahr – über 2 Mio. Pfund – die direkte Konsequenz aus Arbeitsstreitigkeiten ist.
7. **George H.**: Das ist leider wahr.
8. **Susan**: Und der Rückgang des Reingewinns ist noch außergewöhnlicher – über 60%.
9. **George H.**: Die Entscheidung von UC, den Geschäftsbetrieb in Großbritannien umzustrukturieren, ist nicht unbemerkt geblieben. Die Gewerkschaften fanden, daß es nicht die Spur von Verhandlungen gegeben habe, bevor die Firmenleitung die Pläne zur Umstrukturierung des Unternehmens ankündigte. Sie riefen erfolgreich zu einem Warnstreik auf, und der bewirkte für fast drei Wochen beinahe den totalen Stillstand der Produktion. Noch immer halten die Unruhen an.
10. **Susan**: Hätten wir das Produktionssoll nicht durch Überstunden reinholen können?
11. **George H.**: Nicht mit demotivierten Arbeitern und Angestellten!

ANMERKUNGEN

(1) **income statement** ist der amerikanische Ausdruck für "Gewinn- und Verlustrechnung, Aufwands- und Ertragsrechnung".

(2) **profit and loss account** bedeutet ebenfalls "Gewinn- und Verlustrechnung". Dieser Ausdruck wird in Großbritannien benutzt.

(3) **statement of movement of reserves (UK)**: Dieser Begriff, dessen amerikanisches Synynom *retained earnings* lautet, bezeichnet den Gewinn nach Steuern in einem Geschäftsjahr *(financial year [GB], fiscal year [US])*, den ein Unternehmen nicht als Dividende an die Aktionäre auszahlt, sondern der in den Geschäftsbüchern verbleibt.

(4) **retained earnings**: "nicht ausgeschütteter Gewinn, thesaurierter Gewinn, Gewinnvortrag". (Siehe Anmerkung 3.)

CHAPTER 36

12. **Susan:** All the same, I gather from all the documents submitted to me by the accountant that the company is not in a catastrophic position. It should be relatively easy to bring production back to former levels when tensions ease. **(5)**

13. **George H.:** If we increased our sales, we would also be able to reduce stocks, but hardly below £250,000.

14. **Susan:** That's still a lot. Couldn't we improve things further by using the just-in-time method of stock management? **(6)**

15. **George H.:** Not really. Remember that we import our basic raw materials from overseas – cocoa, coffee, sugar... They come in large shipments. We can't take the risk of a stock-out. **(7)**

16. **Susan:** I hadn't thought of that.

17. **George H.:** You will also have noted in the balance sheet that we have no work in progress right now, nor any investment planned. Yet, it would take little to raise our production capacity. **(8)**

18. **Susan:** I was surprised by one item in the balance sheet: the profit and loss account, representing the company's accumulated reserves. They amount to £1,410,000, which is not bad for our size, whereas the long-term debt is negligible – £52,000. What does that represent? **(9) (10)**

19. **George H.:** It's the balance due on the purchase of a new integrated packing unit, five years ago, a few months before the takeover by UC.

20. **Susan:** Until two years ago, UC paid itself a handsome dividend!

21. **George H.:** That's the rule of the game. After all, UC had invested much money in the acquisition of the company. Nevertheless, the size of the existing reserves shows it never looked upon Birtwhistle's as a mere milk cow! **(11)**

KAPITEL 36

12. **Susan:** Jedenfalls entnehme ich all den Dokumenten, die mir vom Buchhalter übergeben wurden, daß sich das Unternehmen in keiner katastrophalen Lage befindet. Es sollte relativ einfach sein, die Produktion wieder auf den früheren Stand zu bringen, wenn sich die Spannungen gelegt haben.
13. **George H.:** Wenn wir mehr verkaufen würden, wären wir auch in der Lage, den Lagerbestand zu vermindern, jedoch kaum unter 250.000 Pfund.
14. **Susan:** Das ist immer noch viel. Könnten wir die Situation nicht noch weiter verbessern, indem wir in unserer Lagerverwaltung die Just-in-Time-Methode anwenden?
15. **George H.:** Nicht direkt. Bedenken Sie, daß wir unsere wichtigsten Rohmaterialien – Kakao, Kaffee, Zucker... – aus Übersee importieren. Sie werden in großen Mengen geliefert. Wir können nicht das Risiko eines Lagerdefizits eingehen.
16. **Susan:** Das hatte ich nicht bedacht.
17. **George H.:** Sie werden in der Bilanz auch bemerkt haben, daß zur Zeit keine Investitionsarbeiten im Gange und auch keine Investitionen geplant sind. Dennoch wäre nur wenig nötig, um unsere Produktionskapazität zu erhöhen.
18. **Susan:** Ein Posten in der Bilanz hat mich überrascht: die Gewinn- und Verlustrechnung, die die Reservebildung des Unternehmens darstellt. Sie belaufen sich auf 1.410.000 Pfund, was gemessen an der Unternehmensgröße nicht schlecht ist, wogegen die langfristige Verschuldung unerheblich ist – 52.000 Pfund. Was bedeutet das?
19. **George H.:** Das ist der fällige Rechnungsbetrag für eine neue integrierte Verpackungseinheit, die vor fünf Jahren gekauft wurde, einige Monate vor der Übernahme durch UC.
20. **Susan:** Bis vor zwei Jahren hat sich UC selbst eine hübsche Dividende gezahlt!
21. **George H.:** So sind die Spielregeln. Schließlich hat UC viel Geld in den Kauf des Unternehmens gesteckt. Trotzdem zeigt die Höhe der bestehenden Reserven, daß UC Birtwhistle niemals bloß "melken" wollte!

ANMERKUNGEN (Fortsetzung)

(5) **accountant:** Fachmann/-frau des Rechnungswesens (z.B. Buchhalter, Kostenrechner, Revisoren, Buchsachverständige, Wirtschaftsprüfer,...). Beachten Sie den Unterschied zu *book-keeper*, der einfach ein "Buchhalter" ist. *Book-keeping* "Buchhaltung". (Vgl. Kapitel 1, Anmerkung 10.)

(6) **just-in-time (JIT):** Eine Methode in der Lagerverwaltung, bei der die Lagerbestände so knapp verwaltet werden, daß immer nur die Teile am Lager sind, die unmittelbar für die Produktion (Rohmaterialien) oder die Auslieferung (Fertigprodukte) benötigt werden.

(7) **stock-out:** "Lagermanko, Lagerdefizit". Synonym: *inventory shortage (US)*. *Shortage* "Defizit, Fehl-, Minderbetrag; Engpaß". Nicht zu verwechseln mit *stock-taking* "Inventur".

(8) **balance sheet:** Vgl. Kapitel 10, Anmerkung 2.

(9) **item:** Hier: "Posten", auch "Punkt" (einer Tagesordnung), "Artikel" (im Handel).

(10) **profit and loss account:** Vgl. Dokument 2 unter *Shareholders' funds*. Taucht der Begriff in der Bilanz eines englischen Unternehmens auf, bezeichnet er die angesammelten Reserven. Dem entspricht in Dokument 1 der Betrag, der in der 3. Zeile unter *statement of movement of reserves* angegeben ist, im Anhang der Gewinn- und Verlustrechnung (Dokument 1).

(11) **milk cow:** Bezeichnung für ein Unternehmen, dessen einziges Interesse der unmittelbare maximale Gewinn ist und für das andere Kriterien unberücksichtigt bleiben. Synonym: *cash cow (US)*. *To milk:* "ausbeuten; 'melken'".

CHAPTER 36

DOCUMENT 1

Birtwhistle's: Profit and Loss Account (1)
(in £ million)

	199.	199. (–1)
Turnover (2)	38.177	40.285
Cost of production sold	31.812	31.103
Other expenses (administrative and R & D)	4.721	4.836
Profit before taxation (3)	1.644	4.346
Tax	.210	.613
Net profit after taxation (4)	**1.434**	**3.733**
Dividends: ordinary shares (5): 18p per share	1.328	3.314
Undistributed surplus (6)	.106	.419
Earnings per share (EPS)	20p	52p
In Notes to financial statements		
Statement of movement of reserves (7)		
– Reserves at beginning of the year	1.304	.885
– Undistributed surplus for the year	.106	.419
– Reserves at end of the year	1.410	1.304

US equivalents
(1) *Income statement, statement of earnings and retained earnings*
(2) *Total sales*
(3) *Earnings before income taxes (EBIT)*
(4) *Net earnings*
(5) *Common stock*
(6) *Undistributed earnings*
(7) *Statement of retained earnings*

DOCUMENT 2   **KAPITEL 36**

Birtwhistle's: Balance Sheet (1)
(in £ million)

Assets	199.	199.(-1)
Tangible fixed assets (2)	2.410	2.535
– Property, plant and equipment	2.410	2.535
– Assets in course of construction (3)	0.000	0.000
– Investments	0.000	0.000
Current assets		
– Stocks (4)	.481	.390
– Debtors (5)	.194	.165
– Cash in bank and on hand	.293	.238
Total assets	**3.378**	**3.328**
Liabilities		
Current liabilities		
– Creditors (6) (less than 1 year)	.101	.123
Other liabilities		
– Provisions for charges and deferred taxation	.085	.094
– Creditors (more than 1 year) and long-term debt	.052	.077
Total liabilities	**.238**	**.294**
Shareholders' funds (7)		
– Called-up (share) capital (8)	1.420	1.420
– Share premium account (9)	.310	.310
– Profit and loss account (10)	1.410	1.304
Total shareholders' funds	**3.140**	**3.034**
Total liabilities and shareholders' funds	**3.378**	**3.328**

US equivalents
(1) *Balance sheet, statement of financial condition*
(2) *Fixed assets*
(3) *Work in process, work in progress*
(4) *Inventories*
(5) *Accounts receivable*
(6) *Accounts payable*
(7) *Stockholders' equity*
(8) *Common stock*
(9) *Paid-in surplus, capital in excess of par value*
(10) *Retained earnings*

CHAPTER 36

EXERCISES

Comprehension

Lesen Sie den Dialog aufmerksam durch. Beantworten Sie dann die nachfolgenden Fragen, und zwar immer in ganzen Sätzen:

1. Why has Susan spent so much time over the company books? **2.** What is the main difference, apart from vocabulary, between the US income statement and its British counterpart, the profit and loss account? **3.** Where is the statement of movement of reserves to be found? **4.** Does Susan prefer the British format? **5.** How can the decline in last year's turnover be accounted for? **6.** What about net profits? **7.** Why couldn't target production be caught up with? **8.** Does this mean for Susan that the company is in a catastrophic position? **9.** Are the basic raw materials processed in the plant easily available in Britain? **10.** Why is Susan surprised by the profit and loss account item in the balance sheet?

Translation

1. Die Grundsätze der Buchhaltung sind in Großbritannien die gleichen wie in den USA. Der Unterschied ist vorwiegend eine Frage des Vokabulars. **2.** Der Aufruf der Gewerkschaft zu einem Warnstreik hat beinahe den Stillstand der Produktion für mehr als zwei Wochen verursacht. **3.** Mir scheint, daß die Produktion leicht wieder auf ihr früheres Niveau gebracht werden kann, wenn es uns gelingt, die Lage zu entspannen. **4.** Um unsere Lagerbestände zu reduzieren, müssen wir mehr verkaufen. **5.** In unserer Branche ist es schwierig, wenn nicht unmöglich, die Just-in-Time-Methode der Lagerverwaltung anzuwenden. **6.** Lieferungen von importierten Rohmaterialien werden nach Tonnen berechnet. **7.** Ein Lagermanko in den Wochen vor Weihnachten wäre katastrophal für unseren Umsatz. **8.** Es wird schwierig sein, die Produktion zu steigern, ohne Investitionen zu planen. **9.** Der Posten "Gewinn und Verlust" in der Bilanz stellt die Gesamtsumme der angesammelten Reserven dar. **10.** Hätte United Chocolate Birtwhistle "melken" wollen, wäre die Verschuldung des Werks heute erheblich und seine Reserven unbedeutend.

KAPITEL 36

LÖSUNGSVORSCHLÄGE

Verständnisübung

1. She wanted to analyse the company's accounts, and, at the same time, become familiar with the way the British present financial documents. **2.** In the profit and loss account, the statement of movement of reserves (*or* retained earnings [US]) is left out. **3.** It is to be found in the Notes to the Financial Statements. **4.** No, she thinks that the US format provides a better overall view of the current financial situation. **5.** It is the direct consequence of labour disputes. **6.** The decrease is even more spectacular, over 60 % compared with the previous year's. **7.** It couldn't be done with demotivated workers and staff. **8.** No. In fact, she thinks that it should be relatively easy to bring production back to former levels when tensions ease. **9.** No, they have to be imported from overseas. **10.** She is surprised because that item, representing the company's accumulated reserves, amounts to £1,410,000.

Übersetzungsübung

1. Accounting principles are the same in Britain as in the US. The difference is mostly a question of vocabulary. **2.** The unions' call for a warning strike has caused a near stoppage of production for more than two weeks. **3.** It seems to me that production should easily be brought back to its former levels if we manage to ease tensions. **4.** To reduce our stocks (*ou* inventories), we must increase our sales. **5.** In our industry, it is difficult, if not impossible, to apply the just-in-time method of stock (*ou* inventory) management. **6.** Shipments of imported raw materials are computed by the ton(ne). **7.** A stock-out (*ou* inventory) shortage in the weeks preceding Christmas would be catastrophic for our turnover (*ou* sales). **8.** It will be difficult to increase production without planning investments. **9.** The profit and loss item in the balance sheet represents the total amount of accumulated reserves. **10.** If United Chocolate had considered Birtwhistle's as a milk cow, today, the latter's debt would be considerable and its reserves negligible.

CHAPTER 36

Application

Erstellen Sie unter Verwendung der richtigen Begriffe eine "amerikanische" Version der in Dokument 1 gezeigten Gewinn- und Verlustrechnung.

Der Kontenplan

Im angelsächsischen Rechnungswesen ist es den Unternehmen freigestellt, ob sie einen Kontenplan *(chart of accounts)* führen oder nicht. Ermessensgrundlage ist hierbei die Frage, ob der Kontenplan mit den Grundsätzen ordnungsgemäßer Buchführung *(Statements of Standard Accounting Practice, SSAP [UK], Generally Accepted Accounting Principles, GAAP [US])* übereinstimmt. Diese Richtlinien werden in Großbritannien vom *Accounting Standards Board* festgelegt, einem mit den Vertretern der sechs größten Accountants-Verbände besetzten Ausschuß.

Der Kontenplan unterliegt der Zustimmung des Fiskus *(inland revenue [UK], internal revenue service, IRS [US])*, gegebenenfalls der britischen Wertpapier- und Investitionskontrollbehörde *(Securities and Investment Board, SIB)* bzw. in den USA der Börsenaufsichtsbehörde *(Securities and Exchange Commission, SEC)*.

 DO!

Avoid controversial topics in a negotiation.
Don't bring up taboo subjects like politics and religion.

KAPITEL 36

Praktische Übung – Lösung

Income statement (*oder* **Statement of earnings and retained earnings**)
(in $ million)

	199.	199. (–1)
Total sales	57.265	60.427
Cost of production sold	47.718	46.654
Other expenses	7.081	7.254
Earnings before income taxes (EBIT)	2.466	6.519
Taxes	.315	.919
Net earnings	**2.151**	**5.600**
Dividends: common stock (27c per share)	1.992	4.971
Undistributed earnings	.159	.629
Earnings per share (EPS)	30c	78c
Retained earnings		
– Retained earnings at beginning of year	1.956	1.328
– Undistributed earnings for year	.159	.628
– Retained earnings at end of year	2.115	1.956

DON'T!

*When you negotiate with the Japanese,
don't be impatient, don't play power games.
Be respectful: self-control is highly valued.*

CHAPTER 37 🎧

Errors of the past

Susan has called a meeting of representatives of local management, production workers and clerical staff, who include: Sid Higginbottom (union representative), George Howard (Financial Manager), Sallie Wilson (a bookkeeper who has been in the company over a dozen years) and Tony Greenhalgh (Production Manager).

1. **Susan:** This get-together is strictly informal. My aim is to present my view of the situation, not only as manager in charge, but as someone new to the company who has analysed the problems with no bias.

2. **Sid H.:** What exactly does that mean?

3. **Susan:** *(Ironically)* Thanks for asking. First, there must be no doubt about my loyalty to UC. At the same time, I want you to know I am fully aware of how you all feel. Now let's consider the facts.

4. **Sid H.:** That's just talk!

5. **Susan:** Certainly not! You must realise that the people at UC don't see the takeover as a success over a 5-year period. They have failed in their initial objective of integrating Birtwhistle's into their structures. Those were the days when 'big was beautiful'. It may no longer be as true. *(Turning to George Howard)* Do you have any comment on the confidential document addressed prior to the meeting to those attending? **(1)**

6. **George H.:** The document recalls the financial background to the takeover and the negotiations leading up to it. Such things are a routine matter in the world of business. I need not repeat what is clearly spelled out.

7. **Sallie Wilson:** At that time, there were rumours about leaks and insider trading. Sounded like those Wall Street scandals you read about in the press or see on TV. **(2)**

8. **Susan:** It is true that there was a leak half-way through the negotiations. That triggered speculation on the company's shares, typical insider trading – although there was no definite evidence of it.

9. **Tony G.:** It must have made the people at UC very angry.

KAPITEL 37

Fehler der Vergangenheit

Susan hat eine Sitzung von Vertretern der örtlichen Firmenleitung, Produktionsarbeitern und Verwaltungspersonal einberufen; dazu gehören: Sid Higginbottom (Gewerkschaftsvertreter), George Howard (Finanzdirektor), Sallie Wilson (eine Buchhalterin, die seit über 12 Jahren im Unternehmen tätig ist) und Tony Greenhalgh (Produktionsleiter).

1. **Susan:** Diese Zusammenkunft ist streng informell. Mein Ziel besteht darin, meine Ansicht über die Situation darzulegen, und zwar nicht nur als verantwortliche Managerin, sondern auch als eine Person, die neu im Unternehmen ist und die die Probleme unvoreingenommen analysiert hat.

2. **Sid H.:** Was bedeutet das genau?

3. **Susan:** *(Ironisch)* Danke für die Frage. Zunächst einmal dürfen keine Zweifel über meine Loyalität gegenüber UC bestehen. Gleichzeitig möchte ich, daß Sie wissen, daß ich mir völlig darüber im klaren bin, wie Sie sich alle fühlen. Nun wollen wir die Tatsachen betrachten.

4. **Sid H.:** Das ist nur Gerede!

5. **Susan:** Bestimmt nicht! Sie müssen erkennen, daß die Leute bei UC die Übernahme nicht als einen Erfolg über einen 5-Jahres-Zeitraum betrachten. Ihr Anfangsziel, Birtwhistle in ihre Strukturen zu integrieren, ist fehlgeschlagen. Das war die Zeit von 'alles was groß ist, ist schön'. Das ist sicherlich so nicht mehr wahr. *(Wendet sich an George Howard)* Haben Sie irgendwelche Bemerkungen zu dem vertraulichen Dokument zu machen, das vor der Sitzung an die Teilnehmer gerichtet wurde?

6. **George H.:** Das Dokument rollt den finanziellen Hintergrund der Übernahme und die Verhandlungen, die zu ihr geführt haben, auf. Solche Dinge sind Routine in der Geschäftswelt. Ich brauche nicht zu wiederholen, was klar ausgesprochen wurde.

7. **Sallie Wilson:** Zu dieser Zeit gab es Gerüchte über undichte Stellen und Insiderhandel. Klang wie diese Wall-Street-Skandale, über die man in der Presse liest oder die man im Fernsehen sieht.

8. **Susan:** Es stimmt, daß es im Verlauf der Verhandlungen eine undichte Stelle gab. Das hat Spekulationen über die Aktien des Unternehmens ausgelöst, typischer Insiderhandel – obwohl es keine definitiven Beweise dafür gab.

9. **Tony G.:** Das muß die Leute bei UC sehr wütend gemacht haben.

ANMERKUNGEN

(1) **'big is beautiful':** Dieser Ausdruck, der in den 80er Jahren populär war, erklärte und rechtfertigte die Welle von Unternehmensaufkäufen bzw. die Konzentration von Firmen, oft in Form riesiger Konglomerate. Heute lautet die Tendenz eher *'small is beautiful'*.

(2) Unter insider trading "Insiderhandel" versteht man den illegalen Kauf oder Verkauf von Aktien durch Mitarbeiter eines Unternehmens oder andere Personen, die geheime Informationen über die Pläne des Unternehmens besitzen.

CHAPTER 37

10. **Susan:** To say the least! They immediately issued a public statement announcing they were suspending the bid. Meanwhile, they continued to purchase stock discreetly until they held over 10 %. Am I right, George? **(3)**

11. **George H.:** Indeed. They were then in a strong minority position. Their next move was to organise a proxy fight to gain full control of the Board. This they did with the help of one of the owners who sold them his stake in the capital. The Board, now in UC's hands, decided to issue 310,000 new shares at £2 each, including a £1 share premium, entirely subscribed by United Chocolate. Next they split shares by five increasing their total number to 7,100,000... **(4) (5) (6) (7) (8)**

12. **Susan:** Thereby strengthening their control.

13. **George H.:** Yes. The rest of the family threw in the sponge and sold out. UC had won! **(9)**

14. **Susan:** Unfortunately, the whole affair had been concluded over the heads of those primarily concerned, those who worked directly for the company. Hence frustrations and a general feeling of discontent which no effort on the part of UC could erase. This is where we stand now.

15. **Sid H.:** What you've forgotten to say is that United Chocolate bowed to sustained pressure from my members, and withdrew its plans to transfer the production of Birtwhistle's Yorkshire fudge to its new plant in Lancashire! And no doubt eventually to close this place down completely...!

KAPITEL 37

10. **Susan:** Gelinde gesagt! Sie haben sofort eine öffentliche Erklärung herausgegeben, in der sie bekanntgaben, daß sie das Angebot vorläufig zurückziehen. In der Zwischenzeit haben sie weiter diskret Aktien gekauft, bis sie über 10% hielten. Stimmt das, George?
11. **George H.:** In der Tat. Sie befanden sich dann in einer starken Minderheitsposition. Ihr nächster Schachzug bestand darin, einen Kampf um die Stimmrechtsvollmacht zu organisieren, um die volle Kontrolle über den Vorstand zu erhalten. Das haben sie mit Hilfe eines Eigentümers gemacht, der ihnen seine Beteiligung am Kapital verkaufte. Der Vorstand, der sich nun in den Händen von UC befand, entschied, 310.000 neue Aktien zu je 2 Pfund einschließlich eines Aktienagios von 1 Pfund herauszugeben, die gänzlich von United Chocolate gezeichnet wurden. Als nächstes haben sie die Aktien in jeweils fünf einzelne aufgesplittet und so deren Gesamtzahl auf 7.100.000 erhöht...
12. **Susan:** Und dadurch ihre Kontrolle verstärkt.
13. **George H.:** Ja. Da hat der Rest der Familie das Handtuch geworfen und seine gesamten Anteile verkauft. UC hatte gewonnen!
14. **Susan:** Leider ist die ganze Sache über die Köpfe derer hinweg beschlossen worden, die primär betroffen waren, nämlich die direkt für die Firma gearbeitet haben. Daher Frustration und ein allgemeines Gefühl der Unzufriedenheit, das durch keinerlei Bemühungen von seiten UC's beseitigt werden konnte. Da stehen wir nun heute.
15. **Sid H.:** Was Sie vergessen haben zu erwähnen, ist, daß United Chocolate sich dem anhaltenden Druck von seiten meiner Mitglieder gebeugt und seine Pläne zurückgezogen hat, die Produktion des 'Birtwhistle Yorkshire Fudge' in das neue Werk nach Lancashire zu verlegen! Und auch die Pläne, dieses Werk zweifellos irgendwann völlig zu schließen...!

ANMERKUNGEN (Fortsetzung)

(3) **bid:** "Gebot, Angebot". *Takeover bid* "Übernahmeangebot"; *to make a cash bid* "ein Bargebot machen", *opening bid* "Eröffnungsgebot", *invitation for bid* "Ausschreibung".

(4) **move:** "Bewegung; Maßnahme, Schritt"; "Schachzug" (beim Schach und auch im übertragenen Sinne). *It's your move* "Sie sind dran".

(5) **proxy fight "Stimmrechtskampf":** Kampf zwischen zwei Aktionärsgruppen innerhalb einer Gesellschaft, wobei jede Seite versucht, durch Gewinnung möglichst vieler Vollmachten zur Vertretung von Aktien ihre eigene Stimmenzahl zu erhöhen.

(6) **stake:** "Beteiligung, Einlage". *To have a stake in a business* "einen Anteil an einem Unternehmen haben".

(7) **share premium:** Der Betrag, der zusätzlich zum Nominalwert *(nominal value [UK], par value [US])* einer Aktie zu zahlen ist, um diese zu kaufen. Im vorliegenden Fall beträgt der Nominalwert der Aktie 1 Pfund, der Ausgabewert 2 Pfund, das Aktienagio (2-1) = 1 Pfund. (Siehe Dokument.) Der Kapitalüberschuß, der durch dieses Aktienagio entsteht, findet sich in der Bilanz unter dem Posten *shareholders' funds*. (Vgl. Kapitel 36, Dokument 2.) Synonym (US): *additional paid-in capital, paid-in surplus*.

(8) **to split (shares):** Das Aufsplittern von Aktien in kleinere Stückelungen, wodurch es zu einer Erhöhung der Aktienanzahl kommt, ohne daß das Nominalkapital steigt.

(9) **the rest of the family** threw in the sponge and sold out bedeutet, daß Birtwhistle, das von diesem Zeitpunkt an zu 100% von UC (GB) kontrolliert wird, zu Birtwhistle Ltd. wird (vgl. Kapitel 4, Dokument).

CHAPTER 37

DOCUMENT

Summary of Birtwhistle's capital ownership before and after takeover

Before takeover: 1,110,000 shares at £1 nominal value.
Total called-up capital : £1,110,000.
About 20 % traded on the Stock Exchange
(3 % of which already owned by United Chocolate Ltd).
The rest in the hands of different members of the family.

After takeover: United Chocolate Ltd controlling 51 %.

1. Issue of 310,000 shares, £1 nominal value, sold for £2, totally subscribed by UC Ltd.
   Total called-up capital: £1,420,000.
   Share premium: £310,000.

2. Capital split: 5 for 1.
   Total number of shares: 7,100,000, £0.20 nominal value.

3. Acquisition of shares still remaining in family hands.
   UC (UK) now controls 100 % of capital.
   Birtwhistle's Plc becomes Birtwhistle's Ltd, a fully-owned subsidiary of UC (UK).

KAPITEL 37

Die "Golden Boys"

Sie waren in den 80er Jahren *(the eighties)* legendär und vielfach Gegenstand der Schlagzeilen *(headlines)* in den Zeitungen.
Der Begriff bezeichnet junge Führungskräfte, die von den verschiedenen Finanzberufen angezogen wurden, die mit der Aufhebung der einschränkenden Bestimmungen der Finanzmärkte *(deregulation)* aufkamen.
Diese Leute haben an den Terminmärkten und mit den berühmten "Schundanleihen" *(junk bonds)*, hochverzinslichen Anleihen geringer Bonität, viel Geld mit Brokerprovisionen *(brokerage fees)* verdient.
Viele von ihnen haben sich wegen Insiderhandels strafbar gemacht.
Seitdem haben sich die Finanzmärkte so organisiert und strukturiert, daß es immer weniger von den "Golden Boys" gibt.
Dennoch wird der Ausdruck nach wie vor für Personen verwendet, die enorm viel Geld verdienen.

CHAPTER 37

EXERCISES

Comprehension

Lesen Sie den Dialog aufmerksam durch. Beantworten Sie dann die nachfolgenden Fragen, und zwar immer in ganzen Sätzen:

1. What is Susan's aim in calling this informal meeting? **2.** Why does Susan say she has analysed Birtwhistle's problems with no bias? **3.** Why don't the people at UC consider the takeover as a success? **4.** How long has the bookkeeper been working for Birtwhistle's? **5.** At the time of the takeover, what did the rumour about leaks and insider trading remind her of? **6.** How did UC react to the leak? **7.** Do we know who was responsible for the leak during the negotiation? **8.** Why did UC continue to purchase Birtwhistle's stock discreetly? **9.** What did they do next? **10.** Was that enough to gain full control of the board?

Translation

1. Als verantwortlicher Manager wünsche ich, die Vertreter der gesamten Belegschaft zu treffen. **2.** Das war die Zeit, als man in der Geschäftswelt dachte, daß alles was groß ist, schön ist. **3.** Das vertrauliche Dokument, das vor der Besprechung an die Teilnehmer gerichtet wurde, rollt den finanziellen Hintergrund der Übernahme auf. **4.** Obwohl es Gerüchte über undichte Stellen und Insiderhandel gab, gab es keinen eindeutigen Beweis dafür. **5.** Spekulationen über die Aktien des Unternehmens, die von diesen Gerüchten ausgelöst wurden, machten die Leute bei UC sehr wütend. **6.** Um die Kontrolle über den Firmenvorstand zu erhalten, mußten sie einen Kampf um die Stimmrechtsvollmacht organisieren. **7.** Sie erhielten die Stimmrechtsvollmacht kleiner Aktionäre. **8.** Einer der Eigentümer verkaufte ihnen schließlich seinen Anteil am Unternehmen. **9.** Die neu ausgegebenen Aktien wurden vollständig von UC gezeichnet, was deren Kontrolle über das Kapital erhöhte. **10.** Nichts konnte die Frustration und die Unzufriedenheit derer beseitigen, die für die Firma gearbeitet haben.

KAPITEL 37

LÖSUNGSVORSCHLÄGE

Verständnisübung

1. Her aim is to present her view of the situation to representatives of local management, production workers and clerical staff. 2. She has analysed Birtwhistle's problems with no bias because she is new to the company. 3. It's because they have failed in their initial objective of integrating Birtwhistle's into their structures over a 5-year period. 4. She has been working for Birtwhistle's for over 12 years. 5. They reminded her of the Wall Street scandals one reads about in the press or sees on TV. 6. They immediately suspended their (takeover) bid. 7. Not exactly. It must have been an insider, although there was no definite evidence of it. 8. They wanted to obtain a strong minority position with over 10 % of the stock in their hands. 9. They organised a proxy fight. 10. Not quite. They also had the help of one of the owners who sold them his stake in the capital.

Übersetzungsübung

1. As manager in charge, I wish to meet (with) the representatives of all personnels. 2. Those were the days when people in the world of business thought that what was big was beautiful. 3. The confidential document addressed, prior to the meeting, to those attending recalls the financial background to the takeover. 4. Although there were rumours of leaks and insider trading, there was no definite evidence of it. 5. Speculation on the company's shares, triggered by those rumours, made the people at UC very angry. 6. To gain control of the board of directors, they had to organise a proxy fight. 7. They received the proxies of small shareholders. 8. One of the owners finally sold them his stake in the company. 9. The issue of new shares was entirely subscribed by UC, which reinforced their control. of the capital 10. Nothing could erase the frustrations and discontent of those who worked for the company.

CHAPTER 37

Application

Erstellen Sie unter Verwendung der richtigen Begriffe eine "amerikanische" Version der in Kapitel 36, Dokument 2, gezeigten Bilanz (Balance Sheet).

DO!

Show determination. Being a tough negotiator will make you respected in negotiations.

DON'T!

Don't forget to smile. 'The smile that wins' is as American as Mom's apple-pie. Besides, many Americans will tell you: 'Take it easy!'

KAPITEL 37

Praktische Übung – Lösung

Balance Sheet (*oder* **Statement of financial condition**)
(in $ million)

	199.	199. (-1)
Assets		
Fixed assets		
– Property, plant and equipment	3.615	3.802
– Work in process	0.000	0.000
– Investments	0.000	0.000
Current assets		
– Inventories	.721	.585
– Accounts receivable	.291	.247
– Cash in bank and on hand	.439	.357
Total assets	**5.066**	**4.991**
Liabilities		
Current liabilities		
– Accounts payable (less than one year)	.151	.184
Other liabilities		
– Provisions for charges and deferred taxation.	127	.141
– Accounts payable (more than one year) and long-term debt	.078	.115
Total liabilities	**.356**	**.440**
Stockholders' equity		
– Common stock	2.130	2.130
– Paid-in surplus (*oder* Capital in excess of par value)	.465	.465
– Retained earnings	2.115	1.956
Total stockholders' equity	**4.710**	**4.551**
Total liabilities and stockholders' equity	**5.066**	**4.991**

CHAPTER 38

Leveraged management buy-out (LMBO) (1)

United Chocolate (UK) has agreed to an LMBO proposal put together by Susan and George Howard, under Yoshi's guidance. Lord Werrett has sent down his private secretary, Timothy Browne, to finalise arrangements with Ronald Giles, a representative of Barclays. Everything has gone well so far. The five of them are having drinks in the lounge of the Crown Inn, and are still talking shop. **(2)**

1. **Susan:** Well, gentlemen, we have taken a long step forward. Our next task will be to persuade all personnels that this is a better solution for them than the purchase of the company by a competitor.

2. **Ronald Giles:** It will require a lot of explaining.

3. **George H.:** We have, Susan and I, already spent some time with employees and workers on the shop-floor to outline our plan. Most understand why UC wants out, though few approve. **(3) (4)**

4. **Susan:** What they most feared was a takeover by a foreign company resulting in massive restructuring and drastic job-cuts...

5. **George H.:** ... and the manufacture of Birtwhistle's Yorkshire fudge over in France maybe! They're a proud lot, you know!

6. **Timothy B.:** The mechanism of an LMBO is not easy to grasp for anyone, and especially the role of a holding company like Birtwhistle Finance Holding as intermediary structure. **(5)**

7. **Ronald Giles:** Nor that of leverage! Many of your older employees may be worried about getting into debt in order to acquire a right of ownership to the company – however small. **(6)**

KAPITEL 38

Leveraged Management Buy-Out (LMBO)

United Chocolate (UK) hat seine Zustimmung zu einem LMBO-Vorschlag gegeben, den Susan und George Howard unter der Leitung von Yoshi ausgearbeitet haben. Lord Werret hat seinen Privatsekretär, Timothy Browne, geschickt, um die Vereinbarungen mit Ronald Giles, einem Vertreter von Barclays, unter Dach und Fach zu bringen. Bis jetzt ist alles gut gelaufen. Die fünf nehmen in der Hotelhalle des Crown Inn einen Drink ein und fachsimpeln bis jetzt noch.

1. **Susan:** Also, meine Herren, wir haben einen großen Schritt nach vorne gemacht. Unser nächster Schritt wird es sein, die gesamte Belegschaft davon zu überzeugen, daß dies eine bessere Lösung für sie ist als der Kauf des Unternehmens durch eine Konkurrenzfirma.
2. **Ronald Giles:** Wir werden vieles erklären müssen.
3. **George H.:** Wir, Susan und ich, haben bereits einige Zeit mit Angestellten und Arbeitern in der Fertigung verbracht, um unseren Plan zu umreißen. Die meisten verstehen, warum UC aufhören will, aber nur wenige billigen es.
4. **Susan:** Was sie am meisten fürchteten, war eine Übernahme durch eine ausländische Firma, die in einer massiven Umstrukturierung und einem drastischen Arbeitskräfteabbau resultieren würde...
5. **George H.:** ... und vielleicht in der Herstellung des 'Birtwhistle Yorkshire Fudge' drüben in Frankreich! Sie haben ihren Stolz, wissen Sie!
6. **Timothy B.:** Der Mechanismus eines LMBO ist für niemanden leicht zu verstehen, und besonders die Rolle einer Holding-Gesellschaft wie der Birtwhistle Finance Holding als Zwischenstruktur.
7. **Ronald Giles:** Und auch nicht die des Leverage-Effekts! Viele Ihrer älteren Angestellten könnten Angst haben, sich zu verschulden, um ein Eigentumsrecht an der Firma – wie klein auch immer – zu erwerben.

ANMERKUNGEN

(1) **leveraged (management) buy-out (LMBO):** Ein durch Leihkapital finanzierter Aufkauf eines Unternehmens (durch dessen Management), wobei die Schulden mit Einnahmen aus dem erworbenen Unternehmen zurückgezahlt werden.

(2) **to send down** sagt der Engländer, wenn jemand aus London in die Provinz geschickt wird. In der anderen Richtung sagt man *to send up*. Ebenso: *to go up* (oder *down*); *to come up* (oder *down*).

(3) **on the shop floor:** "in der Fertigung".

(4) **to want out** ist ein salopper Ausdruck für "beenden, aufhören wollen" (z.B. eine Zusammenarbeit); auch "verlassen; unterbrechen, abbrechen".

(5) Eine **holding company** (amerikanisches Synonym: *proprietary company*) ist eine Handelsgesellschaft (meist eine AG oder eine GmbH), deren Aufgabe im hauptsächlich darin besteht, im Rahmen eines Konzerns als Dachgesellschaft die Geschäftsanteile oder Aktien der abhängigen Unternehmen zu verwalten und den Konzern einheitlich zu verwalten. Im vorliegenden Fall geht das Kapital von *Birtwhistle Ltd* an die Holding-Gesellschaft *Birtwhistle Finance Holding (BFH)* über, die als Werkzeug für den Aufkauf von 51% des Unternehmens durch die Angestellten fungiert. Den Rest hält *United Chocolate Ltd* (vgl. auch Dokument).

(6) **leverage** ist das Verhältnis von Eigenkapital zu Fremdkapital. Der "Leverage-Effekt" erweist sich nur dann als vorteilhaft, wenn die Rentabilität des Betriebs höher ist als die Kosten, die durch die Inanspruchnahme des Fremdkapitals entstehen.

CHAPTER 38

8. **Susan:** A number of them are familiar with what a secured loan is, having bought their homes that way. **(7)**
9. **Timothy B.:** Still, the old puritan ethic remains strong in these parts. **(8)**
10. **Yoshi:** It will be up to the management to explain the many advantages, especially fiscal, involved in such an operation. The fact that they will have a personal stake in the company could be a more powerful incentive than our current profit-sharing plan. **(9) (10)**
11. **Susan:** Count on me to capitalise on such arguments. Nevertheless, we will have to be very honest and say plainly that successful companies or individuals are those who were willing to take risks when they were threatened.
12. **Timothy B.:** UC is committed to farming out some of its own production to Birtwhistle's. *(Slightly condescending)* It will be reassuring for your people to know that they are not going it alone, at least at the beginning. We will gradually disengage ourselves from capital ownership, maintaining – we hope – a mutually beneficial customer relationship. Well, would you care to order another round of drinks? **(11)**
13. **George H.:** By all means! The same for everybody?
14. **Susan:** Is it reasonable?
15. **Ronald Giles:** Come on, Susan! We have worked hard. We need a break. There's more work ahead.
16. **Susan:** *(In her usual earnest tone)* The leadership of our 'young' company will have to display not only managerial skills but imagination and innovation too.
17. **Timothy B.:** We rely on you for that.
18. **Susan:** That's provided you elect me to the chair of Birtwhistle's Ltd!
19. *(All four men unanimously)* Hear, hear! **(12)**
20. **Susan:** *(Unimpressed)* Our main effort will first bear on marketing and on the reinforcement of our sales team. New products will come next if we can prove that our set-up is viable. *(Turning to Timothy)* I am confident that UC will provide its know-how generously.
21. **Timothy B.:** Susan, you already talk like a chairman and managing director!

KAPITEL 38

8. **Susan:** Eine Reihe von ihnen weiß, was ein gesichertes Darlehen ist, denn sie haben ihre Häuser auf diese Weise gekauft.
9. **Timothy B.:** In dieser Gegend herrscht noch immer stark die alte puritanische Ethik.
10. **Yoshi:** Es wird die Aufgabe des Managements sein, die vielen Vorteile zu erläutern, speziell die steuerlichen, die mit solch einer Operation zusammenhängen. Die Tatsache, daß sie einen eigenen Anteil am Unternehmen haben werden, könnte ein viel stärkerer Anreiz sein als Ihr gegenwärtiger Gewinnbeteiligungsplan.
11. **Susan:** Sie können sich darauf verlassen, daß ich aus solchen Argumenten Kapital schlagen werde. Trotzdem werden wir sehr ehrlich sein und klipp und klar sagen müssen, daß erfolgreiche Unternehmen und Einzelpersonen im Fall einer Bedrohung immer diejenigen sind, die bereit waren, Risiken einzugehen.
12. **Timothy B.:** UC ist verpflichtet, einen Teil seiner eigenen Produktion an Birtwhistle zu übergeben. *(Etwas herablassend)* Es wird beruhigend für Ihre Leute sein, zu wissen, daß sie in dieser Sache nicht alleine sind, zumindest am Anfang. Wir werden uns allmählich aus der Teilhaberschaft am Besitz zurückziehen, wobei wir – wie wir hoffen – eine für beide Seiten vorteilhafte Kundenbeziehung aufrechterhalten werden. Also, möchten Sie nicht eine Runde Drinks bestellen?
13. **George H.:** Aber sicher! Für jeden noch mal das Gleiche?
14. **Susan:** Ist das vernünftig?
15. **Ronald Giles:** Kommen Sie, Susan! Wir haben hart gearbeitet. Wir brauchen eine Pause. Es wartet noch weitere Arbeit auf uns.
16. **Susan:** *(In ihrem gewohnten ernsten Tonfall)* Die Führung unserer 'jungen' Firma wird nicht nur Manager-Fähigkeiten, sondern auch Phantasie und innovatives Denken zeigen müssen.
17. **Timothy B.:** Was das angeht, so verlassen wir uns auf Sie.
18. **Susan:** Vorausgesetzt, Sie wählen mich zur Vorsitzenden von Birtwhistle Ltd!
19. *(Alle vier Männer einstimmig)* Bravo!
20. **Susan:** *(Unbeeindruckt)* Unsere Hauptbemühungen beziehen sich zunächst auf das Marketing und die Verstärkung unserer Verkaufsmannschaft. Danach kommen neue Produkte, wenn wir beweisen können, daß unsere Vorgehensweise realisierbar ist. *(Wendet sich Timothy zu)* Ich bin zuversichtlich, daß UC sein Know-how großzügig zur Verfügung stellen wird.
21. **Timothy B.:** Susan, Sie reden bereits wie eine Vorsitzende und geschäftsführende Direktorin!

ANMERKUNGEN (Fortsetzung)

(7) **secured loan:** Ein gesichertes Darlehen, bei dem der Darlehensnehmer *(borrower)* dem Gläubiger *(lender)* Vermögenswerte als Sicherheit gibt, entweder in Form einer Hypothek *(mortgage)* oder eines Pfands *(pledge)*.

(8) **puritan ethic:** Protestantische Grundsätze der Lebensführung, in dieser Region in der Mehrzahl die der Methodisten, die auf der Tugend der Arbeit und des Sparens basieren. Sich Geld zu leihen, bedeutet, über seine Verhältnisse zu leben.

(9) **(fiscal) advantages:** Die von Birtwhistle an seine Holding gezahlten Dividenden sind nicht steuerpflichtig *(non taxable)* und dienen, zumindest zum Teil, zur Rückzahlung der Kredite.

(10) **profit-sharing plan:** Eine Vereinbarung, nach der Angestellte und Arbeiter eines Unternehmens an den Gewinnen der Firma beteiligt werden können.

(11) **to farm out:** "weitervergeben". Synonyme: *to contract out, to subcontract*.

(12) **hear, hear!:** Dieser Ausdruck stammt ursprünglich aus dem Parlament, wird aber heute bei allen Arten von Sitzungen usw. benutzt. Während des Ausrufs wird begleitend mit der Handfläche auf den Tisch geschlagen.

CHAPTER 38　　　　　　　　　　DOCUMENT

Financing of LMBO
and capital structure of Birtwhistle Finance Holding (BFH)

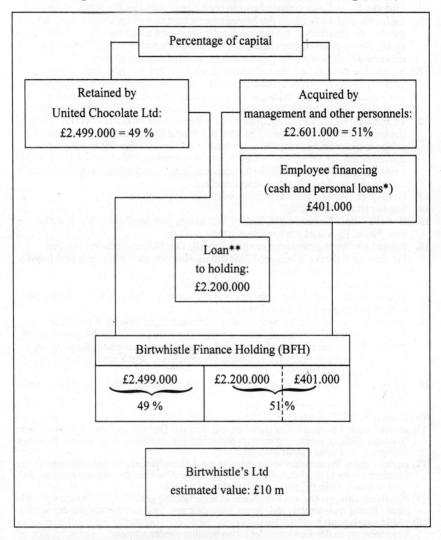

* Secured personal loans from Barclays.

** Loan to holding secured on company property.

KAPITEL 38

Die Beteiligung der Angestellten am Unternehmensgewinn

Im Gegensatz zu anderen Ländern ist in den angelsächsischen Ländern die Gewinnbeteiligung *(profit sharing)* nicht vom Gesetzgeber vorgeschrieben, sondern sie ist das Ergebnis von Verhandlungen, die in den einzelnen Unternehmen oder Berufszweigen, meistens mit den Gewerkschaften im Rahmen von Tarifverträgen *(collective agreements)*, geführt werden.

CHAPTER 38

EXERCISES

Comprehension

Lesen Sie den Dialog aufmerksam durch. Beantworten Sie dann die nachfolgenden Fragen, und zwar immer in ganzen Sätzen:

1. Where is the dialogue taking place? 2. Who are the five persons taking part in the discussion? 3. What was most feared by employees and workers? 4. What is the role played by a holding in an LMBO? 5. According to Ronald Giles and Timothy Browne, why might some of the older employees be worried about getting into debt? 6. How can the LMBO be a powerful incentive to employees? 7. According to Susan, what makes companies or individuals successful? 8. Does UC (UK) plan to retain its share of the holding for long? 9. What does Timothy Browne mean by 'maintaining a mutually beneficial customer relationship'? 10. Are Susan's ambitions clearly expressed at the end of the dialogue?

Translation

1. Der LMBO-Vorschlag ist von Susan und George Howard unter der Leitung von Yoshi ausgearbeitet worden. 2. Der Privatsekretär von Lord Werret ist herausgekommen, um die finanziellen Vereinbarungen unter Dach und Fach zu bringen. 3. Es wird nun Ihre Aufgabe sein, alle Betriebsangehörigen davon zu überzeugen, daß ein LMBO die beste Lösung ist. 4. UC will sich aus dem Kapitaleigentum zurückziehen, wehrt sich jedoch gegen eine Übernahme durch einen ausländischen Mitbewerber. 5. Wenn der LMBO nicht genehmigt wird, bleibt nur noch eine Lösung: verkaufen. 6. Der Leverage-Effekt wird vorteilhaft sein, wenn die Rentabilität der Firma höher ist als die Zinsen, die für das Darlehen gezahlt werden. 7. Das Darlehen an die Holding-Gesellschaft ist durch die materiellen Vermögenswerte des Unternehmens gesichert. 8. Die Angestellten werden von Barclays ein Darlehen erhalten können, um Anteile am Unternehmen zu erwerben. 9. Susan wird ihre Manager-Fähigkeiten zeigen müssen, um zur Vorstandsvorsitzenden gewählt zu werden. 10. Sie erklärt, daß ihre Hauptbemühungen sich zuerst auf das Marketing und die Verstärkung der Verkaufsmannschaft beziehen werden.

KAPITEL 38

LÖSUNGSVORSCHLÄGE

Verständnisübung

1. It is taking place in the lounge of the Crown Inn. 2. They are Susan, George Howard, Timothy Browne, Lord Werrett's private secretary, Ronald Giles, Barclays' representative and Yoshi. 3. It was a takeover by a foreign competitor, resulting in massive restructuring. 4. It's only an intermediary structure controlling the capital, with no commercial or industrial activity. 5. They think they might be influenced by the old puritan ethic. 6. Their right of ownership will give them a personal stake in the company and will therefore stimulate them to work harder. 7. It is their willingness to take risks when threatened. 8. No, it will gradually disengage itself from capital ownership. 9. UC will continue to farm out some of its production to Birtwhistle's as customer and no longer as part owner of the company. 10. Yes, definitely! She hopes to become chairman and managing director of the company.

Übersetzungsübung

1. The LMBO proposal has been put together by Susan and George Howard under Yoshi's guidance. 2. Lord Werrett's private secretary has come down to finalise financial arrangements. 3. It will be up to you now to persuade all personnels that an LMBO is the best solution. 4. UC wants out (*or* wants to disengage itself) from capital ownership but refuses a takeover by a foreign competitor. 5. If the LMBO is not approved, there will be only one solution left: to sell. 6. Leverage will be favourable (*or* positive) if the profitability of the firm is higher than the interests paid on the loan. 7. The loan to the holding company is secured on the company's tangible fixed assets. 8. The employees will be able to obtain a loan from Barclays to acquire company shares. 9. Susan will have to display her managerial skills in order to be elected to the chair of the board (*or* chairman of the board). 10. She states that her main effort will first bear on marketing and on the reinforcement of the sales team.

CHAPTER 38

Application

Bei der folgenden Übung können Sie noch mal ein bißchen mit Zahlen spielen. Ziehen Sie als Referenz die Dokumente der Kapitel 37 und 38 heran.

Question 1: Compute the total number of shares held by personnels after successful completion of the LMBO.

Question 2: Compute the price paid per share.

DO!

**Be careful when you use 'girl' or 'boy' in the USA.
'Girl' can be considered sexist; 'boy' can be considered racist.**

KAPITEL 38

Lösung der praktischen Übung

Frage 1: Total number of shares: 7,100,000.

51 % acquired by personnels, ie: $\dfrac{7,100,000 \times 51}{100}$ = **3,621,000 shares.**

Frage 2: Total amound paid for 51 % of capital:
£2,601,000 (£401,000 + £2,200,000).

Price per share: $\dfrac{2,601,000}{3,621,000}$ ~ **£0.72.**

DON'T!

***Don't address someone as 'Mr',
but always 'Mr So-and-so', or just 'Sir'.***

CHAPTER 39

Diversification (1)

During the informal weekly meeting that she holds with George Howard, the Financial Manager, and Basil Dykes, the Marketing Manager, Susan raises the issue of diversification.

1. **Susan:** Well, I would like us to start thinking of development projects.

2. **Basil Dykes:** I agree with you. Our organisation can't afford not to introduce new products.

3. **Susan:** According to an expert, half of all the profits of all US companies come from products that did not exist ten years ago.

4. **George H.:** Careful! Never forget that small is beautiful! It's always risky for a company to broaden its business portfolio. Let's not sacrifice our profitable core business, however stodgy it may look, to move into glamorous new markets that are experiencing growth! **(2) (3)**

5. **Basil Dykes:** Come on George! Such moves are risky when a company acquires a business that fits poorly with the old one or when it operates in unfamiliar markets.

6. **Susan:** Our ambition is not to get bogged down under a smorgasbord portfolio! We want to stick to our knitting – with apologies to Women's Lib! **(4) (5) (6) (7)**

7. **Basil Dykes:** As marketing manager, it's my job to see that we move into new fields and diversify. There is no doubt in my mind that the field of ice-cream bars has the greatest potential for Birtwhistle.

8. **George H.:** Such a diversification project requires a lot of resources. We would probably be better off if we used our money to improve current products.

KAPITEL 39

Diversifikation

Während der wöchentlich stattfindenden informellen Besprechung, die sie mit George Howard, dem Finanzdirektor, und Basil Dykes, dem Marketing-Leiter, abhält, wirft Susan die Frage der Diversifikation auf.

1. **Susan:** Also, ich hätte gerne, daß wir beginnen, uns Gedanken über Entwicklungsprojekte zu machen.
2. **Basil Dykes:** Ich stimme Ihnen zu. Unsere Organisation kann es sich nicht leisten, keine neuen Produkte einzuführen.
3. **Susan:** Nach Meinung eines Experten kommt die Hälfte aller Gewinne sämtlicher US-Firmen von Produkten, die vor zehn Jahren noch nicht existiert haben.
4. **George H.:** Vorsicht! Vergessen Sie niemals, daß klein schön bedeutet. Es ist für eine Firma immer ein Risiko, seinen Geschäftsbereich zu erweitern. Wir wollen nicht unser profitables Hauptgeschäft opfern, so langweilig es auch aussehen mag, um uns auf glanzvollen neuen Märkten zu betätigen, die gerade ein Wachstum erfahren!
5. **Basil Dykes:** Kommen Sie, George! Ein solches Vorgehen ist riskant, wenn eine Firma ein Unternehmen erwirbt, das schlecht zu ihr paßt oder wenn sie auf Märkten arbeitet, die ihr nicht vertraut sind.
6. **Susan:** Unser Bestreben ist es, uns nicht auf ein zu reichhaltiges Sortiment festlegen zu lassen. Wir möchten unserem Strickmuster treu bleiben – ich hoffe, die Frauenbewegung verzeiht mir!
7. **Basil Dykes:** Als Marketing-Leiter ist es meine Aufgabe, darauf zu achten, daß wir in neue Bereiche vordringen und diversifizieren. Es gibt in meinen Augen keinen Zweifel, daß der Bereich der Eiscremeriegel für Birtwhistle das größte Potential besitzt.
8. **George H.:** Solch ein Diversifikationsprojekt erfordert viele Ressourcen. Wir wären vielleicht besser beraten, wenn wir unser Geld zur Verbesserung bestehender Produkte verwenden würden.

ANMERKUNGEN

(1) **diversification:** Programm einer gezielten Unternehmenspolitik, die unter Berücksichtigung der Produktions- und Absatzstruktur neue Produkte auf neuen Märkten einführen und damit die Zukunft eines Unternehmens sichern will.
(2) **core:** "Kern". Hier: "Haupt-, Basis-". *Hard core* "harter Kern".
(3) **stodgy:** "pappig" (Essen); "langweilig, schwerfällig; trübsinnig".
(4) **to get bogged down:** "festsitzen, nicht weiterkommen" kommt von *bog* "Moor, Sumpf". Merken Sie sich auch *peat bog* "Torfmoor".
(5) **smorgasbord**, schwedisch *Smörgṭsbord*, ist eine aus vielen, meist kalten Speisen bestehende Vorspeisentafel. Im übertragenen Sinne bedeutet es "Sortiment".
(6) **we want to stick to our knitting:** Diese Metapher war in den 90er Jahren Ausdruck einer Unternehmenspolitik, bei der die Beschränkung auf eine etablierte, übersichtliche Produktpalette im Vordergrund stand, nachdem man in den 80er Jahren eine Politik des Wachstums in alle Richtungen verfolgt hatte. Andere Ausdrücke sind *narrowing the focus*, *the urge to purge* oder *back to the basics*.
(7) **Women´s Lib** ist das Kurzwort für *Women's Liberation Movement*.

CHAPTER 39 📼

9. **Susan:** I don't see how our current products can achieve much deeper market penetration. We have cut prices, increased advertising, got our fudge bars into new stores, tried to obtain better shelf position... *(Smiling at George)* And, thanks to you, George, we are in a sound financial position. We should use it.

10. **Basil Dykes:** The ice-cream bar market is not a leap in the dark. On the contrary, we would be moving into a similar product market.

11. **George H.:** It is a new market for us, nevertheless. Do we have the expertise? Strategies that are successful in the marketing of fudge bars may not be applicable to the marketing of ice-cream bars...

12. **Basil Dykes:** *(Interrupting him)* As we have the adequate resources...

13. **George H.:** Your diversification project will not be a good investment if it spreads the company's resources too thin. **(8)**

14. **Basil Dykes:** My point is that we can hope to move in to fill a market gap and thereby strengthen the overall performance of our firm. **(9) (10)**

15. **George H.:** Before making any decision, we all need more information. We need facts and figures. We have to collect the input our company needs such as research ideas, cash, labour, manufacturing processes, market studies...

16. **Susan:** Right! We will also have to see how we will obtain the new product. Will it be through acquisition by taking over a small company which already has experience in that field, or by selling our patent or a licence to produce our bars to someone else? Or will we choose the solution of new-product development by asking our company's research and development department to work on this project? **(11) (12)**

17. **Basil Dykes:** As the costs of developing and introducing new products have climbed, perhaps we should acquire an existing company rather than create our own product...

18. **Susan:** At all events, I'd like you to send me your proposals within the next two months.

KAPITEL 39

9. **Susan:** Ich kann mir nicht vorstellen, wie unsere aktuellen Produkte eine noch höhere Marktdurchdringung erreichen können. Wir haben die Preise reduziert, die Werbung verstärkt, bieten unsere Karamelriegel in neuen Geschäften an, haben versucht, unsere Produkte günstiger in den Regalen zu plazieren ... *(Lächelt George an)* Und dank Ihrer Arbeit, George, befinden wir uns in einer soliden finanziellen Position. Davon sollten wir profitieren.
10. **Basil Dykes:** Der Markt für Eiscremeriegel ist kein Sprung ins Ungewisse. Im Gegenteil, wir würden uns auf einen ähnlichen Produktmarkt verlegen.
11. **George H.:** Es ist für uns trotzdem ein neuer Markt. Haben wir die Fachkenntnisse dafür? Strategien, die im Marketing für Karamelriegel erfolgreich sind, sind möglicherweise im Marketing für Eiscremeriegel nicht anwendbar...
12. **Basil Dykes:** *(Unterbricht ihn)* Da wir die richtigen Ressourcen haben...
13. **George H.:** Ihr Diversifikationsprojekt wird keine gute Investition sein, wenn es die Ressourcen des Unternehmens zu dünn streut.
14. **Basil Dykes:** Worauf ich hinaus will, ist, daß wir darauf hoffen können, eine Marktlücke zu schließen und dadurch die allgemeine Leistung unserer Firma stärken.
15. **George H.:** Bevor wir eine Entscheidung treffen, benötigen wir alle mehr Informationen. Wir brauchen Fakten und Zahlen. Wir müssen die Daten sammeln, die unser Unternehmen braucht, z.B. Forschungsideen, Barbestände, Arbeit, Fertigungsprozesse, Marktstudien...
16. **Susan:** Richtig! Wir werden auch darüber nachdenken müssen, wie wir an das neue Produkt herankommen. Durch Akquisition in Form einer Übernahme einer kleinen Firma, die bereits Erfahrungen in diesem Bereich hat, oder durch den Verkauf unseres Patents oder einer Lizenz für die Produktion unserer Riegel an jemand anderen? Oder werden wir die Lösung einer Produktneuentwicklung wählen, indem wir die Forschungs- und Entwicklungsabteilung unseres Unternehmens beauftragen, dieses Projekt zu bearbeiten?
17. **Basil Dykes:** Da die Kosten für die Entwicklung und Einführung neuer Produkte gestiegen sind, sollten wir vielleicht eher eine bestehende Firma erwerben als unser eigenes Produkt entwickeln...
18. **Susan:** Auf jeden Fall möchte ich, daß Sie mir in den nächsten zwei Monaten Ihre Vorschläge zukommen lassen.

ANMERKUNGEN (Fortsetzung)

(8) **to spread resources thin:** Nicht viel Marge im Einsatz der Ressourcen haben.

(9) **my point is:** "was ich sagen will", "was ich meine". Ebenso: *the point is...* "das Entscheidende ist...", "der springende Punkt ist...". *All right, point taken* "Da hast du recht", "Ich seh´s ein".

(10) **thereby:** "dadurch, hierdurch".

(11) **patent:** "Patent". *To take out a patent* "sich etw. patentieren lassen". *Patent pending* "zum Patent angemeldet".

(12) **licence (oder *license*):** "Lizenz, Genehmigung, Konzession". *Licensee* "Konzessions-/ Lizenzinhaber"; *licensing* "Schank-, Lizenz-, Konzessions-"; *licensing hours* (GB) "Schankzeiten".

CHAPTER 39   DOCUMENT

Minutes of a Board Meeting

Minutes of the special meeting of shareholders, Birtwhistle's Ltd, held in the Rainbow Room at the Crown Hotel at ten o'clock (am).

The special meeting of shareholders was summoned at the request of the Chairman to vote on the LMBO proposal approved by the Board of Directors at its last session.

The Chairman, Lord Werrett, reported on the discussions with the various parties involved that led to the Board's approval of the said proposal. It formalises the financing of the LMBO and the resulting capital structure *(chart appended*)*.

It is the Board's firm conviction that such a plan will:

1. reinforce the employees' commitment to the company in which they will now have a substantial stake.

2. provide capital for needed investments in improved production facilities that will, ultimately, make diversification easier.

In a report to the shareholders, Ms Susan Edwards, Acting Managing Director, described the first concrete steps towards product diversification. Extensive studies have shown that the market for ice-cream fudge bars provides excellent
opportunities.

On behalf of the Assembly, the Chairman thanked Ms Edwards for her invaluable contribution to the company's recovery and proposed her for election to Board membership for a three-year term renewable.

The shareholders present or represented unanimously approved the LMBO proposal and Ms Edwards' election to the Board.

Lord Werrett announced that he would step down from his present position as Chairman and Managing Director of Birtwhistle's at year's end in order to take on new responsibilities on the Board of UC Inc.

In due time, Birtwhistle's Board will elect his successor upon his recommendation and after consultations with representatives of the shareholders.

There being no further business, the meeting was adjourned at twelve o'clock (noon).

* See Chapter 38, Document.

KAPITEL 39

**Eine gelungene Diversifikation:
Eiscremeriegel**

Dank der neuen, von spektakulären Werbeaktionen begleiteten Markteinführung der Eiscremeriegel bekannter Marken wie Lion, Mars usw. hat sich das Speiseeis auf der Beliebtheitsskala einen besonderen Platz erobert. Mit dieser neuen Kreation, zu der sich zunächst die amerikanischen, mittlerweile jedoch auch die europäischen und hier besonders die schwedischen und deutschen Konditoren inspiriert fühlen, können bekannte Süßwarenhersteller nun nicht nur in der Hitze des Sommers, sondern auch zu jeder anderen Jahreszeit, mit einem Produkt auf dem Markt präsent sein, das Verbrauchern eine angemessene Alternative zum klassischen Schokoriegel bietet. Dabei wissen die Hersteller, daß der Kauf eines Eiscremeriegels, wie der eines herkömmlichen Schokoriegels, ein Impulskauf *(impulse purchase)* ist.

Die Diversifikation geht so weit, daß die besagten Riegel nicht mehr nur aus Speiseeis bestehen, sondern man findet auch Riegel aus echter Bitter- oder Vollmilch-Eisschokolade. Die dynamische Entwicklung dieses neuen Sektors profitiert von der Tatsache, daß die meisten Verbraucher lieber zu einem Produkt greifen, das vollständig aus natürlichen Zutaten besteht, als zu Produkten mittelmäßiger Qualität aus pflanzlichen und artifiziellen Bestandteilen.

CHAPTER 39

EXERCISES

Comprehension

Lesen Sie den Dialog aufmerksam durch. Beantworten Sie dann die nachfolgenden Fragen, und zwar immer in ganzen Sätzen:

1. Why can't Birtwhistle's afford not to diversify? **2.** What remark shows that diversification is vital for a company? **3.** What is George Howard wary of? **4.** What is Susan's strategic priority? **5.** Why does she say 'with apologies to Women's Lib'? **6.** Why does Basil Dykes think that the ice-cream bar market is a calculated risk? **7.** Why does George Howard think it is risky, nevertheless? **8.** Why does George Howard not want a decision to be made right away? **9.** What various alternatives does Susan consider? **10.** What deadline does Susan suggest for George Howard's and Basil Dykes's recommendations?

Life cycle of a product

Jedes Produkt kann in seinem Lebenszyklus mehrere Etappen durchlaufen:

Introduction: *Das Produkt wird auf dem Markt eingeführt. Es verkauft sich schlecht, und das Unternehmen erreicht nicht die Rentabilitätsgrenze.*
Growth: *Die Verkaufszahlen für das Produkt steigen schnell an; im gleichen Maße erhöhen sich die Gewinne. Die Konkurrenz bereitet die Einführung ähnlicher Produkte vor.*
Maturity: *Die Verkäufe stagnieren, dann beginnen die Verkaufszahlen zu sinken. Die Gewinne verschlechtern sich. Maßnahmen zur Verkaufsförderung müssen ergriffen und Überlegungen hinsichtlich der Einführung neuer Produkte angestellt werden.*
Decline: *Die Verkaufszahlen sinken rapide und die Gewinne gehen stark zurück.*

Ordnen Sie jeden der untenstehenden Sätze einer der beschriebenen Entwicklungsstufen eines Produkts **(introduction, growth, maturity, decline)** *zu.*

1. Our sales turnover is skyrocketing. **2.** Our market has shrunk. **3.** Our company plans to invest a lot of money in promotion. **4.** Our sales are dipping. **5.** Our sales are growing at a fast pace. **6.** Our research team is preparing a replacement product. **7.** Our sales growth is slowing down. **8.** Our weaker competitors are dropping out. **9.** We're experiencing mushrooming growth. **10.** Our profits are plummeting.

KAPITEL 39

LÖSUNGSVORSCHLÄGE

Verständnisübung

1. Because diversification is becoming increasingly necessary in today's business world. Products reaching the end of their life cycle must be replaced. **2.** In the U.S., half of the profits come from products that did not exist 10 years ago. **3.** He is wary of diversification for diversification's sake. **4.** She wants to keep the focus of Birtwhistle's activities narrow. **5.** Women's Lib rejects the image of women who stay at home and take care of the household. Knitting is considered by 'male chauvinists' as a typically feminine activity. **6.** Because this market is not fundamentally different from that of fudge bars. **7.** Because Birtwhistle's lacks know-how in this field and also because the marketing of ice-cream bars may differ from that of fudge bars. **8.** Because he feels a sound business decision must rest on hard facts, not just ideas. **9.** According to Susan, there are various diversification possibilities: the takeover of a small company, the selling of a licence or patent to another company and the development of the new product by Birtwhistle's own R & D team. **10.** She gives them a two-month deadline.

Lebenszyklus eines Produkts: *Introduction*: 3. *Growth*: 1, 5, 9. *Maturity*: 6, 7. *Decline*: 2, 4, 8, 10.

CHAPTER 39

Application

Ordnen Sie die in der rechten Spalte aufgeführten Ausdrücke bzw. Redewendungen den in der linken Spalte stehenden Bestandteilen einer Rede (Einleitung, Betonung, Einschränkung, Schlußbemerkung usw.) zu.

a. introduction

b. development

c. conclusion

d. complement

e. restriction

f. emphasis

g. alternative

h. deduction

1. still, I feel that
2. this solution is even better
3. in short
4. the aim of our meeting is to
5. whereas most people tend to think that
6. moreover, the forecasts show that
7. generally speaking
8. I do feel that
9. on the other hand
10. apart from that
11. this is undoubtedly true
12. we may go as far as to say that
13. consequently
14. in conclusion
15. my point is that
16. it is one thing to make forecasts, it is another to
17. in a way, yes
18. let me point out that
19. it follows that
20. good morning, ladies and gentlemen

KAPITEL 39

Lösungen

1. e. 2. f. 3. c. 4. a. 5. e. 6. d. 7. b. 8. f. 9. g. 10. d. 11. f. 12. h. 13. h. 14. c. 15. b. 16. g. 17. e. 18. b. 19. h. 20. a.

DO!

'Feeling' (Intuition) *is important.*
It's up to you to judge how quickly you can build rapport with the other party and do business.

DON'T!

Don't expect the English to be as clear,
consistent and cartesian as you would like them to be.
In the land that gave birth to Bacon, Newton and Darwin,
people are aware of changing realities.

CHAPTER 40

The rewards of merit

Six months later, 11 am, in the mahogany-lined boardroom of Birtwhistle's. Susan sits quietly at the end of the table, facing Lord Werrett, Chairman and Managing Director of UC (UK) and of Birtwhistle's Ltd, who is going to open the meeting.

1. **Lord Werrett:** *(Looking satisfied)* Ladies and gentlemen, I am pleased to welcome you. We are here to make important decisions which I have had the opportunity to discuss with each one of you individually in the last few weeks. Before we proceed, I will call upon the Secretary to make a few announcements. Mr Secretary... **(1)**

2. **Secretary:** Thank you, Mr Chairman. Sir Peter Stafford rang me up this morning to apologise for not attending. Sir Peter's flight from Moscow was delayed and he missed the connecting flight to Leeds-Bradford. We have reservations for lunch at the Crown Inn. Transportation to the airport will be available for those who plan to leave today. We will have to confirm room reservations for those staying overnight. That's all, Mr Chairman.

3. **Lord W.:** Thank you, Mr Secretary. First item on our agenda: approval of the minutes of our last meeting which were sent to you in due time. All those in favour please say 'aye'. *(Aye, aye, aye)* No one against, ... or abstaining?... Approved. Second item: Susan Edwards's report on developments in the past six months. The report was appended to the minutes. Susan, will you please summarise the main features? **(2)**

4. **Susan:** Mr Chairman, Ladies and Gentlemen, I just wish to stress that we have made quick progress in restructuring both administrative services and production units to allow greater flexibility and encourage employee involvement at all levels... **(3)**

5. **Lord W.:** I note with pleasure that maximising human resources remains uppermost in your mind. **(4)**

KAPITEL 40

Die verdiente Belohnung

Sechs Monate später um 11 Uhr vormittags im mit Mahagoni ausgekleideten Sitzungssaal von Birtwhistle. Susan sitzt ruhig am Ende des Tisches, gegenüber von Lord Werret, dem Vorsitzenden und geschäftsführenden Direktor von UC (UK) und Birtwhistle Ltd, der die Sitzung eröffnen wird.

1. **Lord Werret:** *(Macht einen zufriedenen Eindruck)* Meine Damen und Herren, ich freue mich, Sie hier begrüßen zu dürfen. Wir haben uns hier zusammengefunden, um wichtige Entscheidungen zu treffen, die ich mit jedem einzelnen von Ihnen in den letzten Wochen persönlich besprechen konnte. Bevor wir fortfahren, möchte ich den Schriftführer bitten, einige Ankündigungen zu machen. Herr Schriftführer...
2. **Schriftführer:** Danke, Herr Vorsitzender. Sir Peter Stafford rief mich heute morgen an und entschuldigte sich dafür, daß er nicht an der Sitzung teilnehmen kann. Sir Peters Flug von Moskau startete verspätet, und er hat den Anschlußflug nach Leeds-Bradford nicht erreicht. Für das Mittagessen sind Reservierungen im Crown Inn vorgenommen worden. Für diejenigen, die vorhaben, heute abzureisen, ist eine Transfermöglichkeit zum Flughafen verfügbar. Für diejenigen, die über Nacht bleiben, müssen wir noch die Zimmerreservierungen bestätigen. Das ist alles, Herr Vorsitzender.
3. **Lord Werret:** Vielen Dank, Herr Schriftführer. Erster Punkt unserer Tagesordnung: Die Genehmigung des Protokolls der letzten Sitzung, das Ihnen rechtzeitig zuging. Alle, die dem Protokoll zustimmen, mögen bitte die Hand heben... Keine Gegenstimmen... Keine Enthaltungen? Genehmigt. Zweiter Punkt: Susan Edwards Bericht über Entwicklungen in den letzten sechs Monaten. Der Bericht befand sich im Anhang zum Protokoll. Susan, würden Sie bitte die Hauptpunkte zusammenfassen?
4. **Susan:** Herr Vorsitzender, meine Damen und Herren, ich möchte nur betonen, daß wir einen schnellen Fortschritt bei der Restrukturierung sowohl der Verwaltungsdienste als auch der Produktionseinheiten gemacht haben, was uns eine größere Flexibilität und eine Steigerung des Engagements der Angestellten auf allen Ebenen ermöglicht...
5. **Lord Werret:** Ich stelle mit Zufriedenheit fest, daß die Optimierung der Personalressourcen Ihr wichtigstes Anliegen bleibt.

ANMERKUNGEN

(1) **to proceed:** "weitergehen, -fahren"; "vorgehen"; "fortfahren". *Proceeding* "Vorgehensweise; Verfahren".

(2) **aye:** "ja". *Ayes and noes:* Bei der Stimmenzählung im Parlament oder anderen Versammlungen die Pro- und Kontrastimmen. *The ayes have it* "Die Mehrheit ist dafür". Bei uns würde man eher sagen: "Heben Sie die Hand": *raise your hand(s)*. Und bestimmt kennen Sie auch: *Ay, ay, sir!* "Jawohl, Herr Kapitän!".

(3) **involvement:** "Beteiligung; Einmischung; Engagement" (für eine Sache). Achtung: *To have an involvement with somebody* "eine Affäre mit jemandem haben". *To be involved in something* "in etw. verwickelt sein".

(4) **uppermost:** wörtlich "oberster, -e, -es". Hier: "von größter Wichtigkeit; Haupt-".

CHAPTER 40 🎞

(Murmurs of approval and 'hear, hear'!)

6. **Susan:** That's the best foundation to build upon. Our productivity is on the rise. So are sales and quarterly profits. We trust that the launching of our new line of ice-cream fudge bars early next year will further boost sales. The Board will be kept informed of progress on a month-to-month basis.

7. **Lord W.:** Excellent, Susan. The next item, discussed at our last board meeting, should be formally endorsed and scheduled: going public to secure outside capital for future investments. **(5)**

8. **Susan:** We're all set for that and we'll get started as soon as we get the Board's signal.

9. **Lord W.:** If our public offering of 25 % of our capital is as successful as I expect in attracting potential investors, Birtwhistle's will be in a position to enlarge its production capacity... My friends, a few months ago I announced my decision to step down from office. The day has come. It is my privilege, with your full support, to propose the name of my successor... Susan, unlike our American colleagues, I find it hard to get used to the word 'chairperson'! May I call upon you to take the chair in my place? Be assured that UC will continue to be supportive – as long as it is in its interest! For a businesswoman of your calibre, that should go without saying! **(6) (7)**

10. **Susan:** Mr Chairman, Ladies and Gentlemen. It's a great honour and a real challenge. **I am deeply moved** and can assure you that I will do my best **to deserve your** confidence.

KAPITEL 40

(Zustimmendes Gemurmel)

6. **Susan:** Das ist die beste Grundlage, auf die man bauen kann. Unsere Produktivität steigt. Ebenso die Verkäufe und die vierteljährlichen Gewinne. Wir hoffen, daß die Einführung unseres neuen Sortiments an Eiscreme-Karamelriegeln Anfang nächsten Jahres die Verkäufe weiter ankurbeln wird. Der Vorstand wird jeden Monat über den Verlauf informiert werden.

7. **Lord Werret:** Hervorragend, Susan. Der nächste Punkt, der auf unserer letzten Vorstandssitzung diskutiert wurde, sollte formal gebilligt und geplant werden: der Gang an die Börse zur Sicherung von Fremdkapital für zukünftige Investitionen.

8. **Susan:** Wir sind alle bereit dafür und werden damit beginnen, sobald wir grünes Licht vom Vorstand bekommen haben.

9. **Lord Werret:** Wenn unser öffentliches Zeichnungsangebot von 25% des Kapitals so erfolgreich potentielle Investoren anlockt wie ich es erwarte, wird Birtwhistle in der Lage sein, seine Produktionskapazität auszuweiten... Meine Freunde, vor einigen Monaten habe ich meine Entscheidung bekanntgegeben, von meinen Ämtern zurückzutreten. Die Zeit ist nun reif. Ich habe die Ehre, mit Ihrer umfassenden Unterstützung den Namen meiner Nachfolgerin vorzuschlagen... Susan, anders als unsere amerikanischen Kollegen kann ich mich nur schwer an das Wort 'chairperson' gewöhnen. Darf ich Sie bitten, statt meiner den Vorsitz zu übernehmen? Seien Sie versichert, daß UC Sie weiterhin unterstützen wird – solange dies im Interesse der Firma liegt! Für eine Geschäftsfrau Ihres Kalibers sollte sich das von selbst verstehen!

10. **Susan:** Herr Vorsitzender, meine Damen und Herren. Es ist mir eine große Ehre und eine wirkliche Herausforderung. Ich bin tief bewegt und kann Ihnen versichern, daß ich mein Bestes tun werde, um mir Ihr Vertrauen zu verdienen.

ANMERKUNGEN (Fortsetzung)

(5) **to go public:** Ein Unternehmen stellt der Öffentlichkeit einen Teil seiner Aktien an der Börse zum Kauf bereit. Für Birtwhistle bedeutet dies die Rückkehr zum Status einer *Public Limited Company (Plc)*.

(6) **public offering:** Ein Unternehmen bietet der Öffentlichkeit neue Aktien zum Kauf an, um sich an der Börse einzuführen. Das britische Äquivalent hierzu ist ein *offer for sale*.

(7) **office:** Hier: "Amt, Funktion". *To take office/to come into office* "Amtstätigkeit aufnehmen", "Amt antreten"; *in virtue of his office* "kraft seines Amtes".

CHAPTER 40 — EPILOGUE

A clipping from the 'Yorkshire Telegraph'

Financial News

Woman in charge at Birtwhistle's

At the last board meeting of Birtwhistle's, Lord Werrett confirmed his resignation – announced six months ago in these columns – from the Chair and Managing Directorship. He proposed as his successor Mrs Susan Edwards, currently Acting Managing Director, who had been elected to full membership of the board earlier this year. The Board unanimously endorsed this proposal.

Susan Edwards, a graduate of Leeds University, with an MBA from Texas A&M, had been working for United Chocolate since she left the university.

She has had substantial international business experience. After a spell in human resources in the UK, she was assigned to the US parent company, first in market research, then as Export Manager for the Pacific Rim countries, based in Los Angeles. She was brought back to the UK as troubleshooter at Birtwhistle's.

The company, acquired by UC (UK) several years ago, had failed to meet expectations.

Birtwhistle's rapid recovery can largely be credited to Susan Edwards. Her energetic action enabled the company to overcome difficulties which, for a long time, had impaired its efficiency.

The LMBO, engineered with the support of its parent company, together with a redeployment of production and marketing, have given new life to a company with deep roots in our community. Many of us still remember the good old Birtwhistle's fudge of our schooldays. It is now on the way to becoming a national product.

The company is also planning to go public at the earliest possible date.

To its new chief, we wish lasting success.

KAPITEL 40

Eine Frage der Etikette

Für alle Bürgerlichen, also nichtadligen Personen *(commoner)* verwendet man als Anrede *Mister*, das in der geschriebenen Form immer *Mr* lautet, jedoch auch dann *Mister* gesprochen wird:
– Mr John E. Martin.
An diesem Beispiel sieht man auch, daß der Vorname immer vor dem Nachnamen genannt wird und der zweite Vorname, sofern ein solcher existiert, als Initiale auftaucht.
Wesentlich formeller und heute sehr selten ist der Ausdruck *Esquire*. Man sagt: – John E. Martin, Esq.
Achtung: Der Vorname wird hinter *Lord* niemals alleine benutzt, sondern immer mit dem Nachnamen: Lord (David) Werret.
Das Gegenteil gilt für *Sir*: Sir Peter (Stafford).

CHAPTER 40

EXERCISES

Comprehension

Lesen Sie den Dialog aufmerksam durch. Beantworten Sie dann die nachfolgenden Fragen, und zwar immer in ganzen Sätzen:

1. Are all the Board members well informed about the decisions to be made?
2. Why isn't Sir Peter attending the meeting? **3.** Where are the Board members supposed to have lunch? **4.** What item always comes first on a board meeting agenda? **5.** Have the members already had a chance to read Susan's report?
6. What does Lord Werrett like especially about Susan's report? **7.** Is Susan pessimistic about the launching of the new line of ice-cream fudge bars?
8. Why is going public an important step for Birtwhistle's? **9.** Does Lord Werrett's decision to resign from the chairmanship come as a suprise to his fellow members?
10. According to Lord Werrett, will there be a limit to UC's support to Birtwhistle's?

Translation

1. Er hätte vom Flughafen aus anrufen können, um sich dafür zu entschuldigen, daß er nicht teilnehmen kann. **2.** Für diejenigen, die über Nacht bleiben möchten, werden im Gasthof Zimmer zur Verfügung stehen. **3.** Das Protokoll faßt die Hauptpunkte zusammen, die während der letzten Vorstandssitzung diskutiert und genehmigt wurden. **4.** Im Anhang des Berichts finden Sie die neusten vierteljährlichen Verkaufszahlen. **5.** Susan wollte nur unterstreichen, daß eine Umstrukturierung der Firma eine größere Flexibilität im Management erlauben würde. **6.** Neue Investitionen werden erforderlich sein, um die Produktionskapazität zu maximieren. **7.** Durch die Einführung einer neuen Produktpalette wurden unsere Verkäufe, ebenso wie unsere Gewinne, gesteigert.
8. Für das Unternehmen bedeutet der Gang an die Börse die Öffnung des Kapitals für auswärtige Investoren. **9.** Der Vorstand hat die Vorschläge gebilligt, die vom Vorsitzenden präsentiert wurden. **10.** Für eine Geschäftsfrau wie Susan ist es die größte Belohnung, Vorsitzende und geschäftsführende Direktorin zu werden.

KAPITEL 40

LÖSUNGSVORSCHLÄGE

Verständnisübung

1. Yes, Lord Werrett has had the opportunity to discuss them with each one individually. **2.** Because his flight from Moscow was delayed, he missed the connecting flight to Leeds-Bradford. **3.** They are supposed to have lunch at the Crown Inn where they have reservations. **4.** The item that always comes first is the approval of the minutes of the previous meeting. **5.** Yes. It was appended to the minutes sent to them before the meeting. **6.** He likes the fact that maximising human resources remains uppermost in her mind. **7.** No. On the contrary, she expects that it will boost sales. **8.** It should enable the company to secure capital for future investments. **9.** No. He had already announced his decision to resign (*or* to step down from office). **10.** Yes, indeed! UC will contine to support Birtwhistle's only as long as it is in its interest.

Übersetzungsübung

1. He could have called (*or* rung up) from the airport to apologise for not attending. **2.** Rooms will be available at the inn for those who want (*or* wish) to stay overnight. **3.** The minutes summarise the main items (*or* issues) discussed and approved during the previous board meeting. **4.** You will find appended to the report the latest quarterly sales figures. **5.** Susan just wished to stress that restructuring the firm would allow greater flexibility in management. **6.** New investments will be needed (*or* necessary) to maximise production capacity. **7.** Our sales, as well as (*or* together with) our profits, have been boosted by the launching of a new range of products. **8.** For the company, going public means opening (*or* the opening of) its capital to outside investors. **9.** The Board has endorsed the proposals put forward (*or* presented) by the Chair(man). **10.** For a businesswoman like Susan, to become Chairman (*or* Chairperson) and Managing Director is the best reward.

CHAPTER 40

Vocabulary Revision (Chapters 31-40)

Vervollständigen Sie die folgenden Sätze (ein oder mehrere Wörter pro Lücke):

1. One way of resisting foreign competition consists in raising (...) duties. **2.** Our supply of (...) materials is guaranteed by long-term contracts on (...) markets. **3.** Quite a few of our products are sold under the distributors' own (...). **4.** A (...) family is one in which both husband and wife work. **5.** The British equivalent of president or chief executive officer is (...). **6.** The profit and loss account item in a British company's balance sheet represents the (...). **7.** When shares are issued above par, the surplus value is called (...). **8.** A loan can be secured by (...) or (...). **9.** With our current products, we cannot hope to achieve much deeper (...) penetration. **10.** Because my plane was delayed by fog, I missed the (...) flight.

DO!

***Be a social mixer: cultivate human contacts at all levels.
They are essential in Britain as well as in the US.***

KAPITEL 40

Lösung der Wortschatzübung

1. customs.
2. raw, commodity.
3. brand names.
4. two-career.
5. managing director.
6. accumulated reserves.
7. share premium (UK), additional paid-in capital, paid-in surplus (US).
8. mortgage, pledge.
9. market.
10. connecting.

 DON'T!

Don't applaud during a board meeting to express approval after a speech. Just say: 'Hear, hear!'.
For more forceful approval, tap the table.

INDEX

Dieser deutsch-englische Index umfaßt die gesamte Wirtschaftsterminologie, die Sie in diesem Kurs kennengelernt haben. Die in der mittleren Spalte angegebenen Zahlen weisen auf das Kapitel hin, in dem der jeweilige Begriff zum ersten Mal aufgetaucht ist. Dahinter finden Sie Angaben zu dem Teil des Kapitels, in dem sich der Begriff befindet. Die Abkürzungen haben folgende Bedeutungen:

Dia:	Dialog
A:	**ANMERKUNGEN**
Dok:	Dokument
I:	Themenbezogene Zusatzinformationen (in den einzelnen Kapiteln mit [i] gekennzeichnet)
Ü:	Übung

DEUTSCH	**KAPITEL**	**ENGLISCH**
A		
Abbau einschränkender Bestimmungen	37 I	deregulation
Abbildung	14 Dia	figure
abbrechen	27 A	to break down
Abendkurse	16 I	night school, evening classes
Abendschule	16 I	night school, evening classes
Abfallbeseitigung	32 Dok	waste disposal
Abfluß (von Kapital usw.)	31 Dok	outflow
Abfolge	24 Dia	sequence
abkühlen	24 Dia	to cool down
Ablauf	9 Dia	working
Ablehnung	3 Ü	refusal
Ablenkungs-	34 Dia	diversionary
abnehmen	11 Ü	to decline
Abrechnung	28 Dia	settlement
abrufen	19 Dia	to retrieve
Absatz	31 Dia	sales
Absatzprognose	21 Dok	sales forecast
abschätzen	6 A	to appraise, to assess
abschließen	9 Dia	to complete
Abschluß	38 Ü	completion
Abschlußprüfung	1 Dia	finals, final examination
abstürzen (Preise)	22 Ü	to plummet
Abteilung	4 Dia	department
abträglich	32 Dok	detrimental
Abwechslung	34 A	diversion
AG (Aktiengesellschaft)	4 A	public limited company, Plc (UK), corporation (US)
Ahnung, keine ~ von etw. haben	20 Dia	not to have a clue
Akademiker	1 Dia	postgraduate (GB), graduate (US)
Akkreditiv, unwiderrufliches	28 A	irrevocable letter of credit

414

Akkreditiv	28	Dia	letter of credit
Akronym	34	Ü	acronym
Aktenschrank	13	A	filing-cabinet
Aktie	4	Dia	share (UK), stock (US)
Aktien	4	A	shares (UK), stock (US)
Aktienagio	36	Dok	share premium (UK), paid-in surplus (US), capital in excess of par value (US)
Aktienbörse	4	Dok	stock exchange
Aktiengesellschaft	5	Dia	corporation (US)
Aktiengesellschaft, eintragen als	5	A	to incorporate
Aktienkapital, aufgerufenes	36	Dok	called-up capital (UK)
Aktionär	4	A	shareholder (UK), stockholder (US)
Aktionärsversammlung einberufen	32	A	to summon a shareholders' meeting
Aktiva	10	A	asset(s)
aktivieren	13	A	to file
Aktivitäten	2	Dia	activity
aktuell	6	Ü	current
aktuell	35	Ü	up to date
Allgemeines Zoll- und Handelsabkommen	31	Dia	GATT (General Agreement on Tariffs and Trade)
Allgemeinwissen	5	Dia	general culture
Amt antreten	40	A	to take office, to come into office
Amt niederlegen	40	Ü	to resign
Amt	40	Dia	office
Amtstätigkeit aufnehmen	40	A	to take office, to come into office
andauern	30	Dia	to last
andauernd	40	Dok	lasting
ändern	21	Dia	to alter
Anerkennung	24	Dok	accreditation
anfordern	28	Dia	to request
Anforderung, auf ~ von	9	Dok	at the request of
Anforderung	34	Dia	demand
Anfrage	13	Dia	enquiry
Angebot	37	Dia	bid
angehen gegen	5	Dia	to counter
angemessen	9	Dok	appropriate
angenehm	27	Dia	congenial
angesammelte Reserven	36	Dia	accumulated reserves, shareholders' funds (UK), stockholders' equity (US)
Angestellte(r)	9	Dia	white collar (worker), staff
angrenzendes Gebiet	31	I	proximity zone
Angst haben	38	Dia	to worry
anhaltender Druck	37	Dia	sustained pressure
Anhang zum Jahresabschluß	36	Dia	note to the financial statements
anhängen	40	Dia	to append
ankurbeln	23	Dok	to boost
Anlage	10	Dok	encl(osure)
Anlage	24	Dia	facilities
Anlaufkosten	13	A	start-up costs
annehmen	9	Dia	to assume

anordnen	13 Dia	to lay out
Anrainerstaaten des Pazifiks	5 Dok	Pacific rim
Anrede	1 I	greetings (correspondence)
anregen	9 Dia	to stimulate, to boost
Anreiz (Leistungs-)	22 Dok	incentive, inducement
Anreiz	38 Dia	incentive
Anreizprämie	26 A	incentive bonus, incentive payment
Anreizsystem (Leistungs-)	26 A	incentive scheme
Anruf	12 Dia	buzz, ring, phone call
anschließen, sich einer Sache	28 Dia	to plug (into)
Anschluß	13 Dia	extension
Anschlußflug	40 Dia	connecting flight
ansetzen	9 Dok	to schedule
ansprechen, Probleme	32 Dia	to raise (problems)
Ansprechpartner	5 Dia	corresponding number
Ansprüche gerichtlich geltend machen	31 A	to enforce one´s claims by suit
Anstecker	15 Dok	lapel pin
Antwort	9 Dok	response, reply
Anwalt	4 Dok	solicitor
appellieren, an jdn.	33 Dia	to call upon s.b.
Arbeit wiederaufnehmen	12 Dia	to resume work
arbeiten	5 Dia	hier: to operate
Arbeiter(in)	9 Dia	blue collar (worker), line
Arbeiterschaft	10 Dia	labour force
Arbeitsabläufe	6 Dok	operations
Arbeitsamt	30 A	labour exchange
arbeitseinsparend	34 Dia	labour-saving
Arbeitsethik	20 I	ethics of work
Arbeitskollege	11 Dia	fellow worker
Arbeitskräfteabbau	38 Dia	job cut
Arbeitslosigkeit	11 Dok	unemployment
Arbeitsniederlegung	11 Dia	work stoppage
Arbeitsplatzrechner	14 Dia	work station
Arbeitsstreit	36 Dia	labour dispute
Arbeitsunfall	26 A	on-the-job accident
arbeitswütig sein	19 Dia	to be a workaholic
Archivierung	13 Dia	filing
arrangieren	40 Dok	to engineer
Artikel (im Handel)	13 Ü	item
Artikel (Zeitungs-)	25 Ü	(feature) article
Atempause	31 Dia	relief
Auf und Ab	32 Dia	rise and fall
Aufbaustudium für Manager	16 Dia	postgraduate management training
Aufenthalt	27 Ü	stay
auffällig	25 Dia	flashy
auffordern, jdn.	35 Ü	to call (on sb.)
Aufgabe, jd.´s ~ sein	32 Dia	to be up (to)
aufgliedern	27 Dia	to break down
Aufgliederung	27 A	breakdown
aufhören	34 Dia	to quit

German	Ref	EN
Aufmerksamkeit erregen	23 Dia	to grab s.o.´s attention
aufrichtig	20 Dia	straightforward
Aufruhr	31 Dia	turmoil
aufschlüsseln	27 Dia	to break down
Aufschlüsselung	27 A	breakdown
aufsplittern, Aktien	37 A	to split (shares)
aufspüren	22 Dia	to ferret out
Aufstellung des unverteilten Reingewinns	36 Dia	statement of movement of reserves (UK), retained earnings statement (US)
Aufteilung	7 Dia	lay-out
Auftrag, in ~ geben (Marktstudie)	18 Ü	to commission (a market study)
Auftrag, jdm. einen ~ erteilen	26 Dok	to place an order with s.o.
auftreten	6 Dia	to arise
aufzeichnen	33 A	to record
ausarbeiten	21 Dia	to devise, to work out
Ausbeute	9 A	output
ausbeuten	36 A	to milk
ausbilden	2 Dia	to train
Ausbildung	2 A	training
Ausbildung von Führungskräften	2 Dia	management training
Ausbildung an der Arbeitsstelle	26 Dia	on-the-job training
Ausbildungszeit	2 A	training period
ausbrechen (Streik)	11 Dia	to break out (strike)
Ausbreitung	24 Dok	proliferation
ausdrücken	37 Dia	to spell out
ausfallen (Maschine)	27 A	to break down
ausführen	19 Dia	to perform
ausfüllen, Formular	9 A	to complete, to fill in (UK), to fill out (US) (a form)
Ausgabe	9 A	output
Ausgaben im Reiseverkehr	31 Dok	tourist spending
Ausgangskorb (Geschäftspost)	13 Dia	out-tray
ausgeben	10 Dok	to issue
ausgeben (Schuldschein)	8 Dia	to issue
ausgeben (Aktien)	37 Dia	to issue
ausgleichen	30 Dia	to offset
Aushang	7 Dia	notice
Ausland, im	34 Dok	abroad
Auslands-	34 Dok	overseas
auslösen	33 A	to trigger
Auslöser	33 A	trigger
ausmachen	23 Dia	to make up
ausnutzen (Gelegenheit)	28 Dok	to take advantage (of)
ausrufen, einen Streik ~	11 Ü	to call a strike
ausscheiden	39 Ü	to drop out
Ausschreibung	37 A	invitation for bids
Außendienst, im	9 Ü	in the field
Außenhandelsdefizit	31 Dok	trade deficit, trade gap
Außenhandelsüberschuß	31 Dok	trade surplus
Außenstände	36 Dok	debtor(s) (UK), account(s) receivable (US)

Außenwerbung	23	Dia	outdoor display
außergewöhnlich	23	Dia	outstanding
Aussichten	3	Dia	prospects
ausspionieren, jdn.	21	A	to snoop on s.b.
Ausstellung	33	Dia	exhibition
austauschen	27	Ü	to switch products
ausüben (Macht)	11	Dok	to wield
Ausverkauf	27	Ü	bargain sale
auswählen	10	Dia	to select
Autobahn	14	Dok	highway (US), motorway (UK)
Autofahrer	11	I	motorist

B

Balkendiagramm	19	Dia	bar-graph
Bankgebühren	28	A	bank charges
Bankgeschäfte	8	Dia	banking operations
Bankguthaben	36	Dok	cash in bank
Bankrott	28	A	bankruptcy
Bankscheck	28	Dia	banker's draft
Banksektor	35	Dia	banking sector
Bankwechsel	28	Dia	banker's draft
Barbestand	36	Dok	cash in/on hand
Bargeld	8	A	cash (in/on hand)
Barmittel	8	A	cash
Barzahlungsrabatt	22	Dok	cash discount, discount for cash
Basis-	39	Dia	core
bearbeiten	9	Dia	to process
bearbeiten	27	Dia	to handle
Bebauungsbestimmung	33	Dia	zoning regulation
Bedenken	18	Ü	misgivings
Bedingungen	3	Dok	terms, conditions
bedrohen	31	Dia	to threaten
beeinträchtigen	40	Dok	to impair
beenden	9	Dia	to complete
befassen, sich ~ mit	24	A	to cope with
Befehlskette	9	I	chain of command
befördern	10	Dia	to promote, to upgrade
Beförderung	10	A	promotion
Befragte(r)	18	Dok	respondent
begierig	20	Dok	eager
beginnen, mit etw. neu ~	16	Dok	to embark
behandeln	9	Dia	to process
behaupten	9	Dia	to claim
behindern	24	Dia	to hamper
beitragsfreie Betriebspension	3	A	non-contributory pension scheme
beitragspflichtige Pensionskasse	3	A	contributory pension scheme
bekannter Markenname	35	Dia	household name
belästigen	21	Ü	to bother
belaufen, sich ~ auf	36	Dia	to amount (to)

418

Belegschaft	10	Dia	labour force
Belegschaftswechsel	12	Dia	(staff) turnover
Belohnung	10	Dia	reward
benutzerfreundlich	19	Dok	user-friendly
Benutzungsgebühr	22	Ü	toll
Berater	9	Dok	consultant
berechnen	32	Ü	to compute
Berechnungen anstellen	19	Dia	to crunch numbers
Bereich	8	Ü	field, area
bereitstellen	8	Dok	to provide
bereitstellen, Geld	23	Dia	to allocate money
bereitstellen, Essen	24	A	to cater for
Bericht erstatten, jdm.	18	Dia	to report (to sb.)
Bericht	19	Dia	report
berufliche Zufriedenheit	3	Dia	job satisfaction
Berufsausbildung	12	I	technical training, vocational training
Berufsberatungszentrum (GB)	1	Dia	Careers Office
Berufserfahrung	6	Ü	professional experience
Berufsstand	4	Dok	profession
Berufung	32	A	summons
beschädigt	14	Ü	damaged
beschimpfen, jdn.	33	Dia	to call (sb.) names
Beschwerde	32	Dia	complaint
beseitigen	37	Dia	to erase
besessen sein	32	Dia	to be obsessed
besitzen	6	Ü	to own
besorgt sein über	32	Dia	to be anxious (about)
Bestechungsgeld	22	Ü	bribe
Bestellformular	13	Dok	order form
Bestimmung	7	Dia	regulation
Bestreben	39	Dia	ambition
Besuch abstatten	27	Dia	to pay a call
Beteiligung (Anteil)	37	Dia	stake
Beteiligung an	40	Dia	involvement in
betonen	10	Dok	to point out, to stress
Betracht, in ~ ziehen	6	Dia	to consider, to take into account
betrauen, jdn.	40	Dok	to assign sb.
betrieblich	32	Dia	operating
betriebliche Vertrauensperson	11	Dia	shop steward
Betriebs-	32	Dia	operating
Betriebseinnahmen	32	A	operating income
Betriebsunfall	10	Dok	labour injury, on-the-job accident
Betriebsverlust	32	A	operating loss
Betriebswirtschaft	16	Dok	business administration
Betrug durch Firmenangehörige	30	I	bonding
betrügen	23	Dok	to highjack
Beurteilung	6	Dia	appraisal, assessment
bevorstehend	25	Dia	impending
Beweis	37	Dia	evidence
bewerben, s. um eine Stelle ~	3	Dia	to apply for (a job)

Deutsch	Seite	Typ	English
Bewerber	1	Dok	candidate, applicant
Bewerbung	3	Ü	application
bewerten	6	A	to appraise, to assess
Bewertung	6	Dia	appraisal, assessment
bewirten	25	Ü	to entertain
bezahlter Urlaub	26	Dia	paid vacation
beziehen, sich ~ auf	38	Dia	to bear (on)
Beziehung	10	Dia	interrelationship
Bezugsrecht auf neue Aktien	3	A	stock option
Bibliothek	19	Dia	library
Bilanz	10	Dia	balance sheet
Bildungsurlaub, einjähriger bezahlter ~ (GB)	20	Ü	sabbatical leave
Bildunterschrift	25	Ü	caption
billigen	33	Dia	to endorse
Billigung	33	A	endorsement
Bleistift	13	Dok	pencil
Bleistiftspitzer	13	Dok	pencil-sharpener
Bluff	26	Dia	bluff
Bonität	30	Ü	credit worthiness
Bonitätsbeurteilung	28	Dia	credit rating
Bonus	23	Dia	bonus
Bonze	34	Ü	big shot
Börse	30	A	stock exchange
Börse, an die ~ gehen	40	Dia	to go public
Börsenaufsichtsbehörde	36	I	Securities and Exchange Commission (SEC) (US)
Börsenschluß	32	Ü	close
Brainstorming	21	Dok	brainstorming
Branche	22	Dia	industry
Briefumschlag	13	Dok	envelope
Britischer Normenverband	7	A	British Standards Institute (BSI)
Brokerprovision	37	I	brokerage fee
Bruttoeinkommen	32	A	gross income
Buchführung	1	A	accounting
Buchhalter	36	A	book-keeper
Buchhaltung	1	A	accounting, book-keeping
Bummelstreik	11	Dia	go-slow
Büro	7	Dok	office
Büroklammer	13	Dia	paper-clip
Büromaterial	13	Dok	stationery
Bürotechnik	14	I	office automation, bureautics

C

Deutsch	Seite	Typ	English
Cash Flow	27	Ü	cash flow
Chancen	21	Dia	odds
Chef	18	Dia	boss
Computer	7	Dia	computer
computergesteuert	7	Dia	computer-controlled

computergestützte Produktionsverwaltung	7	Dia	computerised production management
computergestützte Ausbildung	19	Dok	computer-assisted education
Computernetz	8	A	computer network
computersüchtig sein	19	Dia	to be a computaholic

D

Dach und Fach, unter ~ bringen	38	Dia	to finalise
Darlehensnehmer	38	A	borrower
Datei	19	Ü	file
Daten	14	Dia	data
Datenbank	6	Ü	database
Datenverarbeitung	19	Dia	data processing
Dauerauftrag	28	Ü	standing order
Debitoren	36	Dok	debtor(s) (UK), account(s) receivable (US)
defekt	32	Dia	defective
Defizit	36	A	shortage
Depositenquittung	8	Dia	certificate of deposit (CD)
detailliert	9	Dok	detailed
Devisen	30	A	exchange
Devisenbörse	30	Dia	currency exchange
Devisenkontrolle	31	Dok	currency control
Devisenmakler	30	Dia	trader in currency exchange
Devisenterminhandel	30	A	futures exchange
Dienst	8	Dia	service
Dienst nach Vorschrift	11	Dia	work-to-rule
Dienst(leistung)	28	Dia	service
Dienstalter	7	Dia	seniority
Diplom der philosophischen Fakultät	1	Dia	BA (Bachelor of Arts)
Diplom	1	A	diploma, degree
Diplom in Betriebswirtschaft	17	Dia	Bachelor of Business Administration (BBA)
direkt	20	Dia	straightforward
Direktheit	28	I	directness
Direktverkauf	25	Dia	personal selling, direct selling
Diskette	19	Ü	floppy disk, diskette
Diskontsatz	21	A	discount rate
Diversifikation	6	Dia	diversification
Dividende	4	Dok	dividend
Doktor (Titel)	1	Dia	PhD (Doctor of Philosophy)
Doppelverdiener, Familie der	34	Dia	two-career family
drastische Maßnahmen ergreifen	31	A	to crack down (on)
Drei (Note)	1	A	third (class honours)
Druck ausüben	22	Dia	to squeeze
Drucker	14	A	printer
DTP (Desktop Publishing)	14	Dia	desktop publishing
durch	32	Dia	by means of
Durchblick	26	Dia	savvy
Durcheinander	31	Dia	turmoil
durchführen	18	Dia	to carry out

Durchschlagpapier	13	Dia	flimsy
durchsehen	36	Dia	to go over
durchsetzen	31	A	to enforce
Durchsetzung	31	A	enforcement
Durchsetzung eines Rechtsanspruchs	31	A	enforcement of a right
durchstellen (Anruf)	5	Dia	to put through

E

Echtzeitverarbeitung	6	A	real-time processing
Effizienz	24	Dia	efficiency
Ehemaliger	2	Dok	old-boy
eigenartig	28	Dia	peculiar
Eigenkapital	4	A	shareholders' funds (UK), stockholders' equity (US), capital ownership
Eigenschaft	23	Dia	feature
Eigentum(srecht)	6	Dok	ownership
einberufen	32	A	to summon
einbetten	5	Dia	to integrate
einführen	18	A	to launch
Einführung	18	Dia	launching
Eingabe	9	Dia	input
Eingangskorb (Geschäftspost)	13	Dia	in-tray
Eingangswert	9	Dia	input
eingetragenes Warenzeichen	32	A	registered trade mark
Einhalt gebieten	23	Dok	to curb
Einhaltung (von Bestimmungen)	10	Dok	compliance
Einkäufer	22	Dia	shopper
Einkaufsleiter	27	Dia	purchasing manager
Einkommen	26	Dia	income
Einkommensteuer	4	Dok	income tax
Einlage	37	A	stake
einlösen (Scheck)	8	Dia	to cash
Einmischung	40	Dia	involvement
Einnahmen	10	Dia	return, yield, revenues, income
einrichten	33	Dia	to set up
Einrichtung	24	Dok	setting-up
Einrichtungen	33	Dia	facilities
Eins (Note)	1	Dia	first (class honours)
Einsatzmenge	9	Dia	input
Einsatztruppe	9	I	task force
einschränken	35	Dia	to cut back on
Einsparungen	8	Dia	savings
einstellen	2	A	to hire, to take on, to recruit
Einstellung	2	A	hiring, recruitment
eintreten (in eine Firma)	10	Dia	to join
Einzelhandel	1	Dia	retail distribution, retailing
Einzelhandelsgeschäft	27	Dia	retail store
Einzelhändler	25	Dia	retailer
Einzelkaufmann	4	Dok	sole trader (UK), sole proprietor (US)

einziehen (Forderungen)	28 Dia	to collect
Einziehung	31 Ü	collection
elektronische Post	14 Dia	(E-)mail
Eliteauswahl	2 Dia	"milk round"
Emissionshaus	8 Dok	investment bank (US), issuing house (UK)
Empfänger	14 I	addressee, recipient
Engagement	34 Dia	commitment, involvement
engagieren, jdn.	14 Dia	to get (sb.) involved, to involve sb.
engagiert (sein)	29 Ü	(to be) involved
Entgelt	10 Dia	reward
enthalten, sich	40 Dia	to abstain
entlassen	11 Dia	to dismiss, to lay off, to make redundant
Entlassung	11 A	firing, sacking, dismissal, lay-off, redundancy
entlohnen	10 Dia	to compensate, to reward
entnehmen	9 Dia	to guess, to gather
Entschädigung	26 Dia	compensation
entscheiden, sich für etw.	10 Dia	to opt for
Entscheidungsfindung	9 I	decision making
Entscheidungszentrum	31 I	decision centre
entschieden	40 Dok	energetic
entschuldigen, sich	40 Dia	to apologise
entspannt	20 Dia	relaxed
entspannter Moment	34 Dia	downbeat moment
entwickeln	9 Dia	to develop
entwickeln (konzipieren)	18 Dia	to design
Entwurf (Tätigkeit)	21 Dok	design, designing
Entwurf	23 Dia	rough, draft
entziffern	14 Ü	to decipher
Epidemie	10 Dok	epidemic
erfahren in	6 Ü	conversant with
erfahren	9 Dia	experienced
erfahren	8 Dok	to undergo, to suffer
erfassen	19 Dia	to capture, to grasp
Erfolg haben	16 Dia	to make the grade
erfordern	39 Dia	to require
erfüllen (Bedürfnisse)	10 A	to meet
Ergebnis	18 Dia	finding
ergreifen	25 Dia	to grasp
erhöhen	36 Dia	to raise
Erklärung, öffentliche	37 Dia	(public) statement
Erleichterung	31 Dia	relief
Erlös	6 Dia	profit(s)
Ermittler	18 Ü	investigator
ermöglichen	9 Dok	to enable
Eröffnung, feierliche	25 Dok	grand opening
Eröffnungsansprache	33 Dok	opening statement
erreichen	10 Dia	to achieve
erreichen (Ziel)	23 Dia	to meet (a goal)
erstatten	26 Dia	to reimburse

erstrecken, sich	9 Dok	to extend (over)
Ertrag	6 Dia	profit(s), return, yield
Ertrag aus investiertem Kapital	10 A	return on investment (ROI)
Ertragsrechnung	36 Dia	statement of income
Ertragssumme	22 Dia	rate of return
Erwartungen	24 Dia	expectations
erweisen, sich ~ als	6 Ü	to prove to be
erweitern	33 Dia	to enlarge, to broaden
erwerben	38 Dia	to acquire
Erzeugnis	30 Dia	commodity
Erzwingung	31 A	enforcement
Etikett	32 Dok	label
Europäische Wirtschaftsgemeinschaft	7 A	EEC (European Economic Community)
Europäische Gemeinschaft	7 Dia	EC (European Community)
Europäische Union	7 A	European Union
Eventualfall	28 Dia	contingency
Eventualität	28 Dia	contingency
Examen ohne Prädikat	1 A	pass degree
extern	9 Dok	outside

F

fachsimpeln	35 Dia	to talk shop
Fähigkeiten	6 Ü	skill(s)
Fakturierung	19 Dok	invoicing, billing
Fakultät für Unternehmensmanagement	16 Dia	school of business
fallen	39 Ü	to dip
fällig	36 Dia	due
Fälligkeit	30 I	maturity
Fälligkeitsdatum	30 A	maturity date
Fallstudie	26 Dia	case study
Falsch-	21 Ü	counterfeit
Fälscher	21 Ü	counterfeiter, forger
Fälschung	21 Ü	fake, counterfeit
Faszination	25 Dia	thrill
Fehlbetrag	36 A	shortage
Fehlschlag	18 Dia	failure
fehlschlagen	37 Dia	to fail
Feinheit	24 Dia	sharpness
Ferngespräch	5 Dia	long-distance call
Fernschreiber	14 Dia	telex
Fernunterricht	16 I	distance-learning
fertige Produkte	31 I	manufactured goods, finished goods
fertigen	7 Dia	to make, to manufacture, to produce
Fertigung	6 Dok	operational level, (production) line
Fertigungsverfahren	32 A	manufacturing process
festangestellte Mitarbeiter	11 Dok	(salaried) employee, member of staff, wage-earner
festsetzen	22 Dia	to set
festsitzen	39 Dia	to get bogged down

feuern	11	Dia	to sack, to fire, to dismiss, to lay off, to make redundant
Filiale	8	Dia	branch
Filzstift	13	Dok	felt(-tip) pen
Finanzabteilung	4	Dia	financial department
Finanzbehörde (GB/USA)	36	I	Inland Revenue (UK), Internal Revenue Service, IRS (US)
Finanzbeihilfe	17	A	grant
Finanzdirektor	36	Dia	financial manager
finanzieren	15	Dia	to sponsor
Finanzmanagement	8	Dia	cash management
Finanzmarkt	8	Dia	capital market, financial market
Finanzterminmarkt	30	A	financial futures market
Finanzverwaltung (USA)	27	I	Internal Revenue Service, IRS
Firma	1	Dok	company
Firmenanteile	3	A	stock option
Firmenanwalt	2	A	corporate lawyer
Firmenflugzeug	2	A	corporate jet
Firmenimage	33	Dia	corporate image
Firmenkunde	8	Dok	corporate customer
Firmensitz	2	A	corporate headquarters
Firmensitz haben in	5	Dia	(to be) headquartered in
Firmenvorstand	5	Dok	board (of directors)
Firmenwagen	3	A	company car
fix und fertig	34	Dia	tuckered out
Flexibilität	40	Dia	flexibility
Fließband	24	Ü	assembly line
Flitterwochen	32	Dia	honeymoon
Folgetermin	26	Dok	follow-up date
Fonds für außerordentliche Rückstellungen	28	A	contingency fund, contingency reserve
fordern	11	Dia	to demand
fördern	15	Dia	to sponsor
Forderung	12	Dia	claim
Förderung	9	A	output
Formular	26	Dok	form
Formulierung	18	Dia	wording
Forscher	1	Dia	researcher
Forschung und Entwicklung	6	Dok	research and development
Forschung	1	Dia	research
Forschungsziele	18	Dia	research objectives
Fortbildung	12	Dia	continuing education, further education, adult education
fortfahren	40	Dia	to proceed
Fragebogen	18	Dia	questionnaire
freier Wettbewerb	32	I	free competition
Freistellung	17	Dia	waiver
Fremdkapital	40	Dia	outside capital
Fremdwährung	30	A	foreign exchange
Frist	18	Dia	deadline

führen zu	9 Dia	to lead
führend	8 Dok	leading
Führung	38 Dia	leadership
Führungsebene	34 I	executive level
Führungskraft	3 Dia	executive, manager
Führungsnachwuchs	2 Dia	trainee manager
Führungsspitze	6 Ü	top management
Funktion	2 Dia	function, office
funktionieren	6 Dia	to work
Fusion	11 Dok	merger

G

ganztägig	16 Dok	full-time
Garantie	22 Dok	warranty (US), guarantee (UK)
garantieren	30 Dia	to secure, to guarantee
Gastronomie	24 A	catering
Gebietsvertreter	27 Dia	area representative
Gebot	37 Dia	bid
Gebühr	22 Ü	fee
Gedächtnis, im ~ behalten	30 Dia	to bear in mind
Gefahr	28 Ü	hazard
gefälscht	21 Dok	counterfeit
Gegner	30 Dia	opponent
Gehalt	3 Dia	salary
Gehaltserhöhung	10 A	salary increase
gekreuzter Scheck	8 A	crossed cheque
Geld scheffeln	1 Dia	to rake
Geld aufbringen für	16 Dia	to put up money for
Geld sparen	17 Ü	to save money
Geld aus dem Fenster werfen	21 Dia	to fling money out of the window
Geldmarkt	8 Dia	capital market, financial market
Gelegenheit	8 Dia	opportunity
Gemecker	32 Dia	gripes
Gemeinde	15 Dia	community
genehmigen	5 Dia	to approve, to endorse
Genehmigung	39 Dok	approval
Generaldirektor	6 Dia	chief executive officer (CEO) (US), chairman and managing director (UK)
Generalstreik	11 Dia	full-scale strike
gerechtwerden (Anforderungen)	10 A	to meet
gerichtliche Vorladung	32 A	summons
Gerücht	35 Dia	rumour
Gesamteinkommen	32 A	gross income
Geschäft	2 Dia	business
Geschäft (Laden)	39 Dia	store
Geschäft(sabschluß)	20 Ü	deal, dealing
Geschäftsbank	8 Dok	commercial bank (US), deposit bank (UK)
Geschäftsbereich	39 Dia	portfolio
Geschäftsbücher	36 Dia	company books

426

Geschäftserträge	32 A	operating income
Geschäftsfrau	1 Dia	businesswoman
geschäftsführender Direktor	16 Dia	managing director (MD)
Geschäftsführer	16 Dia	managing director (MD)
Geschäftsinhaber	4 Dok	shopkeeper
Geschäftsjahr	36 A	financial year (UK), fiscal year (US)
Geschäftsmann	3 Dia	businessman
Geschäftspartner	31 Dia	associate
Geschäftsreise, auf ~ sein	14 Dia	to travel, to be away (on business)
Geschäftsverkehr	32 Dia	dealing
Geschmacksprobe	21 Ü	(blind) tasting
Geschmacksprüfung	21 Dia	sensorial evaluation
Gesellschaftskapital	4 A	shareholders' funds (UK), stockholders' equity (US)
Gesetz	4 Dok	law
gesichertes Darlehen	38 Dia	secured loan
gestalten	13 Dia	to lay out
Gestaltung	13 A	lay-out
gesunder Menschenverstand	18 Dia	(common) sense
Gesundheitswesen	33 Dia	public health
Gewerbe	24 Ü	trade
Gewerkschaft	11 Dia	(trade) union (UK), (labor) union (US)
Gewinn	6 Dia	profit(s), return, yield
Gewinn, nicht ausgeschütteter	36 Dia	retained earnings (US), undistributed surplus (UK)
Gewinn, thesaurierter	36 Dia	retained earnings (US), undistributed surplus (UK)
Gewinn vor Steuern	36 Dok	profit before taxation (UK), earnings before income tax, EBIT (US)
Gewinn- und Verlustrechnung (GB)	36 Dia	profit and loss account (UK)
Gewinn- und Verlustrechnung (USA)	36 Dia	income statement, statement of earnings and retained earnings (US)
Gewinnaufschlag	22 Dia	mark-up, profit margin
Gewinnbeteiligung	38 Dia	profit-sharing
Gewinnspanne	22 Dia	mark-up, profit margin
gewöhnen, sich	20 Dia	to adjust to
glanzvoll	39 Dia	glamorous
Gläubiger	38 A	lender
GmbH	4 A	private limited company (UK), corporation (US)
Greenwich-Zeit	5 I	Greenwich Mean Time (GMT)
Grippe	10 Dok	flu
Größe	24 Dia	size
Großhändler	27 A	wholesaler
gründen	5 Dia	to found
Gründer	5 Ü	founder
Grundkapital	4 Dia	capital stock
gründlich	10 Ü	thoroughly
Grundsätze ordnungsgemüßer Buchführung (USA)	36 I	Generally accepted accounting principles, GAAP (US)

427

Grundsätze ordnungsgemäßer Buchführung (GB)	36 I	Statements of standard accounting practice, SSAP (UK)
grünes Licht geben	12 Dok	to give the go-ahead
Gummiband	13 Dok	rubber band
gutheißen	33 Dia	to endorse
Gutschein	25 Dia	(money-off) coupon

H

Haftpflicht	30 I	liability
Haftung	4 Dok	liability, responsability
Haken	31 A	rub
Halbfabrikate	36 Dok	work in progress (WIP)
Handel	5 Dia	trade
handeln	4 Dia	to trade, to negotiate
Handelsbilanz	27 Ü	balance of trade, trade balance
Handelsbilanzüberschuß	31 Dia	trade surplus
Handelskammer	26 Ü	chamber of commerce
Handelsschranke	31 Dok	trade barrier
Handelsspanne	22 Dia	mark-up, profit margin
Handelsware	30 Dia	commodity
Handelswechsel	8 Dia	commercial paper
Händler	30 Dia	trader
Händlerrabatt	22 Dok	trade discount, trade terms
Handwerker	4 Dok	craftsman
Hardliner	31 Dia	hardliner
hart durchgreifen	31 A	to crack down (on)
Haupt-	39 Dia	core, uppermost
Hauptfach	17 Dia	major
Hauptniederlassung	4 Dia	registered/head office, company headquarters (UK), corporate headquarters (US)
Hauptpunkt	40 Dia	main feature
Hauptstraße	11 I	major road (UK), major highway (US)
Hauptverdiener	34 Dia	principle wage-earner
Hauptverkehrszeit	11 Dia	rush hour
Haushaltsgerät	35 A	household appliance
Hausmarkenprodukt	4 Dia	own brand product
Hausratversicherung	35 A	household insurance
Hauswirtschaftslehre	35 A	household economics
Hauszeitung	14 Dia	house magazine
Hedging	30 Dia	hedging
heften	13 A	to staple
Heftklammer	13 Dia	staple
Heftmaschine	13 A	stapler
hektisch	31 Dia	hectic
herausfinden	32 Dia	to find out
herausfordernd	3 Dia	challenging
Herausforderung	6 Ü	challenge
Herausgeber	25 Dok	editor

428

hereinführen, jdn.	7	A	to show s.o. in
hereinschneien	20	Dia	to drop in
herstellen	7	Dia	to make, to manufacture, to produce
herumführen, jdn.	7	Dia	to show (sb.) round
hervorheben	25	Ü	to show off
hervorragende Leistung	34	Dia	excellence
hervorrufen	33	A	to trigger
Hierarchie	9	Dia	hierarchy
High-Tech	14	Dia	high-tech, advanced, state-of-the-art
hinausbegleiten, jdn.	2	Dia	to see (sb.) out, to show (sb.) out
Hintergedanke	35	Ü	ulterior motive
Hintergrund, historischer	35	Ü	(historical) background
Hintergrund	37	Dia	background
Hinterlegungsschein	8	Dia	certificate of deposit (CD)
Hochbegabter	2	Dok	high-flyer
Hochschulabsolvent	1	Dia	postgraduate (GB), graduate (US)
hochspielen	25	Ü	to play up
Hochtechnologie	14	Dia	high-tech, advanced, state-of-the-art
Höflichkeit	27	Dia	courtesy
Höflichkeitsbesuch abstatten	28	Dok	to pay a courtesy call
Höhe, in die ~ schnellen	39	Ü	to skyrocket
höhere Gewalt	30	I	act of God
höherer akademischer Grad in BWL	2	Dia	MBA (Master's Degree in Business Administration)
hohes Tier	34	Ü	big shot
Holding(-Gesellschaft)	38	Dia	holding company (UK), proprietary company (US)
Honorar	10	Dia	reward
Hülle und Fülle, in	34	Dia	galore
Hygiene	7	Dia	hygiene
Hypothek	38	A	mortgage

I

Imitation	21	Dia	knock-off
immaterielle Güter	32	Dia	intangible asset(s)
Implementierung	5	Dia	implementing
implizieren	5	Dia	to imply
Impulskauf	39	I	impulse purchase/buy
Indossament	33	A	endorsement
indossieren, Scheck	33	A	to endorse
Informationen	9	A	information, pieces/elements of information
Informationspaket	4	Dia	information pack
informieren, sich ~ über	35	Dia	to read up on
Inhaberscheck	8	A	bearer cheque
Inhalt	25	Ü	content
Initiative, Sinn für	10	Dia	sense of initiative
Input	9	Dia	input
Insiderhandel	37	Dia	insider trading

Installation	24 Dia	facilities
Intensivkurs	26 Dia	crash course
intern	9 Dia	inner, in-house
Internationaler Normenausschuß	7 A	International Standards Organisation (ISO)
Inventur machen	24 Dia	to take stock of
Inventur	36 A	stocktaking
Investitionsarbeiten im Gange	36 Dia	assets in course of construction (UK), work in process/progress (US)
Investmentbank	8 Dok	investment bank (US), issuing house (UK)
Investmentfonds	27 Ü	unit trust (US), mutual fund (GB)
irreführend (Werbung)	23 Dok	misleading (advertisement, advertising)

J

Jahresabschluß	36 Dia	financial statement
Jahresbericht	4 Dia	annual report
Jahrgang	24 Dia	vintage
Jahrzehnt	11 Dok	decade
jammern	21 Dia	to wail
Just-in-Time-Methode	36 Dia	just-in-time (method of stock management) (JIT)

K

Kaffeepause	6 I	coffee break
kalkuliertes Risiko	30 I	calculated risk
kampfbereit sein	33 Dia	to be up in arms (against)
Kampftruppe, Angehörige der	9 A	line
Kanalisation	33 Dia	sewage system
Kante	32 Dia	edge
Kantine	7 Dok	canteen
Kapital	4 Dia	capital
Kapital, eingefordertes	36 Dok	called-up capital (UK)
Kapital, aus etwas ~ schlagen	33 Dok	to capitalise (on)
Kapitalgesellschaft	5 Dia	corporation (US)
Kapitalmarkt	8 Dia	capital market, financial market
Kapitalverkehr	31 Dok	capital transactions
Kapitalverzinsung	22 Dia	rate of return
Karriere	3 Dia	career
Karriere, steile ~ machen	34 A	to be on the fast track
Karrierist	34 Dia	fast-tracker
Karte für Geldautomat	28 Ü	cashpoint credit card
Kartellgesetzgebung	32 I	antitrust legislation
Kassamarkt	30 A	spot market
Kassenbestand	36 Dok	cash in/on hand
Kassenschlager	21 Dia	blockbuster
kaufen	4 A	to buy, to purchase
Käuferbewußtsein	21 Dia	consumer awareness
Kaufkomfort	29 Dia	consumer convenience

Kaufkraft	22	Dok	purchasing power
Kaufmann	30	Dia	trader
kaufmännisches Personal	14	Dia	commercial people
Kern-	39	Dia	core
Klebeband	13	Dok	self-adhesive tape
Kleber	13	Dok	glue
Kleinigkeit	20	Dia	trifle
Know-how	21	Dok	know-how, skill
Knüller	21	Dia	blockbuster
Kohlepapier	13	Dok	carbon paper
Kollege	4	I	colleague
Kolumne	23	I	column
kombinieren	27	Dia	to combine (with)
Komitee	33	Dia	committee
Kommanditgesellschaft (KG)	4	Dok	limited partnership
Kommilitone	30	A	fellow student
Kommunikation und PR	6	Dok	communication and public relations
Konferenz	27	Dia	conference
Konflikt	6	Dia	conflict
Konfliktlösung	33	Dia	conflict resolution
Konkurrenzkampf	8	Dok	competition
Konkurs	28	A	bankruptcy
Konsequenzen	33	Dia	repercussions
Konsum	5	Dia	consumption
Konsumerismus	21	Dia	consumerism
Kontakt aufnehmen mit	28	Dia	to get in touch (with)
Kontenplan	36	I	chart of accounts
Kontingent	31	Dok	quota
kontrollieren	24	Ü	to monitor
konzentrieren	27	Dia	to concentrate
Konzerngesellschaft	28	Dia	affiliated company, affiliate, subsidiary
kooperative Werbung	29	A	cooperative advertising
Kopist	21	Dia	copycat
Korrekturflüssigkeit	13	Dok	correction fluid
kostendeckend arbeiten	22	A	to break even
kostengünstiger	8	Dia	less costly
Kostenkontrolle	22	Dia	cost control
kostenorientierte Preisgestaltung	22	Dia	cost-oriented pricing
kraft seines Amtes	40	A	in virtue of his office
Krankengeld	26	Dia	sickness benefits
Krankenversicherung	3	A	health insurance, sickness benefits
Kreativabteilung	23	A	creative department
Kreditauskunftei	28	Dia	credit agency, credit bureau
Kreditinstitut	8	Dia	banking institution
Kreditinstrument	8	Dia	financial instrument
Kreditlinie	28	A ·	credit line
Kreditoren	36	Dok	creditor(s) (UK), account(s) payable (US)
Kreditrisiko	28	Dia	credit risk
Kreditwürdigkeit	30	Ü	credit worthiness
Krieg führen	32	Dia	to wage war

Krimskrams	34 Dia	gadget(s)
Krisenmanager	15 Dia	troubleshooter
Krisenplan	28 A	contingency plan
Kriterium	10 A	criterion (Plural: -ia)
Kugelschreiber	13 Dok	ballpoint pen
Kunde	4 Dia	customer, client
Kundendienstmanager	23 Dia	customer service manager
Kundenwerbung	25 A	publicity
künstlerische Gestaltung	23 Dia	artwork
Kurs feststellen	8 A	to quote
Kurs(notierung)	8 Dia	quotation, rate, quote
Kurssicherungsgeschäft	30 Dia	hedging
kurzfristig	8 Dia	short-term, at short notice
Küste(nlinie)	17 Ü	coastline

L

Labor(atorium)	9 Dia	laboratory, lab
Laden (Firma)	17 Dia	outfit, joint, (i.e. company)
Laderampe	7 Dok	loading bay
Lage, sich in der ~ befinden, zu...	28 Dia	to be in a position (to)
Lage	36 Dia	situation, position
Lagerbestände	22 Dok	stock(s) (UK), inventory (-ies) (US)
Lagerdefizit	36 Dia	stock-out, inventory shortage
Lagerhalle	7 Dok	warehouse
Lagermanko	36 Dia	stock-out, inventory shortage
Lagerverwaltung	36 Dia	stock management
Laisser-faire (Politik des)	32 I	laisser-faire, non-interference
Landesgrenze	8 Dia	border, frontier
Landsmann	27 Dia	fellow countryman (-woman)
langfristig	8 Dia	long-term
Laptop	19 Dia	portable computer, laptop (computer)
Lasche	32 Dia	tab
laufende Verbindlichkeiten	36 Dok	current liabilities
Laufenden, auf dem ~ halten	14 Ü	to keep informed about
Lebenslauf	1 Dia	CV (curriculum vitae) (UK), résumé (US)
Lebensmittelbehörde (USA)	21 Dia	Food and Drug Administration (FDA)
Lebensmittelerzeugnisse	7 Dia	food products
Lebensmittelindustrie	1 Dia	food industry, agri-business
Lebensrhythmus	20 Dia	pace
Lebensstandard	30 Ü	standard of living, living standard
legen, sich (spannungen)	36 Dia	to ease
Lehrling	24 Ü	apprentice
Lehrplan	18 Dia	curriculum
leichte Unterhaltung	20 Dia	small talk
leisten	39 Dia	to afford
Leistung	20 Ü	performance
Leistungen im Krankheitsfall	26 Dia	sickness benefits
leistungsabhängige Zulage	23 A	performance-related bonus
Leistungsbewertung	10 Dia	performance evaluation

432

leitender Angestellter	6 Dia	(senior) executive, head
Leiter	1 Dok	manager, director
Leitung	38 Dia	guidance
Leverage-Effekt	38 Dia	leverage
Leveraged Management Buy-Out	38 Dia	leveraged management buy-out (LMBO)
Lieferant	28 Dia	supplier
liefern	14 Ü	to deliver
Lieferung (Ware)	13 Dok	supply (-ies)
Lieferung (Vorgang)	27 Ü	delivery
Lineal	13 Dok	ruler
Listenpreis	22 Dok	list price
Lizenzabkommen	34 Ü	licensing agreement
Lobby	11 Dok	lobby, pressure group
Lobbyist	33 A	lobbyist
locker	20 Dia	informal
Logistik	14 Dia	logistics
Lohn	22 Ü	wage, compensation
Lohnkosten	31 Dia	labour costs
lokale Bildungsbehörde (USA)	17 Dia	local education authority
Lokokauf	32 Ü	spot purchase
Lokomarkt	30 A	spot market
Lokopreis, zum ~ kaufen	30 Dia	to buy spot
Luftfrachtgebühren	31 Ü	air-freight charge
Luftkorridor	34 A	air lane
luxuriös	27 Dia	luxurious
Luxusartikel	22 Dok	luxury product

M

Magister der naturwissenschaftlichen Fakultät	17 Dia	Master of Science (MS)
Management	2 Dia	management (services)
Manager der mittleren Führungsebene	34 I	middle manager
Manager der unteren Unternehmensführung	34 I	junior manager
Manager-Fähigkeiten	38 Dia	managerial skills
Marke	4 Dia	brand
Markenimage	32 Dia	brand image
Markenname	21 Dok	brandname
Markenpräsenz	29 Dia	brand exposure
Markentreue	25 Dia	brand loyalty
Marketing	1 Dia	marketing
Marketing-Mix	22 Dia	marketing mix
Markt	4 Dok	market
Marktanteil	27 Dia	market share
Marktdurchdringung	39 Dia	market penetration
Marktlücke	39 Dia	market gap
Marktstudie	18 Dia	market study, market research

Maßnahme	37	A	move
MBA	2	Dia	MBA (Master's Degree in Business Administration)
Media-Plan	23	Dia	media plan
Meinungsforscher(in)	18	Dok	pollster
Meinungsumfrage	18	Ü	opinion poll
Meinungsverschiedenheit	6	Dia	disagreement
Meister	12	A	supervisor, foreman
melden, sich	11	Dia	to report to (sb.)
Mengen, in großen	36	Dia	in large shipments
Mengenrabatt	22	Dok	quantity discount
Merchant-Bank	8	Dok	merchant bank
Metallspitze	32	Dia	tab
Miete	22	Ü	rent
Mietkauf	30	Ü	hire purchase
Milchkuh	36	Dia	milk cow (UK), cash cow (US)
Minderung	11	Dok	shrinkage
Mindestpreis ansetzen	22	Dia	to set the floor
Mischung	24	Dia	blend
Mißerfolgsrate	21	Dok	failure rate
Mißgeschick	32	Dia	mishap
mißtrauisch	39	Ü	wary
Mitarbeiter der Fertigung	12	A	shop floor, grass roots
Mitbewerber	32	Dia	competitor
Mitglied	11	Ü	member
Modem	14	Dia	modem
modern	22	Dok	high-fashion
modernisieren	22	Dia	to streamline
Monopol	32	I	monopoly
Motivationstrainer	26	Dia	motivational speaker
motivieren	9	Dia	to motivate, to get (sb.) involved, to involve sb.
Motto	17	I	motto
Mühle	24	Dia	grinder
mühsam	19	Dia	tedious
Multi (multinationales Unternehmen)	31	I	worldwide corporation
multinational	13	Dia	multinational
Mund-zu-Mund-Propaganda	25	Dia	grapevine
Muttergesellschaft	4	Dia	parent company

N

Nachfolge-	31	Dia	follow-up
nachlässig mit etw. umgehen	20	A	to trifle with s.th.
Nachname	4	I	surname
Nachteil	25	Ü	drawback
nagelneu	18	Dia	brandnew
Nahrungsmittel	29	Dia	foodstuffs
Namen, im	39	Dok	on behalf of

Nationalstaat	31 I	nation state
Naturschutzvereinigung	33 Dia	environmental organisation
Nebenfach	17 Dia	minor
Nebenstelle	8 Dia	branch
Nennwert	4 A	nominal value (UK), par value (US)
Nettoeinkommen	32 A	net income
Nettogewinn nach Steuern	36 Dok	net profit after taxation (UK), net earnings (US)
Netzwerk, über ein ~ miteinander verbunden	14 Dia	to be networked
Netzwerk	8 Dia	network
neutral	18 Dia	unbiased
Nichterscheinen, unentschuldigtes	9 Dok	absenteeism
Nominalwert	37 A	nominal value (UK), par value (US)
Nonstop-Flug	27 Dia	non-stop flight
notiert (an der Börse)	4 Dok	quoted, listet (on the stock exchange)
Notizblock	13 Dok	note-pad
Null, wieder bei ~ anfangen	24 Dia	to take a clean sheet

O

obere Managementetage	26 A	senior management level
oberster, -e, -es	40 A	uppermost
objektiv	18 Dia	unbiased
obligatorisch	24 Dok	compulsory
öffentlicher Dienst	3 A	civil service
öffentliches Zeichnungsangebot	40 A	public offering (US), offer for sale (GB)
Öffentlichkeitsarbeit	25 Dia	public relations (PR)
OHG (Offene Handelsgesellschaft)	4 A	etwa: partnership
ohnehin	27 Dia	as a matter of fact
Ohren, viel um die ~ haben	9 Dia	to have plenty of work on one´s plate
ökonomisch	8 I	frugal
optimieren	40 Dia	to maximise
Organisation, gemeinnützige	22 I	non-profit organization
Organisationsplan	27 Dok	organization chart
Organisationsschema	5 Dia	organization chart
Overhead-Projektor	27 Dia	overhead projector (OHP)

P

Partner	4 Dok	partner, associate
Partnerbank	8 Dia	partner bank
Partyservice	24 A	catering, caterer
Passiva	10 A	liability (-ties)
Patent, zum ~ anmelden	21 Dok	to take out (a patent)
Patent	32 A	patent
Patent, zum ~ angemeldet	39 A	patent pending
PC	14 Dia	PC (personal computer)
Peripheriegerät	14 A	peripheral
Personal	1 Dia	personnel, staff

Personalchef	4	Dia	director of human resources (DHR), personell manager
Personalentwicklung	16	Dia	staff development
Personalführung	1	Dia	personnel management
Personalverwaltung	1	Dia	personnel management
Personalwesen	3	Dok	human resources
Personengesellschaft	4	Dok	partnership
Personenrufgerät	14	Dia	pager
Pfand	38	A	pledge
Pfund	7	Dia	pound (weight: lb; money: £)
Piepser	14	Dia	pager
Pionierarbeit leisten	5	Dia	to pioneer
Plackerei	24	A	grind
Plakattafel	23	A	hoarding (UK), billboard (US)
Plan	29	Dia	outline
planen	13	Dia	to lay out, to get lined up, to schedule
planmäßige Langsamarbeit	11	Dia	work-to-rule
planmäßiger Flug	20	A	scheduled flight
Planung	20	A	scheduling
Planwirtschaft des Staates	32	I	state interventionism, government interventionism
Platz machen	10	Dia	to give way (to)
Platzkauf	32	Ü	spot purchase
pleite	17	Dia	broke
Post	3	Ü	mail, letter
Postauftrag	30	Ü	mail order
Posten	8	Dia	assignment, job, task
Posten (einer Rechnung)	36	Dia	item
potentiell	16	Ü	would-be, potential
Praktikant	2	A	trainee, intern (US)
Praktikum	2	A	placement (UK), internship (US), training period, on-the-job training
praktische Erfahrung	7	Dia	hands-on experience
Prämie	10	A	bonus
Prämie	22	Ü	premium
Präsentation	23	Dia	brief
Präsident (eines Vorstands)	6	Dia	chairperson
Praxis, in die ~ umsetzen	18	Dia	to implement
Preis ansetzen	8	A	to quote
Preisabsprachen, unerlaubte	32	I	price-fixing
Preisaufschlag	22	Dia	mark-up, profit margin
Preisausschreiben	25	Dia	sweepstake
preisgünstig	17	Ü	advantageous
Preiskrieg	9	I	price war, price-cutting war
Preispolitik	22	Dok	pricing policy
Pressemappe	4	Dia	press book
Pressemitteilung	25	Dia	press release
Primärquelle	19	Dia	primary source
Prinzip	36	Dia	principle
private Toiletten	34	I	private restrooms

Privatkunde	8 Dok	private customer
Privatschule (GB)	2 Dok	public school
Pro- und Kontrastimmen	40 A	ayes and noes
Probe	18 Dok	sample
Probezeit	2 Dia	trial period
probieren	21 Dia	to taste
Problem angehen	22 Dia	to tackle (a problem)
Problem	25 Dia	issue
Produkt	4 Dia	product
Produktbeauftragter	21 Dok	product executive
Produktionsabteilung	9 Dia	operational division, line division, operational department
Produktionsarbeiter	7 Dia	(production) worker
Produktionseinheit	7 Ü	production unit, plant
Produktionsleistung	10 Dok	rate
Produktionsleiter	37 Dia	production manager
Produktkonzept	21 Dia	product concept
profitieren, von etwas	33 Dok	to capitalise (on)
profitieren	32 Ü	to benefit
Programm	27 A	agenda
Protokoll	39 Dok	minutes
Provision	22 Ü	commission
Prozentsatz	38 Dok	percentage
Prozeß	9 A	process
psychologische Preisgestaltung	22 Dok	psychological pricing
Publicity	25 A	publicity
Pulver (Kakao-)	24 Dia	powder
Punkt, direkt auf den ~ kommen	28 I	to come straight to the point
Punkt (einer Tagesordnung)	36 Dia	item

Q

Quäker	5 Dia	quaker
Qualitätskontrolle	24 Dia	quality control
Qualitätskreis	7 Dia	quality circle
Quote	31 Dok	quota

R

Rabatt gewähren	21 Dia	to discount
Rabatt	22 Dok	allowance, rebate
Radiergummi	13 Dok	rubber (UK), eraser (US)
Raffinerie	14 Ü	refinery
Raffinieren	24 Dia	refining
Rang	7 Dia	seniority
Ratenkauf	30 Ü	hire purchase
Ratgeber	8 Dia	adviser
rationalisieren	22 Dia	to streamline
Räumungsverkauf	27 Ü	clearance sale

Deutsch	Seite	Typ	English
rausschmeißen	11	Dia	to sack, to fire, to dismiss, to lay off, to make redundant
Reaktion	22	Dok	response, feedback
Realzeit	8	A	real time
Rechenprogramm	19	A	spreadsheet program
Rechentabelle	19	Dia	spreadsheet
Rechnungsabteilung	23	A	billing (invoicing) department
Rechnungsausstellung	19	Dok	invoicing, billing
Rechnungswesen	1	A	accountancy
Rechnung, in ~ stellen	27	Ü	to charge
Rechtsabteilung	4	Dia	legal department
Redakteur	25	Dok	editor
reduzieren	8	Dia	to reduce, to shrink
Regalposition	39	Dia	shelf position
regeln (Problem)	14	Dia	to sort out
Regelung	7	Dia	regulation
Regierung (USA)	31	Dia	administration
registrieren	33	A	to record
reibungslos	9	Dia	smoothly
Reichtum	32	Dok	affluence
Reichweite	8	Dok	range
Reife	39	Ü	maturity
Reinertrag	32	A	net income
Reinfall	21	Dia	flop
Reingewinn	10	A	net profit, net income, bottom line
reinholen	36	Dia	to catch up (with)
Reinvermögen	36	Dok	net worth
Reise	6	Dia	travel, trip
reisen	14	Dia	to travel, to be away (on business)
Reiseroute	27	Dia	itinerary
Reißzwecke	13	Dok	drawing-pin
Reklamewesen	25	A	publicity
Rendite	22	Dia	rate of return
Rentabilität	6	A	profitability
Rentabilitätsgrenze	22	A	break-even point
Rente	6	A	benefit, retirement
Reparaturbetrug	27	Ü	repair fraud
Reservebildung	36	Dia	accumulation of reserves
reservierte Zuschauertribüne	34	I	reserved box
Reservierung	27	Dia	reservation, booking (UK)
Resonanz	25	Dia	feedback
Resultat	18	Dia	finding
Richtlinien	39	Dok	guidelines
Richtung angeben	22	Dia	to set the tone
Risiko	18	Dia	risk, hazard
Risiko-Management	30	I	risk management
Rohentwurf	27	A	(rough, first) draft
Rohstoffe	32	Dia	raw material(s)
Rückgang	11	Dok	fall, decline, decrease
Rückmeldung	25	Dia	feedback

rücksichtslos	35	Ü	ruthless
Rücktritt	40	Dok	resignation
Rückzahlung	25	Dia	refund
Ruf	32	A	summons
rühmen, sich	11	Dok	to boast

S

Sabbatjahr	20	Ü	sabbatical leave
Sachanlagen	32	A	tangible (fixed) asset(s), property plant and equipment
Sachvermögen	32	A	tangible (fixed) asset(s), property plant and equipment
Saisonrabatt	22	Dok	seasonal discount
Sammelbogen	27	A	recapitulation sheet
sammeln (Informationen)	18	Dia	to collect
Sammeltätigkeit	15	Dia	fund-raising activity
Sanierer	15	Dia	troubleshooter
Schachzug	37	Dia	move
Schaden	33	Dia	damage
Schadenersatz	30	I	damages
schaffen	9	Dia	to develop
Schalter	19	Ü	switch
Schätzung	22	Ü	estimate
Scheck	8	Dia	cheque (UK), check (US)
Scheck ausstellen	8	Dia	to write a cheque
Scheckbuch	8	A	cheque book
Schein (an der Universität)	17	Dia	credit
scheitern	27	A	to break down
Scherz	25	Ü	hoax
Schicht	24	Ü	shift
Schlagzeile	37	I	headline
schlecht durchdacht	32	Dia	ill-conceived
Schlichter	15	Dia	troubleshooter
schließen aus	36	Dia	to gather
Schlußfolgerungen ziehen	15	Ü	to draw conclusions
Schlußformal, formelle	1	I	formal ending, polite ending (correspondence)
Schnellkurs	26	Dia	crash course
schnurloses Telefon	14	A	cordless telephone
schreiben	13	A	to type
Schreibkraft	13	A	typist
Schreibmaschine	13	Dia	typewriter
Schreibtischforschung	18	Ü	desk research
Schreibwaren	13	Dok	stationery
schriftliche Verwarnung	11	Dia	written warning
Schritt	18	Dia	step, stage
Schritt nach vorne machen	38	Dia	to take a step forward
schrumpfen	39	Ü	to shrink
Schuldanerkenntnis, schriftliches	34	Ü	acknowledgement of a debt
Schuldschein	8	A	note of hand, promissory note

German	Ref	English
Schulung	7 Dia	training course
Schulung vor Ort	26 Dia	on-the-job training
Schundanleihe	37 I	junk bond
schützen	32 Dia	to safeguard
schwarzes Brett	34 Ü	bulletin board
Schwelle	22 Dia	floor
schwer einbringliche Forderung	28 Dia	bad debt
schwer einziehbare Außenstände	28 Dia	bad debt
Schwung	20 Dok	buoyancy
sehnen, sich ~ nach	24 A	to crave for
Seite, auf jdn.´s Seite stehen	31 Dia	to side with
Sekretärinnenausbildung	13 Dia	secretarial course
Sekretärinnenschule	14 Dia	secretarial college
Sektor	4 Dia	sector, business, market
Sekundärliteratur	19 A	secondary literature
Sekundärquelle	19 Dia	secondary source
selbstregulierend	32 I	self-regulating
Semesterstunde	17 Dia	semester hour
Server	14 A	server
sich niederlassen	6 Ü	to settle
sich verlassen auf	8 Dia	to rely (on)
Sicherheit	7 Dia	safety
sicherstellen	10 Dia	to ensure
Sicherungsgeschäft abschließen	32 Ü	to hedge
sichtbare Ein- und Ausfuhren	31 Dok	visibles, visible imports and exports
Sitzung	37 Dia	meeting
Skizze	23 Dia	rough
Sofort-	30 A	spot
Sofortpreis	30 A	spot price
Software-Paket	6 Ü	software (package)
Sonderangebot	22 Dok	bargain
Sonderleistungen	3 Dia	fringe benefit(s), perquisite(s) [perk(s)]
Sondervergünstigungen	26 Dia	perquisites, perks
Sorgen	24 Ü	grievance
Sortiment	40 Dia	line
Spannung	34 Ü	strain
Sparkasse	8 Dok	savings bank
Sparkonto	28 Ü	savings account
sparsam	22 Dia	thrifty
Sparsamkeit	8 I	frugality
speichern	13 A	to file, to store
Spesen	26 Dia	expenses
Spesenkonto	34 I	expense account
Spesenrestaurant	27 I	expense-account restaurant
spezialangefertigt	30 Ü	custom (made)
Spezialqualifikation	2 Dia	special qualification
Spitzenmanager	34 I	top manager, senior manager
Staatsdienst	3 A	civil service
Staatsanleihen	28 Ü	government bonds, government securities
Staatsbediensteter	3 A	civil servant (UK), government worker (US)

Stabspersonal	9	A	staff
stagnieren	27	Dia	to remain stagnant
Stammaktien	36	Dok	ordinary share (UK), common (capital) stock (US)
Stand, auf dem neusten	35	Ü	up to date
stark interessiert an	21	Ü	keen (on)
stärken	39	Dia	to strengthen
Statussymbol	6	I	status symbol
Stecker	19	Ü	plug
steigern	8	Dia	to improve, to upgrade
Steigerung	9	Dok	increase
Stelle	1	Dia	job, employment, post, position
Stellenanzeige	1	Dia	job advertisement
stellvertretender Direktor	7	Dia	assistant director
Stenographie	13	Dia	shorthand
Stenotypist(in)	13	A	shorthand-typist
stetig	8	Dok	steady
Steuerabzug	27	I	tax reduction
Steuererleichterung	31	A	tax relief
steuerpflichtig, nicht	38	A	non-taxable
Steuervergünstigung	31	A	tax relief
Steuervorteil	38	Dia	fiscal advantage
stiller Teilhaber	4	Dok	sleeping partner
Stimmrechtskampf	37	Dia	proxy fight
Stipendium	17	Dia	grant, scholarship
Stockwerk	27	Dia	floor
stolz sein auf	6	Ü	to pride oneself (on)
Stoßzeit	11	Dia	rush hour
Strategie	2	Dia	policy
streben nach	34	Dia	to strive for
Streben	6	Dia	quest
Streik	11	Dia	strike
Streikposten	11	Dia	(strike) picket, picketer(s)
Streikpostenkette	11	A	picket line
Streit	11	A	dispute
Streitfrage	25	Dia	issue
Strickmuster, seinem ~ treu bleiben	39	Dia	to stick to one's knitting, back to the basics, urge to purge
Student	1	A	undergraduate
Studienabschluß mit zwei Hauptfächern	2	Dia	joint (honors) degree
Studiengebühren	2	Dia	tuition fees
Studienzeitschrift	18	Dia	study periodical
studieren	1	Dia	to read
System	38	Dia	set-up

T

Tabelle	10	Dia	chart, graph
Tag der offenen Tür	15	Dia	open day
Tagebuch	14	A	diary

Tagesordnung	27 A	agenda
Tarifvertrag	38 I	collective agreement
Taschenkalender	27 A	pocket diary
Tastatur	19 Ü	keyboard
tätig werden als	35 Dia	to act as
Tauschhandel	22 Ü	barter
taxieren	6 A	to appraise, to assess
Team	10 Dia	team
Teepause	6 I	tea break
teilnehmen an	30 Dia	to take part (in)
teilnehmen	27 Dia	to attend
Teilzeit-	16 Dia	part-time
Telefax	14 A	fax
Telefonist(in)	13 Dia	switchboard operator
Telefonkarte	26 Dia	telephone credit-card
Termin	14 Dia	appointment
Termingeschäft abschließen	32 Ü	to sell forward
Terminkalender	14 Dia	diary
Terminkontrakt	30 Dia	futures contract
Terminmarkt	30 Dia	futures market
Terminpreis	30 A	forward price
Terminpreis, zum ~ kaufen	30 Dia	to buy forward
Terminverkauf	32 Ü	forward sale
Tesafilm	13 Dok	Sellotape
Testmarkt	29 Dia	test market
teuer	13 Ü	expensive, dear
Texter	23 Dia	creative writer
Textmarker	13 Dok	highlighter (pen)
Textverarbeitung	6 Ü	word processing
Thema	25 Dia	issue
tippen	13 A	to type
Tischcomputer	19 A	desktop computer
Tischkalender	27 A	desk diary
Tochtergesellschaft	4 Dia	subsidiary, affiliate (US), affiliated company
Tortendiagramm	19 Dia	pie-chart
Totale Qualitätskontrolle	7 Dia	total quality management (TQM)
Trainer	26 Dia	coach, trainer
Transportservice	14 Dia	transport
Traubenlese	24 Dia	vintage
treu	26 Dok	loyal
Treue	12 Dia	(staff, customer) loyalty
Tutor	20 Dok	tutor

U

überarbeitet	19 Dia	overworked
überblicken	36 Dia	to overlook
übereinstimmen, mit jdm.	32 Dia	to agree
Überflieger	2 Dok	high-flyer

Deutsch	Seite	Typ	Englisch
Überfluß	32	Dok	affluence
übergeben an, etwas	6	Dia	to turn s.th. over (to)
Überholspur	34	Dia	fast lane
übermitteln	26	Dok	to convey
Übernahme	35	Dia	takeover
Übernahmeangebot	35	A	takeover bid
übernehmen	35	Ü	to take over
Überproduktion	32	Ü	overproduction
überprüfen	19	Dok	to check
Überprüfung	21	Dok	screening
Überschrift	23	Ü	headline
Übersee, in	34	Dok	overseas
Überstunden	11	Dia	overtime
Übertragung von Kursen per Computer	8	Dia	computerised quote
Übertragungen per Satellit	8	Dia	satellite communications
überweisen (Geld)	8	Dia	to transfer
Überweisung	28	Dia	transfer
überwinden	40	Dok	to overcome
überzeugen	10	Dia	to convince
Überziehung	28	A	overdraft
Umfang	8	Dok	scope
umgehen mit	33	Dia	to handle
Umgruppierung von Arbeitsplätzen	40	Dok	redeployment
Umkleide	24	Dia	locker room
Umlaufvermögen	36	Dok	current assets
Umrechnung in eine andere Währung	30	Dia	conversion
umreißen	38	Dia	to outline
Umsatz	4	Dia	turnover (UK), total sales (US)
umsehen, sich ein bißchen	21	Dia	to snoop around
umstrukturieren	36	Dia	to restructure
Umstrukturierung	36	Dia	restructuring, restructuration
Umtausch	30	A	exchange
Umwelt	6	Ü	environment
Umweltschützer	33	Dia	ecologist
Umweltschutzorganisation	33	Dia	environmental organisation
undichte Stelle	37	Dia	leak
unerfahren	8	Dia	untrained, soft on the edges
Universalversicherung	30	Dia	comprehensive policy
Unruhen	36	Dia	unrest
unsicher	32	Dok	unsafe
unsichtbare Ein- und Ausfuhren	31	Dok	invisibles, invisible imports and exports
unterbrechen	34	Dia	to disrupt
unterbringen, jdn.	5	Dia	to put (sb.) up
Unterhaltung, eine ~ führen	26	Dia	to have a chat
Unternehmen	3	Dia	firm, company (UK), corporation (US), enterprise
Unternehmen gründen	13	Dia	to start up, to create
Unternehmensgründung	13	A	start-up
Unternehmensleiter	6	Dia	chief executive officer (CEO) (US), chairman and managing director (UK)

Unternehmensphilosophie	12 Dia	(corporate) culture
Unternehmenspolitik	10 Dia	business policy
Unternehmerverband	31 A	entrepreneurial association
Unternehmenswelt	2 A	corporate world
Unternehmens-	2 A	corporate
unternehmerisch	31 Dia	entrepreneurial
Unternehmerrisiko	31 A	entrepreneurial risk
Unternehmertum	31 A	entrepreneurial management
Unternehmer	31 A	entrepreneur
unterrichten (anweisen)	5 Dia	to brief
Unterrichtung	5 A	briefing
unterschätzen	21 Dia	to underestimate
unterschiedliche Preisgestaltung	22 Dok	discriminatory pricing
unterstehen, jdm.	11 Dia	to report to (sb.)
unterstützen	15 Dia	to support, to endorse
unterstützen (finanziell)	15 Dia	to sponsor
Unterstützung	33 A	endorsement
Untersuchung	9 Dok	survey
Untertitel	23 Ü	subheadline
unvoreingenommen	18 Dia	unbiased, with no bias
unvorhergesehenes Ereignis	28 Dia	contingency
Unwahrscheinlichkeit	38 Dia	unlikelihood
Unze	9 Ü	ounce

V

Verabredung	14 Dia	appointment
veranlassen	28 Ü	to induce
verantwortlich sein für	8 Dia	to be in charge of
Verantwortung delegieren	14 Dia	to delegate responsibility
verarbeiten	36 Ü	to process
verbergen	22 Dia	to stash away
Verbesserung	9 Dia	improvement
verbieten	21 Dia	to ban
Verbindlichkeiten	36 Dok	creditor(s) (UK), account(s) payable (US)
Verbraucher	1 Ü	consumer
verdanken, zu ~ sein	40 Dok	to be credited to
verdienen an	30 Dia	to gain (by)
verdienen	40 Dia	to deserve
Verdünner für Korrekturflüssigkeit	13 Dok	thinner
vereinbaren, miteinander	34 Dia	to reconcile
Vereinbarung	38 Dia	arrangement
vereinfachen	8 Dia	to simplify
Verfahren	9 A	process
verfassen	14 Ü	to write, to draft
Verfassen einer Werbeanzeige	23 Dia	ad-writing
verfügbar	8 Dia	available
Verfügbarkeit	10 Dia	availability
vergehen (Zeit)	32 Dia	to go by
vergeuden	23 Dia	to squander

Vergünstigung	6	A	benefit
Vergütung	10	Dia	reward, compensation
Verkauf	6	Dia	sale
verkaufen	4	A	to sell
Verkäufer	26	Ü	salesperson
Verkäufer(in)	7	I	shop assistant
Verkaufsautomat	29	Dia	vending machine
Verkaufsförderung	25	Dia	sales promotion
Verkaufskunst	26	Ü	salesmanship
Verkaufsleiter	26	Dia	sales manager
Verkaufsmannschaft	9	I	sales force
Verkaufsstelle, kleine	8	A	outlet
Verkaufswettbewerb	29	Dia	sales contest
verknüpfen	23	Dia	to tie
Verladegebühren	31	Dok	shipping charges
Verlagerung	11	Dok	shift
verlängerbar	39	Dok	renewable
verlassen, sich auf jdn.	23	Dia	to rely (on s.b.)
verlassen, sich darauf ~	28	Dok	to count on
verletzen (Bestimmungen)	33	Dia	to break
Verlosung	25	Dia	sweepstake
Verlust	30	Dia	loss
vermeiden	10	Dia	to avoid
Vermittlerfähigkeiten	33	Dia	skills as a negotiator
vernünftig	10	Ü	sensible
Verpackung	21	Dok	packaging, wrapping, packing
Verpackungspapier	32	Dia	wrapping paper
verpassen	40	Dia	to miss
verpflichten, sich vertraglich	30	Ü	to contract
verpflichten, sich	31	Dia	to pledge (to), to commit o.s.
Verpflichtung	34	Dia	commitment
Verrechnungsscheck	8	A	crossed cheque
Verschachtelung	33	I	interlocking
verschlimmern	10	Dok	to aggravate
verschulden, sich	38	Dia	to get into debt
Verschuldung	4	Dok	debt
versetzen	30	Dia	to remove
Versicherung	30	Dia	insurance
Versicherungsleistung	6	A	benefit
Versicherungsschutz	30	Dia	coverage
Versorgung	32	Dia	supply
verspäten, sich	40	Dia	to delay
Verständigungsbereitschaft	25	Ü	goodwill
verstärken	39	Dok	to reinforce
Verstärkung	38	Dia	reinforcement
verstehen	38	Dia	to grasp
vertagen (Sitzung)	39	Dok	to adjourn (the meeting)
Vertrag	3	Dok	contract
Vertrag abschließen	30	Ü	to contract
Vertragsentwurf	27	A	draft contract

Vertrauen	40 Dia	confidence
Vertreter	37 Dia	representative
Vertriebsabkommen	29 Dia	distribution agreement
Vertriebsnetz	32 Dia	distribution network
Vertriebsstelle	31 Dia	outlet, distributor
Veruntreuung von Geldern	30 I	embezzlement
Verwaltung	8 Dia	management
Verwaltung (mit Kundenkontakt)	8 A	front-office
Verwaltung (ohne Kundenkontakt)	8 Dia	back-office
Verwaltungsabteilung	9 Dia	functional division, staff division, staff department
Verwaltungsaufwand	8 Dia	paper work
Verwaltungsebene	6 Dok	functional level, staff
Verwaltungspersonal	37 Dia	clerical staff
Verzögerung	18 A	delay
Video-Konferenz	14 Dok	video-conferencing
vierteljährlich	40 Dia	quarterly
Vize-Präsident	18 Dia	vice president (VP)
vollberuflich	16 Dok	full-time
Vollstreckung	31 A	enforcement
Vollzeit-	16 Dok	full-time
vollziehen	31 A	to enforce
Vorankündigung	33 A	advance notice
Vorarbeiter	12 A	supervisor, foreman
Voraus-	30 Dia	spot
voraussagen	18 Ü	to forecast
Vorgabe, genaue	21 Dia	specification
Vorgang	9 A	process
vorgehen	40 Dia	to proceed
Vorgehensweise	40 A	proceeding
vorherige Benachrichtigung	33 A	advance notice
vorläufig	15 Dia	tentative, preliminary
Vorleben	33 Dia	record
Vorname	4 I	first name, given name, Christian name
Vorrichtungen	24 Dia	facilities
Vorruhestand	12 A	early retirement
Vorschlag	29 Dia	proposal
vorschlagen	26 Dok	to put forward
Vorschrift	7 Dia	regulation
Vorsitz	38 Dia	chair
Vorsitzende(r)	5 Dok	chairman, chairperson
Vorstadt	32 A	suburb
Vorstädter	32 Dia	suburbanite
Vorstandsmitglied	6 Dia	board member
Vorstandspräsident	6 Dia	chairman of the board
Vorstandssitzung	27 Dia	executive meeting
Vorstandsvorsitzender	5 Dok	president (US), chief executive officer (CEO) (US), managing director (UK)
Vorstellung, sich eine~ von etw. machen	14 Dok	to conceptualise

446

Vorstellungsgespräch	1	Dia	(job) interview
Vorteil	6	A	benefit
Vortrag	26	Dia	lecture
Vorwahl	3	I	local (dialling) code (UK), area code (US)

W

Wagnis	30	I	hazard, risk
wählen	5	Dok	to elect
Wahrscheinlichkeit	30	Dia	likelihood
Währung	32	Dia	currency
Währungsfluktuation	32	Dia	currency (exchange) fluctuation
Waren	27	Ü	goods
Waren austauschen	31	I	to trade
Warenmarkt	32	Dia	commodity (commodities) market
Warenterminmarkt	30	A	commodity/commodities futures market
Warenwechsel	8	Dia	commercial paper
Warenzeichen	4	Dia	trade mark
Warnhinweis	10	Dok	warning
Warnstreik	36	Dia	warning strike
Wartung	22	Dok	maintenance, upkeep
Wartungsvertrag	31	Ü	maintenance contract
Wäscherei	24	Dia	laundry
Wechselverkehr	30	A	exchange
Wegbereiter	5	Ü	pioneer
Weihnachtsgeschäft	14	Ü	Christmas rush
Weinlese	24	Dia	vintage
weiß machen	24	Dia	to blanch
Weiterbildung	12	Dia	continuing education, further education, adult education
weitergeben	32	Dia	to pass on
Weiterverfolgung	31	Dia	follow-up
weitervergeben	38	Dia	to farm out, to contract out, to subcontract
Welthandelsorganisation	31	Dia	World Trade Organization (WTO)
Weltmarkt	8	Dia	global market
Werbekampagne	4	Dia	advertising campaign
Werbemittel, unterschiedliche	25	Dia	promotion mix
Werbepreis	22	Dok	promotional pricing
Werbespot	25	Dia	commercial
Werbungskosten	27	I	entertainment expenses
Werdegang	33	Dia	record
Werk	7	Dia	factory, plant
Werksleiter	7	Dok	factory manager, plant manager
Werkzeug	25	Dia	tool
Wertpapier [festverzinsliches]	8	Dia	bond, debenture (UK)
Wertpapier und Investitionskontrollbehörde	36	I	Securities and Investment Board (SIB) (UK)
Wertpapierhändler	30	Dia	trader
Wettbewerb	8	Dok	competition
Wettbewerbsvorteil	21	Dia	competitive edge

wichtig	5	Dia	relevant (to)
widmen	20	Ü	to devote
Wiederbelebung	40	Dok	recovery
wiedereinstellen	11	A	to reinstate
Wiedereinstellung	11	Dia	reinstatement
wilder Streik	11	Dia	wildcat strike
Wirtschaft	22	Ü	economics (field of study), economy (of a country)
wirtschaftlich	8	I	frugal
Wirtschaftlichkeit	6	A	profitability
Wirtschaftsfakultät	2	Dia	business school
Wirtschaftskrieg	9	I	economic warfare
Wirtschaftsprüfer	1	Dia	chartered accountant (UK), certified public accountant, CPA (US)
wissen, nicht mehr weiter	34	Dia	to be at one's wits' end
Wohl(fahrt)	33	I	welfare
Wohlfahrtsstaat	33	I	welfare state
Wohlstand	32	Dok	affluence
Wohltätigkeitsorganisation	15	I	charity organisation
Wohltätigkeitsveranstaltung	15	Dia	charity event
Wortlaut	18	Dia	wording

Y

Yuppies	23	Dok	Young Urban Professional People

Z

Zahlung, in ~ gegebene Ware	22	Dok	trade-in
Zahlungsbilanz	31	A	balance of payments
Zahlungsempfänger	28	A	payee
zeichnen (Aktien)	37	Dia	to subscribe
zeigen auf	9	Dia	to point (to)
zeitgenössische Tracht	15	Dok	period dress
Zeitlang	40	Dok	spell
Zeitplan	20	Dia	schedule, agenda
Zeitungsausschnitt	40	Dok	clipping
Zeitzone	5	I	time zone
Zerstreuung	34	A	diversion
Ziel	32	Dia	target
Zielsetzung	6	Dia	objective, goal
Zielmarkt	23	Dia	target market
Zins(en)	22	Ü	interest
Zollgebühren	22	Dia	customs duty, tariff
zu Händen (z.H.)	14	Ü	for the attention of
zufriedenstellend	32	Dia	satisfactory
zugunsten von	39	Dok	on behalf of
Zulage	10	A	bonus
Zulieferrampe	7	Dok	delivery bay
zurechtkommen mit	24	A	to cope with, to handle
zurückgehen auf	8	Dok	to go back (to)
zurückgehen	11	Ü	to decline

zurückgreifen auf	8	Dia	to resort (to)
zurücktreten (von einem Amt)	39	Dok	to step down, to resign
zurückziehen, vorläufig	37	Dia	to suspend
zurückziehen	38	Dia	to disengage
zusammenfassen	27	A	to recap(itulate), to sum up, to summarize
Zusammenfassung	27	Dia	recap(itulation)
Zusammenkunft	28	Dok	get-together, meeting
zusammenrufen	32	Dia	to summon
Zusammenschluß	34	Dia	merger
zuschlagen (Tür)	31	Dia	to slam
Zustimmung	33	Dok	acceptance
Zustimmung geben zu	38	Dia	to agree (to)
Zustrom (von Kapital etc.)	31	Dok	inflow
zuverlässig	32	Ü	reliable
Zweck	27	Dia	purpose
Zwei (Note)	1	A	second (class honours)
Zweigstelle	8	Dia	branch
zweite Geige, die ~ spielen	34	Dia	to take second billing

NUMERISCHE STICHWÖRTER

100%ige Tochtergesellschaft	5	Dok	wholly-owned subsidiary

450

Aubin Imprimeur
LIGUGÉ, POITIERS

Achevé d'imprimer en juillet 1996
N° d'édition 1298 / N° d'impression L 51977
Dépôt légal juillet 1996
Imprimé en France